Heaven's Door

Heaven's Door

IMMIGRATION POLICY AND THE AMERICAN ECONOMY

With a new preface by the author
GEORGE J. BORJAS

PRINCETON UNIVERSITY PRESS

PRINCETON AND OXFORD

Copyright © 1999 by Princeton University Press
Published by Princeton University Press,
41 William Street, Princeton, New Jersey 08540
In the United Kingdom: Princeton University Press,
3 Market Place, Woodstock, Oxfordshire OX20 1SY

Second printing, and first paperback printing, with a new preface, 2001
Paperback ISBN 0-691-08896-9

The Library of Congress has cataloged the cloth edition of this book as follows

Borjas, George J.
Heaven's door : immigration policy and the American economy / George J. Borjas.
p.   cm.
Includes bibliographical references and index.
ISBN 0-691-05966-7 (cl : alk. paper)
1. Immigrants—United States—Economic conditions. 2. United States—Emigration and immigration—Economic aspects. 3. United States—Emigration and immigration—Government
policy. 4. United States—Economic conditions—1981–. I. Title.
JV6471.B675   1999   325.73—dc21   99-12997

This book has been composed in Galliard

Printed on acid-free paper. ∞

www.pup.princeton.edu

Printed in the United States of America

2   3   4   5   6   7   8   9   10

TO JANE

WITH LOVE

Mama, take this badge off of me
I can't use it anymore . . .
That long black cloud is comin' down
I feel like I'm knockin' on heaven's door

—Bob Dylan

CONTENTS

IT HAS BEEN A YEAR since *Heaven's Door* was published. And it has been an interesting year, both in terms of the reactions to my book and in terms of how the debate over immigration policy has evolved.

I was not surprised that my book generated interest among participants in the immigration debate and among political commentators.[1] After all, the book addresses topics that are highly contentious and controversial—and these topics evoke a great deal of emotion among most Americans.

I was surprised, however, at the nature of the reaction—as represented by the reviews and comments published in major newspapers and magazines. To a large extent, the reviews can be easily allocated to two extreme camps: the favorable reviewers, who tended to like the book a lot, and the unfavorable reviewers, who disliked the book intensely. As with immigration itself, there seemed to be no middle ground, no subtleties over the type of book that I had written and the type of policies I had proposed. It was often difficult to imagine that the reviewers were referring to the same book. For example, Peter Skerry, who reviewed the book for the *Washington Post,* characterized *Heaven's Door* as a "tour de force in the economics of immigration," and Sylvia Nassar, who reviewed it for the *New York Times,* concluded that it was "impressively researched."[2] In contrast, Jagdish Bhagwati, who reviewed it for the *Wall Street Journal,* declared that the "economics arguments . . . are critically flawed."[3]

In retrospect, and given the fact that the immigrant experience forms an important part of the American psyche, I should have expected those extremes. I thought that *Heaven's Door* made a nuanced argument that could not be easily tagged as fitting into either extreme of the immigration debate. After all, the book stresses that there are *both* benefits *and* costs associated with immigration. The book also argued that if the United States wished to increase the economic benefits from immigration, the country should pursue a different type of immigration policy, a policy that would favor the entry of skilled immigrants. To be sure, I left little doubt as to whether I think the United States should factor in economic considerations in setting immigration policy (it should!). Nevertheless, the subtleties quickly got lost in the mythological mist that enshrouds any discussion of U.S. immigration.

In reflecting over the reaction to *Heaven's Door,* it is clear (at least to me) that the book elicited the most negative responses from reviewers writing for conservative and libertarian publications, such as the *Wall Street Journal* and *Reason.* These publications typically support calls for unrestricted immigration to the United States. The editorial page of the *Wall Street Journal,* for example, is famous (or, depending on one's point of view, infamous) for repeatedly proposing a new constitutional amendment: "There Shall Be Open Borders."

From my perspective, the reaction exhibited by these publications represented a "circling-of-the-wagons" mentality. Rather than evaluating the overall merits of the idea that some restrictions on immigration are probably better than none, and that it might be worth discussing which types of restrictions might be most beneficial, the response was to attack almost every fact reported in the book, to raise questions about the credibility of the findings, and to dismiss the whole enterprise as my misguided attempt to reflect on immigration policy when I failed to fully understand the (obvious?) implications of the fact that the United States is "a nation of immigrants."

Surprisingly, the reviews re-ignited the debate over an empirical observation that I thought had been settled beyond dispute. In particular, some reviewers doubted my claim that there has been a drop in the relative skills of immigrants who entered the United States in recent decades. The empirical validity of this finding, which I first published in the academic literature in 1985 and which has been reexamined by many social scientists in the past decade, is well established. In fact, a panel of scholars assembled by the National Academy of Sciences in 1997 reviewed the evidence, conducted additional empirical research, and concluded that the skills of new waves of immigrants "have been declining relative to that of native-born Americans. This decline appears across a number of measures, including education levels and wages."[4]

Some reviewers claimed that there might not have been a drop in the relative skills of *legal* immigrants who entered the country in the past few decades, but rather that the trends revealed by the Census data were contaminated because the Census enumerates both legal and illegal immigrants (as well as such nonimmigrants as foreign students and business executives temporarily working in the United States). If the presence of illegal immigrants in these data biases the direction of the trends in immigrant skills, the evidence then provides little information about what happened to legal immigration and what should be done about it.

I doubt that the detractors have a valid point. As I showed in *Heaven's Door* (see Figure 2–4), the downward trend in the relative skills of immigrants remains even if one simply examines the trend among non-Mexican immigrants, on the presumption that a large fraction of the illegal immigrants are from Mexico and are relatively unskilled. Moreover, the panel assembled by the National Academy of Sciences itself conducted an empirical analysis of data collected by the Immigration and Naturalization Service (INS) and concluded that "the decline in the relative skills of the foreign-born over the last few decades is not due exclusively to illegal immigrants or nonimmigrants. The data suggest that the relative skills of legal immigrants have also been falling over the period."[5]

A recent study conducted by Guillermina Jasso, Mark Rosenzweig, and James Smith (and published in a volume that I edited for the National Bureau of Economic Research) reexamined the INS data and seems to suggest that the absolute skill level of legal immigrants exceeded that of natives for much of the 1972—95 period.[6] It is worth pointing out, however, that the INS data are particularly ill-suited for documenting trends in immigrant skills. After all, the data do not report the immigrant's actual earnings or educational attainment; instead, one makes a guess about the person's economic potential by using information on the type of job the immigrant held before moving to the United States.[7] For instance, if the immigrant was a medical doctor prior to migrating, one assumes that the immigrant will earn the average salary of doctors in the United States. Needless to say, there is a great deal of error in this measure of the immigrant's potential skills. After all, the immigrant's pre-migration job may have little to do with what that person ends up doing in the United States—particularly if the occupation requires re-licensing, as in the case of medical doctors. Moreover, the Jasso-Rosenzweig-Smith study is itself inconclusive. The relative economic status of the immigrant population depends on the type of statistical fine-tuning that is done to adjust the data for the fact that the Census Bureau changed the way it coded occupations between 1970 and 1980.[8]

Some reviewers also claimed that it was "absurd" to conclude, as I do, that the net economic benefits from immigration are small, probably less than $10 billion a year. This estimate comes from a simple application of the widely used textbook model of a competitive labor market. This is the same model that is typically used to analyze the economic consequences of such government policies as minimum wages and payroll taxes. The market for ideas provides what is perhaps the most convincing argument in favor of my estimate. The immigration area, after all, is highly contentious. If it were that simple to show that the gains from immigration are huge, there would be an audience ready and willing to buy such numbers. My estimates are so "absurd" that not a single academic study has concluded that they are higher—and some studies have concluded that they are lower.

The mischaracterization of the evidence was perhaps most apparent when it came to the issue of whether immigrants had a negative effect on the wages of workers already in the United States. The *Wall Street Journal* review, written by Jagdish Bhagwati, an economic theorist specializing in international trade issues, shows this tendency in a very striking way. Mr. Bhagwati dismissed my evidence ("Mr. Borjas's larger economic claim, that immigration drives down wages, does not survive scrutiny") by claiming that economists Gordon Hanson and Matthew Slaughter showed that U.S. wages are not driven down by immigration. The Hanson-Slaughter work actually demonstrates that immigration does not seem to create wage differentials between states that receive many immigrants and states that do not, a point addressed at length in *Heaven's Door* (see pages 73—78). The concluding paragraph of the Hanson-Slaughter study explicitly describes how their work relates to the question at hand: "The evidence that state-specific endowments shocks do not trigger state-specific wage responses does *not* imply that the United States overall had no wage response to increased immigration" (the emphasis is theirs).[9]

The arguments that Mr. Bhagwati and other reviewers used to quickly dismiss the evidence on the adverse labor market impacts of immigration were further undermined by the unexpected entry into this debate of *the* authority on U.S. economic policy. In February 2000, Alan Greenspan, the chairman of the Federal Reserve, made some remarks linking immigration and inflation that are destined to change the nature of this debate. In Mr. Greenspan's words:

> Imbalances in the labor market perhaps may have even more serious implications for potential inflation pressures. While the pool of officially unemployed and those otherwise willing to work may continue to shrink, as it has persistently over the past seven years, there is an effective limit to new hiring, unless immigration is uncapped. At some point in the continuous reduction in the number of available workers willing to take jobs, short of the repeal of the law of supply and demand, wage increases must rise above even impressive gains in productivity. . . . In short, unless we are able to indefinitely increase the rate of capital flows into the United States to finance rising net imports or continuously augment immigration quotas, overall demand for goods and services cannot chronically exceed the underlying growth rate of supply.[10]

Mr. Greenspan's pronouncement restates the obvious: the laws of supply and demand inevitably imply that a large increase in the supply of workers lowers wages and reduces inflationary pressures. Mr. Greenspan, in effect, partly credits the large immigration flows of the 1990s for the U.S. economy's low inflation rate. Under Mr. Greenspan's astute interpretation, the fact that immigrants lowered wages need not be seen as an adverse impact of immigration; instead, it is a favorable consequence, for it holds inflation in check. Many of those who, in the pre-Greenspan days, had argued strenuously that immigration had little impact on the economic opportunities of native workers now began to argue just as strenuously that immigration fueled economic growth by keeping wages and prices down.[11]

Many of the unfavorable reviewers were so busy questioning the credibility of the facts reported in *Heaven's Door* that they seemed to miss the whole point of the book. The United States will inevitably attract many more immigrants than the country is willing to admit. As a result, choices have to be made. Current immigration policy benefits some Americans (the newly arrived immigrants as well as those who employ and use the services the immigrants provide) at the expense of others (those Americans who happen to have skills that compete directly with those of immigrants). Before deciding how many and which immigrants to admit, the country must determine which groups of Americans should be the winners and which should be the losers. Few of the detractors were willing to take on this question.

Finally, there is an amusing, if unintended, irony in some of the most extreme reviews—particularly those written from a libertarian perspective. Stuart Anderson wrote a review for *Reason* magazine that is worth singling out.[12] Mr. Anderson dismissed my proposal for a skills-based point system by repeating my book's warning that the system would be difficult for bureaucrats to administer, and then added sarcastically: "As if bureaucrats are well suited to handle *any* labor market decisions" (his emphasis). I wonder if Mr. Anderson saw the incongruity in his statement. At the time he wrote the review, he was a high-ranking immigration apparatchik himself—the "director of immigration policy" for the Senate Immigration Subcommittee. His boss, Senator Spencer Abraham, led the charge—presumably with Mr. Anderson's advice—to alter the U.S. labor market for skilled workers by greatly expanding the number of H1-B visas granted to temporary high-tech workers. Does Mr. Anderson truly believe what he writes about bureaucratic incompetence?

In the year that followed the publication of *Heaven's Door*, the immigration debate was dominated by three unrelated events. The first was the media obsession with the saga of Elián Gonzalez, the six-year-old boy who was rescued from the Florida seas on Thanksgiving Day in 1999. His mother died during her attempted escape from Cuba, and Fidel Castro soon made the return of the boy a cause célèbre that dominated the airwaves and the front pages of newspapers for months. Regardless of how one feels about the merits of the case, the Elián Gonzalez saga made an important contribution to the future debate over immigration policy.[13] It illustrated the awesome and arbitrary power that the INS has over the lives of many foreign-born persons residing in the United States. The INS has a great deal of discretion in deciding whether particular aliens should be allowed to remain in the country. And once the agency chooses to pursue a set of clearly defined goals, it seems to be able to achieve those goals with relatively little interference.

There is now, in fact, a healthy debate over the agency's competence in managing U.S. immigration policy. And Congress is seriously considering proposals that would break up the INS into two separate agencies. One agency would be responsible for border protection and enforcement of immigration regulations, while the other would provide naturalization services to legal immigrants already in the United States.

There is much to be said for the proposition that administrative incompetence rules at the INS. Consider, for instance, the agency's record during the Clinton years. At the beginning of Doris Meissner's tenure as head of the INS in 1993, the agency reported that there were just over 3 million illegal aliens residing in the United States. By the year 2000, there were 6 million. This huge increase in the illegal alien population occurred despite much higher expenditures on border enforcement. The INS budget more than tripled from $1.5 billion to $4.8 billion during that time. One could easily argue that there has been a tremendous waste of resources at the agency in recent years—billions of dollars spent on enforcement with little to show for it.

The failure of the INS in enforcing existing immigration laws extends far beyond the agency's flawed stewardship of the U.S. borders. The INS has a huge backlog of persons who are *already* living in the United States and who are waiting to regularize their immigration status and get their green cards. This backlog increased from an "equilibrium" of about 121,000 persons in 1994 to over 1 million by the year 2000. The agency, it seems, cannot even keep up with the *legal* immigrant flow.

Finally, political events in Mexico will inevitably alter the nature of the dialogue over immigration policy in the United States.[14] Over 7 million Mexican immigrants now live in the United States, and an additional 130,000 Mexican legal immigrants and 150,000 illegal immigrants enter the country annually. Soon after his election on July 2, 2000, President Vicente Fox proposed that the two countries share an open border within ten years. There would then be free movement of people and goods.

The Mexico-U.S. wage gap is among the largest wage gaps found between any two contiguous countries in the world. The World Bank reports that an American manufacturing worker earns four times the salary of a manufacturing worker in Mexico and thirty times the salary of an agricultural worker. These income differences ensure that an open border would increase the number of Mexican immigrants.

The new immigrants would probably resemble the Mexican immigrants already in the United States, whose poverty rate exceeds 33 percent. Firms that employ less-skilled labor would gain from having access to an even larger pool of workers. But, as Mr. Greenspan's reiteration of the laws of supply and demand suggests, Mr. Fox's proposals would further erode the economic opportunities available to the most disadvantaged Americans. An open border between Mexico and the United States would surely benefit Mexico and Mexican immigrants. But would it be good for the United States?

In the end, the answers to many of the concerns that drive the debate over immigration policy hinge on the question that I posed at the beginning of *Heaven's Door*, a question that has yet to become a central issue in the modern immigration debate: What do the American people want immigration to do for the United States?

Cambridge, Massachusetts
July 25, 2000

NOTES

1. See, for example, David Warsh, "Rainbow Didn't Just Happen." *Boston Globe*, October 3, 1999; Robert J. Samuelson, "Ignoring Immigration." *Washington Post*, May 3, 2000; and Alan B. Krueger, "Work Visas Are Allowing Washington To Sidestep Immigration Reform." *New York Times*, May 25, 2000.

2. Peter Skerry, "How Immigration Re-Slices the American Pie." *Washington Post,* October 28, 1999; Sylvia Nassar, "A Gloomy View of Immigration." *New York Times,* October 10, 1999.

3. Jagdish Bhagwati, "A Close Look at the Newest Newcomers." *Wall Street Journal,* September 28, 1999.

4. James P. Smith and Barry Edmonston, eds., *The New Americans: Economic, Demographic, and Fiscal Effects of Immigration* (Washington, D.C.: National Academy Press, 1997), p. 185.

5. Ibid., p. 196.

6. Guillermina Jasso, Mark Rosenzweig, and James P. Smith, "The Changing Skills of New Immigrants to the United States: Recent Trends and Their Determinants," in *Issues in the Economics of Immigration,* ed. George J. Borjas (Chicago: University of Chicago Press, 2000), pp. 185–235. Ironically, two of the authors of this study (Jasso and Smith) are responsible for the section in the National Academy of Sciences report that uses exactly the same data to reach seemingly different conclusions.

7. The INS has also commissioned the New Immigrant Survey, which provides detailed information on skills and earnings for the cohort of legal immigrants admitted in July and August of 1996. The mean education of this cohort is only slightly lower than that of natives; see Guillermina Jasso, Douglas S. Massey, Mark R. Rosenzweig, and James P. Smith, "The New Immigrant Survey Pilot (NIS-P): Overview and New Findings about U.S. Legal Immigrants at Admission," *Demography* 37 (February 2000): 127–136. Like the Census data, the New Immigrant Survey suffers from a particular type of inclusion bias. The INS has a huge backlog of persons (436,000 persons in 1996) who are *already* living in the United States and who are waiting for their green cards. Many of these immigrants probably entered the country illegally, probably have lower-than-average skills, and would be included—and rightly so—in Census data. The data collected by the New Immigrant Survey may well have looked quite different if the INS had chosen to substantially reduce the backlog in the summer of 1996.

8. Compare the evidence presented in Figures 5.1A and 5.1B (page 194) of the Jasso-Rosenzweig-Smith study. The unadjusted data show that the average occupational earnings of new immigrants are below those of native workers in twelve of the fourteen years between 1978 and 1991, rise above native earnings in 1992 and 1993, and then fall again below native earnings in 1994 and 1995. Once the authors make a particular (and somewhat arbitrary) adjustment for the change in occupational coding, the data suggests that the occupational earnings of new immigrants is at least as high as that of natives.

9. Gordon H. Hanson and Matthew J. Slaughter, "The Rybczynski Theorem, Factor-Price Equalization, and Immigration: Evidence from U.S. States" (National Bureau of Economic Research Working Paper no. 7074, April 1999, p. 29).

10. Alan Greenspan, "The Revolution in Information Technology" (remarks before the Boston College Conference on the New Economy, Boston, Mass., March 6, 2000).

11. For example, in 1994, Frank Sharry, the executive director of the National Immigration Forum, a pro-immigration advocacy group, claimed that immigrants "increase wages and mobility opportunities for many groups of U.S. workers" (Frank Sharry, "Admitting Newcomers is in the Nation's Best Interests." *Cleveland Plain Dealer,* April 1, 1994). In 2000, he invoked Alan Greenspan to argue that immigrants

"ward off higher inflation and higher interest rates" (Frank Sharry, "Immigrants' Contribution to America." *Business Week*, April 3, 2000).

12. Stuart Anderson, "Muddled Masses," *Reason Magazine*, February 2000, pp. 67–70 .

13. My feelings over the Elián Gonzalez case are made amply clear in my article "Let Elián Remain Free." *New York Times*, January 12, 2000.

14. For a more detailed discussion, see George J. Borjas, "Mexico's One-Way Remedy." *New York Times*, July 18, 2000.

IN ONE SENSE, this is a very personal book. I am, after all, an immigrant. To be more precise, I am a Cuban refugee. My family—like millions of other families who have found themselves in similar circumstances—benefited immensely from being granted the opportunity to live in the United States, giving us access to political privileges and economic opportunities that most people in the world cannot even imagine. And yet this book will surely be interpreted by some as presenting an unfavorable view of the economic impact that immigration has had on this country.

Part of the problem is that the immigration debate, like most debates over social policy, frames the issues in black and white: one must be in favor either of wide-open borders or of highly restrictive immigration policies. Because the political lines are so clearly delineated, many of the participants in the policy debate quickly associate new evidence or new arguments with one of the two opposing camps. However, as with most things in life, there is a large range of policy options in varying shades of gray.

The evidence that I present in this book indicates that immigration imparts both benefits *and* costs on the United States. As a result, the evidence does not support either of the two extremes in the immigration debate. Yet because the book is not a paean to immigration, I fear that it will be quickly pigeonholed as supporting the position of those who view immigration as inherently harmful and want immigration into the United States to be greatly curtailed, or perhaps even stopped altogether. Nothing could be further from the truth.

The typical ode to immigration focuses on the stereotypical anecdotes of the few from the huddled masses who arrive in the United States penniless, and yet go on to win Nobel prizes and lead multinational corporations. Instead, this book presents a great deal of evidence that the bulk of the huddled masses will not go on to win Nobel prizes or lead multinational corporations, and that a fair number of those immigrants tend to have less than favorable impacts on many American workers and taxpayers. In my view, these facts do not necessarily suggest that the United States would be better off without immigration. Rather, they suggest that immigration could be much more beneficial if the country pursued a different type of immigration policy. So before moving to a more detached discussion of how immigration affects the United States and what I think should be done about it, let me start by briefly describing the "immigrant experience" from a very different perspective— my own.

I have been thinking about immigration for a long time. In fact, I remember the first quiet rumblings about *emigración* soon after Fidel Castro rolled his tanks into Havana. I was eight years old. My family had been part of the entrepreneurial class in prerevolutionary Cuba. They owned a small factory that manufactured men's pants. The entire family worked at the factory, and they hired an additional thirty or so employees. Although we lived a comfortable life, the scale of the operation was much too small to allow my family to accumulate much wealth—let alone transfer it out of the country in the pre-Castro days. At the same time, however, the factory was much too threatening for the ideological forces against entrepreneurship and individual incentives. A year or so after Castro's triumphant march into Havana, the factory was confiscated, and my family's means of support suddenly disappeared.

I remember some of the initial gatherings where my family discussed migrating to the United States. I listened attentively as they talked in hushed voices about the mechanics and difficulties of getting a permanent residence visa. The "green card," as that magical piece of paper is commonly known, permits a person to enter the United States permanently. Those conversations, of course, were entirely in Spanish, and it was then that I first heard about *la residencia*—the Cuban jargon for this permit.

At the time, however, my young and impressionable mind did not equate *la residencia* with a bureaucratic piece of paper (which, at that time, was actually green). For in Spanish, *la residencia* also means a substantial-looking place of residence—an estate or a mansion. So my initiation into the intricacies of U.S. immigration policy consisted of discussions of how my family could possibly finagle its way into getting this *residencia* in Miami. What did we have to do to get one? How much would it cost? How would we pay for it?

Needless to say, I quickly began to daydream about the Hollywood lifestyle that life in America entitled a person to. My *residencia* in Miami would surely have dozens of rooms, a swimming pool, beautifully landscaped grounds, and so on.

Probably because of my father's long illness, we were unable to leave Cuba soon after Castro's takeover in 1959. My father died just before the Bay of Pigs fiasco, and it wasn't until after his death that my mother began in earnest the process of filing all the paperwork required to leave the country. Her efforts, and the very generous assistance of the Catholic priests who had taught me in school during the prerevolutionary days, finally paid off on the morning of October 17, 1962, just about a week before the Cuban missile crisis—and the permanent shutdown of the "freedom flights" that had carried tens of thousands of Cubans to a new life in the United States. We boarded a Pan Am propeller plane at the Havana airport and landed in Miami an hour later. Although it is less than two hundred miles from Havana to Miami, it immediately struck me—in those first few minutes—that the two places were quite different. Whereas Cuba was a dark, moody, and frightening place, Miami was bright and bold. Havana was dead, nothing was possible because the prison walls surrounded everything and everyone. Miami was alive!

I remember my disappointment, however, when we arrived at our *residencia*. It was most certainly not the mansion that I had envisioned in my dreams. My mother and I landed in Miami penniless (yes, that old cliché is often true), lived in what social scientists would now kindly call housing for the economically disadvantaged, and faced a difficult trek ahead. Somehow the mansion that I thought we had been promised turned out to be a run-down two-story apartment building. My mother and two of her sisters—as well as a small brood of cousins—shared a small apartment on the second floor. On the left side of the apartment building was the back entrance to a bar, and a freeway overpass dominated the landscape about a hundred feet away. Our situation was quite common in those early days of Miami's Cuban community. Some of our neighbors were former teachers, lawyers, and doctors who worked in factories and waited tables during the day, and then attended various types of schools at night to acquire the training that would allow them to eventually reenter the professions they had left behind.

To this day, I continue to be amazed by the courage and boldness that my mother and millions of others exhibited in picking up the little they had, and starting life again in a foreign country—without knowing the language, the culture, or almost anything about it. They all relied on their unshakable belief that the United States was a far better place, and that even if they themselves could not share in those opportunities, their children surely would. In fact, I have often wondered if I would have been as courageous and bold if I had faced similar circumstances.

Not surprisingly, my interest in migration issues has continued through the years—in college, where I carried out a survey of immigrant households for a sociology class; in graduate school, where my doctoral dissertation addressed issues related to labor mobility; and throughout much of my professional career, a large chunk of which I spent in California, the hot zone of modern immigration. I learned how to be an economist at Columbia University and the University of Chicago, and began my professional study of immigration issues with a strong "Chicago-school" perspective. Because free-market solutions are generally hard to beat, it seems eminently sensible that the United States should place as few restrictions on immigration as possible. I have to admit that my thinking on this issue has changed substantially over the years. As I began to look at the accumulating evidence, I began to appreciate that the immigrants and the native population of the United States might not have the same interests and aspirations, and as a result one had to make a choice as to who mattered more.

This book stresses that immigration generates both costs and benefits for the native-born population of the United States. As a result, perhaps the key theme of the book is that the economic impact of immigration will vary by time and by place, and can be either beneficial or harmful. In other words, the type of immigration policy that the United States pursues matters—and it can matter quite a bit.

And although the book presents a balanced look at the evidence, I have also learned that man cannot live by facts alone. At some point in the debate over any social policy, the facts have to be let out of their moral vacuum. And the facts have to be interpreted in the context of a set of beliefs, values, and a vision of what the United States is about. Facts have little meaning without such a vision, and different visions will inevitably lead to different proposals for reforming immigration policy. As a result, my perspective on the type of policy that the United States should pursue cannot fully escape my immigrant past and the immense sense of wonder and gratitude that I have always held for this country and its people.

I am fully aware that my own immigrant experience and the policy recommendations contained in this book may seem somewhat incompatible to many. Although my family and I entered the country as refugees, my family would have been unable to "pass the test" implicit in the skills-oriented immigration policy that I think would best serve the interests of the United States. There were no college graduates in my family, no wealth to prove that we would not become public charges, no particular skills that would seem "urgently needed." In short, putting aside the refugee circumstance of our entry, we simply would never have gotten a green card, and we would have never had the chance to share in the American dream. Nevertheless, immigration policy should be set in ways that further the national interest, and the nation's interest may simply not coincide with giving any particular person or any particular ethnic group the opportunity to partake in the unrivaled opportunities that the United States has to offer.

Looking back over my immigrant experience, I have come to treasure one important lesson. I was quite wrong in not sufficiently appreciating the beauty and substance of my new surroundings in those first few months after arriving in the United States. In the fall of 1997, during my first visit to Miami in over thirty years, I took a cab from the airport to one of the shiny new hotels scattered over the downtown area, and I asked the driver if he could take a detour to the "old" neighborhood. The apartment building was still there. And, although it had a fresh coat of paint, the house and the neighborhood were still run down. The Cuban refugees who had lived there in the early 1960s, it turned out, had long since moved on. New waves of immigrants, mostly of Haitian origin, now occupied the apartments.

In retrospect, I can see clearly the dreams and aspirations that motivated my family and so many others to move to the United States. The run-down apartment building was indeed a *residencia*, and the streets of that poor Miami neighborhood were paved with gold.

ACKNOWLEDGMENTS

MY STUDY OF THE economic impact of immigration stretches back over almost a twenty-year period. During that time, I have accumulated many debts to friends and colleagues, and it would be almost impossible to thank each of them individually. But a few of the debts stand out in my mind, so I would like to acknowledge them—even if the creditors may not remember what they contributed.

My greatest debt is to Richard Freeman. His steadfast encouragement and genuine enthusiasm for the line of research that I pursued on immigration issues dates back to the very beginning, when the study of such issues were the backwater of the economics profession and barely registered in the debate over public policy. We have discussed most of the questions addressed in this book many times, in many different settings, and from many different angles. We have collaborated on a number of research papers related to immigration issues. And I continue to value and learn from our interaction.

I am also very grateful to Steve Trejo. I have known Steve for twenty years. We are friends and colleagues, and have collaborated on several research projects. He was often the first person I sounded out on a particular idea, and I always learned something from his reaction. Steve also took the time to read carefully an early draft of this book, and he made copious annotations on the manuscript. I have come to trust Steve's judgment greatly, so almost all of his suggestions made it into the final draft.

I have also benefited from research collaborations with other friends and colleagues. They include Bernt Bratsberg, Steve Bronars, Lynette Hilton, Larry Katz, Valerie Ramey, Glenn Sueyoshi, and Marta Tienda. I have learned something valuable from each of these collaborations. And I know that my co-authors will be able to see their influence on the material presented in this book.

Over the past twenty years, I have discussed issues related to the economic impact of immigration in countless academic seminars, conferences, and public policy forums. At most of these events, my work evoked many reactions—sometimes favorable, sometimes less so. Although my memory of who said what at these meetings is dim, I remember specifically benefiting from discussions with Orley Ashenfelter, Gary Becker, Charles Brown, David Card, Ronald Ehrenberg, Rachel Friedberg, Daniel Hamermesh, James Heckman, John Pencavel, Alejandro Portes, James Rauch, Sherwin Rosen, Michael Rothschild, George Schultz, and Pete Wilson.

Several cohorts of students at the John F. Kennedy School of Government also left their mark. The idea for this book began to take shape as I prepared a set of notes for a class that I teach on "The Economic Impact of Immigration." Over time, the notes took on a life of their own as I filled in the details to address the (often skeptical) questions and reactions of the students. The

Kennedy School is an ideal place to teach about immigration because the students often know more about some of these issues than I do. One's perception of what the immigration debate is about is bound to change when the students include a Coast Guard captain who helps control the flow of Haitian and Cuban illegal aliens into Florida, lawyers who represent immigrant-rights groups, an assistant director for investigations at the Immigration and Naturalization Service, reporters who cover immigration issues for national newspapers, a Mexican government official who helps design Mexican immigration policy, and teachers who were part of California's bilingual education program. The students' reactions helped to broaden my horizon and sharpen my arguments.

I am also grateful to those who have generously shared their data and other types of information to help me prepare the book. They include David Autor, Ed Glaeser, Larry Katz, Mark Krikorian, Ronald Lee, Jeffrey Passel, Daniel Stein, and Michael Teitelbaum.

A number of friends and colleagues read parts (or all) of an early draft of the book, and made very valuable comments. They include Peter Brimelow, Daniel Hamermesh, John Isbister, Dani Rodrik, Fred Schauer, and Eric Wanner.

And I am grateful to the National Science Foundation. They have continuously supported my research on immigration since the mid-1980s. Their financial support enabled me to devote my time and effort to conducting a broad investigation of many related issues. This focus would have been impossible without their assistance.

Needless to say, the material contained in this book does not reflect the opinions or interpretations of any of the persons who influenced or helped in its preparation. After all, some of the reactions consisted of sharp disagreements with what I was trying to say.

On a more personal note, I am particularly grateful for the lessons my mother taught me not only about the immigrant experience, but also about many things in life. I do not know how things would have turned out had it not been for her perseverance after we arrived in Miami. She *knew* that she was going to make it—and there was never any looking back. That perseverance is an invaluable trait, particularly when one launches a two-decade investigation into an area that is an emotional and political minefield.

I am also very happy to have been able to share my recollections of the immigrant experience with my children, Sarah, Timothy, and Rebecca. They were a constant source of joy during the years that it took to prepare this book. They would often barge into my office to play at just the right time, when I was stuck in the middle of a particularly difficult section or a computer programming error had just spit out some information that I just knew had to be wrong. Luckily, they were born at a time and in a place where they will not have to worry about the things that I had to worry about as a child. But I have made sure that they understand what the immigrant experience is all about. When my twins were in preschool, the teacher took my wife aside and informed her, in a somewhat concerned tone (this was in the People's Republic of Cambridge, Massachusetts, after all), that the kids seemed to know an awful lot about the evil deeds committed by communist soldiers in Cuba. First lesson: A+.

And, finally, I am grateful to my wife, Jane. She also did not have to live the immigrant experience. And, as a result, she has taught me a great deal about the costs that the uprooted life imposes on the immigrant family. To be sure, these costs are far lower than the gains from moving. But the benefits do not come cheap for immigrants. She has helped me in the preparation of this book in many ways. But, above all, I am most grateful for her love.

Heaven's Door

Reframing the Immigration Debate

IN JANUARY 1979, China's Vice-Premier Deng Xiaoping made a much-celebrated state visit to Washington. At one of the meetings with President Jimmy Carter, both leaders brought along briefing books to guide their discussions. President Carter eventually got to the section that dealt with human rights and began his standard lecture, stressing that China had to learn to respect human rights. Among the specific human rights that concerned the president was the right of Chinese nationals to emigrate. Like most communist countries, China made it extremely difficult for its citizens to leave—presumably because, as a matter of ideology, no workers would ever want to leave a so-called workers' paradise.

"Mr. Vice-Premier," the president said, "the Jackson-Vanik amendment prohibits our granting most-favored-nation status to centrally-managed economies, unless they provide freedom of departure for their own nationals." Deng Xiaoping turned to *his* briefing book, leaned back in his chair, smiled, and asked, "Well, Mr. President, how many Chinese nationals do you want? Ten million? Twenty million? Thirty million?"[1]

Not surprisingly, that exchange marked the end of Jimmy Carter's brief campaign to grant Chinese citizens the right to leave their country.

Deng Xiaoping actually put his finger on one of the two crucial issues facing the United States in the current debate over immigration policy. Suppose that President Carter had replied that the United States was willing to admit ten million Chinese citizens over the next few years. The vice-premier could then have retorted, "Well, Mr. President, which ten million do you want? After all, we have a billion persons to choose from."

And there, in a nutshell, is what the immigration debate is all about. *How many* people should the United States admit? And, since there are many more persons who will want to migrate to the United States than the country is willing to admit, *which* of the visa applicants should the country accept?

The debate over immigration policy has raged throughout the entire span of American history. In 1753, twenty-three years before he signed the Declaration of Independence, Benjamin Franklin ruminated at length about the costs and benefits of German immigration.[2] On the one hand, he wrote, the German immigrants are "the most stupid of their own nation," "few of their children in the country know English," and "through their indiscretion, or ours, or both, great disorders may one day arise among us." But Franklin also appreciated immigration's benefits: German immigrants were "excellent husbandmen, and contribute greatly to the improvement of a country." In the end, Franklin concluded, the benefits could outweigh the costs—*if* the conditions were ripe: "All that seems necessary is, to distribute them more equally, mix them with the English, establish English schools where they are now too thick settled."

American history is dotted with such cost-benefit calculations. In some periods, the calculation encourages the country to adopt an open-door immigration policy, as was the case until 1924. In other periods, the calculation tempts the country to close the door and admit few immigrants, as was the case from 1924 through 1965.

As the twenty-first century begins, the United States is about to embark once again upon a historic debate about the type of immigration policy that the country should pursue. As in the past, the cost-benefit calculus frames the terms of the debate: Who loses from immigration, and by how much? Who gains from immigration, and by how much?

Consider some of the issues at the core of today's immigration debate. There is a great deal of worry, for example, that immigrants make extensive use of social services and do not "pay their way" in the welfare state. There is also anxiety that labor market competition with immigrants has a harmful impact on the economic well-being of some American workers. And there is the traditional concern over assimilation: Will today's immigrants find it harder to assimilate than did earlier waves? Do the large ethnic enclaves that dominate major American cities impede assimilation? Will the presence of hard-to-assimilate immigrants further balkanize the country, leading to undesirable social, economic, and political consequences in the next century?

On the benefit side, it is sometime argued that immigration spurs economic growth, perhaps by contributing to the creation of new industries, as in Silicon Valley. The large-scale migration of less-skilled workers may also reduce the prices that American consumers pay for many goods and services. In short, the size of the economic pie may be greatly increased by immigration, potentially making the entire population of the United States better off. Moreover, immigrants may do jobs that natives refuse to take, so that certain industries in the country—such as California's agriculture industry— would likely disappear if immigrant labor were not available. Finally, some participants in the debate argue that immigrants continually reintroduce ambition and drive into the American economy, helping propel the country forward.

These are all valid issues that should be part of the immigration debate. Unfortunately, they are also the *symptoms* of pursuing particular types of immigration policies. By arguing over the validity of these symptoms—whether immigrants use a lot of welfare, whether consumer prices are lowered by immigration—the immigration debate is, in a sense, worrying about the height of the trees in the forest, rather than about the shape of the forest itself.

The concern over each of these symptoms of immigration—whether harmful or beneficial—can be traced to a single issue: *the American people care about who the immigrants are*. It matters if the immigrants might need social services or if they might instead contribute to the funding of the programs in the welfare state. It matters if the immigrants compete with disadvantaged workers in the labor market and take their jobs away, or if the immigrants do jobs that natives do not particularly want and would go unfilled in the immigrants' absence. It matters if the immigrants "spark" the creative juices in particular industries, or if they simply replicate the talents of the native work force. And, finally, it matters if the immigrants will want to adapt to the social, economic, and political environment of the United States, or if they will fight to maintain their language and culture for several generations.

This book attempts to shift the terms of the immigration debate—away from arguing endlessly over the validity of the particular symptoms, and toward the fundamental questions: How many immigrants does the United States want? And which types of immigrants should the country admit?

By framing the debate in this fashion, I hope to clarify what is really at stake. And what is at stake is nothing less than the conception of what the United States is about. After all, it is futile to think about how many and which immigrants to admit unless one first has some objectives in mind. What is it that the American people want immigration to do for the country? Must immigration provide economic benefits to the native population? Which of the hundreds of millions of foreigners who now live under dire economic conditions or face political and religious persecution should be granted a chance to pursue the American dream? Does the United States want to use immigration as a political tool to further foreign policy goals? In short, what exactly does the United States want to accomplish through immigration?

Even if all Americans agreed on the same set of facts regarding the symptoms of immigration—such as the impact of immigrants on the labor market, on welfare expenditures, or on the gains that accrue to natives—they could still disagree on what to do about it. Some Americans, for instance, might put a lot of weight on what happens to their disposable income when selecting among alternative social policies. These Americans might then perceive the large-scale immigration of less-skilled workers as a boon because it allows them to buy many goods and services—such as vegetables grown in California, a neater lawn, or the services of a full-time nanny—at much lower prices. In contrast, other Americans might care deeply about the impact of immigration on income inequality in the United States, and would view the large-scale migration of less-skilled workers as an unmitigated disaster. This type of migration, after all, would probably have a very harmful impact on the wages of less-skilled native workers. Therefore, the same facts—that immigration of less-skilled workers cuts consumer prices and lowers the wages of less-skilled native workers—would have very different policy implications depending on what Americans wanted immigration to accomplish.

This book is an attempt to delineate the terms of the incipient immigration debate. In the next five chapters, the symptoms of immigration in the short run are evaluated. These chapters summarize the evidence that is most in contention in the debate over immigration policy. What types of immigrants is the United States admitting? How do they do in the labor market? What factors determine the rate of assimilation? What happens to native jobs when immigrants enter the labor market? What is the impact of immigration on the balance sheet of the welfare state? And who benefits and loses from immigration?

The next three chapters evaluate a different set of symptoms—symptoms that have yet to enter the public consciousness, but that are probably much more important. What is the impact of immigration in the long run, as the children and grandchildren of today's immigrants become tomorrow's ethnic groups? Does the melting pot work? Do the differences in skills and economic performance between immigrants and natives, or among the ethnic groups that make up the immigrant population, narrow across generations? How long will it take for the United States to digest the current wave of immigrants?

The last three chapters discuss the policy implications of the evidence. I ask two distinct questions: what should be the objective of immigration policy; and, given that objective, what should the country do about it? I sketch the implications of one particular objective: the maximization of the economic well-being of the native-born population. In my view, this objective has dominated the immigration debate throughout American history. There can obviously be a lot of disagreement among reasonable persons over my choice of such an objective for immigration policy. Even if one disagrees with my choice, however, there is still much to learn by comparing how any proposed immigration policy deviates from the one that the United States would pursue if the country simply wanted to make natives better off.

THE "TOP TEN" SYMPTOMS OF IMMIGRATION

Participants in the debate over immigration policy typically use an array of statistics, many of them drawn from the latest research by economists and other social scientists, as weapons in this debate. Each side in the debate stresses particular symptoms or provides a particular interpretation of the evidence. I begin by listing the top ten symptoms (not necessarily in order of importance) that frame the immigration debate, and that will likely determine its direction.

1. The Number of Immigrants Entering the United States Is at Record Levels

Although the United States has admitted immigrants throughout its entire history, the number of immigrants admitted into the country has fluctuated greatly over time (see Figure 1-1). Eras of heavy migration, for instance, were followed by decades of rest, during which time the immigrant waves were presumably assimilated and incorporated into the American mainstream.

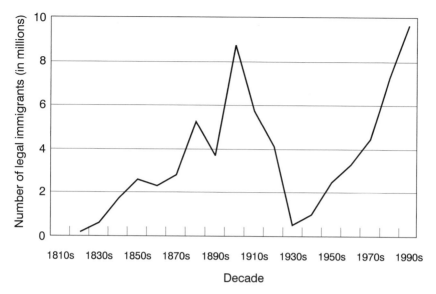

FIGURE 1-1. Legal immigration to the United States, by decade.

Source: U.S. Immigration and Naturalization Service, *Statistical Yearbook of the Immigration and Naturalization Service, 1996* (Washington, D.C. 1997), p. 25.

Note: The total number of legal immigrants for the 1990s is predicted by assuming that nine hundred thousand will be admitted in each of the remaining years of the decade.

Surprisingly, relatively few immigrants (only about ten million) entered the country between 1820 and 1880. The huge flow that has come to be known as the Great Migration began around 1880 and continued until 1924, bringing with it about twenty-six million immigrants. Between 1901 and 1910, at the peak of this unprecedented migration, an average of nine hundred thousand immigrants arrived in the United States each year. The immigration restrictions imposed in 1924, as well as the Great Depression, reduced the immigrant flow to a trickle by the 1930s. Since then, the number of immigrants has increased steadily, with the increase accelerating in the 1970s and 1980s. By the late 1990s, nearly one million persons entered the country legally each year, and another three hundred thousand entered the country illegally.

There is no disagreement over the fact that the absolute number of immigrants entering the country at the end of the twentieth century is at record levels. The country, however, is much larger now than it was in the early 1900s. As a result, some participants in the immigration debate emphasize that the foreign-born share of the U.S. population is much lower now— presumably implying that immigration is not as serious a problem as others make it out to be. In 1910, for example, 15 percent of the population was foreign-born, as compared to "only" 10 percent in 1998. It is worth noting, however, that the foreign-born share of the population has doubled since 1970, when it was just below 5 percent.

Moreover, it is not clear that this particular "spin" of the data accurately describes the demographic impact of immigration. Much more relevant is the fact that immigration in the 1990s played a near-record role in determining population growth in the United States. Because of the increasing number of immigrants and the lower fertility rate of American women, immigration in the 1990s, as in the early 1900s, accounted for at least a third of the change in population.[3] Therefore, immigration in the 1990s had a historic impact, at least in terms of determining the changes that are occurring in American social and economic life. And this impact clearly justifies calling the large immigrant wave that began to enter the United States after 1965 the *Second Great Migration*.

2. The Relative Skills and Economic Performance of Immigrants Have Declined

In 1960, the average immigrant man living in the United States actually earned about 4 percent more than the average native man. By 1998, the average immigrant earned about 23 percent less.

The worsening economic performance of immigrants is partly due to a decline in their relative skills across successive waves. The newest immigrants arriving in the country in 1960 were better educated than natives at the time of arrival; by 1998 the newest arrivals had almost two fewer years of schooling. As a result of this growing disadvantage in human capital, the relative wage of successive immigrant waves also fell. At the time of entry, the newest immigrants in 1960 earned 13 percent less than natives; by 1998, the newest immigrants earned 34 percent less.

In short, there has been a precipitous decline—relative to the trend in the native population—in the average skills of the immigrant flow reaching the United States. This historic change in the skill composition of the immigrant population helped rekindle the debate over immigration policy, and is the source of many of the symptoms of immigration that are stressed in this debate.

Although the direction of the overall trend in the relative skills of immigrants is clear, it would be a mistake to interpret the trend as indicating that every immigrant who entered the country in the 1980s and 1990s is relatively less skilled. The immigrant population is highly bifurcated: there are many immigrants with few skills and many immigrants who are highly skilled. In other words, immigrants tend to be lumped at both ends of the skill distribution. But the "bump" at the bottom end has become much more pronounced over time. By the late 1990s, almost 40 percent of the immigrants were in the bottom two deciles of the native wage distribution, and only 14 percent were in the top two deciles.[4] In other words, the relative decline in the average economic performance of immigrants is mainly due to a very large increase in the number of immigrants at the bottom of the skill distribution.

3. Immigrant Earnings Will Continue to Lag Behind

The worsening economic performance of immigrants at the time of entry might not be a cause for concern if their economic disadvantage diminished over time, as immigrants assimilated and acquired skills valuable to American employers. However, the economic gap between immigrants and natives may not narrow substantially during the immigrants' working lives.

The historical experience suggests that the process of economic assimilation—the acquisition of skills, such as English language proficiency, that American employers value—narrows the wage gap between immigrants and natives by about 10 percentage points in the first two decades after arrival. Immigrants who entered the United States after 1980 had a 25 percent wage disadvantage at the time of entry. If these recent arrivals experience the same rate of economic assimilation as did earlier waves, the wage gap between recent immigrants and natives will remain at about 15 percentage points throughout much of the immigrants' working lives. Put differently, the most recent immigrant waves will probably suffer a substantial economic disadvantage for decades to come.

4. National Origin Matters

The increase in immigration in recent decades can be attributed partly to changes in U.S. immigration policy. Prior to 1965, immigration was guided by the national origins quota system, which granted visas mainly to persons originating in Western European countries, particularly Great Britain and Germany. The 1965 Amendments to the Immigration and Nationality Act (and subsequent revisions) repealed the national origin restrictions, increased the number of available visas, and made family ties to persons already living in the United States the key factor that determines whether a visa applicant is admitted into the country.

As a consequence of these shifts and of major changes in economic and political conditions in the source countries, there was a substantial change in the national origin mix of the immigrant flow (see Figure 1-2). Over two-thirds of the legal immigrants admitted during the 1950s originated in Europe or Canada, one-quarter in Latin America, and only 6 percent in Asia. By the 1990s, only 17 percent of the immigrants originated in Europe or Canada, almost half in Latin America, and 30 percent in Asia.[5]

These changes have generated a great deal of concern over the link between immigration and the ethnic and racial composition of the U.S. population.[6] In 1970, the population was 5 percent Hispanic, 1 percent Asian, and 12 percent black. A recent projection concluded that by the year 2050 the population will be 26 percent Hispanic, 8 percent Asian, and 14 percent black.[7] If nothing else, the Second Great Migration has altered the "look" of the United States in ways that were unimaginable in 1970.

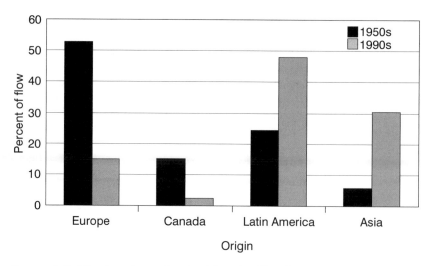

FIGURE 1-2. The changing national origin mix of immigrants.
    Source: U.S. Immigration and Naturalization Service, *Statistical Yearbook of the Immigration and Naturalization Service, 1996* (Washington, D.C., 1997), p. 25.
    Notes: "Latin America" includes all countries in the Western Hemisphere other than Canada. The data for the 1990s include only the 1991–96 period.

There are also huge differences in economic performance among national origin groups. Immigrants from El Salvador or Mexico earn 40 percent less than natives, while immigrants from Australia or South Africa earn 30 to 40 percent more. To some extent, these differences in economic performance among national origin groups mirror the dispersion in skills across the populations of the source countries. Immigrants who originate in countries that have abundant human capital and higher levels of per capita income tend to do better in the United States.

In view of the sizable skill differentials across ethnic groups, it is not surprising that the changes in the national origin mix of immigrants induced by the 1965 Amendments—away from the industrialized countries and toward developing countries—can explain the decline in the economic performance of successive immigrant waves. Put differently, there would not have been a decline in the relative skills and earnings of immigrants if the national origin mix of immigrants had remained the same in recent decades.

The strong link between national origin and economic performance raises an important—*and disturbing*—problem for immigration policy. Because national origin and immigrant skills are so closely related, any attempt to change one will inevitably change the other.

5. *Immigration Harmed the Economic Opportunities of the Least Skilled Natives*

Immigrants cluster geographically in a small number of cities and states. In 1998, almost three-quarters of the immigrants lived in only six states (California, New York, Texas, Florida, New Jersey, and Illinois). In contrast, only a third of the native-born lived in those states.

This geographical clustering suggests that one may be able to measure the impact of immigration on the labor market opportunities of native workers by comparing natives who reside in cities with large numbers of immigrants (such as San Diego) to natives who reside in cities where few immigrants live (such as Pittsburgh). The available evidence indicates that these "spatial correlations" are extremely weak: if one city has 10 percent more immigrants than another, the native wage in the city with more immigrants is perhaps .2 percent lower. This finding has led many observers to conclude that immigration has little impact on native employment opportunities.

It turns out, however, that a weak spatial correlation does not necessarily indicate that immigrants have a numerically inconsequential impact on the well-being of native workers. Suppose, for example, that immigration into California lowers the earnings of natives in California substantially. Native workers are not likely to stand idly by and watch their economic opportunities evaporate. Many will move out of California into other regions, and persons who were considering moving to California will now move somewhere else instead. These native population flows effectively diffuse the adverse impact of immigration on California's labor market over the entire economy. In the end, all native workers are worse off from immigration, not simply those who happened to live in the areas where immigrants clustered.

There is evidence that the flows of native workers within the United States—as well as the flows of native firms looking for cheap labor—have indeed responded to immigration. Because of these responses, the labor market impact of immigration must be measured at the national level, rather than at the local level.

Between 1980 and 1995, immigration increased the number of high school dropouts by 21 percent and the number of persons with at least a high school diploma by only 4 percent. During that time, the wage of high school dropouts relative to that of workers with more schooling fell by 11 percentage points. The disproportionate increase in the number of workers at the bottom end of the skill distribution probably caused a substantial decline in the relative wage of high school dropouts, accounting for perhaps half of the observed drop. In other words, immigration seems to have been an important contributor to the rise in income inequality in the United States, depressing the economic opportunities faced by the least skilled workers.

6. Immigration Had a Severe Fiscal Impact on the Affected States

In 1970, immigrants were slightly less likely to receive public assistance than natives. By 1998, immigrants had a much higher chance of receiving welfare: almost a quarter of immigrant households were receiving some type of assistance, as compared to 15 percent of native households.

Two distinct factors account for the disproportionate increase in welfare use among immigrant households. Because more recent immigrant waves are relatively less skilled than earlier waves, it is not surprising that more recent immigrant waves are also more likely to use welfare than earlier waves. In addition, the welfare use of a specific immigrant wave increases over time (both in absolute numbers and relative to natives). It seems that the assimilation process involves not only learning about labor market opportunities, but also learning about the income opportunities provided by the welfare state.

There is little doubt, therefore, that immigrants are making increasing use of public assistance programs. This trend, as well as the expense of providing immigrants with a host of public services, particularly education, has added a new and potentially explosive question to the immigration debate: do immigrants "pay their way" in the welfare state? A comprehensive study by the National Academy of Sciences concluded that immigration raised the annual taxes of the typical native household in California by about $1,200 a year.[8] The fiscal impact of immigration on the affected states, therefore, can be quite severe.

The welfare reform legislation enacted in 1996 gives states much greater leeway in setting benefit levels. States, in effect, are now freer to compete in the "market" for welfare recipients. It seems that immigrant-receiving states, such as California, have a huge incentive to race to the bottom as they attempt to reduce the fiscal burden imposed by the immigration of less-skilled workers.

7. The (Measurable) Net Economic Gains from Immigration Are Small

To see how natives gain from immigration, first think about how the United States gains from foreign trade. When the United States imports toys made by low-wage Chinese labor, workers in the American toy industry suffer wage cuts and perhaps even lose their jobs. These losses, however, are more than offset by the benefits accruing to consumers, who can now buy toys at lower prices.

Consider now the analogous argument for immigration. Immigrants increase the number of workers in the economy. Because of the additional competition in the labor market, the wage of native workers falls. At the same time, however, native-owned firms gain because they can now hire workers at lower wages, and many native consumers gain because the lower labor costs lead to cheaper goods and services. As with foreign trade, the gains accruing to the persons who use or consume immigrant services exceed the losses suffered by native workers, and hence society as a whole is better off.

Although some participants in the immigration debate claim that these gains from immigration are large, the facts are quite different: all of the available estimates suggest that the annual net gain is astoundingly small, less than .1 percent of GDP. In the late 1990s, this amounted to a net gain of less than $10 billion a year for the entire native population, or less than $30 per person.

Immigration, however, does more than just increase the total income accruing to natives. Immigration also induces a substantial redistribution of wealth, away from workers who compete with immigrants and toward employers and other users of immigrant services. Workers lose because immigrants drag wages down. Employers gain because immigrants drag wages down. These wealth transfers may be in the tens of billions of dollars per year.

These facts suggest a new prism for looking at the immigration debate. Immigration can be viewed as an income redistribution program, a large wealth transfer from those who compete with immigrant workers to those who use immigrant services or buy the goods produced by immigrant workers. The debate over immigration policy, therefore, is not a debate over whether immigration increases the size of the economic pie in the United States. Rather, the immigration debate is essentially a debate over how the pie is split.

Immigration may also benefit or harm the United States through what are called externalities. After all, immigration expands the size of the market. It can introduce many new interactions among workers and firms, and expose Americans to a variety of new products, such as the rich variety of ethnic cuisine that dominates major American cities. These potential benefits, however, are tempered by increased congestion or by a higher potential for ethnic conflict. Most of these externalities, however, are hard to measure, and the calculation of their benefit or harm will often be in the eye of the beholder.

8. Ethnic Skill Differentials May Persist for at Least Three Generations

In 1998, 11 percent of the U.S. population was "second-generation"—born in the United States but with at least one foreign-born parent. By the year 2050, the share of second-generation persons will increase to 14 percent, and an additional 9 percent will be composed of the grandchildren of current immigrants. The economic impact of immigration obviously depends not only on how immigrants adapt, but also on the adjustment process experienced by their offspring.

The historical experience of the children and grandchildren of the First Great Migration provides important lessons about the long-run consequences of immigration. That migration introduced substantial ethnic skill differentials into the United States: 97 percent of French immigrants knew how to read and write some language, as compared to 80 percent of Greek immigrants, and 45 percent of Mexican immigrants.

These differences helped determine the skills and economic performance of the children and grandchildren of the First Great Migration. A 20 percentage point difference in literacy rates among two immigrant groups in 1910, for instance, implied a one-year difference in educational attainment in the second generation, and a half-year difference in educational attainment in the third. Similarly, a 20 percent wage differential between two immigrant groups in 1910 implied a 12 percent wage differential in the second generation, and a 5 percent wage differential in the third. In rough terms, about half of the average skill differential between any two groups in the first generation persists into the second, and half of the differential remaining in the second generation persists into the third.

The historical lesson is clear: the skill differentials found among today's immigrants become the skill differentials found among tomorrow's ethnic groups. If past history is any guide, national origin will still determine the economic performance of the grandchildren of the Second Great Migration at the end of the twenty-first century. In short, ethnicity matters in economic life, and it matters for a very long time.

9. Ethnic Spillovers Influence the Social Mobility of Immigrant Groups

The characteristics of the ethnic environment, which I will call ethnic capital, influence the skills and economic performance of the children in the ethnic group, above and beyond the influence of the parents. These characteristics include the culture, attitudes, and economic opportunities that permeate the ethnic networks.

Exposure to an advantaged ethnic environment—in the sense that the environment has abundant human capital—has a positive influence on the children in the group, while exposure to a disadvantaged environment has a negative influence. Ethnic capital creates a type of stickiness in the process of social mobility, making it difficult for persons in disadvantaged ethnic groups to move up and for persons in the advantaged ethnic groups to move down. In other words, the skill differences across ethnic groups will tend to persist across generations because continued exposure to a particular set of socioeconomic traits and outcomes "spills over" and influences one's life.

The available evidence suggests that the skills of the children of immigrants are affected not only by the skills of their parents, but also by measures of the group's ethnic capital, such as the mean education or wage of the ethnic group in the parental generation. In fact, the impact of ethnic capital on social mobility may account for half of the persistence in ethnic skill differentials across generations. Because the children of particular ethnic groups tend to follow in the *group's* footsteps, ethnic capital effectively lowers the flame under the melting pot from a full boil to a slow simmer. In a sense, ethnic capital makes it hard to escape the economic fate implied by one's ethnic background.

10. Ethnic Ghettos Incubate Ethnic Differences and Slow Down the Melting Pot

There is a growing realization that the segregation of young African Americans into poor neighborhoods helped create the black underclass by depriving these young men and women of particular types of role models, and of the social and economic contacts that provide valuable information about many types of economic opportunities.[9] The segregation of blacks into poor neighborhoods helps feed a vicious cycle that makes it all the more difficult to escape the ghetto.

There is also a great deal of residential segregation among ethnic groups in the United States. Persons of Mexican ancestry live near other persons of Mexican ancestry, persons of Italian ancestry live near other persons of Italian ancestry, and so on. Because few of the persons in disadvantaged ethnic groups can afford to escape the ethnic ghetto, these enclaves make it easy for ethnic capital to influence the social mobility of the persons who reside in those ghettos, and help to perpetuate the socioeconomic differences observed across ethnic groups from generation to generation.

Ethnic ghettos are an important feature of many American cities at the end of the twentieth century. The immigrants in the Second Great Migration live, work, and raise their children in these ghettos. These neighborhoods provide the social and economic networks that will influence the lives of the children and grandchildren of these immigrants far into the next century. The stage has already been set for a new chapter in the history of ethnic America.

IMPLICATIONS FOR IMMIGRATION POLICY

So what should the United States do? It is important to get one piece of common sense out of the way quickly: the "top ten" symptoms of immigration listed above—*by themselves*—have no policy implications whatsoever. In other words, there are no policy implications inherent in the facts that immigrants use a lot of welfare or reduce the earnings of less-skilled workers or that ethnic enclaves hamper the assimilation process.

This approach to the immigration debate goes against the grain of most discussions of social policy reform. Typically, those who argue over the parameters of a particular social policy take sides by grasping onto a specific fact, and from that fact they immediately infer some policy reform that the country should pursue. In my view, this way of thinking about the evolution of social policy is just plain wrong.

To see why, single out a particular symptom of immigration over which there is little disagreement: immigrant use of welfare is high. The policy implications of this fact depend crucially on what the United States is trying to accomplish. If the goal of immigration policy were to ensure that immigration did not place a fiscal burden on the native population, this symptom would surely imply that the United States should take steps to restrict the entry of potential welfare recipients. If, in contrast, the goal of immigration policy were to help the poorest persons in the world, this symptom has no policy relevance—it is the price that the country is willing to pay to achieve a particular humanitarian objective. And the country would want to accept even more immigrants who could become potential welfare recipients.

In the end, a debate over the policy implications of what is known about the economic impact of immigration cannot be based on the evidence alone. *Any policy discussion requires explicitly stated assumptions about what constitutes the national interest.* It is the combination of the evidence with an assumption about what Americans desire that permits an informed debate over the type of immigration policy that the United States should pursue. In an important sense, the top ten symptoms of immigration resemble Pirandello's characters in search of an author. These symptoms are looking for a policy to recommend, but cannot find one unless the American people first ask, and answer, the bigger question, What should immigration policy accomplish?

Of course, answering this question is very difficult, even when the debate is restricted purely to the economic issues that tend to frame the immigration debate. To see why, divide the world into three distinct constituencies: the current population of the United States (or "natives"), the immigrants themselves, and those who remain in the source countries.[10] To draw policy conclusions from the symptoms of immigration, one has to know whose economic welfare the United States should try to improve when setting policy—that of natives, immigrants, the rest of the world, or some mix thereof. The policy implications implied by the symptoms depend crucially on whose interests the United States cares most about.

By framing the issue in this fashion, the tradeoffs implicit in immigration policy are made crystal clear. The native population probably benefits a great deal when the United States admits high-quality scientific workers, but the people left behind in the source countries probably lose a lot. Similarly, immigrants benefit when immigration policy favors the entry of their relatives, but natives may lose because this policy does not screen the new entrants and might let in many persons who qualify for social services.

It is probably impossible to come up with an immigration policy where all the relevant parties benefit.[11] As a result, the United States will have to make difficult choices.

In my view, any serious discussion of immigration policy must begin with the choice of a weighting scheme that values the costs and benefits that accrue to each of the three groups—the natives, the immigrants, and the rest of the world. And any assignment of weights among these groups inevitably raises a number of moral issues. Is it just to favor some persons over others? Is it fair to deny some persons the opportunity to join in the American dream? Is it right to make some natives pay for the benefits that immigration imparts to other natives?

I will address these issues in due course, but for now let's suppose that somehow the country has decided that the main objective of immigration policy should be to increase the economic well-being of the native population. That decision resolves the issue of how to weigh the costs and benefits accruing to the three groups. But there is still another question to answer: What exactly is it about natives that the country cares about? Does the country want to pursue an immigration policy that maximizes the per capita income of natives, without regard to how the economic pie is split? Or does the country want to pursue an immigration policy that does not increase the social and economic inequities that already exist in the United States?

Each of these decisions leads to a different interpretation of the symptoms of immigration. And, as a result, each permutation of what the American people determine to be the national interest generates a different recommendation for the type of immigration policy that the country should pursue.

Suppose for the sake of argument that the goal of immigration policy is indeed to maximize the economic well-being of the native population. And suppose that native economic well-being depends both on per capita income and on the distribution of income in the native population. In effect, the United States wants immigration to make the country wealthier, but it does not want immigration to greatly increase the amount of inequality in the society.

How many and which types of immigrants should the country then admit? The evidence presented in this book, I conclude, can be used to make a strong case that the United States would be better off by adopting an immigration policy that favored skilled workers. And a plausible argument can also be made that the country would be better off with a slight reduction in the number of immigrants.

It is useful to view immigration policy as a formula that gives "points" to visa applicants on the basis of various characteristics, and then sets a passing grade. The variables in the formula determine *which* types of persons will be admitted, while the setting of the passing grade determines *how many* persons will be let in. In 1965, the United States began to use an admissions formula that, to a large extent, had only one variable—whether the visa applicant had a family member already residing in the United States. The immigrant flow would be much more skilled if the United States, like other immigrant-receiving countries, expanded the admissions formula to include not only family connections, but such other factors as education, age, and English proficiency.

And how many immigrants should the country admit? In theory, the United States should admit an immigrant as long as the contribution made by the immigrant exceeds the costs imposed by the immigrant. Unfortunately, it is difficult to come up with the "magic number" unless one becomes much more specific about how to balance the facts that immigration increases the size of the economic pie *and* changes how the pie is split. Those who care about economic efficiency will typically want to see more immigrants: the greater the number of immigrants, the greater the gains to employers (through lower wages) and consumers (through lower prices). Those who care about distributional issues will typically want to see fewer immigrants: the greater the number of immigrants, the greater the dislocation in labor markets, and the greater the losses suffered by those who compete with immigrant workers.

In a typical year of the 1980s and 1990s, the United States admitted 730,000 legal immigrants, 200,000 illegal aliens, and over 100,000 refugees. In other words, the immigrant flow (net of refugees) consisted of around one million immigrants per year. This flow was disproportionately composed of less-skilled workers, and had a disproportionately severe impact on economic opportunities at the bottom end of the skill distribution. I suspect that an annual flow of one million immigrants is probably too large—regardless of whether the losers are at the bottom or at the top of the skill distribution. Such a large flow can substantially depress the economic opportunities of workers who compete with immigrant labor. A good place to start the process of converging to the "magic number" might be to let in 500,000 immigrants per year—which happens to roughly correspond with the recommendation made by the Commission on Immigration Reform in 1997.

The United States is about to embark on a historic debate, a debate that will determine who can partake in the American dream during the twenty-first century. Because the immigration debate has historically focused on economic issues, this book will inevitably emphasize the economic impact of immigration. Let me admit at the outset, however, that economic factors— *by themselves*—should not decide the outcome of this debate. But they will play an important role. Economics, after all, helps frame answerable questions about immigration: Who benefits? Who loses?

In the end, the objective of immigration policy will reflect a political consensus that inevitably incorporates the conflicting social and economic interests of various demographic, socioeconomic, and ethnic groups, as well as political and humanitarian concerns. Perhaps after debating these issues, the American people will place the economic concerns aside, and choose an immigration policy that stresses the humanitarian or political consequences of immigration.

Such a resolution of the debate does not diminish the value of entering a discussion that informs the country about the economic consequences of immigration. A wise and stable political consensus requires that the American people be fully aware of the price they will have to pay if the United States chooses to adopt an immigration policy that minimizes or ignores economic considerations.

The Skills of Immigrants

As NOTED EARLIER, the debate over immigration policy focuses almost exclusively on arguing over whether the symptoms of immigration are real or imagined. There is, for example, a great deal of concern because welfare use may run high among many immigrant groups. Some workers worry about the adverse impact that immigration might have on their employment opportunities. And many Americans fret over the social and cultural impact of immigration when immigrants are very "different" and have little potential for assimilating—either socially or economically—into the mainstream.

All of these concerns reflect a simple fact. The American people care about who the immigrants are, and it matters if the immigrants are likely to become public charges, if they speak little English, if they increase competition in the labor market, or if they find it hard to adapt to the United States.

If nothing else, decades of social science research have established an irrefutable link between human capital—a person's endowment of ability and acquired skills—and a wide array of social and economic outcomes, ranging from earnings potential to criminal activity, work effort to drug abuse, and family stability to life expectancy. In view of this strong link, it is not surprising that the United States cares about whether the immigrant population is composed of skilled or unskilled workers. The skill composition of the immigrant population—*and how the skills of immigrants compare to those of natives*—determine the social and economic consequences of immigration for the country.

The connection between immigrant skills and the fiscal impact of immigration is obvious. The many programs that make up the welfare state tend to redistribute resources from high-income workers to persons with less economic potential. Skilled workers, regardless of where they were born, typically pay higher taxes and receive fewer social services. As a result, highly skilled immigrants would probably have a negligible impact on the cost of social insurance programs—and might even contribute to their funding. From a fiscal point of view, therefore, skilled immigrants are probably a very good investment.

Skilled immigrants may also assimilate quickly. They might be more adept at learning the tools and "tricks of the trade" that can increase the chances of economic success in the United States, such as the language and culture of the American workplace. Moreover, the structure of the American economy changed drastically in the 1980s and 1990s, and now favors workers who have valuable skills to offer. It seems, therefore, as if skilled immigrants have a head start in the race for economic assimilation.

The skill mix of immigrants also determines which native workers are most affected by immigration. Unskilled immigrants will typically harm unskilled natives, while skilled immigrants will harm skilled natives. As this chapter documents, a large number of the immigrants in the Second Great Migration are relatively unskilled, and could be expected to have an adverse impact on the economic opportunities of less-skilled natives. It should not be too surprising that public opinion polls typically report that low-income Americans are the ones most opposed to immigration. In 1995, 70 percent of high school dropouts believed that immigration should be decreased from its present level, as compared to "only" 48 percent of those with a graduate education.[1]

Finally, the skills of immigrants determine the economic benefits from immigration. The United States benefits from international trade because it can import goods that are not available or are too expensive to produce in the domestic market. Similarly, the country benefits from immigration because it can import workers with scarce qualifications and abilities. Think, for example, of the great culinary benefits that immigration has offered restaurant-goers in most large American cities.

If immigrants were just like American workers—that is, if they had the same mix of doctors and accountants, beauticians and bricklayers, and gardeners and lawyers that Americans already have—the gains from immigration would not be very large. Immigrants would have little to contribute to economic life because they would essentially replicate what already exists. The economic gains from immigration multiply when immigrants are very different from natives. The United States has much to gain when the human capital and physical resources that immigrants bring complement those that already exist. Immigrants can then produce goods and services that are not currently available, or produce existing goods and services at much lower prices.

For example, the admission of many unskilled immigrants, who often end up in the service sector of the economy, might allow skilled natives to specialize in doing what they do best. The skilled natives could then devote all their time and effort to writing software programs and designing electronic equipment, and avoid such time-consuming tasks as housekeeping and child-raising. Similarly, importing many skilled immigrants (such as a cluster of world-class scientists in a field where the United States is not dominant) might unleash a flowering of scientific discovery that could have beneficial repercussions throughout the entire economy.

But the economic gains from immigration gains do not come out of thin air. The factory owners who can now hire cheaper laborers, the universities and think tanks that can now hire cheaper mathematicians, and those Americans who consume the garments and formulas that the laborers and mathematicians produce gain substantially. At the same time, the native laborers who had been producing (or who could have been producing) those garments and the native mathematicians who had an exclusive monopoly over producing mathematical formulas now face stiffer competition in the labor market—and lower wages.

TABLE 2–1
The Changing Skills of the Immigrant and Native Populations, 1960–98

	1960	1970	1980	1990	1998
Native men					
Percent who are high school dropouts	53.0	39.7	23.3	11.9	9.0
Percent who are college graduates	11.4	15.4	22.8	26.4	29.8
Percent with at least a master's degree	—	—	—	9.2	9.9
Immigrant men					
Percent who are high school dropouts	66.0	49.0	37.5	31.4	33.6
Percent who are college graduates	10.1	18.6	25.3	26.6	28.3
Percent with at least a master's degree	—	—	—	12.9	12.5
Percent hourly wage differential between immigrant and native men	4.2	0.0	−9.2	−15.0	−23.0
Native women					
Percent who are high school dropouts	46.1	35.3	19.7	9.2	6.6
Percent who are college graduates	9.7	11.5	17.9	23.6	28.5
Percent with at least a master's degree	—	—	—	7.7	8.7
Immigrant women					
Percent who are high school dropouts	61.8	47.9	34.6	25.9	24.5
Percent who are college graduates	5.6	9.7	17.5	23.0	28.7
Percent with at least a master's degree	—	—	—	8.0	8.8
Percent hourly wage differential between immigrant and native women	3.4	3.0	−1.7	−5.0	−12.1

Sources: Calculations from the 1960–90 Public Use Microdata Samples of the U.S. Census and the pooled 1996–98 Current Population Surveys (Annual Demographic Files).

Note: The data refer to salaried workers who are twenty-five to sixty-four years old and are employed in the civilian sector.

In sum, the costs and benefits from immigration are intrinsically linked to the skills of immigrants, and to how those skills compare with the skills of natives. As a result, debating over the validity of some of the symptoms of immigration is somewhat fruitless. Instead, the immigration debate should be directly confronting one of the central questions in immigration policy: *Whom should the United States let in?*

THE TREND IN IMMIGRANT SKILLS

The relative educational attainment and the economic performance of the immigrant population in the United States changed markedly—and for the worse—in the last half of the twentieth century (see Table 2-1).[2] In 1960, immigrant workers, on average, earned more than native workers. By the 1990s, the educational attainment and wages of immigrants lagged far behind.[3]

The extent of this decline is remarkable. In 1960, for instance, 66 percent of immigrant men were high school dropouts, and 10 percent were college graduates. This educational mix was somewhat worse than that of native men, where 53 percent were high school dropouts, and 11 percent were college graduates. But immigrants actually earned about 4 percent *more* than natives. By the late 1990s, both groups were still just as likely to have a college degree, but immigrants were far more likely to be high school dropouts (34 percent of immigrants lacked a high school diploma, as compared to only 9 percent of natives). Partly as a result of the widening gap in educational attainment between the two groups, the earnings advantage enjoyed by immigrant workers in 1960 vanished and turned into a huge disadvantage, with immigrants earning about 23 percent less than natives by 1998.[4]

These data summarize the key trends in the skills and economic performance of the average immigrant and average native worker in the United States. A better understanding of the gap between the two groups can be obtained by comparing their wage distributions. Figure 2-1 illustrates the fraction of immigrant workers found in each of the ten deciles of the native wage distribution. If immigrants had the same wage distribution as natives, 10 percent of the immigrant work force would be found in each of the deciles. In 1960, there was little difference between the wage distribution of immigrants and natives: roughly 10 percent of the immigrants fell into each of the ten deciles of the native wage distribution. By 1998, however, immigrants were very likely to be in the bottom deciles. Almost 40 percent of the immigrants were in the bottom two deciles of the native wage distribution, and only 14 percent placed in the top two deciles.

The comparison of the immigrant and native skill distributions also reveals an interesting fact. Throughout the 1970s and 1980s, there was some bifurcation in the immigrant population: there were a lot of immigrants at both the top and the bottom of the skill distribution. This bifurcation became much less pronounced over time, with the slight overrepresentation of immigrants at the top of the distribution disappearing by the 1990s. In 1970 and 1980, for example, roughly 11 percent of the immigrants were in the top decile of the native wage distribution. By the late 1990s, however, only 8 percent of the immigrants were in the top decile. Overall, the post-1960 deterioration in the relative economic performance of the average immigrant is almost entirely due to a large increase in the proportion of immigrants at the very bottom rung of the U.S. economic ladder.

A MATTER OF INTERPRETATION

The dramatic decline in the relative economic performance of immigrants is the result of many different factors. Two distinct questions play a central role in any discussion of this trend:

- How do the skills of the immigrant waves admitted in the 1980s and 1990s compare to the skills of the waves admitted in the 1950s and 1960s?
- What happens to the economic performance of immigrants as they assimilate into the United States?

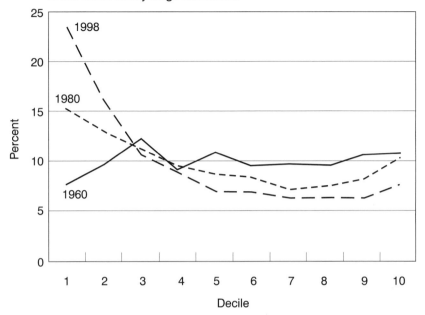

FIGURE 2-1. Changes in the wage distribution of immigrant men.

Sources: George J. Borjas, "The Economic Analysis of Immigration," in *Handbook of Labor Economics*, vol. 3, ed. Orley Ashenfelter and David Card (Amsterdam: North-Holland, forthcoming 1999), tab. 3; and additional calculations from the pooled 1996–98 Current Population Surveys (Annual Demographic Files).

Note: The data refer to salaried men who are twenty-five to sixty-four years old and are employed in the civilian sector.

To see why it is crucial to distinguish between these two questions, consider the data illustrated in Figure 2-2, which compares the economic performance of various waves of immigrants as of 1990. At that time, the newest immigrants (those who arrived after 1984) earned 32 percent less than natives; immigrants who arrived in the early 1970s, and had been in the country almost twenty years, earned about 9 percent less; and immigrants who arrived in the early 1960s, and had been in the country almost thirty years, earned about 9 percent more. The trend is clear and unmistakable: immigrants who have been in the country longer do better. How should this trend be interpreted, however?

The "assimilationist" interpretation argues along the following lines.[5] Newly arrived immigrants tend to perform poorly in the U.S. labor market because they lack skills that are rewarded by American employers, such as being proficient in the English language, and know little about the structure of the labor market. New immigrants may not even know which industries are growing and which are contracting, or which geographic regions offer the best job opportunities and which offer stagnant or declining labor mar-

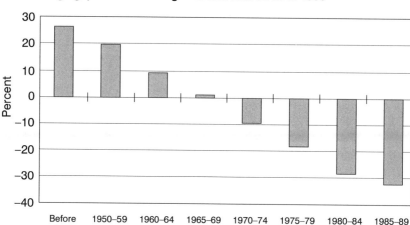

FIGURE 2-2. Wage differentials between immigrants and natives in 1990, by year of entry.

Source: Calculations from the 1990 Public Use Microdata Sample of the U.S. Census.

Note: The data refer to salaried men who are twenty-five to sixty-four years old and are employed in the civilian sector.

kets. As immigrants acquire these skills and learn about alternative jobs, the wage gap between immigrants and natives will probably narrow. If, in addition, only the most driven and most able persons have the ambition and wherewithal to pack up, move, and start life anew in a foreign country, one should not be too surprised if immigrants eventually overtake natives in terms of their earnings potential.

This interpretation of the data snapshot in Figure 2-2 provides a very optimistic appraisal of the economic contribution of immigrants. After all, the low wage of the most recent arrivals—the 32 percent wage gap at the time of entry—is a short-run phenomenon. Over the next two decades, this wage disadvantage will narrow, disappear, and turn around, so that even these low-wage immigrants will be quite productive in the long run.

There is, however, another interpretation of the same data, one that is much less upbeat about the future.[6] Suppose that today's newly arrived immigrants are inherently less skilled than those who arrived twenty years ago. The poor economic performance of recent arrivals may then indicate that the newest immigrants have few skills and little economic potential and hence will *always* have low earnings, while the economic success enjoyed by the earlier arrivals may indicate that the earlier waves were always better skilled and had greater economic potential. Because of these intrinsic differences in skills across immigrant waves, one cannot use the current labor market experiences of those who arrived twenty or thirty years ago to forecast the future earnings of newly arrived immigrants.

In short, the 1990 data snapshot yields an incorrect picture of the adaptation process experienced by immigrants if there are skill differentials among immigrant cohorts at the time of their entry into the United States. Shifts in immigration policy, such as a change in the rules used to award entry visas, could generate such skill differentials. After all, pursuing a policy that favors the admission of skilled workers probably leads to a more skilled immigrant flow than a policy that favors relatives of U.S. residents. There are also huge skill differences among workers originating in different countries, so any policy shift that alters the national origin mix of immigrants will also generate skill differences across immigrant cohorts. Finally, many immigrants decide to return to their home countries after testing the waters in the United States. Suppose that the returnees are the ones who find that things did not work out as expected, and have disproportionately low wages. At the time the data snapshot is taken, the earlier waves have been "weeded out" and will have higher average earnings than more recent waves—even if no economic assimilation ever takes place.

The profound difference between these two interpretations of the same data has played and continues to play a major role in the immigration debate. Consider, for example, Carl C. Brigham's notorious *Study of American Intelligence*, first published in 1923.[7] Brigham was a highly respected academic at Princeton University, who later in his career helped develop the Scholastic Aptitude Test (SAT), the standard aptitude test used by admission offices in most American colleges and universities. Part of Brigham's influential study described the trends in immigrant "intelligence" as measured by the scores on IQ tests given to army recruits during World War I. This study, along with many others, probably helped fuel the debate over immigration that culminated in the restrictive legislation enacted in 1924.[8]

The army data indicated that foreign-born recruits who had been in the United States for less than five years had an "average mental age" of eleven years, while recruits who had been in the country for at least twenty years had an average mental age of almost fourteen years. Brigham interpreted these data simply and provocatively: "The average intelligence of succeeding waves of immigration has become progressively lower." He further attributed this trend to the relative decline in the number of "Nordic" immigrants in the United States: "The intellectual superiority of our Nordic group over the Alpine, Mediterranean and negro groups has been demonstrated."[9]

There is little disagreement over the validity of the army data: immigrants who had been in the United States longer did have higher IQ scores. Brigham's notorious contribution was to *interpret* this correlation as indicating that earlier immigrant waves were just smarter. But it was almost inevitable that measured IQ scores would increase as immigrants assimilated into the United States, becoming more comfortable with the English language and "learning" the types of responses that the army psychologists were expecting. In other words, an alternative explanation of the same data is that IQ increased the longer the immigrants lived in the United States.

Brigham, however, was certainly not the last person to interpret trends in immigration by filtering the data through a particular—and often ideological—lens. Consider, for example, the Urban Institute's widely publicized attempt in 1994 to "set the record straight" on immigration. The Urban Institute study, which many in the media interpreted as a pro-immigration essay,[10] compares the incomes of various immigrant waves as of 1990 and notes:

> For households headed by immigrants entering the U.S. before 1980, household income averages about $40,900 a year—almost 10 percent greater than native households. But income for households headed by immigrants who entered in the 1980s averages only $31,100.[11]

In other words, the 1990 data snapshot shows immigrants who have lived in the United States longer earning more. This positive correlation leads the Urban Institute researchers to conclude that "*immigrant socioeconomic status improves with time in the United States,*" and that "data for immigrants who have been in this country for at least 10 years suggest that over time immigrants increasingly resemble natives."[12] The optimistic policy inference is clear: one need not be too concerned about the substantial economic disadvantage of recently arrived immigrants because in a decade or two these immigrants will do just as well as, if not better than, the native-born. The Urban Institute study, however, ignores the more pessimistic interpretation of the same data: the newest immigrants are inherently less skilled than the earlier arrivals.

The history of the immigration debate shows that ideas matter. The interpretation imposed upon a fundamentally ambiguous piece of evidence can have a major impact on social policy. As a result, it is crucial to understand the trends in immigrant economic performance and to predict what these trends portend for the future. To do this right, one has to disentangle differences in skills across immigrant cohorts from the skill accumulation that occurs as a given cohort assimilates into the United States.

THE NEW IMMIGRATION VERSUS THE OLD IMMIGRATION

Are the immigrant waves arriving today as skilled as those that arrived twenty or thirty years ago? As illustrated above, this question has a long—and less than honorable—history in the immigration debate. The checkered history of this question, however, does not diminish its relevance for evaluating the economic impact of immigration, or for thinking about the type of immigration policy that the United States should pursue.

It turns out that one can provide a convincing answer by contrasting the skills and economic performance of the most recently arrived immigrants enumerated in the 1960 or 1970 Census with the skills and economic performance of the most recently arrived immigrants enumerated in later surveys.[13]

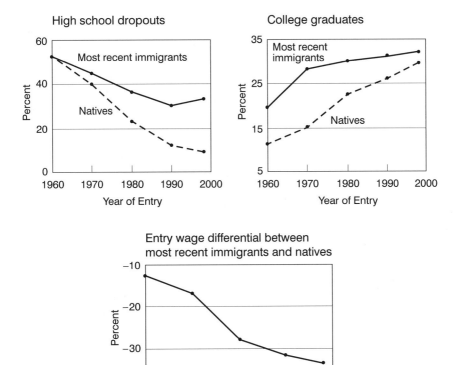

FIGURE 2-3. The changing skills of successive immigrant waves, 1960–98.

Sources. Calculations from the 1960–90 Public Use Microdata Samples of the U.S. Census and the pooled 1996–98 Current Population Surveys (Annual Demographic Files).

Notes. The data refer to salaried men who are twenty-five to sixty-four years old and are employed in the civilian sector. The sample of "most recent immigrants" consists of persons who arrived in the country in the five-year period prior to the survey.

This type of comparison isolates the trend in the skill level of successive immigrant cohorts (see Figure 2-3).

The trend in educational attainment is striking. In 1960, 53 percent of natives were high school dropouts; by 1998, only 9 percent of natives lacked a high school diploma. In contrast, 52 percent of the immigrants admitted in the late 1950s were high school dropouts at the time of arrival, as compared to 33 percent of the immigrants admitted in the late 1990s. In short, the immigrants who had just entered the country in 1960 were slightly *less* likely to be high school dropouts. By 1998, the newest immigrants were almost four times more likely to be high school dropouts.

In contrast, even though the fraction of new immigrant workers who were college graduates rose steadily over the period, the fraction of natives who were college graduates rose even faster. In 1960, the typical immigrant admitted was almost twice as likely as a native worker to be a college graduate. By 1998, the immigrant advantage in college graduation rates had mostly disappeared.

In view of these trends in educational attainment, it is not surprising that the *entry* wage gap between immigrant and natives widened substantially. The immigrants who had just entered the country in 1960 earned 13 percent less than natives at the time of arrival. By 1980, the newest entrants earned 28 percent less than natives; and by 1998, the newest entrants had a 34 percent wage disadvantage.[14] As long as one is willing to interpret relative wages as a measure of relative skills, the relative skills of successive immigrant waves declined precipitously in the post-1965 period.

It is worth noting that these data, based on surveys collected by the Bureau of the Census, do not distinguish between legal and illegal aliens, nor do they distinguish between refugees and other legal immigrants. One could then argue that the statistical evidence does not provide any guidance for immigration policy because it pools very disparate groups. It might be the case, for example, that the decline in relative skills was due entirely to the entry of illegal aliens. It would then be fruitless to change the parameters that regulate the entry of legal immigrants to correct a problem that was not there in the first place.

It is not difficult to get a rough picture of what the long-run trend might look like in the legal, nonrefugee population. About half of the illegal aliens originate in Mexico.[15] Although Mexicans also make up the largest national origin group in the legal immigrant population, it might be worth investigating the direction of the trend in the sample of non-Mexican immigrants (where illegal immigration presumably plays a much smaller role). It turns out that the relative wage of successive immigrant cohorts declined even among non-Mexican immigrants (see Figure 2-4). Similarly, over 90 percent of the refugees admitted in the 1970s and 1980s originated in one of thirteen countries.[16] One can then analyze the trends in the sample of immigrants who did *not* originate in these countries. Again, the evidence is irrefutable: the relative entry wage of immigrants who are not Mexicans and who did not originate in the main refugee-sending countries declined substantially between 1960 and 1990.

Moreover, a recent report issued by the National Academy of Sciences used data collected by the Immigration and Naturalization Service to calculate a measure of skills for three specific cohorts of legal immigrants—the waves admitted in 1977, 1982, and 1994.[17] At the time of entry, each legal immigrant is asked about his or her occupation.[18] This information can be used to calculate the "average occupational earnings," the earnings in the occupation that employs the typical immigrant. It turns out that the typical legal immigrant admitted in 1977 worked in an occupation that offered $21,300 a year (in 1979 dollars). By 1994, the typical latest arrival worked in an occupation that offered only $19,600. Over a seventeen-year period, therefore, the entry earnings potential of successive immigrant waves—as measured by occupa-

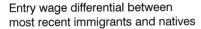

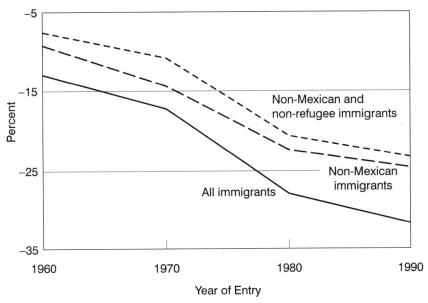

FIGURE 2-4. Mexican immigration, refugees, and the declining relative wage of immigrants.

Source: Calculations from the 1960–90 Public Use Microdata Samples of the U.S. Census.

Notes: The data refer to salaried men who are twenty-five to sixty-four years old and are employed in the civilian sector. The sample of "most recent immigrants" consists of persons who arrived in the country in the five-year period prior to the survey.

tional earnings—had fallen by 8 percent. The lesson is clear: the declining skills of immigrants are a consequence of the policies that regulate *legal* immigration.

ECONOMIC ASSIMILATION

The most important feature of immigration in the post-1965 period has been a significant deterioration in the economic performance of successive immigrant waves. Relative to natives, the "new" immigrants are not as skilled or as economically successful as immigrants who came in earlier waves. The policy reaction to this trend might depend on whether the entry wage disadvantage disappears over time, as the immigrants assimilate in the American economy and acquire skills and information valuable in the American labor market. It turns out, however, that this is often not the case, particularly for the most recent arrivals.

One can get a sense of the rate of economic assimilation by measuring how the wage gap between natives and a specific wave of immigrants narrows over

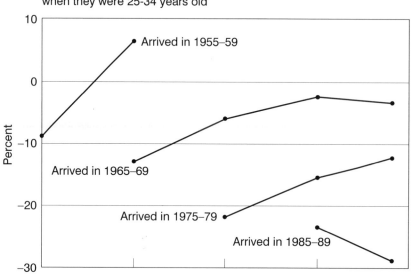

Relative wage of immigrants who arrived
when they were 25-34 years old

FIGURE 2-5. Economic assimilation.

Sources: George J. Borjas, "The Economic Analysis of Immigration," in *Handbook of Labor Economics*, vol. 3, ed. Orley Ashenfelter and David Card (Amsterdam: North-Holland, forthcoming 1999), tab. 2; and additional calculations from the pooled 1996–98 Current Population Surveys (Annual Demographic Files).

Notes: The data refer to salaried men who are employed in the civilian sector. Each cohort is tracked across surveys, with the age of the immigrant and native workers changing over time. For example, the workers who entered between 1975 and 1979 were twenty-five to thirty-four years old in 1980, thirty-five to forty-four years old in 1990, and forty-three to fifty-two years old in 1998.

time. For example, one can use the decennial Census data to calculate the wage differential between newly arrived immigrants and natives as of 1970, recalculate the wage gap between these same two groups ten years later in the 1980 Census, and recalculate it again twenty years later in the 1990 Census (see Figure 2-5).

Consider the group of immigrant men who arrived in the late 1960s at a relatively young age (they were twenty-five to thirty-four years old in 1970). These immigrants earned 13 percent less than comparably aged native workers at the time of entry. Move forward in time ten years to 1980, when both the immigrants and the natives are thirty-five to forty-four years old. The wage gap between the two groups has narrowed to 6 percentage points. Move forward in time again to 1990, when both immigrants and natives are forty-five to fifty-four years old. The wage gap between the same immigrants and natives declined further, to 2 percent. Finally, move forward in time to 1998, when the two groups are fifty-three to sixty-two years old. It turns out that the wage gap did not narrow any further in the 1990s. Overall, the process of economic assimilation reduced the initial wage disadvantage of these immigrants by about 10 percentage points over a thirty-year period. Because this immigrant cohort had a relatively high entry wage, the process of economic assimilation allowed the immigrants to narrow the wage disadvantage substantially, and to almost "catch up" to natives.

The young immigrants who arrived after 1970, however, face a much bleaker future—simply because they start out with a much greater disadvantage. Consider those who arrived in the late 1970s. They entered the country with a 22 percent wage disadvantage. By the late 1990s, twenty years after arrival, these immigrants were still earning 12 percent less than natives. The situation is even gloomier for those who arrived in the late 1980s. They started out with a 23 percent wage disadvantage, but the wage gap actually grew, rather narrowed, during the 1990s. If the historical experience is used to extrapolate into the future, these cohorts should be able to eventually narrow the gap, but by 10 percentage points, so these immigrants will earn much less than natives throughout their working lives.

The evidence, therefore, suggests that most of the immigrants who arrived in the 1970s and 1980s will not accumulate sufficient human capital to close the skills gap. Interestingly, this was not always the case. The young immigrants who entered the country in the late 1950s had a 9 percent wage disadvantage at the time of entry. By 1970, however, these immigrants had experienced substantial wage growth, sufficient not just to catch up to natives, but to actually surpass them. In the first ten years after entry, the relative wage of this immigrant cohort grew by 15 percentage points, far above the growth rate experienced by the post-1965 cohorts.[19] In short, the waves of immigrants who made up the Second Great Migration had lower starting wages *and* lower rates of economic assimilation.

Is Economic Assimilation Desirable?

Many participants in the immigration debate implicitly assume that economic assimilation—the process of human capital accumulation that narrows the wage gap between immigrants and natives—is socially desirable, and is something that policymakers might want to encourage and even nurture.

The question of assimilation, whether economic or cultural, has always played a major role in the immigration debate. Prior to the 1960s, there was a clear consensus that *E Pluribus Unum* (From Many, One), the motto of the United States seal, should be the guiding theme of public policy regarding assimilation. Sadly, that consensus no longer exists. Moreover, the multicultural political rhetoric of the 1980s and 1990s often denigrated the notion of cultural assimilation with such sound bites as "Death by English" or "Cultural assimilation, cultural acculturation . . . or cultural assassination!"[20] Martha Farnsworth Riche, director of the Bureau of the Census in the Clinton administration, succinctly, and perhaps inadvertently, unveiled part of the hidden political agenda of the multiculturalists: "Without fully realizing it, we have left the time when the nonwhite, non-Western part of our population could be expected to assimilate to the dominant majority. In the future, the white Western majority will have to do some assimilation of its own."[21]

Of course, the notion of economic assimilation differs somewhat—*but only somewhat*—from the loss of an immigrant's language and culture that the multiculturalists deplore. Some observers probably wish that the United States offered a social and economic environment where immigrants could maintain their cultural and social identity, yet at the same time make rapid economic progress. In order to experience economic assimilation, however, an immigrant will often have to acquire skills that are valued by American employers, such as learning the English language, adopting the norms of the American workplace, moving to economically vibrant areas that might be quite distant from the ethnic enclave, entering nontraditional occupations, and so on. Each of these activities helps to weaken the link between the immigrant's foreign past and his or her American future. In an important sense, therefore, many immigrants must pay a price for economic progress: they have to discard the attributes, habits, and characteristics that can hamper the chances of making it in the American economy, and pick up the ones that enhance those chances.

Ironically, from a purely economic point of view, it is unclear that the United States is better off by encouraging the immigrant population to assimilate rapidly. On the one hand, the process of assimilation helps narrow the economic gap between immigrants and natives, reducing the drain on many social services. The rapid assimilation of disadvantaged immigrants would also lower the chances that this population, clustered in poor ethnic ghettos, would become a new underclass, the potential source of a great deal of social conflict. On the other hand, the economic gains from immigration are largest when the skills of immigrants most complement those of natives. The quicker immigrants become like American workers, the faster those gains vanish.

I suspect, however, that the cost of addressing the social and economic problems created by a large underclass of immigrants (and their descendants) greatly exceeds the economic gains that arise from production complementarities between immigrant and native workers. After all, the available evidence indicates that these productivity gains are quite small. A simple cost-benefit calculation would then suggest that the United States would be better off by encouraging rapid economic assimilation, making it easier for immigrants to acquire the skills and human capital that increase their marketability and acceptability in their newly adopted country.

Needless to say, assimilation is not purely, or even mainly, an economic phenomenon. Delaying the process of cultural assimilation also has significant—and potentially much more serious—social and political consequences. One need not travel far to see the intrinsic dangers that a country faces when it has numerically large, culturally distinct, and linguistically separate minorities. The de facto political segmentation of Canada provides an illuminating example—an example that Americans ignore at their peril.[22]

Economic Assimilation and the English Language

After arriving in the United States, immigrants add to their human capital in many ways. They might return to school, they might enroll in on-the-job training programs, or they might devote some time and effort to learning about the types of jobs and economic opportunities offered by American employers in different cities and industries.

Perhaps the most important part of the assimilation process is the acquisition of English language proficiency. It would seem that English proficiency is economically beneficial because bilingual immigrants have many additional opportunities: they can look for jobs both inside and outside the ethnic enclave. In fact, a great deal of evidence shows that immigrants who understand and speak English earn more than those who do not. Hispanic immigrants who speak English earn 17 percent more than those who do not, even after adjusting for differences in education and other socioeconomic characteristics between the two groups.[23] And as much as half of the relative wage growth experienced by immigrants in the first twenty years after arrival may be attributed to the gains from learning the English language.[24]

Nevertheless, a large number of immigrants do not bother or are unable to learn the English language. In 1990, for example, 37 percent of the immigrants who had been living in the United States for at least ten years did not speak English "very well."[25] In view of the apparently very high returns to being bilingual, it is worth asking why more immigrants do not make the necessary investment.

The economic payoff to becoming bilingual *for a particular immigrant* may have little to do with the wage differential that exists between immigrants who speak English and immigrants who do not. English proficiency and earnings might be correlated simply because more able workers are likely to both speak English *and* earn more. Put differently, the 17 percent wage advantage enjoyed by Hispanics who speak English does not necessarily imply that a newly arrived Hispanic immigrant would increase his or her earnings by 17 percent by learning English.

The economic returns to learning English are also influenced by the extreme clustering of immigrants in ethnic enclaves, such as the Cubans in Miami's Little Havana and the Mexicans in the barrios of East Los Angeles. Immigrants in these enclaves may have little to gain from becoming bilingual, simply because most of their social and economic exchanges are with persons who share the same ethnic and linguistic background. Almost half of the Cubans who arrived in the Mariel boatlift in 1980, for instance, worked for Cuban employers in 1986.[26] In fact, the wage gap between Hispanics who know English and Hispanics who do not is 26 percent in counties where there are few Hispanics, but only 11 percent in counties that have a large Hispanic population.[27] As a result, immigrants who live in an area where they can find many compatriots who share their culture and language are much less likely to learn English.[28]

In sum, the larger and more geographically segregated the ethnic group becomes, the less likely that persons in that group will become proficient in the English language, and the less likely that the group will be fully integrated into American economic life.[29]

The historical data from the last half of the twentieth century provide a somewhat pessimistic appraisal of the contribution that the Second Great Migration made to the skill endowment of the U.S. work force. It seems that the later waves of immigrants do not perform as well in the labor market as the earlier waves. Moreover, the earnings of an immigrant wave do not grow rapidly enough to permit most recent immigrants to ever overcome their economic disadvantage.

Because these conclusions can easily be—and have been—used to justify various types of exclusionary immigration policies, it is worth investigating if conceptual or data problems taint my interpretation of the evidence. Put differently, are there other interpretations of the data that would give a more optimistic picture of the trends in immigrant skills?

Changes in the U.S. Wage Structure

Much of the discussion in this chapter presumes that a worker's wage is a good measure of the worker's human capital, the stock of marketable skills and abilities. This assumption, frequently made in economic studies of the labor market, implies that one can interpret a change in the relative wage of one group as a change in its relative skills.[30]

There are many other factors that can change the average wage of a group of workers over time, and these factors have nothing to do with the skill composition of the group. A worker's wage, after all, depends not only on his or her human capital, but also on how the labor market rewards that human capital. For instance, the worker's wage depends not only on how much schooling the worker has, but also on the rate of return to education. If macroeconomic conditions increase the demand for highly skilled workers, the returns to human capital also increase, and the average wage of skilled workers rises relative to that of unskilled workers. In contrast, if there is a drop in the demand for skilled workers, the returns to human capital fall, and the average wage of skilled workers falls relative to that of unskilled workers. It is possible, therefore, for changes in macroeconomic conditions to change the wages of immigrants and natives by different amounts, even if the human capital of the two groups has remained constant over time. It would then be wrong to interpret the drop in the entry wage of immigrants as a decline in relative skills.

In fact, the 1980s and 1990s witnessed a historic shift in the U.S. wage structure, and this shift did not affect all skill groups equally.[31] In particular,

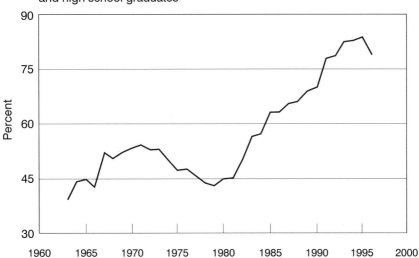

FIGURE 2-6. Changes in the wage structure, 1963–96.

Source: Lawrence F. Katz and David H. Autor, "Changes in the Wage Structure and Earnings Inequality," in *Handbook of Labor Economics*, vol. 3, ed. Orley Ashenfelter and David Card
(Amsterdam: North-Holland, forthcoming 1999).

Note: The wage differentials give the differences in weekly earnings among salaried men
who are eighteen to sixty-five years old and are employed full time in the civilian sector.

there was a large rise in income inequality. For instance, college graduates
earned 43 percent more than high school graduates in 1979 (see Figure 2-
6). By 1995, college graduates earned 84 percent more than high school
graduates. In fact, a great deal of evidence indicates that wage inequality
increased even within groups of workers who had the same schooling and
labor market experience, and among workers employed in the same industries
and occupations.

There is little disagreement over the basic fact: wage inequality rose spec-
tacularly in the 1980s. There is, however, a lot of disagreement over *why* this
occurred. The list of usual suspects includes the following:

1. *The deunionization of the American labor force*. In 1970, 24 percent of workers
were unionized; by 1997, only 14 percent were unionized.[32] Because unions typically prop up the wages of workers with relatively less schooling, the phenomenon
of the vanishing union might account for some of the decline in the real wage of
less-educated workers.

2. *Skill-biased technological change*. Technological change increases the productivity of the work force, and the type of technological change associated with the
information age, such as the introduction of the personal computer, is believed to
have increased the productivity of skilled workers the most.

3. *The globalization of the American economy.* Trade and immigration have made American workers more vulnerable to labor market conditions in other countries. There is some evidence suggesting that the opening up of the market to these outside influences had a particularly adverse effect on less-skilled workers.

Although all of these factors, as well as others, seem to account for part of the increase in wage inequality, there is no consensus over how to apportion "blame" among the possible causes.[33]

Regardless of the cause, these changes in the wage structure likely had a differential impact on the economic status of immigrant and native workers. The evidence clearly shows that immigrants have less schooling than natives. Because the U.S. labor market valued education more in the 1980s and 1990s, the relative wage of immigrants would have fallen *even if immigrant skills had remained constant.* In other words, the changes in the wage structure could, in principle, account for much of the decline in the relative wage of successive immigrant cohorts and for the sluggish wage growth experienced by a particular immigrant cohort during the 1980s.

This alternative interpretation of the downward trend in the relative wage of immigrants has important implications for the immigration debate. It is one thing to say that immigrant wages are declining because the immigrant population is becoming relatively less skilled. It is quite another to claim that the decline in immigrant wages is due to changes in macroeconomic conditions—changes that might be reversed within the next decade or two.

However, the changes in the U.S. wage structure—large as they were—cannot account for the declining relative economic status of immigrants. After all, the educational attainment of successive immigrant waves did fall relative to that of the native population. Because educational attainment is a "real" measure of a worker's skills, there must have been some decline in the relative skills of immigrants during the period of the Second Great Migration.

Moreover, the available evidence suggests that the drop in relative wages across successive immigrant cohorts was much too large to be explained by the changes in the wage structure. In a sense, these changes in the wage structure imply that different skill groups experienced different levels of "wage inflation": the wages of highly skilled workers rose at a faster rate than the wages of the less-skilled.

It turns out, however, that there was a decline in the entry wage of successive immigrant cohorts, even after adjusting the data for the changes in the wage structure (see Figure 2-7). For example, the immigrants who arrived in the late 1960s earned 17 percent less than natives at the time of entry. One can calculate the "real" wage of these workers in 1980 and 1990 by using a skill-specific wage deflator (based on a worker's education and age).[34] If the wage structure had not changed, the immigrants who entered in the late 1970s would have earned 25 percent less than natives at the time of entry, while those who arrived in the late 1980s would have earned 29 percent less. In other words, the change in the wage structure was not sufficiently large to generate the very large decline in the relative entry wage of successive immi-

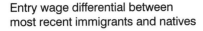

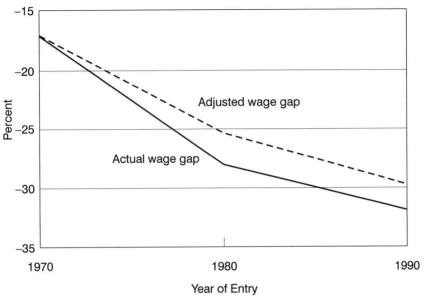

FIGURE 2-7. The entry wage of immigrants, adjusted for changes in the wage structure.

Source: George J. Borjas, "The Economics of Immigration," *Journal of Economic Literature* 32 (December 1994), pp. 1674, 1678.

Notes: The data refer to salaried men who are twenty-five to sixty-four years old and are employed in the civilian sector. The sample of "most recent immigrants" consists of persons who arrived in the country in the five-year period prior to the survey.

grant cohorts between 1970 and 1990. In fact, the increase in wage inequality accounts for only about 15 percent of the observed drop in the entry wage.[35]

The Out-Migration of Immigrants

Many immigrants decide to return to their countries of origin—or perhaps migrate elsewhere—after spending a few years in the United States. It is estimated that about 22 percent of the two million legal immigrants who arrived between 1970 and 1974 were not living in the United States by 1980.[36] And the population projections of the Bureau of the Census routinely assume that 195,000 foreign-born persons leave the United States every year.[37]

The fact that many immigrants leave the country means that the relative wage growth experienced by a particular immigrant wave over time may not measure the rate of economic assimilation. Consider, for example, the immigrants who arrived in the late 1960s. The 1970 Census enumerates the immigrants from this cohort who survived their first few years in the United States, the 1980 Census enumerates those who survived their first decade, and the

1990 Census enumerates those who survived their first twenty years. Over time, the existing sample of immigrants from this cohort becomes more select because it includes an ever-higher proportion of "survivors."

Suppose that the return migrants tend to have relatively low earnings. The tracking of a particular immigrant cohort across Censuses will then indicate that relative wages are increasing even if *no* economic assimilation actually takes place. After all, the low-wage immigrants are being systematically weeded out and they will not show up in the later surveys. The rate of economic assimilation that can be calculated from the available data would then be "too big." Suppose, in contrast, that the out-migrants are the successes, the immigrants with the highest wages. One might then see the relative wage of an immigrant cohort fall over time—simply because the later surveys are "overpopulated" by low-wage immigrants. And the estimated rate of economic assimilation would be too low.

Despite the potential importance of out-migration for the interpretation of wage trends in the immigrant population, very little is actually known about it. In recent decades, the United States has not collected any systematic data on the out-migration of either native- or foreign-born persons.[38] Few studies attempt to count the number of out-migrants, and even fewer attempt to determine which types of immigrants leave.[39] Put bluntly, there is no systematic evidence that can be used to assess how out-migration taints the rates of economic assimilation discussed earlier in this chapter.

Despite the lack of data, two general observations can be made. First, if one wishes to argue that the "true" rate of economic assimilation is much higher than what the available data suggest, then one would also have to argue that the immigrants who leave the United States have above-average wages. In other words, it is the "successes" who leave the country, not the "failures." Second, it is mathematically difficult for the true rate of economic assimilation to be much higher than what is actually measured if only a third of the immigrants leave. For instance, an exercise conducted in the recent National Academy of Sciences report assumed that a third of the immigrants leave and that the returnees earn 30 percent more than those who stay.[40] The mathematics of the problem would then imply that the immigrants who arrived in the 1980s and 1990s—*and* stay in the United States—would still not experience enough economic assimilation to ever catch up with native workers.

Summing Up

So what do the data say? A large proportion of the immigrants who entered the United States in the post-1965 period are relatively unskilled; they do not perform well in the American labor market; and there is little hope that they will reach economic parity with native workers during their lifetimes. These indisputable facts lie at the core of the debate over the symptoms of immigration. And, as I show in subsequent chapters, these trends are responsible for the rekindling of the debate over immigration policy in the United States.

National Origin

THE RELATIVE DECLINE in the skills and economic performance of immigrants in the post-1965 period is striking and irrefutable. A question remains: why did this decline occur? A great deal of evidence points to a single—and disturbing—culprit: the changing national origin mix of the immigrant population. Between the 1960s and the 1990s, the United States experienced a historic shift in the national origin mix of its immigrant population, away from the "traditional" Western European source countries and toward developing countries. It turns out that there are huge differences in the skills of immigrants who belong to different ethnic groups, with immigrants who originate in developing countries typically having a much harder time in the U.S. labor market.

The link between immigrant skills and national origin brings to the forefront a number of unpleasant questions with potentially explosive ramifications for the immigration debate. After all, this link places the difficult issues of race and ethnicity right in the center of the debate, and forces Americans to ask why race and ethnicity are such important determinants of economic performance.

The history of the immigration debate is not reassuring about how U.S. social policy typically handles these issues. The last great debate over immigration policy took place in the early 1920s, with the issues of ethnicity and skills playing a prominent role. This debate culminated with President Calvin Coolidge's proclamation that "America must be kept American," and with the United States adopting an openly discriminatory immigration policy that banned the entry of persons from Asia and awarded most entry visas to persons originating in Germany or Great Britain.

I do not argue—and I certainly do not believe—that the link between ethnicity and economic performance provides a rationale for turning back the clock, and shifting to an immigration policy that awards entry visas on the basis of national origin. At the same time, however, one should be candid about the long-run implications of pursuing a policy that seeks to improve the skills of immigrants. Such a policy would have a major impact on the national origin mix of the immigrant population. Because national origin and immigrant skills are so intimately related, any attempt to change one will inevitably change the other.

TRENDS IN IMMIGRATION

In many ways, the first and last decades of the twentieth century are bookends to a remarkable era in American immigration history. As the century began, there was a resurgence of mass immigration. This First Great Migration was halted by restrictive immigration policies enacted in 1924, and the restrictions stood until 1965. As the century ends, there is a new resurgence of mass immigration, a Second Great Migration.

Nearly twenty-six million immigrants entered the United States between 1880 and 1924, the period that roughly spans the First Great Migration. At its height, between 1901 and 1910, almost nine million immigrants entered the country. Prior to 1880, the United States had never admitted three million immigrants in any single decade.

In addition to the huge increase in the number of immigrants, the "new" immigrants that made up the First Great Migration came from nontraditional source countries: they came from Poland, Russia, and Italy, and not from Great Britain, Germany, or Sweden. And there was a strong perception—fueled by "evidence" from the army IQ tests—that the new immigrants were not as able, had less economic potential, and would find it hard to assimilate.

These symptoms of the First Great Migration, whether imagined or real, provided the backdrop for the immigration debate that culminated in 1924 with the enactment of the national origins quota system.[1] For the first time in American history, there would be numerical caps on immigration. The system allotted 150,000 annual visas for persons originating in the Eastern Hemisphere. These visas were allocated on the basis of national origin, with each country's share depending on the representation of that ethnic group in the U.S. population as of 1920. As a result, Germany and the United Kingdom received almost two-thirds of the available visas. Immigration from Asia was effectively banned. Until the early 1960s, for instance, India and the Philippines were each allotted one hundred visas annually. Finally, few persons migrated from Latin America. Although the national origins quota system did not set a numerical limit on migration from Western Hemisphere countries, the migration of Latin Americans may have been discouraged through administrative means, such as consular officials simply refusing to grant entry visas to the applicants.

The rekindling of the immigration debate at the end of the twentieth century had its roots in the 1965 Amendments to the Immigration and Nationality Act. The 1965 Amendments and subsequent minor legislation repealed the national origins quota system, set a worldwide numerical limit (507,000 visas in 1996), and enshrined a new objective for awarding entry visas among the many applicants: the reunification of families. The United States sets aside the bulk of the visas (62 percent in 1996) for certain persons who have relatives already residing in the country, including the adult children and siblings of U.S. citizens, as well as the spouses and minor children of permanent resident aliens. "Immediate" relatives of U.S. citizens—such as spouses, parents, and minor children—are exempt from the numerical limits, and are entitled to immediate entry. In the mid-1990s, 32 percent of the immigrants entered with an "immediate relative" visa that did not count against the limit, and over 70 percent entered through one of the family reunification provisions of the law.[2]

The policy shifts in the 1965 Amendments had a profound impact on the number of legal immigrants. Even though only 250,000 legal immigrants entered the country annually during the 1950s, almost one million were entering by the 1990s. Moreover, many persons come into the country illegally. The INS estimates that five million illegal aliens lived in the country in 1996, and around 300,000 join their ranks every year.[3] As a result of these trends, the proportion of foreign-born persons in the population began to rise rapidly, from 4.7 percent in 1970 to 7.9 percent in 1990 and 10 percent in 1998.

The 1965 Amendments also changed the national origin mix of the immigrant population (see Table 3-1). Over two-thirds of the legal immigrants admitted during the 1950s originated in Europe or Canada, 25 percent in Latin America, and 6 percent in Asia. By the 1990s, only 16 percent originated in Europe or Canada, 49 percent in Latin America, and 32 percent in Asia.[4] In fact, the "Top Ten" list of immigrant-sending countries in the 1950s and 1990s have few countries in common. Eight of the countries in the Top Ten between 1991 and 1996 (the Philippines, Vietnam, China, the Dominican Republic, India, Korea, El Salvador, and Jamaica) were not important source countries as recently as the 1950s.

It would be wrong to "blame" only the 1965 Amendments for the shifting national origin mix of the immigrant flow. Immigrants will not come to the United States unless they gain from the move—even if visas are freely available. During the early 1960s, for example, the United Kingdom was allocated over 65,000 quota visas per year, but the annual flow averaged fewer than 28,000 persons. In short, immigration policy and economic conditions in the United States are not the only factors that influence the decisions of potential migrants; economic and political conditions in the source countries also play a role.

Finally, there is an uncanny similarity in the key issues that fueled the immigration debates at the beginning and end of the twentieth century: a rapid increase in the number of immigrants, a huge change in their ethnic mix, and the perception that the new immigrants do not do as well as the earlier ones.[5] American history has already revealed how immigration policy responds when these "fundamentals" play themselves out in the political arena. The national origins quota system was not born out of thin air; it was the political consensus that was reached after thirty years of debate to address the real or perceived problems. The current immigration debate revolves around the same issues. Will history repeat itself? *Should it?*

NATIONAL ORIGIN AND THE DECLINE IN IMMIGRANT SKILLS

The changing ethnic mix of immigrants plays a crucial role in understanding the economic impact of immigration, and how that impact changes over

TABLE 3–1

Sources of Legal Immigration to the United States (percent distribution)

Country of birth	1951–60	1971–80	1991–96
Europe	52.7	17.8	14.5
Germany	19.0	1.7	0.1
Greece	1.9	2.1	0.2
Ireland	1.9	0.3	0.9
Italy	7.4	2.9	0.2
Poland	0.4	0.8	2.1
United Kingdom	8.1	3.1	1.5
Asia	6.1	35.3	31.8
China	0.4	2.8	4.4
India	0.1	3.7	3.9
Iran	1.0	1.0	1.3
Korea	0.2	6.0	1.9
Philippines	0.8	7.9	5.7
Vietnam	0.0	3.8	5.2
Americas	39.6	44.1	50.2
Canada	15.0	3.8	1.5
Mexico	11.9	14.3	26.9
Cuba	3.1	5.9	1.5
Dominican Republic	0.4	3.3	4.2
Haiti	0.2	1.3	1.9
Africa	0.6	1.8	3.4
Oceania	0.5	0.9	0.5

Source: U.S. Immigration and Naturalization Service, *Statistical Yearbook of the Immigration and Naturalization Service, 1996* (Washington, D.C., 1997), pp. 27–28.

time. There are huge differences in educational attainment and economic performance among immigrant groups (see Table 3-2). In 1990, immigrants from Mexico or Portugal had only about eight years of schooling, while immigrants from such diverse countries as Egypt, India, and the United Kingdom had around fifteen years (as compared to thirteen years for native workers). Similarly, immigrants from El Salvador and Mexico earned 40 percent less than natives, while immigrants from Germany and Canada earned 25 percent more. In short, national origin matters.

It is tempting to dismiss many of these differences by noting that some of the groups have been in the United States for many years, while other groups are relatively recent arrivals. For example, the typical German immigrant has been in the United States far longer than the typical Korean immigrant. Because residence in the United States improves skills and enhances economic performance, one would expect that the groups originating in the traditional source countries would earn more than the more recent arrivals. However,

TABLE 3–2
Education and Wages of Immigrant Men, by Country of Birth, 1990

Country of birth	Years of schooling	Percent wage differential between immigrants and natives
Europe		
Germany	13.9	24.5
Greece	11.8	–0.9
Italy	10.9	16.1
Poland	12.8	–0.3
Portugal	8.3	–3.1
U.S.S.R.	14.2	6.2
United Kingdom	14.6	37.2
Asia		
Cambodia	10.2	–30.8
China	12.8	–21.3
India	15.9	17.6
Korea	14.3	–12.0
Laos	10.0	–32.4
Philippines	14.1	–5.9
Vietnam	12.3	–18.9
Americas		
Canada	13.8	24.0
Cuba	11.7	–15.3
Dominican Republic	10.3	–29.2
El Salvador	8.6	–39.7
Haiti	11.2	–30.2
Jamaica	12.0	–11.2
Mexico	7.6	–39.5
Africa		
Egypt	15.6	12.2
Ethiopia	14.0	–21.0
Nigeria	15.8	–18.9
Australia	15.2	33.0
Native-born workers	13.2	—

Source: George J. Borjas, "The Economics of Immigration," *Journal of Economic Literature* 32 (December 1994), p. 1686.

Note: The data refer to salaried men who are twenty-five to sixty-four years old and are employed in the civilian sector.

the huge ethnic differences in economic performance persist even among immigrants who have been in the country for over ten years. Long-time immigrants from Italy or Poland earn about 20 percent more than natives, while those who originated in Guatemala or the Dominican Republic earn 20 percent less.[6]

There are, therefore, large differences in education and wages among ethnic groups. There was also a major change in the ethnic mix of the immigrant

TABLE 3–3

Link between National Origin and the Decline in the Relative Wage of Immigrants

	Percent of immigrants born in region		*Percent wage differential between immigrant and native men*
	1970	1990	
Region of birth			
Asia	10.8	25.3	−4.4
Europe and Canada	60.8	20.5	18.1
Mexico	10.0	24.9	−40.1
Other Latin America	13.8	22.2	−22.4
Other	4.6	7.1	−16.4
Actual wage gap in 1970			0.0
Actual wage gap in 1990			−15.8
Predicted wage gap in 1990 if the immigrants had the 1970 national origin mix			0.2

Source: James P. Smith and Barry Edmonston, eds., *The New Americans: Economic, Demographic, and Fiscal Effects of Immigration* (Washington, D.C.: National Academy Press, 1997), p. 191.

Note: The wage differentials for each of the ethnic groups are measured as of 1990.

population since 1960. And there was a huge decline in the relative skills and economic performance of immigrants. It is only natural to suspect that these events are linked—that the changing ethnic mix might have something to do with the decline in immigrant skills. It turns out that this suspicion is right on target.

The 1997 report of the National Academy of Sciences shows how easy it is to link the changing national origin mix of immigrants and the decline in immigrant economic performance (see Table 3-3).[7] In 1990, workers from Europe or Canada made up 21 percent of the immigrant work force, and earned 18 percent more than natives. Workers from Asia made up 25 percent of the immigrant work force, and earned 4 percent less than natives. Workers from Mexico made up 25 percent of the immigrant work force, and earned 40 percent less than natives. And workers from other Latin American countries made up 22 percent of the immigrant work force, and earned 22 percent less than the average native. Overall, the average immigrant earned 16 percent less than the average natives.[8]

In 1970, the national origin mix of immigrant workers was quite different: 61 percent originated in Europe or Canada, 11 percent in Asia, 10 percent in Mexico, and 14 percent in other Latin American countries. By using the information on how each of these groups fared in the labor market, one can predict what the average wage of immigrants would have been in 1990 if their national origin mix had been the same as it was in 1970. As Table 3-3 shows, there would have been no wage gap between immigrants and natives in 1990 in this counterfactual world.[9]

This simple exercise leads to a striking conclusion: *the decline in immigrant economic performance can be attributed to a single factor, the changing national origin mix of the immigrant population*. Put differently, the United States would not have witnessed a decline in the relative economic performance of immigrants if the ethnic mix of immigrants had not changed.

WHY DOES NATIONAL ORIGIN MATTER?

The economic importance of national origin raises a number of important questions for the immigration debate. Can the United States pursue an immigration policy that increases the skills of the immigrant population without greatly altering the ethnic diversity of the flow? Should social policy encourage the narrowing of ethnic differences over time, or should the government simply let these differences play themselves out in the marketplace? Are the socioeconomic differences observed among ethnic groups at the time of entry setting the stage for ethnic differences in the second and third generations—ethnic differences that may play a dominant role in the United States well into the twenty-first century? Before these questions can be addressed, one first has to understand why national origin has such a profound influence on economic outcomes.

International Differences in Human Capital

To some extent, the differences in skills and economic performance across immigrant groups in the United States mirror the skill differences that exist across the populations of the source countries (see Figure 3-1). The typical adult man has completed two years of school in Haiti, five years in Mexico, seven years in the Philippines, and eleven years in Hungary.[10] It is not hard to see how these differences in educational attainment could be transmitted to the immigrant flow. Suppose, for instance, that immigrants were randomly drawn from the population of the source countries. The average Mexican immigrant would then have the same education as the average Mexican in the population, the average Filipino immigrant would have the same education as the average Filipino, and so on. Not surprisingly, highly educated immigrant groups tend to originate in countries where the population is highly educated. The trend line illustrated in Figure 3-1 suggests that each additional year of education in the source country is associated with a .9-year increase in the education of immigrants.[11]

In one sense, the 1965 Amendments "redistributed" visas from advanced, industrialized economies to developing countries. Because the average educational attainment in developing countries is below that of industrialized economies, the immigrants arriving in the 1980s and 1990s would then tend to be less educated than the immigrants arriving in the 1950s. For example, in 1970, the average immigrant originated in a country where the average person had 7.7 years of schooling. By 1990, the average immigrant origi-

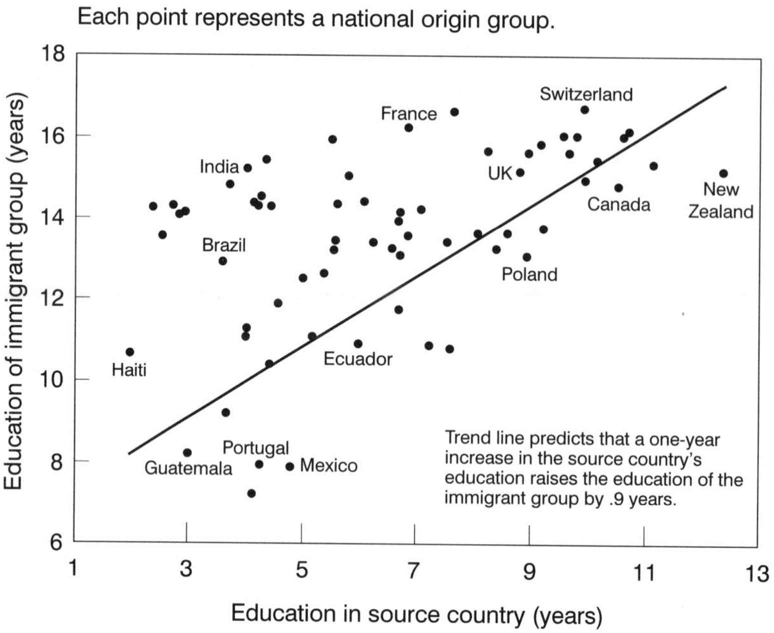

Each point represents a national origin group.

FIGURE 3-1. Relation between the education of immigrants and the education of the source country's population.

Sources: Robert J. Barro and Jong-Wha Lee, "International Comparisons of Educational Attainment," *Journal of Monetary Economics* 32 (December 1993), 363–394; and calculations from the 1990 Public Use Microdata Sample of the U.S. Census

Notes: The education data for the source country refer to the number of years completed by adult men in 1985. The education data for immigrants refer to the number of years completed by salaried men who are twenty-five to sixty-four years old and employed in the civilian sector. The trend line comes from a regression that is weighted by the sample size of the national origin group.

nated in a country where the average person had only about six years of schooling.[12] In short, the educational attainment of the source country represented by the average immigrant dropped by almost two years between 1970 and 1990.

It is well known that an additional year of schooling increases earnings by at least 5 percent in the United States.[13] As a result, the shift in the national origin mix toward countries where the population has less formal schooling could easily account for a 10 percent drop in the relative earnings of immigrants.

Not only does the human capital of workers differ across countries, but national origin also determines the ease with which this human capital can be transferred to the United States. There are major differences between industrialized economies and developing countries in industrial structures and in the types of jobs available, so workers acquire different types of skills in different countries. It does not seem farfetched to assume that the skills acquired in advanced economies tend to be equally useful in other industrialized economies and are, therefore, more easily transferable to the U.S. labor market. In contrast, the skills acquired in developing countries are much less useful in an industrialized setting.

There is, in fact, a strong positive correlation between per capita income in the source country and the earnings of immigrants in the United States—even after adjusting for differences in the educational attainment of the immigrant groups (see Figure 3-2).[14] A group of immigrants who originate in a rich country will earn more than a similarly educated group originating in a poor country—suggesting that the skills acquired in the rich country are valued more by American employers. The trend line indicates that a doubling of per capita income in the source country is associated with an increase in immigrant earnings of about 15 percent.[15]

Because visas were redistributed to poorer countries after 1965, there was a dramatic drop in the per capita income of the source country of the typical immigrant in the United States. In 1970, the average immigrant came from a country with a per capita GDP of $8,400 (in 1985 dollars). By 1990, the typical immigrant came from a country with a per capita income of only $5,500, a drop of 35 percent.[16] This decline in the level of "economic development" embodied in the average immigrant would alone account for a 7 percent drop in the relative earnings of immigrants over the period.

SELF-SELECTION

Immigrants are not randomly chosen from the populations of the countries of origin. Consider, for instance, the migration of Mexicans to the United States. Even though it is very large (seven million Mexican-born persons lived in the United States in 1997), it is still small when compared to the Mexican population. In 1997, Mexico's population was ninety-eight million, so that fewer than 7 percent of Mexicans had chosen to move to the United States.

It would be hard to blame restrictive immigration policies for Mexico's relatively low emigration rate. The U.S.-Mexico border is notoriously porous, and can be crossed illegally by almost anyone who really wants to. Moreover, per capita income in the United States is more than three times that of Mexico, even after adjusting for differences in purchasing power.[17] In view of the potentially large gains from migrating to the United States, the question is not why so many Mexicans emigrate, but rather, *Why do so few move?*

The answer is simple—although it comes as a shock to most Americans. Not everyone in the world wants to live in the United States. The group of immigrants who end up in the United States is self-selected from the population of the source countries. And because of this self-selection, the typical immigrant who reaches the United States will be different from the typical person who chooses to remain in the source country.

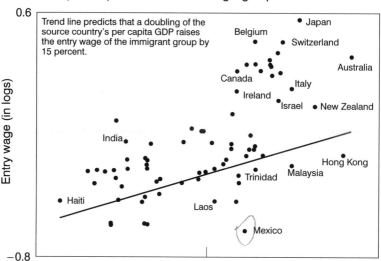

Each point represents a national origin group.

FIGURE 3-2. Relation between the entry wage of immigrants and per capita income in the source country, adjusted for differences in educational attainment among groups.

Source: Based on George J. Borjas, "The Economic Progress of Immigrants," in *Issues in the Economics of Immigration*, ed. George J. Borjas (Chicago: University of Chicago Press, forthcoming 2000), tab. 6.

Notes: Per capita GDP is measured as of 1985, and is adjusted using the purchasing-power–parity basis. The entry wage gives the age-adjusted 1990 wage for immigrant men who arrived between 1985 and 1989. The trend line comes from a regression that is weighted by the sample size of the national origin group. The regression also includes a measure of income inequality in the source country (the Gini coefficient), distance from the United States, and the educational attainment of the immigrant group in 1990.

There has been a long-standing debate over the nature of the process that filters out the immigrants from the population of the source countries. One extreme view is illustrated by Benjamin Franklin's remark that German immigrants are "the most stupid of their own nation."[18] At the other extreme stands General George Patton's colorful exhortation to his troops on the eve of the American invasion of Sicily on July 9, 1943: "When we land, we will meet German and Italian soldiers whom it is our honor and privilege to attack and destroy. Many of you have in your veins German and Italian blood, but remember that these ancestors of yours so loved freedom that they gave up home and country to cross the ocean in search of liberty. The ancestors of the people we shall kill lacked the courage to make such a sacrifice and continued as slaves."[19]

Why do relatively few persons bother to migrate to the United States? Mainly because it is costly to immigrate. The costs include the expense of transporting the household across thousands of miles and looking for new employment, as well as the psychological burden of leaving family and friends behind and of becoming aliens in a strange land. As a result, the immigrants are typically the persons who have the most to gain from moving—because only those who gain the most would be willing to incur the substantial migration costs.

Does the United States, then, attract the most skilled workers from any given source country, or the least skilled workers?[20]

Suppose that workers make the migration decision by comparing the economic opportunities provided by the source country with those provided by the United States. Consider first a group of workers who live in a country where the payoff to human capital is low, so that highly skilled workers do not earn much more than less-skilled workers. This situation is common in many Western European countries, such as Sweden, where the welfare state and other social policies tend to equalize the income distribution—taxing the highly skilled and subsidizing the less-skilled. As long as persons migrate to countries that provide the best economic opportunities, the workers who have the most to gain by moving to the United States are the workers with above-average skills. The United States benefits from a brain drain.

Alternatively, consider workers living in countries where the payoff to human capital is quite high. The rewards to skills are often substantial in many developing countries, such as Mexico and the Philippines.[21] These high rewards to skills partly account for the very unequal distributions of incomes observed in those countries, where the skilled earn substantially more than the less-skilled. Highly skilled workers in these countries often face better economic opportunities than they would face if they migrated to the United States, while less-skilled workers can barely rise above the subsistence level. As long as persons migrate to countries that provide better economic opportunities, the skilled workers in these countries have little incentive to leave. It is the least skilled who want to emigrate, and the immigrant flow will be composed of workers with below-average skills.

As long as economic considerations matter in the migration decision, skills tend to flow to those markets that offer the highest value. The United States is then likely to attract highly skilled workers from some countries (those where the returns to skills are low), and unskilled workers from others (those where the returns to skills are high).

There is, in fact, a negative correlation between measures of the source country's rate of return to skills and the economic performance of immigrants in the United States (see Figure 3-3). In particular, immigrants earn less if they originate in countries where there is a great deal of income dispersion—as measured by the widely used Gini coefficient.[22] The income distribution in Mexico, for instance, is much more dispersed than the income distribution in the United Kingdom—and part of this dispersion arises because the rate of return to skills is much higher in Mexico than in the United Kingdom.[23] The trend line in Figure 3-3 suggests that this difference in the return to skills generates a 30 percent wage differential between the two

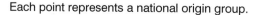

Each point represents a national origin group.

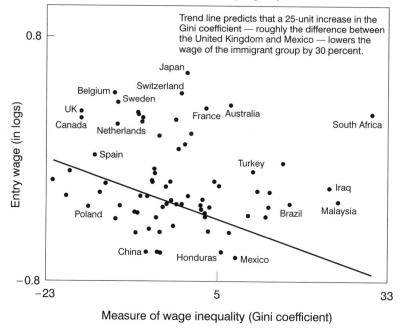

Measure of wage inequality (Gini coefficient)

FIGURE 3-3. Relation between the entry wage of immigrants and income inequality in the source country.

Source: Based on George J. Borjas, "The Economic Progress of Immigrants," in *Issues in the Economics of Immigration*, ed. George J. Borjas (Chicago: University of Chicago Press, forthcoming 2000), tab. 6.

Notes: The Gini coefficient measures income inequality in the source country in 1980. The entry wage gives the age-adjusted 1990 wage for immigrant men who arrived between 1985 and 1989. The trend line comes from a regression that is weighted by the sample size of the national origin group. The regression also includes the (log) per capita GDP in the source country and distance from the United States.

groups. In other words, an important part of the sizable wage gap between Mexican and British immigrants (which was around 125 percent in 1990) arises because different types of persons choose to leave those two countries.[24]

In sum, immigrants originating in developing countries will typically have less human capital for a number of reasons. Workers in developing countries tend to have less education than their counterparts in the industrialized economies; the less-skilled in the developing countries sometimes have the greatest incentive to migrate to the United States; and the human capital acquired in developing economies is harder to transfer to an industrialized setting.

Employment Discrimination

My discussion of the sizable wage differentials among ethnic groups has not yet mentioned the possibility that some groups face systematic employment discrimination in the American labor market. This omission might seem odd because the discrimination argument is commonly invoked to explain why some racial and ethnic groups have relatively low incomes. In my view, however, there is little evidence to suggest that such systematic discrimination can account for the poor economic performance of many immigrant groups.

To begin with, it turns out that a large part of the average wage differential between immigrants and natives can be explained by differences in educational attainment between the two groups. In 1990, for instance, the schooling gap between immigrants and natives accounted for half of the 23 percent wage differential between the two groups.[25] Although one may be tempted to "blame" other social and cultural forces in American society for the lower educational attainment of some minority groups, this explanation is certainly not credible in the case of immigrants. The median age at migration is around thirty, so most immigrants completed their schooling years before they ever set foot in the United States. It would be difficult to blame the education gap between immigrants and natives on the pernicious impact of segregated and underfunded schools in America's inner cities and ethnic ghettoes.

Moreover, there is growing evidence that the descendants of the most disadvantaged immigrant groups, such as Mexicans, do *not* earn less than non-Hispanic whites—once one adjusts for differences in educational attainment between the groups. Workers of Mexican ancestry born in the United States earned about 28 percent less than non-Hispanic whites in 1990. Practically all of this wage differential can be traced back to differences in human capital between the groups, particularly educational attainment and proficiency in the English language.[26] Equally striking, persons of Asian ancestry born in the United States actually earn *more* than non-Hispanic whites.[27] Again, it would be difficult to explain this wage differential in terms of a discrimination story—unless the discrimination is against the white majority.

Although there is a tendency to attribute many of the problems faced by disadvantaged minority groups to discriminatory forces operating at many levels of American society—and although this argument might even be right in some cases—the explanation carries little weight when it comes to immigrants. Many immigrants from developing countries earn less not because of discrimination, but because they are less skilled.

ETHNICITY AND ASSIMILATION

As shown above, national origin plays a crucial role in determining the skill level of immigrants at the time of entry. Not surprisingly, there is also a great deal of dispersion in the rate of wage growth experienced by the various ethnic groups (see Table 3-4).[28] Some immigrant groups experience rapid wage growth, while other groups do not exhibit any wage growth at all. For example, the earnings of British immigrants who entered the United States in the late 1970s grew by about 27 percent in the first ten years after arrival (relative to the growth experienced by comparably aged natives), while the

TABLE 3–4

Economic Assimilation of Immigrants Who Arrived in
1975–79, by Country of Origin

Country of origin	Percent wage growth in first ten years, relative to natives
Europe	
Greece	11.6
Ireland	44.5
Italy	17.0
Portugal	10.4
Spain	−5.4
United Kingdom	26.7
Americas	
Brazil	−15.9
Canada	19.0
Cuba	10.6
Dominican Republic	7.8
Jamaica	13.9
Mexico	−6.0
Asia	
China	16.3
Korea	24.7
Laos	−4.8
Philippines	25.7

Source: Based on George J. Borjas, "The Economic Progress of Immigrants," in *Issues in the Economics of Immigration*, ed. George J.
Borjas (Chicago: University of Chicago Press, forthcoming 2000),
tab. 3.

Notes: The data refer to salaried men who are employed in the
civilian sector. The immigrants were twenty-five to thirty-four years
old at the time of entry. The rate of wage growth is calculated relative to that experienced by comparably aged native workers.

earnings of Portuguese immigrants grew by 10 percent and those of Laotian
immigrants fell by 5 percent.

Do the ethnic differences in economic performance disappear over time
as the immigrant groups assimilate in the United States, or do they widen?
If the immigrant groups that had the highest entry wages also experienced
the fastest wage growth, there would be a divergence in economic performance across ethnic groups. The groups that entered doing well would then
end up doing even better in the long run, and leave the low-wage groups far
behind. However, if the groups with the highest entry wages had the slowest
wage growth, the wages of different immigrant groups would converge over
time—although the convergence might take several decades.

Figure 3-4 shows the actual relation between entry wages and subsequent
wage growth (over the first ten years in the United States) for the immigrant
groups that entered the United States in the late 1970s. Each point in the
figure represents an immigrant cohort defined by national origin and age at

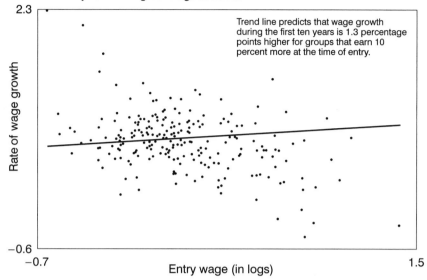

Each point represents an immigrant cohort, defined by national origin and age at arrival.

Trend line predicts that wage growth during the first ten years is 1.3 percentage points higher for groups that earn 10 percent more at the time of entry.

Rate of wage growth

2.3

−0.6

−0.7

Entry wage (in logs)

1.5

FIGURE 3-4. Relation between wage growth in the first ten years and the entry wage.

Source: Based on George J. Borjas, "The Economic Progress of Immigrants," in *Issues in the Economics of Immigration*, ed. George J. Borjas (Chicago: University of Chicago Press, forthcoming 2000), tab. 4.

Notes: The data refer to the age-adjusted entry wage and wage growth experienced by immigrant men who entered the United States between 1975 and 1979. The trend line comes from a regression that is weighted by the sample size of the national origin group.

arrival.[29] The trend line drawn in the figure summarizes the nature of the correlation between entry wages and relative wage growth.[30] This trend line has a very slight positive trend, indicating that immigrant groups with the highest entry wages were also the ones with the fastest subsequent wage growth. Although the positive correlation is not very strong, the evidence suggests that, if anything, high-wage groups are also the groups who most improve their economic performance in subsequent years. As a result, there is no evidence that the ethnic differences in economic performance disappear over the lifetime of the immigrant generation. If anything, the assimilation process may well magnify some of those ethnic differences.

Although the data clearly show that high-wage immigrant groups experience slightly faster wage growth as they assimilate, there is a great deal of confusion both in academic studies and in the public debate over the meaning of this correlation. The confusion arises because different persons use different definitions of economic assimilation, and, not surprisingly, reach very different conclusions. One common approach, for example, is to compare the wage growth of different immigrant groups *after* adjusting for differences in educational attainment across the groups.[31] It turns out that there is a strong *negative* correlation between entry wages and subsequent wage growth once one

Each point represents an immigrant cohort,
defined by national origin and age at arrival.

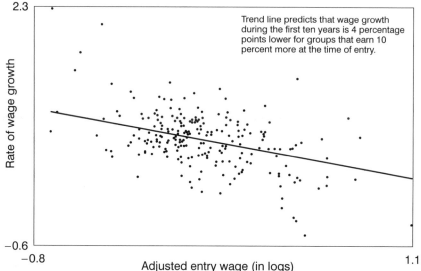

FIGURE 3-5. Relation between wage growth in the first ten years and the entry
wage, adjusted for differences in educational attainment.

Source: Based on George J. Borjas, "The Economic Progress of Immigrants," in *Issues in
the Economics of Immigration*, ed. George J. Borjas (Chicago: University of Chicago Press,
forthcoming 2000), tab. 4.

Notes: The data refer to the age-adjusted entry wage and wage growth experienced by immigrant men who entered the United States between 1975 and 1979. The trend line comes from
a regression that includes the educational attainment of the group in 1980, and is weighted
by the sample size of the national origin group.

adjusts for differences in educational attainment (see Figure 3-5).[32] In other
words, if all ethnic groups had the same education at the time of entry, those
groups with the highest entry wages would experience the slowest subsequent
wage growth. As a result, the wages of ethnic groups that are equally skilled
at the time of entry tend to converge over time.

The typical participant in the immigration debate then faces an important
question: which definition of assimilation makes more sense? The answer to
this question will generally depend on the context in which it is being asked.
For some purposes, the definition of assimilation that does not adjust for
differences in skills among immigrant groups may be more relevant, while
for other purposes, the adjusted correlation may be more useful.

From the perspective of immigration policy, however, I think that the unadjusted correlation illustrated in Figure 3-4 is far more relevant. Although
it is of interest to know that immigrants who have similar skills (but belong
to different national origin groups) eventually end up with the same wage,
this type of "conditional" convergence has little significance for measuring
the economic impact of immigration. The economic impact of immigration

depends on how the *actual* skills of immigrants compare with the *actual* skills of natives. It is this contrast that determines the labor market impact of immigration, and the gains and losses to the overall economy.[33]

Ethnic Enclaves and Economic Assimilation

The economic characteristics of the source country are not the only factors that determine the economic performance of immigrants in the United States. National origin groups also differ in the ways that they choose to assimilate. In particular, some groups have well-developed and thriving ethnic enclaves in many American cities. These enclaves presumably ease the transition between the old and the new.

In 1990, the typical Mexican immigrant lived in a metropolitan area where 11 percent of the population were Mexican-born, the typical Cuban lived in one where 15 percent of the population were Cuban-born, and the typical Pole lived in one where almost 1 percent of the population were Polish-born. One commonly used measure of geographic clustering, called the exposure index, measures the overrepresentation of immigrants in particular localities by calculating the number of immigrants found in the "average" metropolitan area relative to what one would expect to find if immigrants were randomly distributed (see Table 3-5). For example, even though the typical Mexican immigrant lives in a metropolitan area where the population is 11.2 percent Mexican, only 2.3 percent of the U.S. population are Mexican-born. The exposure index then takes on a value of 5 (or 11.2 divided by 2.3). In other words, the typical Mexican lives in a locality where there are five times as many Mexicans as one would expect to find if the Mexican population were randomly sorted across the United States. The exposure index varies a lot among national origin groups, from 1 for immigrants born in Germany, to 4 for those born in Vietnam, to 12 for those born in Haiti, to 41 for those born in Cuba.

It is reasonable to suspect that this geographic clustering affects the economic performance of immigrant groups—although it is not clear in which direction these effects should go. Many observers of the immigrant experience, particularly those who use a sociological perspective, argue that the geographic clustering of immigrants, and the "warm embrace" of the enclave, helps immigrants escape the discrimination that they would otherwise encounter in the labor market.[34] This argument would suggest that clustering helps: immigrants who live in ethnic enclaves should do better than those who do not.

One can also argue, however, that the clustering can have adverse economic effects. The ethnic enclave creates incentives for immigrants *not* to leave and *not* to acquire the skills that might be useful in the larger national market. In other words, the clustering may effectively hinder the move to better-paying jobs by reducing the immigrants' incentives to learn the culture and language of the American labor market. In a sense, immigrants who live and work in an ethnic enclave are working in a "one-company" town.

TABLE 3–5
Ethnic Clustering of Immigrants, by Country of Origin, 1990

Country of birth	Percent of U.S. population that belongs to the immigrant group	Exposure index
Europe		
Germany	0.33	1.3
Greece	0.09	2.9
Ireland	0.07	3.5
Italy	0.22	3.7
Poland	0.45	5.6
Portugal	0.10	33.4
United Kingdom	0.29	1.4
Americas		
Canada	0.30	1.9
Cuba	0.37	40.9
Dominican Republic	0.18	15.4
El Salvador	0.25	7.4
Jamaica	0.17	7.4
Mexico	2.25	5.0
Haiti	0.12	12.4
Asia		
Cambodia	0.06	6.5
China	0.27	4.8
India	0.26	2.2
Philippines	0.49	4.6
Vietnam	0.28	4.2

Source: Calculations from the 1990 Public Use Microdata Sample of the U.S. Census.

Note: The exposure index measures the overrepresentation of immigrants in the metropolitan area where the typical immigrant resides. As an example, the exposure index for Mexico equals 5 because the typical Mexican immigrant lives in a metropolitan area where there are five times as many Mexican immigrants as one would expect to find from a purely random allocation.

In my view, the existing evidence suggests that residential segregation does not benefit immigrants.[35] There is, for instance, a negative correlation between the rate of economic assimilation and the geographic clustering of the immigrant group (see Figure 3-6).[36] If an immigrant group that is segregated completely in one state were randomly redistributed throughout the country—so that its geographic distribution looked just like that of natives—the wage of this group would rise by another 16 percentage points over the first ten years.

As noted earlier, geographic clustering reduces the rate of economic assimilation partly because it reduces an immigrant's incentives to learn the English language. The clustering of immigrants in ethnic enclaves thus raises the possibility of a vicious cycle in the long-run economic development of

Each point represents an immigrant cohort, defined
by national origin, year of arrival, and age at arrival.

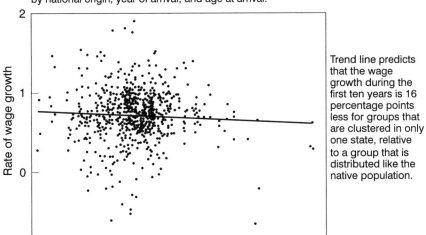

Trend line predicts
that the wage
growth during the
first ten years is 16
percentage points
less for groups that
are clustered in only
one state, relative
to a group that is
distributed like the
native population.

FIGURE 3-6. Relation between wage growth in the first ten years and residential segregation.

Source: Based on George J. Borjas, "The Economic Progress of Immigrants," in *Issues in the Economics of Immigration*, ed. George J. Borjas (Chicago: University of Chicago Press, forthcoming 2000), tab. 7.

Notes: The data refer to the age-adjusted wage growth experienced by immigrant men. The measure of residential segregation is the Herfindahl index at the state level. The trend line comes from a regression that is weighted by the sample size of the national origin group. The regression also includes the (log) per capita GDP in the source country, income inequality in the source country (as measured by the Gini coefficient), distance from the United States, and indicators for the calendar year of migration and age at arrival of the immigrant groups.

the ethnic group. Immigrants who live in ethnic enclaves have few incentives to make the effort and devote the resources required to learn English. This decision, however, may have serious and damaging long-run repercussions. Many immigrants cannot attempt to sell their resources in the national market and will have lower earnings. The ethnic enclave's warm embrace becomes an economic stranglehold. Unless this vicious cycle is broken, the immigrant population could easily end up in an impoverished ethnic enclave throughout the immigrants' working lives—unwilling *and* unable to escape and assimilate into the larger economy.

In view of these adverse effects, it is not surprising that many immigrants may have endorsed the English for the Children initiative (also known as Proposition 227) in California's 1998 elections. This proposition effectively ended the misguided use of bilingual education for teaching immigrants in

California's public schools. Throughout much of the 1980s and 1990s, California's bilingual education program mandated that immigrant children be taught almost all their school subjects in the children's native language, with perhaps a thirty-minute English lesson during the school day. In short, immigrant children were "sheltered" in their native language for many years—never given the chance to become fully fluent either in their native language or in English.

According to exit polls conducted by the *Los Angeles Times,* nearly two-thirds of whites and Asians supported the proposition, as well as over 40 percent of Hispanics.[37] The high social and economic cost of social policies designed to enhance the "hold" of the ethnic enclave was obvious to many of the affected families—even if the cost was not apparent to the politicians and educators who created and nurtured this policy.

NATIONAL ORIGIN AND THE POINT SYSTEM: THE CANADIAN EXPERIENCE

Until 1961, Canadian immigration policy, like that of the United States, only permitted the entry of persons born in a few selected countries, such as the United Kingdom, Ireland, and the United States, or of persons who were dependents of Canadian residents. Major policy changes in the 1960s repealed the national origin restrictions and introduced the point system, a visa allocation scheme that awards entry permits to applicants who meet certain skill restrictions.

For the most part, visa applicants who do not have close relatives already residing in Canada must pass a "test" given by the Canadian immigration authorities.[38] This test asks about the applicant's age, education, proficiency in English and French, occupation, and a host of other factors, and each answer is "graded." For instance, applicants who are twenty-one to forty-four years old get ten points, while applicants over the age of forty-nine get zero points. Applicants who have a graduate or professional degree get sixteen points, while those who are high school dropouts get zero points. Applicants also get points for working in "favored" occupations, for being fluent in either English or French, for having arranged employment, and for having relatives already residing in Canada. At the end of the test, the points are added up and applicants who score at least 70 points out of a total of 112 may qualify for an entry visa.[39]

Not surprisingly, this "filtering" has a major impact on the skills and economic performance of immigrants in Canada vis-à-vis their counterparts in the United States. Immigrants in Canada—relative to Canadian natives—have higher skills and higher wages than immigrants in the United States.[40] In 1980, for example, the newest immigrant arrivals in the United States earned about 28 percent less than natives, and had almost one less year of schooling. In contrast, the newest immigrant arrivals in Canada earned 16 percent less than natives, and had one more year of schooling.[41]

In short, the Canadian point system "works" because it generates a more skilled immigrant flow. But how exactly does it accomplish this goal?

The point system could increase immigrant skills by attracting more productive immigrants from each source country. For example, the entry of less-skilled Irish immigrants is greatly restricted by Canada, and hence one might expect that Irish immigrants in Canada would be relatively more skilled than Irish immigrants in the United States. The point system might also increase skills because it restricts the entry of most persons from developing countries. Less than 1 percent of Mexico's adult male population has completed a secondary education.[42] By not awarding any points to persons who lack a high school diploma, the point system effectively closes the Canadian border to most Mexicans. The point system, therefore, might work because it alters the national origin mix of immigrants. Under the point system, immigrants are much more likely to originate in industrialized than in developing countries.

Surprisingly, there is little difference in skills and economic performance between immigrants in Canada and immigrants in the United States *within national origin groups* (see Figure 3-7).[43] Immigrant groups that are highly educated in Canada are also highly educated in the United States. Similarly, the high-income immigrant groups in Canada are also the high-income groups in the United States. Overall, there is no evidence whatsoever that Canada attracts relatively more skilled workers from a particular source country.

So how is it that immigrants in Canada are, on average, more skilled than immigrants in the United States? The answer is simple and provocative: the point system works not by attracting more skilled immigrants from each source country, but by changing the national origin mix of the immigrant population. In the 1980s, for instance, only 12 percent of the immigrants reaching the United States originated in Europe or Canada. In contrast, 30 percent of the immigrants entering Canada originated in Europe or the United States. Similarly, 47 percent of the immigrants entering the United States originated in Latin America, but only 16 percent of the immigrants in Canada originated there.[44]

It might seem odd that the point system does not change the average skills of immigrants who originate in a particular source country. But it is not entirely clear why it should. As I have emphasized, the people who choose to leave a particular source country are the ones who have the most to gain by leaving. If economic conditions in a source country "drive out" the most skilled, then it does not really matter much whether these immigrants end up in the United States or in Canada.[45] Regardless of which country accepts them, immigrants from that particular source country will tend to be relatively skilled. In contrast, if economic conditions in a source country drive out the less skilled, immigrants from that country will tend to be relatively unskilled. But the point system prevents the entry of most of those immigrants into Canada.

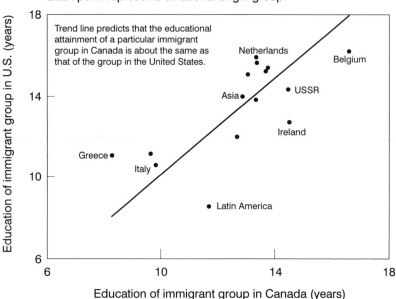

Each point represents a national origin group.

FIGURE 3-7. Relation between the educational attainment of immigrants in the United States and in Canada.

Source: George J. Borjas, "Immigration Policy, National Origin, and Immigrant Skills: A Comparison of Canada and the United States," in *Small Differences That Matter: Labor Markets and Income Maintenance in Canada and the United States*, ed. David Card and Richard B. Freeman (Chicago: University of Chicago Press, 1993), pp. 31–32.

Note: The trend line comes from a regression that is weighted by the sample size of the national origin group.

In other words, although the intention of the point system might be to increase the skills of immigrants belonging to a particular ethnic group, this is not what actually happens. The Canadian point system has little effect on the education or relative wages of specific national origin groups.[46] Instead, the point system redistributes visas across source countries—away from the developing countries and toward the more industrialized economies.

The adoption of a skills-based point system, therefore, raises a difficult and emotional political problem. This type of point system is the primary policy tool recommended by those who argue that the United States should be admitting a more skilled immigrant flow. The system is easy to explain and easy to administer. If the Canadian experience is any guide, the adoption of a skills-based point system will greatly alter the national origin mix of the immigrant population admitted into the United States.

The Canadian experience teaches a subtle, but crucial, lesson: It is extremely difficult to unlink the questions of immigrant skills and national origin. The two are intimately related, and addressing the problems raised by one of these issues will inevitably have an effect on the other. Few participants in the immigration debate advocate a return to a type of national origins quota system. Nevertheless, a return to some variation on this theme might well be an inevitable consequence of adopting policies that seek to improve the skills of the immigrant population.

It is then easy to see how the immigration debate can easily degenerate into a futile argument over race and ethnicity. Those who value the current diversity of the immigrant flow—or who, for political reasons, want to see a marked change in the racial and ethnic composition of the population—will surely ascribe the worst of motives to anyone who argues that the United States might want to improve the skills of its immigrant population. Typically, accusations of racism—and the ugly prospect of Stalinist-like media show "trials" where the accused must publicly atone for their alleged sins—are enough to silence most Americans who believe that admitting large numbers of unskilled immigrants is not in the national interest.[47]

Nevertheless, facts are facts, and an unskilled immigrant flow *does* have many undesirable economic and social repercussions. A skills-based point system would provide a simple mechanism for screening the visa applicants. If the United States wishes to adopt some type of point system, the American people will have to come to terms with an unpleasant reality. To some extent, the point system would mark a de facto acceptance of the kinds of national origin restrictions that characterized U.S. immigration policy prior to the 1965 Amendments.

The Labor Market Impact of Immigration

DO IMMIGRANTS HARM the employment opportunities of native workers? If so, how large is the loss in the economic well-being of natives? And are all native groups equally affected by immigration?

These questions have always been at the core of the immigration debate. In 1852, soon after the potato famine unleashed a new wave of Irish and British immigration, an observer described the connection between immigration and wages in a way that, with minor casting changes in the ethnic origin of the characters, could easily have been written a century and a half later:

> Great Britain is now pouring upon us in a full tide the surplus . . . of her population. The ocean, which once separated us, steam has contracted to a span . . . we are now virtually two contiguous countries. . . . To expect that, in two countries thus situated, without any special direction of public policy towards maintaining some barrier between them, the pressure of population, the profits of capital, and the wages of labor can long remain very unequal, would be as idle as to believe that, without the erection of a dam, water could be maintained at two different levels in the same pond. Throw down the little that remains of our protective system, and let the emigration from Great Britain and Ireland to our shores increase . . . and within the lifetime of the present generation, the laborer's hire in our Atlantic states will be as low as it is in England. Our manufactures would flourish then, as those of Great Britain flourish now; cheap labor is the only requisite for placing them upon the same level.[1]

Throughout the history of the immigration debate, therefore, immigration restrictions have been justified, at least publicly, by arguing that those restrictions improve the economic well-being of native workers. In fact, public opinion polls indicate that native workers disapprove of immigration (typically by very large margins) mainly because they perceive or fear that immigrants reduce wages or take away jobs.[2]

It turns out, however, that this is one of those contentious issues where there is a wide gulf—actually more of a deep chasm—dividing public opinion and the findings from academic studies. Although many researchers have tried, it has proved surprisingly difficult to document that immigration has a sizable adverse effect on native workers.[3] In a 1990 review of these studies, I concluded that "the methodological arsenal of modern econometrics cannot find a single shred of evidence that immigrants have a sizable adverse impact on the earnings and employment opportunities of natives in the United States."[4] An academic survey published in 1995 states that "the effect of immigration on the labor market outcomes of natives is small."[5] And the 1997 National Academy of Sciences report argued that "the weight of the empirical evidence suggests that the impact of immigration on the wages of competing native workers is small."[6] This kind of consensus is rare indeed in social science, particularly when many workers keep insisting that immigrants harm their economic opportunities and when the commonsense intuition behind the economic laws of supply and demand suggests that an increase in the number of workers should reduce the wage.

This chapter presents a revisionist interpretation of the available evidence. I conclude that the native workers' apprehensions are not completely misguided, since many of them—particularly those at the bottom of the skill distribution—have much to fear from the entry of large numbers of less-skilled immigrants.

Put differently, I question the validity of much of the evidence that is typically marshaled by those who claim that immigrants do not affect native economic opportunities. Much of this evidence is based on comparisons of the labor market outcomes of native workers who reside in cities with large numbers of immigrants (such as Los Angeles and San Diego) with the outcomes of natives who reside in cities where few immigrants live (such as Atlanta and Pittsburgh). These "spatial correlations" often suggest that the average native wage is somewhat lower in labor markets where immigrants tend to cluster— but the wage differential between the markets may be so small that it is not worth worrying about.

But a weak spatial correlation does not necessarily prove that immigrants have a benign impact on the employment opportunities of native workers. Suppose, for example, that immigration into San Diego reduces the earnings of native workers there substantially. Native workers will probably react. Many will move out of the San Diego area to other cities, and workers who were considering moving to San Diego will move somewhere else instead. As natives respond to immigration by voting with their feet (creating what has been called "the new white flight"), the adverse impact of immigration on the San Diego labor market will be transmitted to the entire economy.[7] In the end, all native workers will be worse off because of immigration, not just those who reside in the "immigrant cities."

In this chapter, I argue that the economic impact of immigration at the national level may be quite important. The 1980s witnessed a substantial increase in the wage gap between high school dropouts and workers with more education. The decade also witnessed the entry of large numbers of less-skilled immigrants. It turns out that almost half of the decline in the relative wage of high school dropouts may be attributed to immigration.

The dramatic increase in wage inequality that occurred in the 1980s and 1990s raises serious social, economic, and political concerns for the United States. And the fact that part of this increase can be linked to immigration raises equally serious concerns about immigration policy.

In an important sense, the United States pursues social policies that have conflicting goals. Presumably, the objective of many of the redistribution policies enshrined in liberal political ideology and implemented through the welfare state—from public assistance programs to the earned income tax credit—is to redistribute income to less-skilled workers and to improve their economic status.

At the same time, immigration policy has tacitly encouraged the admission of very large numbers of less-skilled workers—either by insisting that only family connections matter when awarding entry visas, or by looking the other way as millions of "unscreened" illegal aliens cross the border. This type of immigration policy probably aggravates the social and economic problems faced by workers at the bottom of the income distribution, and helps undo—and perhaps even unravel—many of the benefits that would have accrued from the redistributive policies aimed at improving their economic status.

IMMIGRATION AND LOCAL LABOR MARKETS

Immigrants in the United States tend to settle in a limited number of states and cities. And this clustering seems to have increased over time. In 1960, 60 percent of the immigrants lived in one of the six main immigrant-receiving states: California, New York, Texas, Florida, New Jersey, and Illinois. By 1998, about 72 percent of immigrants lived in those states, with 32 percent living in California alone. This extreme geographic concentration reflects both the immigrants' propensity to enter the United States through a limited number of gateway cities (such as Los Angeles and New York) and the fact that immigrants—unlike natives—do not seem to move much around the country. Once immigrants enter one of the gateway cities, they tend to stay there.[8]

Much can be learned about the economic impact of immigration by paying particularly close attention to California, the state heaviest hit by the Second Great Migration (see Figure 4-1). Remarkably, California was not an important immigrant-receiving state in 1950. At that time, only 12 percent of adult Californians were foreign-born, as compared to 21 percent in New York and 15 percent in New Jersey.[9] Prior to 1970, the immigrant share of the adult population was either declining or stable in California, in the other immigrant-receiving states, and in the rest of the United States. Since 1970, however, this share tripled in California (rising from 10 to 32 percent between 1970 and 1998), more than doubled in the other immigrant-receiving states (from 8 to 18 percent), and rose much less in the rest of the country (from 3.0 to 5.6 percent). In a very real sense, therefore, the post-1965 resurgence of immigration is a California phenomenon.

The geographic clustering of immigrants is even more remarkable when one looks at specific cities. In 1990, 42 percent of immigrants lived in just five metropolitan areas (Los Angeles, New York, Miami, Chicago, and Anaheim), but only 13 percent of natives lived in those localities. And, not sur-

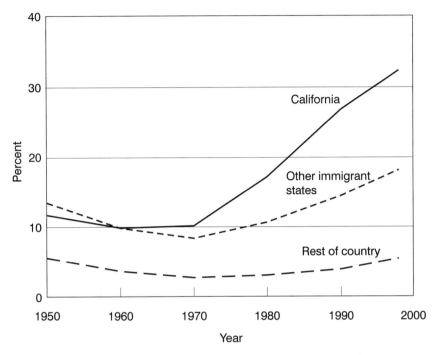

FIGURE 4-1. Percentage of adult population that is foreign-born, 1950–98.

Sources: George J. Borjas, Richard B. Freeman, and Lawrence F. Katz, "How Much Do Immigration and Trade Affect Labor Market Outcomes?" *Brookings Papers on Economic Activity* 1 (1997), p. 5; and additional calculations from the pooled 1996–98 Current Population Surveys (Annual Demographic Files).

Notes: The "other immigrant states" are New York, Texas, Florida, Illinois, and New Jersey. The "adult population" contains persons who are eighteen to sixty-four years old.

prisingly, California's cities were hit particularly hard by the influx. Between 1980 and 1990, the foreign-born share rose from 25 to 40 percent in Los Angeles, 15 to 28 percent in Anaheim, and 14 to 22 percent in San Diego.[10]

The impact of immigration on the local labor market depends not only on how many immigrants enter the locality, but also on how the skills of those immigrants compare to the skills of natives who already work there. The differences between the skill distributions of immigrants and natives in California vis-à-vis the rest of the country have become much more pronounced over time (see Figure 4-2). Prior to 1970, California's immigrant population had a slight overrepresentation of college graduates, and a slight underrepresentation of high school dropouts. In 1950, for example, California was home to 10 percent of all immigrants, to 9 percent of immigrants who were high school dropouts, and to 12 percent of immigrants who were college graduates. By the late 1990s, the situation was strikingly different. California was home to 32 percent of all immigrants, to almost 40 percent of the immigrants who were high school dropouts, and to 28 percent of the immigrants who were college graduates. It would seem, therefore, that if one wishes to find

Percent of immigrants in a particular
education group who live in California

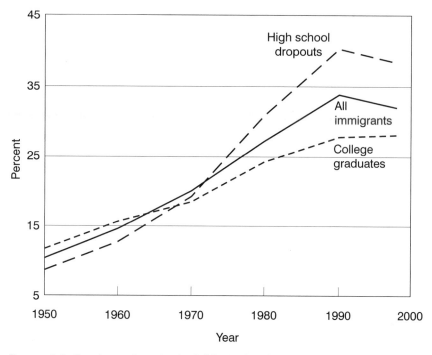

FIGURE 4-2. Immigrant clustering in California, by educational attainment, 1950–98.
   Sources: Calculations from the 1950–90 Public Use Microdata Samples of the U.S. Census
and the pooled 1996–98 Current Population Surveys (Annual Demographic Files).
   Note: The data refer to persons who are eighteen to sixty-four years old.

an adverse impact of immigration on the economic opportunities of native
workers, a fruitful place to begin might be the post-1965 trend in the economic status of California's less-skilled native workers.

REGIONAL DIFFERENCES IN NATIVE WAGES AND EMPLOYMENT

What happens when immigration increases the supply of workers in a particular labor market? The traditional approach to this question—the one that has
greatly influenced the direction of the immigration debate—takes a myopic,
short-run perspective. The entry of immigrants into the local labor market
should lower the wage of competing workers (workers who have the same
types of skills as immigrants) and perhaps increase the wage of complementary workers (workers whose skills become more valuable because of immigration). For example, an influx of foreign-born laborers reduces the economic opportunities for laborers who already live in the locality—all laborers

now face stiffer competition in the labor market. At the same time, highly skilled natives may gain substantially. They pay less for the services that laborers provide, such as painting the house and mowing the lawn, and natives who hire these laborers can now specialize in producing the goods and services that better suit their skills.

This short-run perspective, however, can be very misleading. Over time, natives—both those who live in the city targeted by immigrants as well as those living in other cities—will likely respond to the entry of immigrants. It is not in the best interest of native-owned firms or native workers to sit still and watch immigrants change economic opportunities. All natives now have incentives to change their behavior in ways that take advantage of the altered economic landscape.

For example, native-owned firms see that cities flooded by less-skilled immigrants tend to pay lower wages to laborers. Employers who hire laborers will want to relocate to those cities, and entrepreneurs thinking about starting up new firms will find it more profitable to open them in immigrant areas. In other words, immigration increases the returns to capitalists in the affected cities, and capital will naturally flow to those areas where the returns are highest. The flow of jobs to the immigrant receiving hit areas helps cushion the adverse effect of immigration on the wage of competing workers in these localities.

These capital flows create difficult problems if one wants to measure the labor market impact of immigration by comparing economic opportunities in different cities. After all, the jobs that flow into the immigrant areas are moving from someplace else—the job gains in the immigrant areas are another city's actual or potential job losses. These capital flows help dampen the adverse effects of immigration on the immigrant cities, while worsening economic conditions in the nonimmigrant cities. Because the capital flows tend to equalize economic conditions across cities, intercity comparisons will not be very revealing: the capital flows effectively diffuse the impact of immigration to the national economy. In the end, all laborers, regardless of where they live, are worse off because there are now many more of them.

The forces that tend to equalize employment opportunities across labor markets are reinforced by the fact that native workers will also respond. Laborers living in Michigan or Mississippi were perhaps thinking about moving to California before the immigrants entered that state. These laborers quickly learn that immigration has reduced their potential wages in California. As a result, many will decide to remain where they are or move elsewhere—and some Californians might actually find it worthwhile to incur the cost of leaving the state to search for better opportunities. The migration of native workers within the United States, in effect, accomplishes what the immigrant flow, with its tendency to cluster in a small number of gateway cities, could not—a "spreading out" of the additional workers over the entire nation, rather than in just a limited number of localities. And again, a comparison of the employment opportunities of native workers in California and other states might show little or no difference because, in the end, immigration affected *every* city, not just the ones that actually received immigrants.

If nothing else, the possibility that native-owned firms and native workers might respond to immigration, and effectively diffuse the impact of immigration over the national economy, should make one wary of measuring the impact of immigration from comparisons of economic conditions in different cities. Nevertheless, almost all existing discussions of the labor market impact of immigration rely precisely on these types of spatial correlations, the relation between native labor market outcomes in an area and a measure of immigrant penetration in that area.[11] The native response to immigration suggests that these spatial correlations are probably most meaningful in the period immediately after the immigrants enter the labor market, but become essentially meaningless in the long run, as firms and native workers take advantage of the economic changes unleashed by immigration.

The Statistical Evidence

So what do the empirical studies that compare native economic opportunities across cities conclude? Well, to put it kindly, these studies offer something for everyone. If one believes that immigrants adversely affect native economic outcomes, the evidence reported in some reputable academic publications substantiates that claim.[12] If, in contrast, one believe that immigrants do not change native economic outcomes—or perhaps even improve them—there are equally reputable academic studies substantiating *that* claim.[13] In fact, the conflicting findings sometimes even appear in the same study.

To illustrate the inherent instability of the spatial correlation approach, consider the evidence provided by two recent—and somewhat encyclopedic—studies (see Table 4-1).[14] These studies correlated changes in the weekly earnings of native workers over a ten-year period with the increase in immigration that occurred over that period in a particular locality (either a state or a metropolitan area). So, for example, the impact of immigration on native wages would be obtained by correlating the change in the native wage between 1980 and 1990 with the change in the number of immigrants in the locality over the same period.

The most striking characteristic of the statistical results is the huge dispersion in the estimated effects, making it extremely difficult to generalize about the impact of immigration on labor market outcomes. The sign of the spatial correlation seems to change erratically over time. The correlation between changes in native earnings and immigration is positive and large in some decades and negative and large in others. If one interprets these spatial correlations as measures of the impact of immigration on native wages, the entry of one more immigrant for every ten native workers increases the wage of native men by 6 percent if the immigrants entered in the 1960s, increases it by 1 percent if the immigrants entered in the 1970s, and reduces it by 1 percent if the immigrants entered in the 1980s. A similar change in the num-

TABLE 4–1
Summary of Results from the Spatial Correlations Approach

	Percent change in the wage of native workers if there is one more immigrant per ten native workers					
	Men			Women		
	1960–70	*1970–80*	*1980–90*	*1960–70*	*1970–80*	*1980–90*
State data: All natives	5.9	0.7	–1.0	2.0	3.7	–0.2
Metropolitan area data						
High school dropouts	—	–0.7	5.7	—	–6.4	6.0
High school graduates	—	–2.6	2.2	—	1.1	7.1
Some college	—	0.2	3.7	—	0.3	6.9
Metropolitan area data, adjusted for possibility that immigrants cluster in high-wage areas						
High school dropouts	—	–8.7	9.3	—	–22.5	9.9
High school graduates	—	–7.9	8.3	—	–4.5	9.9
Some college	—	–6.3	5.9	—	–3.2	8.7

Sources: The state-level results are drawn from George J. Borjas, Richard B. Freeman, and Lawrence F. Katz, "How Much Do Immigration and Trade Affect Labor Market Outcomes?" *Brookings Papers on Economic Activity* 1 (1997), p. 24. The metropolitan area results are drawn from Robert F. Schoeni, "The Effect of Immigrants on the Employment and Wages of Native Workers: Evidence from the 1970s and 1980s" (photocopy, RAND Corporation, March 1997), Tabs. 1, 2, 3, and refer to white workers.

ber of immigrants reduces the wage of native men who are high school graduates by 3 percent in the 1970s, but increases it by 2 percent in the 1980s.

One potential problem with the spatial correlation approach is that immigrants are not randomly distributed across the United States. Immigrants "pick" only certain labor markets and avoid others. If the areas where immigrants cluster, such as California, have done well in some time periods and poorly in others, this would produce a spurious correlation between immigration and economic outcomes. Put differently, when California's economy booms—as it did for much of the postwar era—there is a built-in positive correlation between immigration and the economic status of natives, and it will seem as if immigrants help economic conditions in that state.

The statistical problem created by this spurious correlation is one of causality: is California's economy booming because immigrants entered the state, or did immigrants pick California because the state's economy was booming? It turns out, however, that when the spatial correlation approach attempts to correct for this statistical problem, the evidence is even more confusing.[15] Adjusting the data for the possible two-way causality *increases* the dispersion in the estimated spatial correlations. An additional immigrant for every ten natives now reduces the wage of native high school graduates by 8 percent if the immigrants entered in the 1970s, but increases it by 8 percent if the immigrants entered in the 1980s.

In short, one can pick and choose from the very diverse spatial correlations reported in a single study and conclude—by picking the "right" period, the "right" group, and the "right" methodology—that immigration has either a hugely beneficial or a very harmful impact on the labor market opportunities of native workers.

But why does the sign of the spatial correlation switch between the 1970s and the 1980s? The 1980s witnessed major changes in the U.S. wage structure, with the wage gap between skilled and unskilled workers increasing rapidly during the period. It also turns out that there was a major change in the *regional* wage structure in the 1980s—a change that is not well understood and that probably has little, if anything, to do with immigration.[16] The top panel of Figure 4-3 shows the striking nature of this change by illustrating the relation between the wage growth experienced by a particular state in the 1980s and that state's wage growth in the 1970s.[17] One need not use fancy statistical techniques to see the obvious: there is a strong negative correlation in wage growth by state across the two decades.[18] In other words, the states where the wage grew the fastest in the 1970s were the states where the wage grew most slowly in the 1980s.

Little is known about why this change in the regional wage structure occurred. But it did, and the fact that it did has crucial implications for interpreting the spatial correlation between native labor market outcomes and immigration. After all, *the same states* continued to receive large numbers of immigrants in the 1970s and 1980s (see the bottom panel of Figure 4-3).[19] So consider what happened during this period. The same states continued to receive large numbers of immigrants, but the states with the fastest wage growth in the 1970s became the states with the slowest wage growth in the 1980s. So, for example, if the immigrants entered the states where the wage grew relatively fast in the 1970s, they must have entered the states where the wage grew relatively slowly in the 1980s. As a result, it is inevitable that the sign of the spatial correlation between wages and immigration switched over the period. An observer will then draw different inferences about the impact of immigration by estimating spatial correlations in different decades. Unless one can net out the impact of the shift in the regional wage structure (and that would require an understanding of *why* the shift occurred in the first place), it is literally impossible to pry out the economic impact of immigration from spatial correlations.

A somewhat different approach appears in an influential case study of the Mariel immigrant flow.[20] On April 20, 1980, Fidel Castro declared that Cuban nationals wishing to move to the United States could leave freely from the port of Mariel. By September 1980, about 125,000 Cubans had chosen to undertake the journey. Almost overnight, the Mariel "natural experiment" increased Miami's labor force by 7 percent. It turns out that labor market trends in Miami between 1979 and 1981—in terms of wage levels and unemployment rates—were similar or better than those experienced by such cities as Los Angeles, Houston and Atlanta, cities that did not experience the

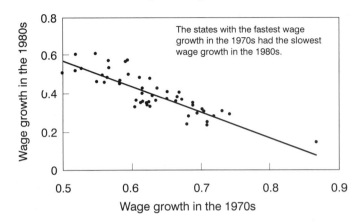

The regional wage structure

The states with the fastest wage growth in the 1970s had the slowest wage growth in the 1980s.

Wage growth in the 1980s

Wage growth in the 1970s

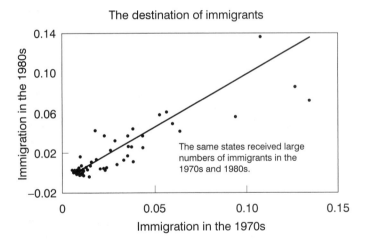

The destination of immigrants

The same states received large numbers of immigrants in the 1970s and 1980s.

Immigration in the 1980s

Immigration in the 1970s

FIGURE 4-3. Change in the regional wage structure and immigration.

Source: Based on George J. Borjas, Richard B. Freeman, and Lawrence F. Katz, "How Much Do Immigration and Trade Affect Labor Market Outcomes?" *Brookings Papers on Economic Activity* 1 (1997), pp. 18, 19.

Notes: The wage growth in the top panel refers to the percent change in the weekly wage of native working men during the decade. The measure of immigration in the bottom panel is the change in the number of immigrants per native worker during the decade. The trend lines come from regressions that are weighted by the population of the state. The data refer to persons who are eighteen to sixty-four years old.

TABLE 4–2
Immigration and the Miami Labor Market

	The Mariel flow		The Mariel flow that did not happen	
	Before (1979)	After (1981)	Before (1993)	After (1995)
Unemployment rate in Miami				
Whites	5.1	3.9	4.9	3.9
Blacks	8.3	9.6	10.1	13.7
Unemployment rate in comparison cities				
Whites	4.4	4.3	5.4	4.1
Blacks	10.3	12.6	11.5	8.8

Sources: The 1979–81 data are drawn from David Card, "The Impact of the Mariel Boatlift on the Miami Labor Market," *Industrial and Labor Relations Review* 43 (January 1990), p. 251. The 1993–95 data are drawn from Joshua D. Angrist and Alan B. Krueger, "Empirical Strategies in Labor Economics," in *Handbook of Labor Economics*, vol. 3, ed. Orley Ashenfelter and David Card (Amsterdam: North-Holland, forthcoming 1999), tab. 7.

Note: The comparison cities are Atlanta, Houston, Los Angeles, and Tampa-St. Petersburg.

Mariel flow (see Table 4-2).[21] For instance, the unemployment rate for Miami's blacks rose from 8.3 to 9.6 percent between 1979 and 1981, but the black unemployment rate in a set of comparison cities was rising even faster, from 10.3 to 12.6 percent, presumably because of changing economic conditions. The obvious inference: the *Marielitos* did not adversely affect the employment opportunities of African Americans in the Miami area.

Although the case study of the Mariel flow seems to estimate the impact of immigration from a natural experiment set in motion by Fidel Castro, there is an important sense in which the Mariel study is simply calculating yet another spatial correlation. The impact of immigration is still being estimated by comparing the native labor market in a city flooded by immigrants with native labor markets in other cities.

Moreover, recent research has raised some questions about the interpretation of the evidence generated by the "experimental approach" implicit in the Mariel study.[22] Consider, in particular, the impact of immigration that can be estimated from yet another natural experiment involving Cuba and the Miami labor market.

In the summer of 1994, economic and political conditions in Cuba were ripe for the onset of a new boatlift of refugees into the Miami area, and thousands began the hazardous journey. To prevent the rafters from reaching the Florida shores, the Clinton administration ordered the Coast Guard to redirect all the refugees to the American military base in Guantanamo Bay.

As a result, relatively few of the potential migrants were able to migrate to Miami.[23]

One can replicate the methodological design of the Mariel study by comparing Miami's labor market conditions (relative to those of control cities) before and after "the Mariel boatlift that didn't happen." It turns out that this nonevent may have had a substantial impact on Miami's unemployment rate—particularly for blacks (again, see Table 4-2).[24] The black unemployment rate in Miami rose from 10.1 to 13.7 percent between 1993 and 1995, as compared to a decline from 11.5 to 8.8 percent in a set of comparison cities. If one interprets this finding in the traditional way, it would seem to indicate that a phantom immigrant flow had a substantial harmful impact on the economic opportunities of black native workers. And this raises an important question: can one confidently interpret the evidence from the Mariel boatlift that *did* happen as indicating that immigration had little impact on Miami's labor market?

One way to interpret the confusing mosaic of spatial correlations estimated for the 1960–90 period is that the economic impact of immigration on native labor market outcomes simply changes over time and varies by sex. In other words, the spatial correlations provide the "right" estimates of the labor market impact of immigration, but it just happens that this impact varies a great deal. In one period or for one group, immigration reduces native economic opportunities; in another period or for another group, it has no effect; and in yet other periods and for yet other groups, it improves native opportunities. If this were a correct interpretation of the evidence, the historical record would provide virtually no information about the future effects of immigration on native economic outcomes. It seems that a different story is needed to understand how immigration affects different labor markets in different time periods. And one would be left wondering which story to use to predict the economic impact of the next immigrant wave.

I interpret these spatial correlations differently: they do not measure the impact of immigration on the native labor market. Put bluntly, the spatial correlations are completely uninformative.

Do Native Workers Vote with Their Feet?

The main problem with the spatial correlation approach is that it ignores the possibility that natives respond to the changing economic environment. Is there any evidence that native workers do, in fact, respond to immigration?

Because of the significance of the underlying issues, it is not surprising that there is a heated debate on this question. This debate involves not only the usual arcane technical and data issues, but also exposes a fundamental disagreement over how the problem should be approached conceptually.[25]

There is clear and unambiguous evidence of a *potential* relation between immigration and native migration decisions (see Figure 4-4).[26] The resur-

Percent of U.S. population living in California

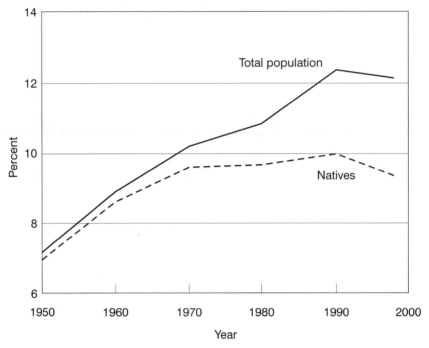

FIGURE 4-4. Trends in California's population, 1950–98.

Sources: George J. Borjas, Richard B. Freeman, and Lawrence F. Katz, "How Much Do Immigration and Trade Affect Labor Market Outcomes?" *Brookings Papers on Economic Activity* 1 (1997), p. 27; and additional calculations from the pooled 1996–98 Current Population Surveys (Annual Demographic Files).

Note: The data refer to persons who are eighteen to sixty-four years old.

gence of immigration in the United States began circa 1968, when the policy changes in the 1965 Amendments became effective. It seems natural, therefore, to measure the impact of immigration by contrasting pre-1970 changes in the residential location of the native population with post-1970 changes.

Not surprisingly, the share of natives who lived in California, the major immigrant-receiving state, was rising rapidly prior to 1970. What is surprising, however, is that the share of natives living in California barely budged between 1970 and 1990, and declined somewhat during the 1990s.[27] Nevertheless, California's share of the total population kept rising continuously until 1990, from 7 percent in 1950 to 10 percent in 1970 and 12 percent in 1990. Put differently, an extrapolation of the population growth that existed before 1970—*before the resurgence of immigration*—would have predicted the state's 1990 share of the population quite accurately. But while natives pouring into the state fueled California's population growth before 1970, immigrants alone fueled the post-1970 growth.

But how should this fact be interpreted? One interpretation is that around 1970, for reasons unknown, Americans simply changed their mind about the magnetic attraction of sun, surf, and silicon, and stopped moving to California. In other words, had it not been for immigration, California's rapid population growth would have stalled in the 1970s and 1980s. An alternative—and more provocative—interpretation is that immigration into California essentially "displaced" the population growth that would have occurred in the immigrants' absence, and this displacement effectively diffused the economic impact of immigration from California to the rest of the country.

The relation between California's population trends and immigration is not unique. Consider what happened to Miami's population after the entry of the Mariel flow in 1980.[28] Miami's population was growing at an annual rate of 2.5 percent in the 1970s, as compared to a growth rate of 3.9 percent for the rest of Florida. After the arrival of the *Marielitos*, Miami's annual growth rate slowed to 1.4 percent, as compared to 3.4 percent in the rest of Florida. As a result of this slowdown in the relative number of persons moving to the Miami area, the actual population of Dade County in 1986 was roughly the same as the pre-Mariel projection made by the University of Florida.

In both California and Miami, therefore, an observer who was familiar with the demographic trends of the region *prior* to the entry of immigrants could have almost perfectly predicted what the region's population would have been at some future time. Remarkably, the observer did not need to know that each of these regions would experience an unexpected and sizable increase in immigration.

Despite these trends, there remains substantial disagreement over whether native workers, in fact, vote with their feet. Figure 4-5 illustrates the relation between the change in a state's native population over the 1970–90 period and the change in the number of immigrants in that state over the same period.[29] There obviously exists a strong positive correlation between native population growth and immigration: states that are growing are growing in every dimension. In fact, the trend line suggests that the number of natives living in a particular state grows by eight persons for every ten immigrants who move into that state. This positive correlation has been interpreted to imply that natives do not respond to immigration, or even that perhaps natives respond by moving to areas penetrated by immigrants.[30]

But this interpretation may be wrong. The population of some states, such as California, has been growing rapidly for quite some time, while the population of other states, such as Iowa, Ohio, and Rhode Island, has been relatively stagnant. The fact that both natives and immigrants move to California, and not to Iowa, need not indicate that immigration "causes" the native population in California to grow. It may just suggest that all workers would rather live in places where the economy is growing and the sun is shining.

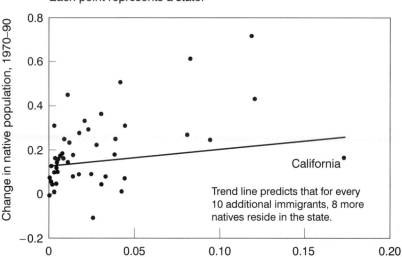

Each point represents a state.

FIGURE 4-5. Relation between immigration and the change in the native population.

Source: George J. Borjas, Richard B. Freeman, and Lawrence F. Katz, "How Much Do Immigration and Trade Affect Labor Market Outcomes?" *Brookings Papers on Economic Activity* 1 (1997), p. 30.

Notes: The "change in native population" gives the annualized 1970–90 change in the number of natives as a fraction of the state's population in 1970. The "change in immigrant population" gives the annualized 1970–90 change in the number of immigrants as a fraction of the state's population in 1970. The trend line comes from a regression that is weighted by the population of the state.

It seems, therefore, that the data need to be adjusted for preexisting "magnetic effects" that attract persons to some states. This can be done by comparing the state's rate of population growth *before and after* the resurgence of immigration. Figure 4-6 illustrates this relationship, which looks at a state's population growth in 1970–90 relative to that state's growth in 1960–70. For instance, each data point in this figure links the number of natives who moved into a particular state (relative to the number of natives who had been moving there prior to the entry of immigrants) with the number of immigrants who chose to move into that state (again, relative to the number of immigrants who had been moving there prior to 1970). These data can then be used to assess how the state's population growth from 1970 through 1990 deviated from the state's preexisting trend.

Figure 4-6 shows that the correlation between native population growth and immigration—relative to the long-run trend—is clearly negative.[31] The trend line suggests that the native population declined by about eight persons for every ten immigrants who moved into the state, relative to what the state could have expected from its long-run trend. This conceptual approach,

Each point represents a state.

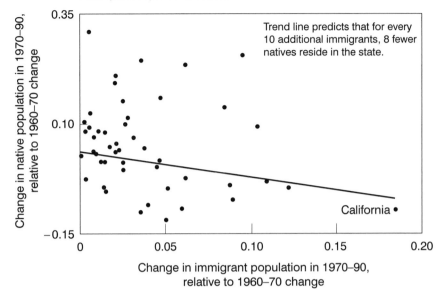

FIGURE 4-6. Relation between immigration and the change in the native population, relative to pre-immigration trend.

Source: George J. Borjas, Richard B. Freeman, and Lawrence F. Katz, "How Much Do Immigration and Trade Affect Labor Market Outcomes?" *Brookings Papers on Economic Activity* 1 (1997), p. 30.

Notes: The "change in native population" gives the annualized 1970–90 change in the number of natives as a fraction of the state's population in 1970 minus the 1960–70 change in the number of natives as a fraction of the state's population in 1960. The "change in immigrant population" gives the annualized 1970–90 change in the number of immigrants as a fraction of the state's population in 1970 minus the 1960–70 change in the number of immigrants as a fraction of the state's population in 1960. The trend line comes from a regression that is weighted by the population of the state.

therefore, suggests that natives more than just voted with their feet. Natives, in fact, stampeded out of the immigrant-receiving states.

In the end, whether one finds that natives move into or out of immigrant-receiving states depends on how the question is posed. One conceptual approach ignores the state's preexisting trends in population growth, and finds that the same states "attract" both immigrants and natives. This approach, however, suffers from a severe flaw: it ignores the fact that different states had different rates of population growth prior to the surge in immigration.

An alternative approach looks at a state's population growth relative to the trend that existed in the preimmigration period, and finds a considerable native response, with natives moving out of (or avoiding) the immigrant-receiving states. This approach, however, also has its problems. It assumes that the preexisting population trends would have continued in the absence of immigration.

It is impossible to determine conclusively how the regional distribution of the American population would have evolved if the Second Great Migration had never occurred, so some assumption is inevitably required to establish a hypothetical baseline. If one is willing to assume that the preexisting trends would have continued, the evidence suggests that the native response to immigration helped diffuse much of the economic impact of immigration over the entire country.

Which Natives Voted with Their Feet?

The migration response of native workers would completely diffuse the impact of immigration on particular localities if the natives who moved—or who chose not to move—belonged to the "right" skill groups. An influx of less-skilled immigrants into California should curtail the migration of less-skilled natives into that state, and should push some of the less-skilled natives who already lived there out. The entry of less-skilled immigrants into California, therefore, should alter the distribution of educational attainment among the native workers who remain there.

As one might suspect, the number of native college graduates relative to the number of high school dropouts rose much faster in California than in other parts of the country, and this trend accelerated after 1970 (see Figure 4-7). As California's population of less-skilled workers surged with immigration—making it harder for less-skilled natives to "make it" there—the natives who remained in California tended to be much better educated.

In sum, it seems that natives do vote with their feet when one views the impact of immigration from a long-run perspective. Moreover, this native response may be sufficiently large to diffuse much of the effect of immigration from the affected regions to the entire economy. As a result, it should not be surprising that spatial correlations between immigration and native economic outcomes behave erratically. Put simply, the local labor markets penetrated by immigrants are probably the wrong place to look if one wants to measure the impact of immigration on the employment opportunities of native workers.

Do Firms Respond to Immigration?

Native workers are not alone in responding to the changes in the economic environment induced by immigration. Native-owned firms—as well as capital flows from abroad—will also want to take advantage of these changes.

It is well known that immigrants enter occupations and industries that differ from the occupations and industries that employ the native work force (see Table 4-3). Not surprisingly, immigrants are more concentrated in the less-skilled occupations and industries. Many immigrants work in farming, in service jobs, as private household workers, and as operators and fabricators.

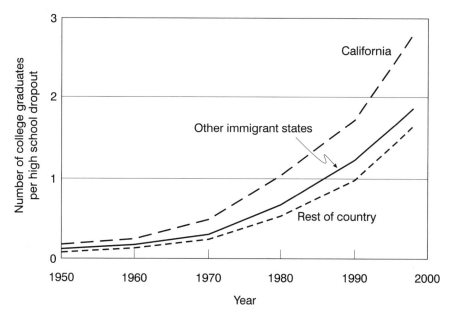

FIGURE 4-7. The educational distribution of native persons, by region, 1950–98.
   Sources: Calculations from the 1950–90 Public Use Samples of the U.S. Census and the pooled 1996–98 Current Population Surveys (Annual Demographic Files).
   Notes: The "other immigrant states" are New York, Texas, Florida, Illinois, and New Jersey. The data refer to persons who are eighteen to sixty-four years old.

There are relatively more immigrants in the agricultural sector, in manufacturing, and in wholesale and retail trade. In contrast, immigrants are underrepresented in white-collar jobs, such as managerial and professional specialties, administration, and sales. Part of the differences in these occupation and industry distributions can obviously be attributed to the lower educational attainment of immigrants.

   The fact that immigrants and natives, on average, do somewhat different types of jobs leads many to conclude that immigrants do not harm native employment opportunities because "immigrants take jobs that natives do not want." In my view, this inference is not justified. Even though the occupational distributions of immigrants and natives differ, there is also a great deal of overlap. It is certainly true that 15 percent of immigrant workers are operators and fabricators, but so are 11 percent of natives. Similarly, 28 percent of native workers are managers and professionals, but so are 21 percent of immigrants. A more sensible inference may well be that immigrants take jobs that natives do not want *at the going wage.* In other words, it might be the case that natives might not want to work in some of the jobs that immigrants have. This does not say, however, that natives would refuse to work in those jobs if the immigrants had never arrived and employers were forced to raise wages to fill the positions.

TABLE 4–3
Occupations and Industries Employing Immigrants and Natives, 1995

	Percent of immigrants employed in occupation or industry	Percent of natives employed in occupation or industry	Percent of workers in occupation or industry who are foreign-born
Occupation			
Managerial and professional specialty	21.2	28.2	7.6
Technical and related support	2.5	3.2	7.7
Sales	9.4	12.1	7.9
Administrative support, including clerical	9.7	15.4	6.4
Precision, production, craft, and repair	11.7	11.0	10.5
Operators and fabricators	14.9	10.5	13.5
Handlers, equipment cleaners, helpers, and laborers	5.7	4.2	12.9
Private household	2.1	0.5	31.5
Service (excluding private household)	17.4	12.5	13.3
Farming, forestry, and fishing	5.4	2.5	19.4
Industry			
Agriculture	5.0	2.3	19.0
Mining	0.3	0.6	5.1
Construction	6.4	6.6	9.7
Manufacturing	20.2	16.2	12.0
Transport, communication, and utilities	5.3	7.2	7.5
Wholesale trade	4.4	3.9	11.0
Retail trade	17.7	16.5	10.5
Finance, insurance, real estate	5.0	6.3	7.9
Services	33.4	35.1	9.5
Government	2.3	5.2	4.5

Source: George J. Borjas, Richard B. Freeman, and Lawrence F. Katz, "How Much Do Immigration and Trade Affect Labor Market Outcomes?" *Brookings Papers on Economic Activity* 1 (1997), p. 8.

Moreover, if immigrants indeed took jobs that natives did not want, the nonwage aspects of the jobs employing the typical immigrant and those employing the typical native would differ significantly. For instance, one might expect immigrants to face more unpleasant working conditions. There is no evidence whatsoever to suggest that this is the case. In fact, the available evidence indicates that immigrants and natives have roughly similar working conditions.[32] The typical native works in a job that has 4.6 injuries per hundred workers annually, while the typical immigrant works in one that has 4.4 injuries. Similarly, about 8 percent of both immigrants and natives are employed in the midnight shift.

Immigration does tend to change the skill composition of the work force in the immigrant-receiving area, possibly altering the industrial structure of the region. Industries that employ workers who "look like" the immigrants will find it cheaper to hire in the immigrant region, and these industries will expand. Moreover, competing firms located in other states (or even abroad) will see the profit opportunities opened up by immigration, and will choose to move to or invest in the immigrant-receiving areas.

TABLE 4-4
Employment Growth in Immigrant Industries, 1970–90

| | *Annual percent change in employment* | | |
	California	*Other immigrant states*	*Rest of country*
Industries that are immigrant-intensive	2.5	1.3	1.5
Manufacturing	1.7	0.1	0.6
Personal services	2.2	1.2	0.9
Industries that are not immigrant-intensive	2.8	2.4	2.4
Professional services	3.2	2.9	2.8
Transportation, communications, and utilities	2.3	1.9	2.0

Source: George J. Borjas, Richard B. Freeman, and Lawrence F. Katz, "How Much Do Immigration and Trade Affect Labor Market Outcomes?" *Brookings Papers on Economic Activity* 1 (1997), p. 9.
Note: The "other immigrant states" are New York, Texas, Florida, Illinois, and New Jersey.

It turns out that employment growth in immigrant-intensive industries has been much stronger in California than in other parts of the country (see Table 4-4).[33] The immigrant-intensive industries are those that employ a disproportionately large number of immigrants, such as manufacturing or personal services. Between 1970 and 1990, employment in these industries rose at a 2.5 percent annual rate in California, as compared to a 1.3 percent annual rate in other immigrant-receiving states and a 1.4 percent annual rate in the rest of the country. In fact, manufacturing employment was stagnant everywhere in the United States except in California. In contrast, employment growth in the industries that do not employ many immigrants was much more similar across the various regions. Employment in professional services, for instance, grew at about 3 percent annually throughout the entire United States.

Obviously, the influx of less-skilled immigrants is not the only factor that determines the evolution of industries in different parts of the country. Many other things matter: the tax policies of state and local governments, the quality of local schools, zoning regulations, and so on. Nevertheless, there seems to be some evidence suggesting that the industrial structure of California adjusted to the post-1965 immigrant influx.

These observed changes in the industry mix provide yet another channel for diffusing the impact of immigration away from the areas that received the immigrants. Less-skilled natives employed by manufacturing firms in Georgia, for example, may have suffered job losses and wage reductions from competition with California's manufacturing firms, who may have expanded and lowered prices because of the increased supply of immigrants. In the end, these responses by capitalists and entrepreneurs—who are always seeking out investment opportunities where they can earn the best return—help to fur-

ther diffuse the adverse impact of immigration from California to other labor
markets.

THE NATIONAL LABOR MARKET

By now, the message should be clear. Because natives respond to changes in
the economic environment, it will be difficult, if not impossible, to detect
the impact of immigration by looking at economic conditions in the local
areas hardest hit. The responses by native workers and by native capitalists
ensure that the adverse (or beneficial) effects of immigration are diffused to
the rest of the country, so one may have to look at the national labor market
to discern if immigration indeed had an impact.

The "factor proportions" approach compares a nation's actual supplies of
workers in particular skill groups to those it would have had in the absence
of immigration, and then uses outside information on how relative wages
respond to changes in the relative supplies of workers to calculate the wage
consequences of immigration.[34] To give a very simple example, suppose that
in the absence of immigration there would have been one unskilled worker
per skilled worker in the national economy. Immigration changes this "factor
proportion" so that there are now, say, two unskilled workers per skilled
worker. Such a change in factor proportions will probably change the wage
gap between skilled and unskilled workers. In particular, the abundance of
unskilled workers in the postimmigration period should widen the gap. If
existing economic research provided a measure of the responsiveness of relative wages to changes in factor proportions, one could then use this estimate
to simulate the impact of immigration on the wage gap between skilled and
unskilled workers in the national economy.[35]

Many studies of the American labor market—studies that have little to do
with immigration—indeed report that increases in the relative supply of less-
educated workers reduce their relative wages.[36] Similar evidence has been
documented for labor markets in many other countries, including Great Britain, Canada, South Korea, and Sweden.[37] In other words, the laws of supply
and demand play an important role in the national labor market: an increase
in the relative number of a particular skill group will typically lower its relative wage.

A practical difficulty with this approach is that one has to define which
group of workers is "skilled" and which group is "unskilled"—and, inevitably, some arbitrariness will enter the calculations. Studies that use the factor
proportions approach often assume that workers with the same educational
attainment belong to the same skill groups.[38] It turns out, however, that
one obtains very different estimates of the economic impact of immigration
depending on how the skill groups are defined.

Table 4-5 summarizes the results from this type of simulation, using two
alternative classifications of the skill groups. Initially, define workers who are

TABLE 4–5
The Impact of Immigration on the National Labor Market

	Definition of "unskilled" versus "skilled"	
	High school dropouts versus all other education groups	High school graduates versus college graduates
Number of unskilled immigrants who arrived between 1979 and 1995 per hundred unskilled natives	20.7	5.6
Number of skilled immigrants who arrived between 1979 and 1995 per hundred skilled natives	4.1	4.3
Percent wage differential between skilled and unskilled natives in 1979	30.1%	30.4%
Percent wage differential between skilled and unskilled natives in 1995	41.0%	49.5%
Percent of the change in the wage gap between skilled and unskilled natives attributable to immigration	44.0%	4.7%

Source: George J. Borjas, Richard B. Freeman, and Lawrence F. Katz, "How Much Do Immigration and Trade Affect Labor Market Outcomes?" *Brookings Papers on Economic Activity* 1 (1997), pp. 47,62.

Note: The percent wage differentials refer to the log point wage differential between the two groups.

high school dropouts to be "unskilled," and all other workers to be "skilled." In 1980, workers with at least a high school education earned about 30 percent more than high school dropouts, and this gap grew to 41 percent by 1995.[39]

How much of the widening in this wage gap can be attributed to immigration? Between 1979 and 1995, immigration increased the supply of workers who were high school dropouts by 21 percent, but increased the supply of workers with at least a high school diploma by only 4 percent.[40] In other words, immigration changed the factor proportions in the American labor market—generating a relative abundance of less-skilled workers. The available evidence on how relative wages respond to changes in relative supplies implies that immigration reduced the relative wage of high school dropouts by about 5 percentage points.[41] In other words, about 44 percent of the widening wage gap between high school dropouts and high school graduates can be attributed to the large impact of immigration on the relative number of high school dropouts.

An alternative definition of the skill groups, however, suggests that immigration had a much smaller effect on the employment opportunities of native workers. Define the unskilled group to consist of workers who are high school graduates and the skilled group to consist of workers who are college graduates.[42] Using this definition, post-1979 immigration increased the supply of unskilled workers by only 6 percent, and that of skilled workers by 4 percent. In other words, immigration did not change factor proportions by much. As a result, even though the wage gap between these two groups grew by 19 percentage points between 1979 and 1995, immigration accounts for little of this increase.

It should not be too surprising that the adverse impact of immigration falls mainly on workers at the very bottom of the skill distribution. The United States admitted about twenty-five million legal and illegal immigrants between 1965 and 1995. But this increase in the number of workers was not evenly balanced across education groups. While immigration increased the supply of high school graduates or college graduates only moderately, it led to a remarkable spike in the number of high school dropouts.

Needless to say, the conclusion that immigration may account for nearly half of the decline in the relative wage of high school dropouts is controversial. And, to some extent, the critics have a point. In an important sense, the factor proportions approach—the approach that predicts a strong link between the wages of less-skilled workers and immigration at the national level—is unsatisfactory. The approach does not estimate the impact of immigration on the labor market by directly observing how immigrants affect some workers and not others. Rather, the factor proportions approach simulates the impact of immigration. It takes as "fact" the level of responsiveness between relative wages and relative supplies uncovered by many economic studies—and then uses this measure of responsiveness to mechanically predict the consequences of immigration. The simulation, therefore, relies heavily on a theoretical framework that describes how the U.S. labor market translates changes in the number of workers into changes in their wages. As a result, the approach has been criticized for relying on theoretical models to calculate the effect of immigration on native employment opportunities.[43]

On the one hand, this criticism is valid. The factor proportions approach certainly relies on a theory of how the labor market works. If this theory is wrong or if one has the wrong estimate of how wages respond to an increase in the number of workers, the estimated impact of immigration is also incorrect. On the other hand, a great deal of evidence shows that relative supplies *do* affect relative wages. Further, the cross-city comparison of native employment opportunities has failed to reveal with any degree of precision the impact that immigration has on the wage structure. Finally, the factor proportions approach is not alone in relying on a theory of how the labor market works. In the end, *any* interpretation of statistical correlations between immigration and the labor market outcomes of native workers—and particularly any use of these data to predict the outcomes of shifts in immigration policy—requires a story. This story would indicate how immigration alters the economic environment, and thereby affects the employment opportunities of particular groups of native workers. The factor proportions approach tells a very specific story of the labor market—a story that has been used successfully to address many issues in social and economic policy—and relies on that story to estimate the impact of immigration on the wage structure.

IMMIGRATION AND TRADE

The emotional debate over the increased globalization of the U.S. economy—including the debate over NAFTA—focused almost exclusively on economic issues. How does trade affect the jobs and wages of American workers? Do international differences in labor standards and environmental regulations give some countries a competitive edge?

The economic impacts of immigration and trade are closely linked. After all, both immigration and trade help connect the American labor market with the labor markets of other countries. They both increase the "effective" labor supply of particular groups of workers in the United States. Every time a Japanese-made car is unloaded at a Southern California dock, the country is essentially importing, say, 350 hours of engineering know-how, 250 hours of less-skilled labor, and so on. In other words, one can interpret the entry of this automobile into the United States as equivalent to the immigration of workers with particular skills.

Trade between the United States and other countries began to rise markedly after 1970—at about the same time that the Second Great Migration began. In 1970, the ratio of exports and imports to GDP stood at 8 percent; by 1996, this ratio had risen to about 19 percent. And much of this increase can be attributed to trade with developing countries. By 1996, nearly 40 percent of all imports came from these countries.[44]

During the 1980s and 1990s, immigration disproportionately increased the labor supply of less-skilled workers in the United States. But how did foreign trade change labor supply? Not surprisingly, the United States tends to export different types of goods from those it imports.[45] The workers employed in the importing industries tend to be less educated, while the workers employed in the exporting industries tend to be well educated. Put simply, imports hurt the less-skilled while exports help the skilled. The huge trade deficit that has persisted since the early 1980s—with the value of imports greatly exceeding that of exports—can then be interpreted as generating a disproportionate increase in the number of less-skilled workers in the U.S. labor market.

Because both immigration and trade change the nation's effective labor supply, one can estimate the impact of trade on the wage gap between skilled and unskilled workers by calculating the total number of worker-hours implicit in the observed trade flows. It turns out that immigration changes effective labor supply by a great deal more than trade, so that the two have very different effects on the income distribution. Between 1980 and 1995, the wage of high school dropouts relative to that of workers with more schooling fell by 11 percentage points. The immigration of large numbers of high school dropouts can account for almost half of this decline in the relative wage. Trade, however, can account for only 10 percent of the decline.[46]

Although this calculation suggests that immigration has a far larger impact than trade on the wage structure, one should be cautious about the interpretation. After all, trade can have a substantial impact on the wages of American workers even if the foreign goods never actually reach the United States. Suppose that a Chinese firm begins producing Boston Red Sox T-shirts and informs the Red Sox souvenir stands that it can provide the product at a lower price than American producers. The souvenir stands will then inform the American manufacturers that they have to meet the new price to keep their business. The American firms, in turn, will tell their workers that they can stay competitive only if the workers accept a wage cut. If the workers accept the wage cut, the American firms maintain their hold on the T-shirts market—but the wages of these workers were effectively set by economic conditions in Beijing. If the workers do not accept the pay cut, the American companies will no longer be competitive, and the American workers lose their jobs as the production of Red Sox T-shirts moves abroad. In short, the *threat* of trade may be sufficient to ensure that labor market conditions in the United States are affected by labor market conditions in the countries that produce competing goods.

Moreover, both trade and immigration allow a country to employ resources that are scarce within its borders—and the same economic incentives that drive global trade flows motivate workers to move across international borders. If the United States did not import cheap toys from China, the country would want to import less-skilled workers to produce those toys in the domestic market. Similarly, if there were no immigration, the United States would want to import the types of goods that are now produced by immigrants. As a result, the "small" effects of trade on wages might be larger if there were no immigration, and the effects of immigration would be larger if there were no trade.[47]

Nevertheless, it is probably safe to conclude that immigration probably has a much larger economic impact in the long run. After all, if the United States stopped trading with its foreign partners, trade would no longer influence the effective labor supply in the American labor market. The goods that were imported in the past decade have long since been consumed, and trade leaves no "footprint." Immigration, however, increases the labor supply permanently. Even if the United States were to stop admitting immigrants tomorrow, the economic impact of past immigration would continue throughout the immigrant's working life—and beyond, as the children and grandchildren of immigrants entered the labor market.

The Economic Benefits from Immigration

THE SECOND GREAT MIGRATION had an adverse impact on the economic well-being of less-skilled native workers. But even though natives at the bottom rung of the economic ladder lost from immigration, other natives gained. Who were these winners? Why did they benefit? And were the benefits large enough to outweigh the losses suffered by the less-skilled?

This chapter describes how natives benefit from immigration, provides a back-of-the-envelope calculation of these benefits, and describes the rough outlines of an immigration policy that would maximize the economic benefits. Natives benefit because there exist production complementarities between immigrant workers and natives: immigrants bring in skills and abilities that may be scarce in the United States. As a result, the economic benefits from immigration are larger when the productive abilities of immigrants are very different from those of natives. Moreover, it turns out that the gains accruing to the winners are larger than the losses suffered by the losers. On net, therefore, the country benefits from immigration.

The net benefit is small, however—probably around $10 billion annually. This quantity, however, does not account for the impact of immigration on the cost of providing public assistance and other social programs. This fiscal impact will be documented in the next chapter. Moreover, the $10 billion net benefit masks a substantial redistribution of wealth induced by immigration, from workers who compete with immigrants to persons who use or consume immigrant services. In other words, while immigration might increase the size of the economic pie slightly, it also changes the way the pie is split.

This perspective on the economic consequences of immigration clarifies what is at the core of the immigration debate. The debate is not over whether the country as a whole is better off—the net gain seems to be much too small to justify such a grand social experiment. The debate is really over the fact that some people gain substantially, while others lose. In short, the immigration debate is a tug-of-war between the winners and the losers.

How Do Natives Benefit from Immigration?

Natives benefit from immigration in many ways. For example, immigrants increase the demand for goods and services produced by native workers and firms. Immigrants, after all, buy cars, order pizza, call the plumber, and go to the supermarket—and native-owned firms and native-born workers are more than willing to provide these services to new consumers. The firms see opportunities for higher profits, and the workers see opportunities for additional jobs.

Immigration may also increase the productivity of some native workers. Less-skilled immigrants, for example, can conduct many of the service tasks in a modern industrialized economy, and thereby free up time for native workers to devote to the activities where they are most productive.

Immigration can lower the prices of many goods and services, benefiting American consumers. Illegal alien labor is plentiful and cheap in Southern California. In 1997, the going wage for a full-time live-in maid in the San Diego area was less than $200 a week (plus room and board)—far below the price of equivalent services in other parts of the country. These illegal aliens surely improve the economic well being of the many native households who hire them to tend the garden, do household chores, and care for the children.

Finally, immigrant entrepreneurs open up firms, create jobs, and possibly make a large contribution to economic growth. Their long list includes the Hungarian-born Andrew Grove, a founder and long-time CEO of Intel Corporation, *Time* magazine's 1997 Man of the Year, the French-born Philippe Kahn, CEO of Borland International, and the late Cuban-born Roberto Goizueta, CEO of Coca-Cola. Foreign-born persons also receive a disproportionately large number of the Nobel prizes awarded to American scientists: 26 percent in chemistry, 31 percent in economics, 32 percent in physics, and 31 percent in medicine.[1] American universities, laboratories, and manufacturers probably gain substantially from the discoveries and intellectual contributions made by these Nobel laureates.

To measure accurately the economic gains from immigration, one needs to list all the possible channels through which immigration transforms the economy: immigration changes the prices of goods and services, the employment opportunities of workers, the number of jobs in native-owned firms, and the number of jobs in immigrant-owned firms. This exhaustive list can then be used to estimate what the gross domestic product of the United States would have been if the country had not admitted any immigrants. The comparison of this counterfactual GDP with the actual GDP yields the increase in national income directly attributable to immigration. And the calculation can also determine how much of the increase in national income accrues to natives, as opposed to being paid directly to immigrants in return for their services.

Obviously, this sort of computation is a very difficult task, and this explains why most discussions of the economic benefits from immigration shy away from actually estimating the size of the benefits. Instead, many observers simply discuss the potential sources of the economic benefits, do a lot of hand waving, and often insinuate that these benefits must be very large. On the rare occasions when actual numbers are provided, there is seldom any documentation to substantiate the often-exaggerated claims. For example, George Gilder, the author of the 1981 bestseller *Wealth and Poverty*, boldly proclaims that "without immigration over the last 50 years, I would estimate that U.S.

real living standards would be at least 40 percent lower."[2] If one takes this number seriously, it would seem that the Second Great Migration contributed over $3 trillion annually to national income in the late 1990s.

It is difficult to calculate the *measurable* benefits from immigration because no such calculation can be made unless one has a model of the U.S. economy detailing how the various sectors of the economy operate and are linked together. One can then simulate how the economy changes when the labor market is flooded by millions of new workers, and use this simulation to examine the ripple effects of immigration on other sectors of the economy. Without such a theoretical framework to guide one's thinking, it is impossible to determine if natives benefit from immigration, and by how much.

It is best to start off, therefore, by describing how immigration benefits the economy in the simplest "textbook model" of a free-market economy. As every student who has ever had to sit through more than a week's worth of introductory economics well knows, this standard model—supply and demand—is the main ingredient in the tool kit of economists. The model is used extensively to understand and estimate the economic consequences of government policies in many areas, such as lowering trade barriers, increasing the minimum wage, reducing the capital gains tax, and changing price supports for agricultural products.

In this model of the U.S. labor market, wage and employment levels are set by the interplay between the supply of workers and the demand for workers.[3] When wages are high, many persons want to work, but few firms are looking for workers. When wages are low, few persons want to work, but many firms are competing for their services. The labor market balances out the conflicting interests of workers and firms, and sets employment and wage levels so that persons who want to work at the going wage can find jobs.

Immigrants enter this economy and suddenly increase the number of workers available. In the short run, the rest of the economy is unaffected by immigration. In particular, the capital stock of the United States—in terms of its land, machines, and other physical productive resources—remains as it was before the immigrants arrived.

So what happens in this highly stylized model when immigrants enter the labor market? And, more important, what happens to the income that accrues to the native population as a result of immigration?

To see how natives gain from immigration, first consider how the country gains from foreign trade. When the United States imports toys made by low-wage Chinese labor, workers employed in the domestic toy industry undoubtedly suffer wage cuts and perhaps even lose their jobs. These losses, however, are more than offset by the benefits accruing to consumers, who can now benefit from the lower prices induced by the additional competition. An important lesson, worth remembering when thinking about the gains from immigration, is that if international trade is to benefit the economy as a whole, some sectors of the economy typically lose. In short: no pain, no gain.[4]

Consider now the analogous argument for immigration. Suppose initially that all workers, whether immigrants or natives, are equally skilled. Because immigrants increase the number of workers, there is additional competition in the labor market and the wage of native workers falls. At the same time, however, native-owned firms gain because they can now hire workers at lower wages, and many native consumers gain because the lower labor costs eventually lead to cheaper goods and services. As with foreign trade, the gains accruing to the persons who use or consume immigrant services exceed the losses suffered by native workers, and hence society as a whole is better off. This does *not* mean that every native-born person in the United States is better off. It simply means that the dollar value of the gains accruing to users of immigrant services exceeds the dollar value of the losses suffered by native workers. The difference between what the winners win and what the losers lose is called the *immigration surplus,* and it gives the gain in national income accruing to natives as a result of immigration.[5]

Immigration, therefore, has two distinct consequences and these consequences propel the immigration debate. The nation, as a whole, gains from immigration. In other words, immigration increases the size of the economic pie available to natives. Immigration also redistributes income—from native workers who compete with immigrants to those who hire and use immigrant services. Immigration changes the way the economic pie is split between workers and firms.

This perspective also shows that the benefits from immigration arise *because* immigrants reduce the wage that native workers get paid. Without the pain suffered by the workers who compete with immigrants, no gains would accrue to the employers who do the hiring or to the consumers who do the buying. Ironically, even though the immigration debate views the possibility that immigrants lower the wage of native workers as a very harmful consequence, the economic benefits from immigration might not exist otherwise.

WHO WINS AND WHO LOSES?

So what does this highly stylized model of the labor market actually imply about the size of the immigration surplus? The model, in fact, generates a specific formula that can be used to estimate the immigration surplus in any free-market economy.

Immigration surplus as a fraction of GDP = .5 × labor's share of national income × percent drop in native wage due to immigration × fraction of labor force that is foreign-born.[6]

Labor's share of national income in the United States is about 70 percent—and there is very little disagreement about this statistic.[7] The fraction of immigrants in the work force is about 10 percent—and again there is little disagreement about this number. So the only uncertainty in calculating the size of the immigration surplus arises over the impact of immigrants on the native wage. The evidence presented in the last chapter suggests that a 10 percent increase in the number of workers would probably lower the wage by about 3 percent.[8]

By plugging these numbers into the formula (or .5 × .7 × .03 × .1), one can calculate that immigration increased the income of natives by about .1 percent (that is, one-tenth of one percent) of GDP. In 1998, national income was about $8 trillion, so that the presence of twenty-five million foreign-born persons in the United States increased the income of the native population by a grand total of $8 billion, or less than $30 per native-born person.

Even though the immigration surplus is astonishingly small, immigration can still have a substantial economic impact. Immigration redistributes wealth from labor to capital. To get an idea of how large this redistribution can be, recall that 70 percent of GDP goes to workers (with the rest going to the owners of the firms), and that natives make up 90 percent of the population. Therefore, native workers take home about 63 percent of GDP in the form of wages and salaries. If immigration reduces native wages by 3 percent, the share of GDP accruing to native workers falls by 1.9 percentage points (or .63 times .03). In an $8 trillion economy, native earnings would drop by about $152 billion.

These lost earnings do not vanish into thin air. They represent an income transfer from workers to users of immigrant services—the employers of immigrants and the consumers who buy the goods and services produced by immigrants. These winners get to pocket the $152 billion *plus* the immigration surplus—because immigrants produce goods that generate additional profits for the employers. The total windfall going to the winners totals $160 billion, or about 2 percent of GDP.[9] In short, the small immigration surplus of $8 billion hides a sizable redistribution of wealth from workers to the users of immigrant labor.

These calculations are obviously sensitive to what one assumes about the impact of immigration on the wage of native workers (see Table 5-1). If the native wage is not budged by the entry of immigrants, the immigration surplus is zero, and there is no redistribution of income from workers to capitalists. If immigration reduces the wage of natives substantially, natives *as a group* gain more from immigration, but the net gains still seem small. Suppose, for example, that immigration reduced the wage of native workers by as much as 10 percent. The immigration surplus would be only about $28 billion per year, but the redistribution would be incredibly large. Immigration would then be responsible for a transfer of wealth of about $500 billion from labor to capital.

The fact that the immigration surplus is tiny in the context of an $8 trillion economy, particularly when compared to the large wealth transfers, probably explains why the immigration debate emphasizes the potentially harmful labor market impacts rather than the overall increase in native incomes. In other words, the debate stresses the distributional issues (the transfer of

TABLE 5–1

The Immigration Surplus, Assuming All Workers Have Similar Skills and the Capital Stock Is Fixed

Immigrants increase the size of the labor force by 10 percent and the:	Billions of dollars		
	Loss to native workers	Gain to native users of immigrant services	Immigration surplus
Native wage does not change	0.0	0.0	0.0
Native wage falls by 3 percent	151.2	159.6	8.4
Native wage falls by 5 percent	252.0	266.0	14.0
Native wage falls by 7 percent	352.8	372.4	19.6
Native wage falls by 10 percent	504.0	532.0	28.0

Note: The simulation assumes that 70 percent of national income accrues to workers, and that the total GDP of the United States is $8 trillion.

wealth from workers to capital) rather than the gains in economic efficiency (the larger economic pie).

The large redistribution of wealth might also explain why free immigration policies have strong and powerful allies in many segments of American society. Employers and other users of immigrant services have much to gain because immigration reduces labor costs. The large gains accrue mainly to a relatively small number of persons and firms, so this minority can be expected to be vocal and aggressive in its defense of an open border. At the same time, even though many native workers may be affected adversely by immigration, the workers are much less homogeneous and not well organized. As a result, those who are on the losing end will probably find it difficult to present a cohesive front against immigration policies that harm their economic well-being.

As I will show in the next chapter, there is also a great deal of concern over whether immigrants "pay their way" in the welfare state. In addition to the economic effects of immigration on native productivity and on consumer prices, there are also fiscal gains or losses accruing from immigration: immigrants contribute to tax revenues but may also be responsible for increased expenditures on many social programs. Before one can conclude that the United States benefits from immigration, therefore, the immigration surplus has to be compared with estimates of the fiscal cost of immigration. Because the immigration surplus is probably around $10 billion annually, the *net* economic benefits from immigration (which take into account the fiscal impact of immigration) are very small, and there could conceivably be a net loss.

Although this economic model underlying the calculation of the immigration surplus is widely accepted—and, in fact, forms the underlying framework for the calculations contained in the widely cited report by the National Academy of Sciences—many participants in the immigration debate often confuse the calculation of the gains and losses.[10] In 1997, for instance, Senator Spencer Abraham, chair of the Subcommittee on Immigration, wrote a *Wall Street Journal* editorial that quoted the economist who headed the National Academy of Sciences panel as saying that "due to the immigrants who arrived since 1980, *total* gross national product is about $200 billion higher each year." In a dizzying display of Beltway arithmetic, Senator Abraham then inferred that "recent immigrants will add $2 *trillion* to the nation's GNP over the course of the 1990s."[11]

This conclusion is quite surprising since the immigration surplus is less than $10 billion a year. The "trick" is that the senator forgot to mention that most of that $2 trillion increase in GDP goes to the immigrants themselves in the form of wages and salaries. Many participants in the immigration debate might welcome the fact that immigrants make substantial economic gains by being in the United States. But many other participants might also want to know exactly what is in it for the "average" native. And the answer is short and simple: not much.

DO BLACKS BENEFIT FROM IMMIGRATION?

Although immigration raises slightly the per capita income of the native population, some native groups, such as the workers who compete with immigrants, suffer losses, and some subgroups of the native population may suffer very large losses. One group that is of particular concern is the native-born black population. Much of the debate over social policy since the 1960s has involved programs that have a disproportionate effect on black economic well-being, such as the debates over affirmative action and welfare reform. And although black workers have made substantial economic strides in the past few decades, the median white man still earned 38 percent more than the median black man in 1997.[12]

It is of great interest, therefore, to determine if immigration—which itself is an income redistribution program—has a disproportionately harmful effect on the black population. It turns out that African Americans are likely to lose from immigration for two distinct reasons. First, it is the employers who receive the bulk of the benefits from immigration. Because blacks own a relatively small proportion of the capital stock of the United States, they are greatly underrepresented in the "hiring class." As a result, blacks have less to gain from immigration than whites.

Moreover, because post-1965 immigrants tend to be disproportionately less skilled, they are much more likely to compete with black workers than with white workers. Even by the late 1990s, black educational attainment lagged behind that of whites. In 1998, for example, only 7 percent of native whites were high school dropouts, as compared to 13 percent of native blacks. Because blacks and immigrants are relatively more similar than whites and immigrants, any adverse impact of immigration on competing workers will fall hardest on the population of native-born African Americans.

A simple calculation illustrates how blacks might lose from immigration simply because they own little of the nation's productive resources. Blacks make up slightly over 10 percent of the work force in the United States. If blacks also owned 10 percent of the land and physical capital of the country, the losses to black labor, the gains to black-owned firms, and the immigration surplus accruing to black natives would all be 10 percent of the respective quantities for the entire country. So blacks, on net, would gain about $800 million (10 percent of the $8 billion immigration surplus), black workers would lose about $15.2 billion (10 percent of $152 billion), and black capitalists would gain about $16 billion (10 percent of $160 billion).

Blacks, however, do not own 10 percent of the capital stock in the country. In fact, the black-white gap in assets and wealth is far greater than the black-white wage gap that has been the focus of so much attention. Blacks own only about 3 percent of the capital stock in the United States, far below their population representation.[13] So consider the impact of immigration on the black population. Because blacks make up about 10 percent of the native work force, black workers lose $15 billion. Because blacks own only 3 percent of the nation's capital stock, however, the gains accruing to black-owned firms are only $5 billion. As a group, therefore, black natives lose about $10 billion. In 1998, there were about thirty-three million black natives residing in the United States. It seems that immigration reduced the income of the average black native by about $300 per year.[14]

PROBLEMS WITH THE CALCULATION OF THE IMMIGRATION SURPLUS

Calculating the immigration surplus requires the use of an economic model that describes how the economy adjusts when immigrants "shock" the U.S. labor market. Because economic models present a highly simplified version of the true labor market, a number of restrictive assumptions have to be built into *any* calculation of the immigration surplus. It is possible, therefore, that the small immigration surplus calculated earlier may be the result of the restrictive assumptions built into the textbook model of the labor market.

What if Immigrants Increase the Capital Stock?

A key assumption in the calculation was that the physical capital stock of the United States did not change as a result of immigration. This means that immigrants did not bring any capital into the economy, and hence did not engage directly in job creation. But it is well known that many immigrants open up firms, often hiring their compatriots—and that some of these firms are hugely successful. In 1990, for example, about 7 percent of both immigrants and natives were self-employed. Moreover, the relative number of entrepreneurs is quite large in some national origin groups: the self-employment rate is 10 percent for Canadian immigrants, 15 percent for Greek immigrants, and 18 percent for Korean immigrants.[15]

These entrepreneurial activities by immigrants directly increase the size of the capital stock in the United States, and would seemingly generate much greater economic gains for natives. It turns out, however, that the immigration surplus might actually *decline* if immigrants also expanded the nation's capital stock.

To see why, imagine what the U.S. economy would look like if there had been no immigration in the past few decades. There would then be around one hundred million native workers and a capital stock that would be completely owned by natives.[16] These native workers and capitalists could jointly generate a GDP of, say, $7 trillion, and this entire GDP would accrue to the native population.

Suppose now that the United States decides to admit only immigrants who qualify for "investor visas," where the successful visa applicants must promise to invest in the country. Immigrants will then increase both the size of the labor force and the capital stock. As an extreme example, suppose that the United States decides to double its labor force and admit one hundred million (adult) immigrants, and that each immigrant is required to bring in just enough capital so that the country's capital stock also doubles.

Since both the number of workers and the capital stock have doubled, it is reasonable to expect that national income will also double, to $14 trillion.[17] One can think of this type of immigration as replicating the original American economy—there now are two identical economies running side by side. One economy is native-run: natives own the capital and hire native workers. The other is immigrant-run: immigrants own the capital and hire immigrant workers. Each of these parallel economies generates a GDP of $7 trillion annually. The natives get to keep the $7 trillion that they produced, and the immigrants get to keep the $7 trillion that they produced.[18]

In this hypothetical example, natives have nothing to gain from immigration. By bringing in their own capital, immigrants have effectively created a parallel economy that essentially distributes all the national income produced by immigrants to the immigrants themselves (that is, to the immigrant workers and the immigrant capitalists).

This example helps to illustrate an important lesson: the immigration surplus arises only when immigrants are sufficiently different from natives, and are able to complement natives in the production process. If immigration doubles both capital and labor, immigrants are exactly like natives and there are no complementarities to be exploited.

Even though the example stresses the possibility that the capital stock changes only because immigrants themselves bring in capital, there are other channels through which immigration alters the amount of capital in the U.S. economy. As immigrants enter the United States, the relative abundance of labor increases the profits that accrue to those who own the firms. Over time, these higher profits encourage additional capital flows from both foreign and domestic investors, increasing the amount of capital in the United States and reducing the gains from immigration to native-owned firms.[19]

The message is striking: the estimated short-run immigration surplus of $8 billion annually would be even *smaller* if the capital stock of the United States adjusted to the immigration influx. Put differently, in the long-run, as the capital stock inevitably adjusts to the changed economic environment, the immigration surplus will tend to become smaller and smaller, and in the end natives may be neither better off nor worse off because of immigration.[20]

What if Immigrants Do Not Lower the Wage of Native Workers?

The calculation of the immigration surplus also assumed that immigrants do have an impact on the earnings of native workers—a 10 percent increase in the number of workers reduced the native wage by 3 percent.

Many participants in the immigrant debate often argue that there is no evidence whatsoever that immigrants harm the employment opportunities of native workers. The Urban Institute's attempt at "setting the record straight," for example, concludes that "immigration has no discernible effect on wages overall. . . . Wage growth and decline appear to be unrelated to immigration."[21] And the late Julian Simon's "interpretation of the literature" is that there is only "a minor negative effect."[22]

Ironically, those who typically take this stand are often the ones who stress the beneficial aspects of immigration, and who advocate a more open immigration policy. They are in for a shock: *there is no immigration surplus if the native wage is not reduced by immigration.* In other words, if some workers are not harmed by immigration, many of the benefits that are typically attributed to immigration—higher profits for firms, lower prices for consumers—cease to exist. As I pointed out earlier, no pain, no gain.

What if Immigrants Generate Externalities?

Some economists believe that an increase in foreign trade generates a number of intangible benefits for the aggregate U.S. economy.[23] As goods produced abroad enter the country, American producers are exposed to ideas and technologies that increase the productivity of native workers and firms. This spillover of valuable information and knowledge, or "positive externalities" in the jargon of economics, could well increase the gains from trade substantially.

Immigration, too, expands the size of the market. It will almost certainly enable many new interactions among workers and firms, so that both native workers and native-owned firms might potentially learn valuable information without paying for it. American workers gain when their immigrant counterparts conduct a familiar task in a different but more efficient way. American firms also gain, because they can now use the social and information networks that link immigrants and the source countries to better market their products in foreign markets. And American consumers gain when immigrants introduce goods and services that the consumers never knew they wanted, but now cannot do without. The economic value of all this new information would have been lost if the U.S. economy had remained smaller and more insular. In short, diversity pays because it may make Americans more productive, and because it introduces new modes of thinking and more efficient ways of delivering goods and services.[24] These positive externalities could substantially increase the benefits from immigration—well above the $8 billion immigration surplus implied by the standard textbook model of the labor market, a model where all such externalities are assumed away.

Although these intangibles are believed to be important by many observers of the immigrant experience, there is *no* empirical evidence supporting their existence, let alone measuring their magnitude. One could also argue that it would be difficult for immigrants to generate many of these externalities in an economy as large as that of the United States, particularly in an era when information travels instantaneously across national borders. In principle, American workers and firms could conceivably obtain much of the knowledge that potential immigrants presumably possess—*and that Americans do not*—by surfing the information highway for a few minutes.

There is yet another difficulty with the belief that accounting for positive externalities would substantially increase the size of the immigration surplus. Although many Americans benefit from the ways in which immigration alters the social and economic environment, many other Americans do not. Put bluntly, a positive externality to some may well be a negative externality to others. The sweet perfumes emanating from Thai restaurants (my personal favorite) might be considered an unpleasant stench by those who dislike what the new cuisine has done to the look, feel, and smell of American cities.

In the end, the problem with stressing externalities in the immigration debate is that although they might exist and could be very important, it is extremely difficult to measure their impact. Would Intel—or an Intel look-alike—never have been incorporated if Andrew Grove had remained in Hungary? How would the computer industry have evolved if Federico Faggin, the Italian-born physicist who built the first microprocessor, had not moved to California? Would California's population in the late 1990s be a third smaller if there had been no immigration, and what value would the American people attach to driving on that state's freeways and visiting its parks and beaches if they were a lot less crowded? What would be the impact of removing all the cultural and linguistic barriers that now hamper social and economic exchanges among large segments of the American population? What would be the political structure of the world today if Enrico Fermi had not migrated to the United States on the eve of World War II, and carried out the first self-sustaining nuclear chain reaction on the campus of the University of Chicago in 1942?

None of these questions can be answered with objective evidence. The case for or against the externality is essentially a case based on one's very subjective beliefs about how immigrants affect certain parts of the social, political, and economic environment. Immigration probably generates both positive and negative externalities for the United States, and both types of externalities have the potential to be very important. But there is little to be gained—and a lot of potential mischief to be had—by basing important social policy decisions on "facts" that can never be measured objectively, far less verified. In the absence of any systematic evidence on the impact of these externalities, therefore, it is wise to emphasize the gains that can be quantified, and the best available evidence indicates that the immigration surplus is quite small.[25]

IMMIGRANT SKILLS AND THE GAINS FROM IMMIGRATION

The economic model used to calculate the immigration surplus ignored the skill differentials that exist between (as well as within) the immigrant and native populations. But post-1965 immigration increased the number of less-skilled workers in the United States disproportionately.

These skill differentials raise two interesting questions. First, does the size of the immigration surplus change substantially when these skill differences are taken into account? The answer, it turns out, is no. The second question is more subtle, but also more important: *could* the net gains from immigration increase substantially if the United States pursued a different type of immigration policy, favoring one skill group over the other? Put differently, which type of immigrant flow, skilled or unskilled, would generate the largest increase in the per capita income of natives?

Accounting for Skill Differentials

Suppose there are two types of workers, skilled and unskilled.[26] Even though the labor market now contains "only" two groups of workers, the calculation of the immigration surplus requires a lot more information. In particular, one needs to know how the wage of each skill group responds to immigration, and how the wage of workers in one skill group responds to changes in the size of the other group. There is a great deal of uncertainty—and little consensus—about the value of these effects in the academic literature.[27] As a result, the calculations of the immigration surplus typically use a range of reasonable values, presumably bracketing the "true" gains that accrue to natives in the United States.

In the last chapter, I defined the skill groups in terms of educational attainment. One can also define the skill groups in terms of the placement of workers in the income distribution. By definition, half of the native workers are above the median native income, and half are below. A natural classification defines native workers who earn more than the median income as skilled, and native workers who earn less than the median as unskilled. About 70 percent of the immigrant workers in the late 1990s were below the median of the native wage distribution and would be classified as unskilled by this definition.

The simulation of this economic model suggests that immigration reduces the income of all native workers in the short run, regardless of which skill group they belong to, but that capitalists gain substantially (see Table 5-2). Depending on the responsiveness of wages to immigration, the total income accruing to skilled native workers falls by 1.0 to 3.9 percent, the income accruing to unskilled workers falls by 1.4 to 4.4 percent, and the income accruing to capitalists rises by 3 to 10 percent. The *net* gain to the country, however, is small: the immigration surplus is between $7 billion and $21 billion. In the long run, as the capital stock adjusts, either because immigrants bring in their own capital or because capital moves into the United States to take advantage of the changed economic environment, the immigration surplus becomes even smaller, and the skilled workers gain while the unskilled workers lose.

This simulation teaches two basic lessons. Because immigrants are disproportionately less skilled, it is the less-skilled natives who pay the price of immigration. Immigration can again be viewed as a redistribution program that transfers a substantial amount of wealth away from the workers who compete with immigrants to the natives who have skills or physical resources that benefit from the presence of immigrants. Second, the immigration surplus is small even when skill differences between immigrants and native are taken into account. Regardless of what assumptions are made, immigrants increase the net income of natives by less than $20 billion annually—a miniscule amount in the context of an $8 trillion economy.[28]

The Immigration Surplus and the Skill Composition of Immigrants

This type of simulation raises a provocative question: is the per capita income of the native population in the United States increased most by admitting skilled workers, unskilled workers, or some mix of the two groups?

For the sake of argument, suppose that the native population were evenly divided between skilled and unskilled workers: fifty million skilled and fifty million unskilled workers.[29] If the skills of immigrants were identical to those of natives—that is, if 50 percent of the immigrants were skilled—native workers would have nothing to gain from immigration. To see why, suppose that immigration doubled the size of the labor force, to one-hundred million skilled and one-hundred million unskilled workers. The United States would then consist of two parallel economies, each with one-hundred million workers (half skilled and half unskilled) and each producing the same national income as the original native economy. Natives, therefore, would not gain by admitting immigrants who simply replicated the economy's preexisting conditions. As I have stressed throughout, natives benefit only if immigrants are different. It is these differences that introduce the production complementarities responsible for the immigration surplus.

TABLE 5–2
The Immigration Surplus When the Skills of Immigrants Differ from Those of Natives

	Percent change in the total income of			*Immigration surplus (in billions of dollars)*
	Skilled workers	*Unskilled workers*	*Capitalists*	
Short-run: The capital stock is fixed				
Wage of native workers is not very responsive to immigration	−1.0	−1.4	+3.0	6.8
Wage of native workers is very responsive to immigration	−3.9	−4.4	+10.3	21.2
Long-run: The capital stock adjusts to immigration				
Wage of native workers is not very responsive to immigration	+0.4	−0.9	—	1.9
Wage of native workers is very responsive to immigration	+0.9	−2.4	—	3.9

Notes: The skill groups are defined in terms of the placement of workers in the native wage distribution. Workers above the median native wage are "skilled," and workers below the median native wage are "unskilled." The simulations assume that total GDP in the United States is $8 trillion; 50 percent of native workers are skilled; 30 percent of immigrant workers are skilled; skilled workers' share of national income is .525; unskilled workers' share is .175; and capital's share is .3. One set of calculations assumes that wages are not very responsive to immigration. The elasticity of the skilled wage with respect to the number of skilled workers is then −.3, and the elasticity of the unskilled wage with respect to the number of unskilled workers is −.5. The other set assumes that wages are very responsive to immigration. The elasticities under this assumption are −.8 and −1.5, respectively. In all simulations, the elasticity of the skilled wage with respect to the number of unskilled workers is set at .05.

If immigrants differ from natives, the size of the immigration surplus then depends on just how different immigrants are. Natives have the most to gain when immigrants are the most different—so the immigration surplus is maximized when the immigrant flow is composed exclusively of unskilled or exclusively of skilled immigrants. If half of the natives were skilled, there would be no particular advantage (from the perspective of generating the largest gains) to admitting either an all-skilled or an all-unskilled immigrant flow.

The incentive for pursuing an immigration policy that selects between these two extreme policy options arises when native workers are either predominantly skilled or predominantly unskilled. The work force of the United States is predominantly skilled, particularly when compared with workers in most other countries. Production complementarities would then imply that skilled natives have much to gain when less-skilled immigrants enter the country. It seems, therefore, that if the country wishes to maximize the immigration surplus it should pursue a policy that admits only unskilled workers.

Immigration, however, also affects the bottom line of native-owned firms. Firms that use less-skilled workers in production, such as sweatshops and large parts of the service sector, gain from the entry of the less-skilled. However, other firms—and perhaps even *most* firms—might be better off with skilled immigrants. There is some consensus among economists that there is more complementarity between skilled workers and the machines that are now used widely in the production process than between unskilled workers and those machines.[30] In other words, physical capital "goes with" skilled workers. It would not be surprising, therefore, if most firms gained more if the immigrant flow were composed of skilled workers.

There then exists a conflict between the type of immigrant the "typical" native worker would like to see and the one the "typical" native-owned firm would like to see. The typical native worker would be better off with unskilled immigrants, while the typical firm would be better off with skilled immigrants. This conflict can be resolved only by measuring how much native workers gain from unskilled immigration and how much employers gain from skilled immigration, and by comparing the value of the two calculations.

A simulation of the U.S. economy suggests that the per capita income of natives would rise substantially if the country switched from the current immigration policy, which admits a mix of skilled and unskilled workers, to one that admitted only skilled workers (see Table 5-3). The short-run immigration surplus from a policy where 30 percent of the immigrant flow is skilled ranges between $7 and $21 billion, depending on the responsiveness of the wage to immigration. This surplus would rise to between $42 and $126 billion if the immigrant flow were composed exclusively of skilled workers, but would rise to only between $8 and $24 billion if the immigrant flow were composed exclusively of unskilled workers. Therefore, the economic benefits—*for the nation as a whole*—from pursuing a policy that attempted to maximize the immigration surplus could be sizable.

It is worth reflecting on the implications of this economic perspective for the history of immigration policy in the United States. Prior to 1924, there were few restrictions preventing the migration of persons to the country, and this policy allowed the entry of tens of millions of poor and less-skilled Europeans. It is often argued that the First Great Migration greatly benefited the country; it provided an engine for economic growth as the United States built its industrial base and reached across the country to fulfill its Manifest Destiny.[31]

In view of this historical experience, why should things be any different now? If both the United States and the immigrants prospered from the First

TABLE 5–3
The Immigration Surplus and Immigration Policy (immigration surplus in billions of dollars)

	Policy option		
	All immigrants are unskilled	*30 percent of immigrants are skilled*	*All immigrants are skilled*
Short-run: The capital stock is fixed			
Wage of native workers is not very responsive to immigration	8.4	6.8	42.0
Wage of native workers is very responsive to immigration	22.4	21.2	126.0
Long-run: The capital stock adjusts to immigration			
Wage of native workers is not very responsive to immigration	8.0	1.9	8.0
Wage of native workers is very responsive to immigration	20.0	3.9	20.0

Notes: Same as Table 5–2.

Great Migration, is it not reasonable to expect this symbiotic relationship to continue? Put bluntly, why worry?

The problem is that the historical experience of a century ago probably has little relevance for the contemporary experience. The United States has changed radically, and what was beneficial then need not be beneficial now.

In fact, the *same* economic model may suggest that the country benefits from skilled immigration in some periods, but from unskilled immigration in others. The economic case for skilled immigration rests partly on the notion that skilled workers and capital are highly complementary *in modern industrialized economies.* The entry of skilled workers makes the machines and microprocessors that are now widely used in production much more valuable. These machines are mostly native-owned, and the admission of skilled immigrants increases the country's wealth through this interaction between skilled immigrants and machines.

But the relation between skills and machines need not be the same in other periods, and was probably very different a century ago. Skilled workers and machines were probably substitutes, not complements, at the time of the First Great Migration. A recent historical analysis concludes that "many of the major technological advances of the nineteenth century . . . substituted physical capital, raw materials, and unskilled labor, as a group, for highly skilled artisans."[32] As an example, consider the technological changes that occurred in shoe manufacturing. For centuries, highly skilled artisans, called cordwainers, made shoes by hand, without the use of any machinery. The shoe factory replaced the skilled cordwainer with machines and with unskilled workers who operated those machines. The entry of unskilled immigrants during the First Great Migration may then have "greased the wheels" of the industrialization process, and greatly increased the value of the physical capital that was in use at the time. In short, the fact that admitting less-skilled immigrants a century ago benefited the United States *then* does not imply that the same type of immigration will benefit the country *now*.

LESSONS FOR THE POLICY DEBATE

The production complementarities that exist between immigrants and natives raise the net income of natives in the United States by a relatively small amount. In the late 1990s, this immigration surplus was somewhere around $10 billion a year. Even though the average native gains somewhat from immigration, this does not mean that everyone in the country gains. There are distinct groups of winners and losers. The winners are the people who employ or use immigrant services, and achieve their economic goals at lower costs. The losers are the people who compete with immigrant workers, and experience a corresponding reduction in their income. In practical terms, post-1965 immigration has shifted income away from less-skilled natives toward highly skilled natives and owners of capital.

Because the net gains from immigration are so small, it is very unlikely that these gains play a crucial role in the immigration debate. *The economic impact of immigration is essentially a distributional impact.* In theory, it is possible to redistribute income from the winners to the losers so as to make every native in the United States better off. In fact, such redistribution seldom takes place: the winners remain winners, and the losers remain losers.

The debate over immigration policy, therefore, is not a debate over whether the entire country is made better off by immigration. The country can be made better off because of the production complementarities that immigrants introduce into the economy, but the per capita gain for the native population is inconsequential. And, as the next chapter shows, these gains could even be outweighed by the cost of providing social services to immigrants.

The immigration debate is best viewed as a political struggle between those who win and those who lose. Simply put, immigration changes the way the economic pie is split—and this undeniable fact goes a long way toward explaining why some segments of society favor the entry of large numbers of immigrants, while other segments want to curtail or cut off the immigrant flow.

This cost-benefit approach to immigration also provides a basis for re-formulating immigration policy. Suppose that the United States chooses to pursue a policy that maximizes the per capita income of its native population. One would then conclude that the United States should admit only skilled workers. This skill-biased immigration policy would also minimize the adverse distributional impact of immigration—immigration would narrow, rather than widen, the income gap between skilled and unskilled workers. And, finally, this type of immigration policy would relieve the fiscal impact of immigration, since more skilled workers use fewer government services and pay higher taxes. It seems, therefore, that there exists a very strong *economic* case for pursuing an immigration policy that uses skill filters to award entry visas.

Many, if not most, participants in the immigration debate would passionately disagree with the notion that the objective of immigration policy should be to maximize the per capita income of natives. In a democracy, immigration policy will inevitably reflect a political consensus that incorporates the conflicting desires of numerous interest groups. And, in the United States, in particular, where the immigrant experience helps define what it means to be an American, the weight of history and tradition plays an important and deeply felt role in framing the issue of immigration. To decide what type of immigration policy the United States should pursue, therefore, the American people must first decide who it is that they want to be.

Regardless of what objectives the United States chooses to pursue, however, I would still argue that the calculation of the immigration surplus and of the distributional impact of immigration is extremely useful for three distinct reasons. First, economic considerations matter—and, often enough, they matter more than most other considerations. Second, the economic impact of immigration is measurable, so the questions posed by the immigration debate can be argued over facts rather than over ideology or emotional attachment to the mythic history embodied in Emma Lazarus's famed refrain of "Give me your tired, your poor, . . . The wretched refuse of your teeming shore." Finally, people living in a democratic society should be fully informed about what they are giving up when they choose to pursue immigration policies that minimize or ignore economic considerations.

Immigration and the Welfare State

THE HISTORICAL DEBATE over immigration policy in the United States and in many other host countries has focused primarily on two issues: How well do immigrants adjust to their new surroundings? And do immigrants take jobs away from native workers? The growth of the welfare state added an explosive new question to this debate: do immigrants pay their way in the welfare state?

We should be concerned over the link between immigration and welfare for two reasons. First, the relatively generous safety net provided by the welfare state may attract a different—and less skilled—type of immigrant. Put differently, generous welfare programs can create a magnet that influences the migration decisions of persons in the source countries, changing the type of person who wishes to migrate to the United States and increasing the cost of maintaining the welfare state.

The potential magnetic effects of welfare raise fundamental questions about both the political legitimacy and economic viability of the welfare state. Who is entitled to the safety net that American taxpayers pay for? And can the United States afford to extend that safety net to the rest of the world?

Second, the empirical link between immigration and welfare is indisputable. Immigrant participation in welfare programs rose steadily after 1965. By the 1990s, immigrants received a disproportionately large share of the welfare benefits distributed, and had a severe fiscal impact on some immigrant-receiving states, particularly California.

In 1996, Congress responded to the clamor by enacting welfare reform legislation that denied many types of means-tested assistance to noncitizens. However, the most draconian provisions of this legislation—such as removing immigrants already in the United States from the rolls of some programs—were never enforced. If nothing else, this episode suggests that it is difficult to address the problems raised by immigrant use of welfare by reforming welfare policy. In the end, the problems raised by the potential link between immigration and welfare may have to be addressed by going to the source, and reforming immigration policy.

TRENDS IN WELFARE USE

In the 1970s and early 1980s, it was widely believed that immigrant households were not heavy users of welfare programs. By the late 1980s, however, the perception had changed: there was a growing realization that immigrant participation in many types of public assistance programs was increasing rapidly.[1] This perspective so greatly influenced the debate over welfare reform that some of the key provisions in the welfare reform bill enacted by Congress in 1996 (officially known as the Personal Responsibility and Work Opportunity Reconciliation Act) specifically banned immigrants from receiving particular types of aid. Why did immigrant participation in welfare programs rise? And was the concern that culminated in the welfare reform legislation valid?

The U.S. Census began to collect information on receipt of cash benefits in 1970. The cash benefit programs included Aid to Families with Dependent Children (AFDC), Supplemental Security Income (SSI), and the general assistance program.[2] The Census, however, does not contain any information on receipt of in-kind transfers, such as food stamps or Medicaid. The total cost of all means-tested programs exceeded $345 billion in 1994, with the cash benefit programs accounting for less than a quarter of the total cost.[3]

In 1970, immigrants were slightly less likely to receive cash benefits than natives (see Figure 6-1).[4] By 1980, the direction of this welfare gap had turned around, and immigrants were about 1 percentage point more likely to receive public assistance. By 1998, over 10 percent of immigrant households received cash benefits, as compared to only 7 percent of native households.

The rising welfare use in the immigrant population masks two distinct trends. First, more recent immigrant waves are more likely to use welfare than earlier waves (again, see Figure 6-1).[5] In 1970, only 5.5 percent of the newest immigrant households (those who had been in the country fewer than five years) received cash assistance, much less than the welfare use found among native households. By 1998, the newest immigrant arrivals were much more likely to receive cash benefits than native households. These trends in welfare use exactly mirror the differences in relative skills that exist among successive immigrant waves, with the most recent waves being the least skilled.

Second, and more surprising, the longer that immigrants live in the United States, the more likely they are to use welfare (see Figure 6-2). Consider, for instance, the group of immigrant households that arrived between 1965 and 1969, when the head of the household was between eighteen and thirty-four years old. At the time of entry, 3 percent of these immigrants received cash assistance, as compared to 5 percent of comparably aged native households. One can track these immigrants and natives over time, and the data show that by 1998 8 percent of the immigrant households received cash assistance, as compared to less than 7 percent of native households.[6]

Why do immigrant households assimilate into welfare? It could be argued that newly arrived immigrants in the 1960s and 1970s refrained from joining the welfare rolls because they did not want to jeopardize their stay in the United States or their applications for naturalization—and thereby reduce the possibility of sponsoring the entry of family members. After all, immigration law has long called for the deportation of anyone who is a "public

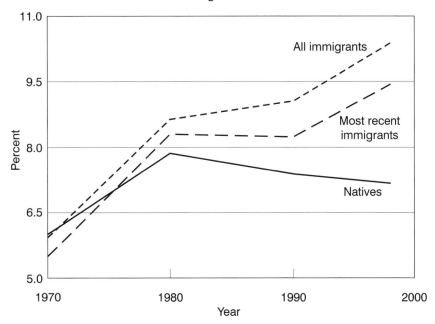

FIGURE 6-1. Trends in receipt of cash benefits, 1970–98.

Sources: George J. Borjas, "Immigration and Welfare, 1970–1990," *Research in Labor Economics 14* (1995), p. 255, and additional calculations from the pooled 1996–98 Current Population Surveys (Annual Demographic Files).

Notes: The data refer to households where the head of the household is at least eighteen years old. The sample of "most recent immigrants" consists of persons who arrived in the country in the five-year period prior to the survey.

charge." One might then expect that welfare use would jump after the five-year residence period required for naturalization. However, it seems that the participation rate of immigrants in welfare programs keeps rising well after the immigrants could have become citizens, making it unlikely that the public charge provision in immigration law was a strong deterrent to welfare use.[7]

It might also be the case that the longer the immigrant household lives in the United States, the more it learns about key aspects of welfare programs—raising the household's propensity to enter the welfare system. In other words, assimilation involves not only learning about labor market opportunities, but also about the opportunities provided by the welfare state.

Overall, the Census data paint a disturbing picture of the long-run trends in immigrant use of cash benefits.[8] But, as noted above, cash benefit programs account for a minor fraction of the cost of welfare programs. The available evidence indicates that immigrants are more likely to participate in almost every single one of the major means-tested programs (see Table 6-1). In

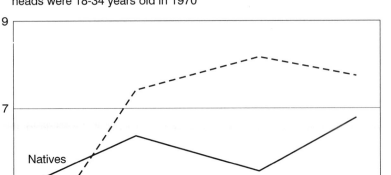

Percent receiving cash benefits; the household
heads were 18-34 years old in 1970

FIGURE 6-2. Assimilation into welfare.

Sources: George J. Borjas, "Immigration and Welfare, 1970–1990," *Research in Labor Economics* 14 (1995), p. 261; and additional calculations from the pooled 1996–98 Current Population Surveys (Annual Demographic Files).

Note: The cohorts are tracked from survey to survey, with the age of the household head changing over time. In particular, the household heads were twenty-eight to forty-four years old in 1980, thirty-eight to fifty-four years old in 1990, and forty-six to sixty-two years old in 1998.

1998, 10 percent of immigrant households received food stamps, as compared to 8 percent of native households. And 20 percent of immigrant households were covered by Medicaid, as compared to 13 percent of native households. In short, almost a quarter of immigrant households received some type of assistance, as compared to 15 percent of native households.[9] Because of their disproportionate presence in the welfare rolls, immigrant households accounted for 14 percent of the cost of means-tested programs even though they only made up 9 percent of the households in the United States.[10]

As with other economic outcomes, there are large differences in welfare propensities among national origin groups (see Table 6-2). Fewer than 10 percent of the households originating in Germany, India, or the United Kingdom receive some type of assistance, as opposed to a quarter of those originating in El Salvador or Nigeria, a third of those originating in Cuba

TABLE 6–1
Participation in Public Assistance Programs, 1998

	Percent participating in program	
	Native households	Immigrant households
Cash programs		
Public assistance or welfare	3.8	5.7
Supplemental Security Income	4.1	5.6
Noncash programs		
Energy assistance	2.7	1.9
Food stamps	7.6	10.3
Housing assistance	4.7	6.0
Medicaid	13.1	20.3
Any type of assistance	15.4	22.4

Source: Calculations from the pooled 1996–98 Current Population Surveys (Annual Demographic Files).

Note: The data refer to households where the head is at least eighteen years old.

or Mexico, and almost 60 percent of those originating in the Dominican Republic or Laos.

A cursory scan at the cross-country differences suggests that immigrants originating in refugee-sending countries exhibit much higher rates of welfare participation. Over half of the households originating in Cambodia or Laos, and about a third of those originating in Vietnam, Cuba, or the former Soviet Union, received some type of assistance. The welfare use of refugee households remains high even after a decade in the United States.

The high propensity of refugee households to enter and stay in the welfare system may be the result of misguided government policies designed to ease the transition of refugees into the United States. Persons who enter the country as refugees have immediate access to a wide array of social services and programs that neither other legal immigrants nor natives qualify for. For instance, needy refugees who cannot qualify for AFDC, SSI, or Medicaid, can apply for special refugee cash assistance or medical assistance. In fiscal year 1995, the cost of the refugee resettlement program neared $400 million.[11] The quick introduction of the refugee population to the many benefits provided by the welfare state can have a profound and long-lasting impact.

Because refugees became an increasingly important part of immigration between 1970 and 1990, it is tempting to attribute much of the increase in immigrant welfare use over this time to the growth of the refugee population.[12] This inference, however, is incorrect (see Table 6-3). Welfare use is high even among nonrefugee immigrant households: 21 percent of such households received some type of assistance in 1998.

TABLE 6–2
Differences in Welfare Use Among National Origin Groups, 1998

Country of birth	Percent of households receiving some type of assistance	Percent of households receiving some type of assistance after ten years in the United States
Europe		
Germany	7.8	7.8
Greece	10.4	10.2
Ireland	5.8	5.6
Italy	12.9	13.3
Poland	7.8	6.8
Portugal	16.8	18.0
USSR	37.1	20.7
United Kingdom	9.7	9.5
Asia		
Cambodia	47.9	46.6
China	17.5	19.4
India	5.6	5.6
Japan	9.7	8.6
Korea	17.3	22.3
Laos	59.1	46.0
Philippines	13.4	13.2
Vietnam	28.7	22.8
Americas		
Canada	9.9	11.7
Cuba	30.7	28.6
Dominican Republic	54.9	58.0
El Salvador	25.2	25.9
Haiti	20.2	19.4
Jamaica	22.7	19.3
Mexico	34.1	33.6
Africa		
Egypt	16.2	20.5
Nigeria	25.7	32.8

Source: Calculations from the pooled 1996–98 Current Population Surveys (Annual Demographic Files).

Note: The data refer to households where the head is at least eighteen years old.

It is also tempting to dismiss the problem by blaming elderly immigrants, who are known to be very heavy users of the SSI program. This inference is also incorrect (again, see Table 6-3). About 21 percent of immigrant households that do not contain any elderly persons receive some type of assistance, as compared to 16 percent of comparable native households.

It is interesting to note that the political debate over immigrant welfare use often revolves around the issue of whether immigrants use welfare more

TABLE 6–3
Welfare Use, by Type of Household, 1998

	Percent receiving some type of assistance	
	Natives	Immigrants
All households	15.4	22.4
Refugee households	—	28.5
Nonrefugee households	—	21.4
Households that do not contain any persons over age sixty-five	15.5	20.6
Nonrefugee households that do not contain any persons over age sixty-five	—	20.0

Source: Calculations from the pooled 1996–98 Current Population Surveys (Annual Demographic Files).

Note: The data refer to households where the head is at least eighteen years old.

often or less often than natives. This comparison implicitly adopts a particular yardstick for measuring immigrant failure or success.

In an important sense, however, this comparison misses the point. Suppose that immigration policy succeeded in exactly replicating the distribution of skills and income opportunities already present in the native population, so that immigrants used welfare exactly as often as natives. Should this type of immigration policy be considered successful from the perspective of the debate over immigration and welfare? I doubt it. After all, this immigration policy would have increased the size of the welfare population considerably, adding to the difficult—and seemingly intractable—social and economic problems of the disadvantaged population in the United States. One could just as easily argue that the debate should use a very different yardstick: should immigrants be on welfare *at all*?

Welfare Recipiency versus Welfare Dependence

There is little doubt that by the 1990s, immigrants used welfare much more often than natives. But is immigrant participation in welfare programs permanent or transitory? Put differently, does the high usage rate among immigrant households arise because many immigrants receive welfare for very short periods, or because some immigrants remain on welfare for a very long time?

The distinction between short-run recipiency and long-run dependency is quite important from a policy perspective. The social and economic implications of admitting immigrants who have short-term needs differ greatly from those of admitting immigrants who are permanently caught in the web of welfare dependence.

Over the short term, many immigrants may well need additional resources to tide them over the hard times encountered as they adjust to life in the United States. This transitional help—mostly provided by families, and sometimes by charitable organizations or governments—is typically not very expensive, and has few, if any, long-run repercussions on the immigrant's social and economic status.

In contrast, being a long-time welfare recipient greatly reduces economic opportunities, both because the recipient is not accumulating labor market experience and because employers probably interpret the long-term dependency as a sign of some underlying problem. Welfare dependency also helps to isolate the household from the economic and social mainstream. Some observers, in fact, associate long-run welfare use with a number of costly social pathologies, including the breakdown of the family unit.[13]

Although there is no conclusive evidence that part of the immigrant population may be trapped in a pattern of long-term dependence, there are reasons to be concerned. Since the mid-1980s, the Bureau of the Census has tracked samples of both immigrant and native households for thirty-two month periods.[14] The thirty-two–month sample period is clearly not sufficiently long to determine whether welfare recipients are in "short-term" or "long-term" spells of welfare use, but the data are instructive. On average, immigrants are more likely to enter the welfare rolls during the sample period. In the early 1990s, for instance, 42 percent of immigrants had at least one spell of welfare during the thirty-two–month period, as compared to 34 percent of natives. Once on welfare, moreover, immigrants stayed enrolled longer.

Because of the higher incidence and the longer duration of welfare spells, immigrants spent a much larger fraction of the sample period receiving some type of public assistance. In fact, about 12 percent of immigrants and 8 percent of natives received welfare benefits for at least twenty-six of the thirty-two months. Although this evidence should be interpreted cautiously, it is suggestive of a long-term welfare problem in the immigrant population.

Why Are Immigrants More Likely to Receive Welfare?

Immigrants are typically less educated, they typically have larger households, and their households typically contain a larger number of younger persons and older persons—the very groups that are particularly prone to need and use welfare. It turns out that much of the welfare gap between immigrants and natives can be attributed to differences in these observable socioeconomic characteristics between the two groups.

In the early 1990s, the fraction of immigrants on welfare exceeded that of natives by about 7 percentage points (see Figure 6-3). What happens to this welfare gap if one compares the typical immigrant household with a native household of the same size? Adjusting for household size alone reduces the

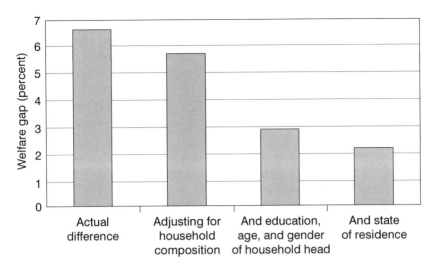

FIGURE 6-3. Determinants of the welfare gap between immigrants and natives.
Source: George J. Borjas and Lynette Hilton, "Immigration and the Welfare State: Immigrant Participation in Means-Tested Entitlement Programs," *Quarterly Journal of Economics* 111 (May 1996), pp. 590–591.

welfare gap to 6 percentage points. If one further adjusts for differences in the educational attainment, age, and gender of the household head, the welfare gap falls to 3 percentage points. And, finally, if one further adjusts for state of residence, the welfare gap falls to 2 percentage points.[15] In short, it is not being an immigrant per se that leads to high welfare use. Rather, it is the socioeconomic characteristics of the immigrant population.

It is tempting to dismiss the *actual* and large welfare gap between immigrants and natives by emphasizing that the *adjusted* welfare gap is quite small. This emphasis, however, is somewhat questionable. It is interesting to know that it is not the immigrant experience that leads to high welfare use: if only immigrants had more schooling, or had smaller households, or lived in different states, their welfare use would be roughly similar to that of natives. But from a cost-benefit perspective—the perspective that stresses the bottom line for the typical native person—what matters is the actual welfare use of the immigrant population. The typical American taxpayer benefits little from knowing that immigrant households headed by high school dropouts do not use welfare any more often than native households headed by high school dropouts—particularly if high school dropouts dominate the immigrant population.

The fact that socioeconomic characteristics matter greatly in determining the welfare gap between immigrants and natives has an important, if controversial, implication for immigration policy. Put bluntly, a small number of observable socioeconomic characteristics can be used to evaluate the chances that a particular visa applicant will eventually become a welfare recipient.[16]

In other words, to the extent that the United States cares about the cost of providing public assistance to the immigrant population, there exists a simple policy tool that can screen the pool of visa applicants and greatly minimize the impact of immigration on expenditures in welfare programs.

WELFARE MAGNETS

Welfare programs in the United States—though not generous by Western European standards—stack up pretty well when compared to the standard of living in most of the world's developing countries. In 1996, the typical AFDC household with two children in California received $7,200 in cash benefits.[17] This household probably qualified for food stamps worth another $3,000 annually. And if this household also participated in the Medicaid program, it received additional benefits valued at over $6,500. At the same time, per capita income in China was $3,200, in Colombia it was $6,000, and in the Philippines it was $3,000.[18]

Income differences across countries influence a person's decision of whether to move to the United States—regardless of whether these differences arise in the labor market or in the safety net provided by the welfare state. As a result, there are good reasons to be concerned with the possibility that generous welfare programs might attract a particular type of immigrant. After all, welfare programs will probably attract persons who qualify for subsidies and repel persons who have to pay for them. A strong magnetic effect, combined with an ineffective border control policy, can literally break the bank.

In addition, immigration can easily fracture the political legitimacy of the social contract that created and sustains the welfare state. No group of native citizens—whether in the United States or in other immigrant-receiving countries—can reasonably be expected to pick up the tab for subsidizing hundreds of millions of "the huddled masses." Milton Friedman neatly summarized the unmistakable implications of the welfare state's magnetic effects: "It's just obvious that you can't have free immigration and a welfare state."[19]

Welfare programs can generate three distinct types of magnetic effects. For instance, there exists the possibility that welfare attracts persons who otherwise would not have migrated to the United States. Although this is the magnetic effect that comes up most often in the immigration debate, it is also the one for which there is no empirical support—and the hardest one to corroborate.

It is doubtful that many immigrants would willingly volunteer the information that they came to the United States to collect SSI benefits or Medicaid. In fact, it is possible that most immigrants arrived in the country without fully knowing all of the income opportunities available to them—either in the job market or in the welfare state. But they quickly learn about them, and the least skilled immigrants, who probably face the least attractive job opportunities, realize that they qualify for many types of public assistance, ranging from cash payments to subsidized housing to medical benefits. One would then observe that many of the unskilled immigrants eventually enter the welfare rolls. But the welfare state need not have been the magnet that attracted those persons in the first place. It would then be extremely difficult to figure out what fraction of immigrants responded to the allure of welfare programs.

The magnetic attraction continues even after the immigrants enter the country. After all, welfare programs may discourage immigrants who fail in the U.S. labor market from returning to their home countries. In the absence of a welfare state, some of those immigrants would realize that they had been too optimistic about their chances in the United States, and would decide to return home. The welfare state provides alternative income opportunities, which might be far better than those they would have in the source countries.

It is difficult to determine if the safety net alters the out-migration behavior of immigrants for the simple reason that the United States does not collect any official data on how many or which types of persons leave the country. One can easily walk across from San Diego to Tijuana without filling out a form or even encountering the Border Patrol. As a result, the available estimates of the out-migration rate probably reflect a great deal of measurement error. Nevertheless, the estimates reported by the Immigration and Naturalization Service indicate that 34 to 38 percent of the immigrants who arrived in the early 1900s, when there was no welfare state, eventually left the United States, as compared to only about 22 percent of the immigrants who arrived in the 1980s.[20] Although this evidence is consistent with the possibility that the welfare state might deter some immigrants from leaving the United States, many other factors may also be at work.

The National Longitudinal Surveys of Youth provide more direct evidence of this type of magnetic effect.[21] Since 1979, the Bureau of Labor Statistics (BLS) has collected annual data on a sample of over twelve thousand young men and women who were fourteen to twenty-two years old when the survey began. Some of these young persons are foreign-born or have parents who are foreign-born. Because of the nature of the data, the BLS made a concerted effort at tracking these workers from year to year, and the surveys contain information on which respondents left the United States. By 1993, about 10 percent of the immigrants in this sample had left the country. Interestingly, the probability of leaving the United States was much smaller for foreign-born families that received public assistance. It seems, therefore, that welfare deters out-migration.[22]

Finally, the magnetic effects of welfare may influence the geographic sorting of the immigrant population in the United States. There are huge differences in welfare benefits across states. Consider, for example, the interstate differences in AFDC benefits (see Figure 6-4).[23] In 1970, California's benefit level matched that of the median state. By 1990, California's benefits were (almost) the most generous in the nation: 20 percent larger than in New York, 136 percent larger than in Florida, and almost 280 percent larger than in Texas.[24]

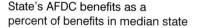

State's AFDC benefits as a
percent of benefits in median state

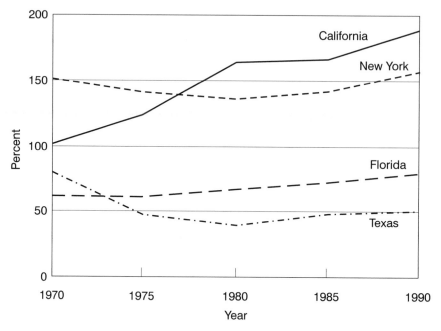

FIGURE 6-4. AFDC benefits in the main immigrant-receiving states, 1970–90.
Source: U.S. House of Representatives, *Background Material and Data on Programs within the Jurisdiction of the Committee on Ways and Means* (Washington, D.C., 1996), pp. 666–667.
Note: The data refer to the maximum benefits received by a family of three.

These differences might influence where immigrants and natives choose to live and place a substantial fiscal burden on relatively generous states.

To see how interstate differences in welfare benefits can affect the location decisions of *both* immigrants and natives, suppose that all migration is motivated by the search for higher incomes. Persons born in the United States and living in a particular state often find it expensive to move across states. The migration costs include not only the expense of transporting the family and the household goods to the new location, but also the burden of separating from families, friends, and social networks. These "psychic costs" probably dwarf the monetary cost of transporting the household across states. If it is indeed very costly to move, the existing interstate differences in welfare benefits may not be large enough to motivate many natives to pick up and migrate to another state. And, in fact, there is little evidence to suggest that interstate differences in welfare benefits generate a magnetic effect in the native population.[25]

In contrast, immigrants are a self-selected sample of persons who have chosen to bear the monetary and psychic costs of the geographic move. Suppose

TABLE 6-4

Geographic Clustering in California, by Receipt of Cash Benefits
(percent of households living in California)

	Did not receive cash benefits		Received cash benefits	
	1980	1990	1980	1990
Native households	9.7	9.6	11.2	11.5
Immigrants who arrived in the last five years				
All households	30.1	28.9	36.9	45.4
Nonrefugee households	31.2	30.0	37.4	43.7
Non-Mexican households	24.9	23.6	34.4	44.2
Households that are neither Mexican nor refugees	25.5	24.4	32.7	40.5

Source: George J. Borjas, "Immigration and Welfare Magnets," *Journal of Labor Economics* (forthcoming 1999), Tab. 2.

that once the costs of moving to the United States are incurred, it costs little to choose one particular state over another. In other words, once a person decides to migrate from Poland to the United States, it costs about the same to migrate to New York as it costs to migrate to California. Newly arrived immigrants will then tend to live in the "right" state. In other words, given that they have chosen to incur the costs of moving, they might as well move to those states that maximize their income opportunities. This perspective has an interesting implication: while welfare recipients in the native population are stuck in the state where they were born, welfare recipients among new immigrants should be heavily clustered in the states that offer the highest benefits.

Does such a clustering of immigrant welfare recipients actually take place? It does, and it became more pronounced as California's benefit level rose relative to that of other states (see Table 6-4). By 1990, California was home to 10 percent of the natives who did not receive cash benefits and to 12 percent of the natives who did. Among new immigrants, however, California was home to 29 percent of the ones who did not receive cash benefits and to 45 percent of the ones who did. The different residential choices made by the welfare recipients in the native and immigrant populations suggest that there may indeed be a purposive clustering of less-skilled immigrants into California.[26]

Obviously, there are many other factors that one should take into account before interpreting these data as conclusive evidence of a magnetic effect. For instance, California has a large refugee population and these refugees, mainly from Southeast Asia, have very high welfare participation rates. One could argue that many refugees end up in California not because of magnetic effects, but because of political decisions made by the federal government, by the states, and by the charitable agencies that sponsor their entry and administer the resettlement process. California is also home to almost 60 percent of the Mexican immigrants who live in the United States. California's geographic proximity to Mexico and the extensive links introduced by family ties and ethnic networks probably dominate their location decision.[27] Nevertheless, there is "excess" geographic clustering in the welfare population even among nonrefugees and among non-Mexicans.

Overall, the evidence suggests that there might be something to the idea of "welfare magnets," particularly when it comes to the geographic clustering of immigrant welfare recipients in particular states. The policy changes enacted in the 1996 welfare reform legislation provide a natural laboratory for better evaluating the importance of these magnetic effects. After all, the welfare reform legislation gives states far more latitude in setting benefits. If magnetic effects are indeed a problem, the main immigrant-receiving states will soon be leading the "race to the bottom," as they attempt to minimize the fiscal burden imposed by the purposive clustering of immigrants in those states that provide the highest benefits.

ETHNIC NETWORKS AND WELFARE

The geographic clustering of immigrants in a small number of states and cities has fostered the creation and growth of ethnic networks that transmit information about life in the United States to potential migrants in the source countries. These ethnic networks are often credited with providing valuable information about job market opportunities to the new immigrants. But do they also provide information about welfare programs?

Case studies of the Russian and Chinese communities leave little doubt that they do.[28] Russian- and Chinese-language newspapers often print detailed reports about the application process and eligibility requirements for particular programs. In fact, there are "Dear Abby"–style columns in newspapers that help readers with welfare problems. And bookstores in Taiwan, Hong Kong, and the United States sell a Chinese-language book that contains a thirty-six page guide to SSI and other benefits. Put simply, these ethnic publications do what they are supposed to do: provide valuable information about life in the United States to interested readers. And part of their job is to include valuable information about the publicly provided services that many of the readers might potentially qualify for.

It also turns out that different national origin groups in the immigrant population tend to use different types of welfare programs.[29] In the early 1990s, for example, even though Mexican immigrants were 50 percent more likely to receive energy assistance than Cuban immigrants, Cuban immigrants were more likely to receive housing subsidies than Mexican immigrants. Part of this dispersion arises because different groups tend to cluster in different parts of the country, and different states provide different services. But even after accounting for this fact (and for differences in the socioeconomic characteristics of the groups), there remains an interesting pattern. All else being equal, the more often a national origin group has been exposed to a particular type of program in the past, the more likely that newcomers in that group will also enroll in that program. In fact, if two national origin groups differ by 10 percentage points in the rate at which they enroll in a particular program, such as housing benefits, newly arrived immigrants belonging to those two groups will also be roughly 10 percentage points apart in their enrollment rate. There is effectively a one-to-one transmission of the propensity to participate in particular programs from one wave of immigrants to the next.[30] In short, ethnic networks—just like the ethnic media—do their job: they transmit valuable information to newcomers, including information about the welfare state.

WELFARE REFORM

The U.S. Congress has reacted to these disturbing trends in immigrant welfare use by making it increasingly more difficult for immigrants to qualify for some types of public assistance. Beginning in 1980, immigrants began to be subject to so-called deeming requirements, where the sponsors' income is "deemed" to be part of the immigrant's application for particular types of assistance. This deeming procedure obviously reduces the chances that new immigrants will qualify for welfare. The initial deeming rules applied only to SSI and lasted only three years, but were later expanded to AFDC and other programs.

In 1996, Congress tightened the eligibility requirements substantially by including a number of immigrant-related provisions in the welfare reform legislation. In fact, almost half of the $54 billion savings attributed to the welfare reform bill can be traced directly to the restrictions on immigrant use of welfare.[31] As signed by President Clinton, the legislation contained two key provisions:

1. Immigrants who entered the United States after August 22, 1996, the "post-enactment" immigrants, were prohibited from receiving most types of public assistance. The ban is to be lifted when the immigrant becomes an American citizen. Most noncitizens present in the country on August 22, 1996, the "preenactment" immigrants, were to be removed from the SSI and food stamp rolls within a year.

2. Postenactment immigrants are subject to stricter deeming regulations. The eligible income and assets of the immigrant's sponsor are deemed to be part of the immigrant's application for most types of public assistance, and the deeming period was extended for up to ten years.[32]

One can interpret the first of these provisions as setting up a five-year waiting period before postenactment immigrants can qualify for public assistance. After five years in the United States, the immigrant can apply for naturalization, and, if the application is successful, the ban on immigrant use of welfare is lifted. Partly because of the increasing importance in the distinction between citizens and noncitizens, there was a rapid rise in the number of immigrants who wished to become naturalized in the early 1990s. In 1991, the INS received only 207,000 petitions for naturalization; in 1996, the INS received 1.3 million such petitions.[33]

In an important sense, the welfare reform legislation embodied the idea that the problem with immigrant use of welfare lies in welfare policy, not in immigration policy. However, even before President Clinton signed the legislation, the rumblings had begun that the restrictions on immigrants were onerous, inhumane, unjust, and would be changed soon after the 1996 presidential election.

These restrictions brought together a number of powerful interest groups—all of which lobbied hard for their repeal. State governors and mayors could read between the lines of the welfare reform bill: hundreds of thousands of current (and future) immigrants on the federal welfare rolls would, more likely than not, become charges of states and local governments. Disabled immigrants, for example, who collected federal SSI dollars before 1996, would not stop being disabled; their disability would now simply become the responsibility of state and local governments. Immigrant-rights organizations stressed the unfairness and injustice in a piece of legislation that singled out legal immigrants who paid taxes and could be drafted during a military crisis. Finally, the media began to air frequent stories of very ill immigrants who received letters from the Social Security Administration notifying them that their benefits would be cut off within months.

Many of the immigrant-related provisions of the legislation were never enforced. The balanced budget agreement reached in 1997 between President Clinton and the Republican-controlled Congress repealed the most draconian aspects of the legislation, such as ejecting the preenactment immigrants from the SSI and food stamp programs. The mandated waiting period for postenactment immigrants, however, remained on the books as of 1998.

The partial unraveling of this major piece of social legislation is illuminating. There is little disagreement over the fact that immigrant use of public assistance grew rapidly in the past three decades. So it is hard to argue that the immigrant provisions in the welfare reform bill were based on faulty data or analysis. Congress saw an actual problem—rising welfare use by immigrants—and tried to do something about it.

However, the political system finds it difficult, if not impossible, to dismantle many parts of the welfare state. It seems that the American people do not wish to bear the political, social, and economic costs of removing immigrants already in the United States from the welfare rolls. It is naïve, after all, to assume that there are no long-run consequences from denying immigrants access to prenatal care, food stamps, and housing assistance. In the end, it is probably easier *and* cheaper to reduce the welfare costs of immigration not by "ending welfare as we know it," but by reforming immigration policy instead.

DO IMMIGRANTS PAY THEIR WAY?

Even though the link between immigration and welfare raises many cultural and political questions, the immigration debate has focused mainly on the bottom line: do immigrants pay their way in the welfare state? This emphasis is unfortunate because, in the end, the true cost of immigrant participation in welfare programs has little to do with the bottom line in the ledger sheet. Through the early 1990s, for example, expenditures on the AFDC program totaled about $25 billion annually. As the raging policy debate over welfare showed, that debate was *not* over $25 billion. Rather, it was over the possibility that welfare reduces work incentives, that it encourages the breakdown of the family unit, that it gives women incentives to bear children out of wedlock, and that it creates a mindset of dependence in the recipients. These are the worrisome consequences of the AFDC program that were at the heart of the debate over welfare reform, and these should be the same consequences that worry observers of the immigrant experience.

Nevertheless, the sign of the bottom line in the ledger sheet has played a prominent role in the immigration debate. And like most accounting exercises, this one is fraught with questionable assumptions—assumptions that effectively determine the answer to the question. In the early 1990s, for example, a widely publicized study by the Urban Institute concluded that immigrants paid over $27 billion more in taxes than it cost to provide them with schooling and welfare services, while an equally publicized study by economist Donald Huddle for the Carrying Capacity Network, an anti–population growth group, claimed that the net costs of immigration exceeded $40 billion.[34]

These studies reached different conclusions because they made different assumptions. The Urban Institute's claim that immigrants generated a $27 billion fiscal surplus assumed that immigrants do not increase the cost of *any* of the programs that were not included in their calculations—for example, that immigrants increase expenditures on schools and welfare, but do not increase the cost of maintaining national parks, providing sanitary services, and building and keeping up roads. At the other end of the spectrum, Donald Huddle claimed that for every six immigrants who entered the country, one native was displaced from his or her job and joined the welfare rolls. Both sets of calculations suffer from a simple problem: they build in obviously false assumptions. There is no evidence, for instance, that immigration drives a large number of natives onto the welfare rolls. And it is implausible that immigrants do not increase the cost of running the thousands of government programs that lie outside the scope of the welfare state.

In 1990, Congress appointed a Commission on Immigration Reform to evaluate the nation's immigration policies. This commission, in turn, requested the National Academy of Sciences to examine the contentious issue of whether "immigrants pay their way." The National Academy report provided two separate studies of the fiscal consequences of immigration.[35] These studies stand as the most careful investigations of this controversial subject.

The Short Run

The first of the two studies conducted by the National Academy considered the short-run impact of immigration on the fiscal ledger sheet of states and local governments—that is, the fiscal impact during a particular fiscal year. For two major immigrant-receiving states, California and New Jersey, the National Academy conducted an item-by-item accounting of expenditures incurred and taxes collected, and calculated how immigration affected each of these entries.[36]

This itemization led to some surprising conclusions. California attracts a disproportionate number of the welfare recipients in the immigrant population, and provides a wide array of expensive services, ranging from generous welfare assistance to a world-class system of public universities to a sophisticated and well-maintained system of roads and freeways. It turns out that immigration increased the state and local taxes of the typical native household in California by $1,174 annually.[37]

It is important to state precisely what this startling number means. Suppose there were a counterfactual world where immigration had been prohibited at some point in the past, so that the entire population of California in the mid-1990s was native-born. And suppose that in this counterfactual world all other social and economic indicators in California, such as the frequency of garbage collection and the layout of the freeway system, would have been the same as they actually were in the early 1990s. The tax bill for the typical native household in California would then have been almost $1,200 lower.

The cost-benefit calculation for New Jersey is less dramatic. Because New Jersey provides fewer state and local services, and because New Jersey attracts a different type of immigrant (more skilled and less prone to use government services), immigration increased the annual tax bill of New Jersey's typical native household by only $229.

These results can be extrapolated nationwide, but the answers clearly depend on whether one uses the New Jersey or the California experience. In other words, is the typical immigrant in the country more like California's or more like New Jersey's? And are the typical government services provided by other states more like California's or like New Jersey's? Regardless of the baseline, immigration imposes a fiscal burden in the short run. Each native household in the United States pays between $166 and $226 more in annual taxes because of immigration.

Much of the short-run fiscal impact of immigration arises because of expenditures in public schooling. In California alone, about $1.7 billion was spent on educating the children of illegal aliens in 1993.[38] Immigrant families tend to have more children than native families. And the schooling provided to immigrant children—such as bilingual education—is often more expensive than the schooling provided to natives. The National Academy concluded that schooling costs accounted for over one-third of the tax burden immigrants imposed on California, and for two-thirds of the burden they imposed on New Jersey.[39]

Because schooling plays such a key role in determining the fiscal burden, the short-run calculations face a serious conceptual difficulty. Although providing schooling to immigrant children today is costly, such expenditures generate future benefits, including larger salaries and higher tax payments. A more complete accounting of the fiscal impact of immigration, therefore, must take into account not only the short-run impact, but also the long-run effects that both immigrants and their descendants have on the fiscal ledger sheet.

The Long Run

Consider what happens when the United States admits an immigrant today. The country incurs some short-run costs, such as public assistance and building additional infrastructure. The immigrant, however, pays some taxes and helps fund part of these activities.[40]

Over time, the immigrant's income and tax contribution grow as economic assimilation takes place. More important, the immigrant will have American-born children. As these children grow up, the country will incur a variety of costs, particularly in terms of putting the children through school. These children, however, will themselves eventually grow up, work, and pay taxes, and their taxes (collected at some point in the future) might cover part of the current expenditures. The children of immigrants will themselves have children, and so on.

The National Academy tried to estimate the long-run fiscal impact by considering what happens over the three hundred years following the entry of a particular immigrant into the country. Figure 6-5 illustrates, in present value terms, the net contribution made by the immigrant and his or her descendants in each year of the three hundred–year period.[41] Initially, the immigrant creates a burden for the taxpayer. The burden suddenly turns into a surplus in the year 2016, after the immigrant has been in the country for about twenty years. Adding up over the three hundred years suggests that, in the long run, admitting one immigrant today yields an $80,000 total fiscal surplus at the national level. Therefore, despite the substantial short-run fiscal burden, it seems that immigration is a pretty good deal.[42]

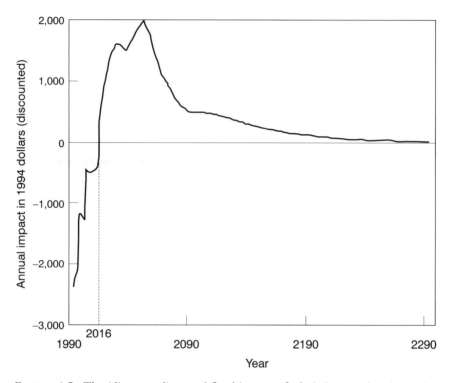

FIGURE 6-5. The (discounted) annual fiscal impact of admitting one immigrant in 1994 over the next three centuries.

Source: James P. Smith and Barry Edmonston, eds., *The New Americans: Economic, Demographic, and Fiscal Effects of Immigration* (Washington, D.C.: National Academy Press, 1997), p. 341.

Notes: The calculations use an annual discount rate of 3 percent. The $80,000 fiscal net gain is obtained by aggregating the discounted annual impacts.

The long-run approach is conceptually superior to the short-run simulation because it takes account of the future returns to investing in immigrant human capital. In fact, Figure 6-5 suggests that there is no fundamental inconsistency between the two approaches: in the short run, there is a fiscal burden; in the long run, there are net gains.

Before one fully accepts the $80,000 figure for the net fiscal gain from immigration, it is worth investigating exactly how the long-run simulation was conducted. It turns out that a key assumption differentiating the two approaches involves the future fiscal policy of the federal government. As shown in Figure 6-5, the fiscal burden turns into a fiscal surplus in the year 2016. A close reading of the fine print in the National Academy report reveals why this happens. The simulation assumes that the federal government will finally get the courage to put its fiscal house in order in the year 2016, and pass a huge tax increase to ensure that the debt problem does not worsen thereafter.[43]

In one important sense, this assumption builds in the conclusion: immigration is beneficial because the country can spread the pain of a large tax bill over a larger population. In fact, the National Academy also conducted a simulation assuming that the federal government would continue its current tax-and-spend proclivities. In this alternative scenario, the $80,000 net benefit quickly turned into a $15,000 net loss.[44] And the logic that makes the assumption so beneficial from the native taxpayer's point of view is a double-edged sword: The economy grew its way out of the budget deficit in the 1990s. A long period of economic expansion would presumably allow the United States to also grow its way out of the debt problem. Immigration would then generate huge fiscal losses for natives, as they would have to share the fiscal savings generated by economic growth with more people.

An additional problem with the long-run simulation is that three hundred years is a long time indeed. In fact, if one shortens the "long run" to the fifty-year period after the immigrant enters the country, the $80,000 net gain dwindles to just over $11,000.[45] The Industrial Revolution was not even a glimmer in someone's eye at the end of the 1600s, and any economic prediction made back then about the United States today would surely have been seriously off the mark. In my view, the calculations that stress the short-run fiscal impact are much more believable because they do not rely on any assumptions about the future of fiscal policy. And recent attempts at forecasting economic trends do not engender a great deal of confidence that even the National Academy of Sciences can make credible predictions about the fiscal condition of the United States thirty years from now, let alone at the end of the twenty-third century.

In the end, the debate over the fiscal impact of immigration faces a dilemma. The short-run approach obviously ignores fundamental parts of the cost-benefit calculation—and may well overstate the adverse fiscal impact of immigration over the long haul. The long-run estimates, however, are full of false assumptions, and these assumptions drive the result of a substantial net fiscal gain.

Moreover, even if the long-run calculations were roughly right—in the sense that an additional immigrant would generate an extra $80,000 over the next three hundred years—there is still an important political calculus to consider. Even in this very optimistic scenario, the United States would suffer short-run losses for about twenty years. The economic benefits that might begin to show up after the year 2016 provide little comfort to the households that lived in California in the 1990s: they had to pay an additional $1,200 a year in taxes because of immigration.

The Bottom Line

The measurable net economic benefits from immigration to the American economy are relatively small, probably around $10 billion a year. These economic benefits arise because immigrants introduce skills that partly complement those of natives. Before concluding whether immigration benefits or harms the United States, one has to contrast these net economic benefits with the fiscal impact. The fiscal impact of immigration, however, depends on whether one uses the short-run or long-run calculations.

Consider first the short-run fiscal impact. The typical native household pays somewhere between $166 and $226 in additional taxes because of immigration. There are approximately ninety million native households in the United States, so the national fiscal burden lies somewhere between $15 billion and $21 billion per year. In the short run, therefore, there seems to be little support for the argument that immigration is a great boon for the country. If anything, the available data suggest that immigration may even be responsible for a small net loss.

In the long run, each immigrant admitted contributes about $80,000 over the next three hundred years. At a 3 percent real rate of return, this is equivalent to a yearly annuity of about $2,400. There were approximately twenty-six million immigrants in the United States in 1998, so the national net gain is about $60 billion per year. Adding this fiscal impact to the immigration surplus, the economic benefits from immigration could begin to add up—perhaps to around $70 billion annually. But, as I argued earlier, the validity of these long-run predictions is questionable. If, for example, the "long run" refers to the fifty-year period after the immigrant arrives, the $11,000 gain over the next fifty years is equivalent to a yearly annuity of less than $450. The national fiscal surplus would then be on the order of $12 billion per year, and the total gains from immigration would run around $20 billion per year.

In my view, the cost-benefit approach teaches an important lesson. After accounting for the impact of immigration on the productivity of native workers and firms and on the fiscal ledger sheet, immigration probably has a small *net* economic impact on the United States.

The cost-benefit approach clearly suggests that issues other than the sign of the bottom line will determine the direction of the immigration debate. After all, this bottom line is neither overwhelmingly positive nor overwhelmingly negative—and a prudent person would probably conclude that it is pretty close to zero. Some of these other issues may be economic, such as the large redistribution of wealth induced by immigration. Some may be political, such as the redistribution of political power that immigration can bring about. And some may be social and cultural, such as the impact of immigration on ethnic diversity and on the cultural cohesion of American society.

Social Mobility across Generations

THE ECONOMIC IMPACT of immigration depends both on how immigrants do in the labor market and on the adjustment process experienced by the immigrant household across generations. In the late 1990s, about 10 percent of Americans were "second-generation," or born in the United States with at least one foreign-born parent. By the year 2050, the share of second-generation persons will increase to 14 percent, and the grandchildren of current immigrants will make up an additional 9 percent of the population.[1]

The traditional view of the mobility experienced by immigrant households across generations is vividly embodied in the melting pot metaphor: Immigrants are molded from a collection of diverse national origin groups into a homogeneous native population in a relatively short time, perhaps two generations.[2] This "assimilationist" perspective long dominated the thinking of many observers of the immigrant experience.

Beginning with the 1963 publication of Nathan Glazer and Daniel Moynihan's *Beyond the Melting Pot*, however, a lot of modern sociological research argues that this metaphor does not correctly portray the ethnic experience in the United States. Glazer and Moynihan conclude that "the American ethos is nowhere better perceived than in the disinclination of the third and fourth generation of newcomers to blend into a standard, uniform national type."[3] This revisionist approach suggests that many of the cultural and economic differences that exist among immigrant groups—as well as between immigrants and natives—are transmitted to their children, so that the diversity found among today's immigrants becomes the diversity found among tomorrow's ethnic groups.[4]

Ironically, and from a purely economic perspective, it is not clear that the United States would be better off if the melting pot operated at breakneck speed, quickly assimilating the new immigrants and churning them out as clones of native workers. After all, diversity pays—the economic gains from immigration are maximized when the immigrant population differs most from the native population. The productivity gains from immigration would then be larger if the United States pursued policies that hampered and delayed the assimilation of immigrants, policies that lowered the flame under the melting pot. If the melting pot were to operate at full boil, the only way that the country could replenish the productivity gains from immigration would be to keep admitting more and more immigrants.

Of course, this perspective is much too narrow and misses the point. The net economic gains from immigration are quite small even in the first generation, when the immigrants are most different from native workers. Moreover, the economic, social, and political consequences of delaying assimilation could be disastrous. The ethnic conflicts that mark many regions of the modern world, for instance, often originated centuries ago, and their consequences still fester. One does not have to be a very astute observer of the human condition to learn that it pays to have a cohesive social fabric. Therefore, it is probably in the national interest of the United States to pursue policies that spur substantial intergenerational progress by immigrant households, and that reduce the importance of ethnicity in determining socioeconomic outcomes in future generations.

In this chapter, I argue that there is a strong positive correlation between the socioeconomic outcomes experienced by ethnic groups in the immigrant generation and the outcomes experienced by their children and grandchildren. Those ethnic groups that do well in the immigrant generation do well in the second and third generations as well. The melting pot, it seems, does not work as rapidly as one might wish. As a result, the ethnic differences that characterize the immigrants of the Second Great Migration will probably dominate American society for much of the twenty-first century.

The Children of Immigrants

The economic fate of the descendants of the immigrants who entered the United States in the 1980s and 1990s is yet to be decided. Nevertheless, one can look at the historical experience of earlier immigrant waves to make informed guesses about what might happen in the future.

There is a widespread—and false—perception that the economic performance of the children of immigrants far surpasses that of their parents. This perception originated in studies that compared the earnings of various generations of Americans at a particular point in time, such as the 1970 decennial Census (see Figure 7-1).[5] This Census allows the precise identification of two generations of Americans: the immigrant generation and the second generation.[6] The generation of the remaining persons in the population (that is, of the native-born who had both parents born in the United States) cannot be determined exactly, but I will refer to them as third-generation Americans.

In the 1970 Census snapshot, it turns out that second-generation workers earn substantially more than other workers: 12 percent more than immigrants and 16 percent more than workers in the third generation. And other surveys—conducted both before and after 1970—confirm this pattern. In 1940, for example, second-generation workers earned 5 percent more than immigrants and 26 percent more than third-generation workers. And in 1998, second-generation workers earned 38 percent more than immigrants and 7 percent more than third-generation workers. Figure 7-1 also reveals a striking trend: even though second-generation workers earned more than other workers at each point in time, the second-generation advantage over the third has declined substantially over time.

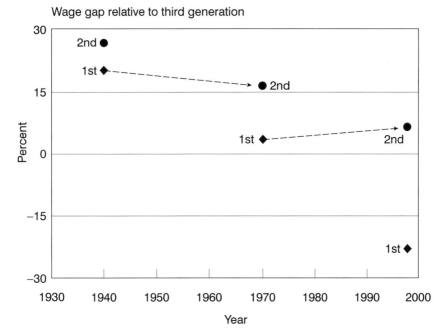

FIGURE 7-1. Relative wages of first and second generations, 1940, 1970, and 1998.

Sources: George J. Borjas, "The Intergenerational Mobility of Immigrants," Part 1, *Journal of Labor Economics* 11 (January 1994), p. 125; and additional calculations from the pooled 1996–98 Current Population Surveys (Annual Demographic Files).

Notes: The data refer to salaried men who are twenty-five to sixty-four years old and are employed in the civilian sector. The "third generation" contains all workers who are U.S.-born and have U.S.-born parents.

The relative economic success of the second generation in each of these data snapshots *seems* to imply that second-generation Americans earn more than both their parents and their children. A common interpretation of this finding is that the children of immigrants are "hungry" and have the drive and ambition that ensure economic success—and that this hunger is lost once the immigrant household becomes fully Americanized in the third generation. If this interpretation were correct, the concern over the skill level of the immigrants in the Second Great Migration may be misplaced. In a few decades, their children will outperform not only the immigrants but the third-generation workers as well.

However, the empirical evidence provided by a snapshot of the U.S. labor market at a point in time does not necessarily justify this conclusion. After all, the family ties among the three generations identifiable in a particular cross-section are very tenuous. For example, many of the immigrants enumerated in the 1998 Current Population Survey just recently arrived in the country, and it would be impossible for them to have American-born children who are already participating in the labor market. Second-generation Americans of working age can only be descendants of immigrants who have been in the country for at least two or three decades. As a result, most of the immigrants enumerated in 1998 are unlikely to be the parents of the second-generation workers enumerated at the same time. Because there are skill differences across immigrant waves, and because some of these differences are probably transmitted to the immigrants' children, the wage gap between first- and second-generation workers in a cross-section does not correctly portray the economic mobility that occurs across generations.

Moreover, the workers who can be identified as members of the so-called third generation are a motley collection of various ethnic groups, whose presence in the United States may date back fifty years or more than two hundred years. It is biologically impossible for these workers to be direct descendants of the immigrants enumerated in a particular cross-section. For example, this would require that working-age immigrants enumerated in 1998 (most of whom arrived in the 1980s and 1990s) have American-born grandchildren who are also of working age.

In short, the fact that second-generation workers earn more than other workers *at a particular point in time* does not imply that second-generation workers earn more than both their parents and their children. To calculate the improvement in economic status between the first and second generations, one has to link parents and children, rather than compare persons belonging to different generations at a given point in time.

Tracking the immigrant household over the years can approximate this linkage. For instance, the 1940 Census provides information on the economic performance of the immigrants present in the United States at that time. These immigrants are presumably the parents of the second generation workers enumerated in the 1970 Census. Similarly, the 1970 Census provides information on the economic performance of immigrants in 1970. In turn, these immigrants are probably the parents of the second-generation workers found in the Current Population Surveys in the late 1990s. By comparing the economic performance of immigrants in 1940 with the economic performance of the second generation in 1970—or the economic performance of immigrants in 1970 with that of the second generation in the 1990s—one can determine the economic progress experienced by the children of immigrants.[7]

It turns out that immigrants in 1940 earned about 20 percent more than third-generation workers, while second-generation workers in 1970—who are presumably the children of these immigrants—earned only about 16 percent more than third-generation workers. It seems, therefore, that immigrant households experienced slightly *less* wage growth over the 1940–70 period than the typical third-generation worker. In contrast, immigrant households experienced slightly faster wage growth between 1970 and 1998. Immigrants in 1970 earned 4 percent more than third-generation workers, while the second-generation workers in 1998 earned 7 percent more than third-generation workers.

Overall, the historical experience of the 1940–98 period does not seem to indicate that the second generation experiences "exceptional" economic progress—relative to the rest of the economy. Depending on the immigrant wave, the intergenerational progress experienced within an immigrant household was only slightly slower or slightly faster than that experienced by the so-called third generation—the bulk of native-born persons in the United States.

REGRESSION TOWARD THE MEAN

The modest change in average economic status that seems to occur between immigrants and their children confounds two distinct factors. It seems reasonable to suspect that the second generation enjoys a head start in its earnings capacity or economic status that is not experienced by any other generation. This "extra" push arises because the human capital of second-generation workers is particularly likely to differ from that of their parents. After all, second-generation Americans are typically the first members of the family to graduate from American schools, the first to benefit from having English as a native tongue, and the first to know about the workings of the U.S. labor market prior to getting their first jobs.

There is something else going on at the same time, however. It is well known that the relation between the skills of parents and children, regardless of whether the parents are foreign- or native-born, is driven by a phenomenon known as regression toward the mean.[8]

Even though the children of highly successful parents are themselves likely to be successful, it is unlikely that the children will be as successful as their parents. For example, the children of Fortune 500 CEOs have a nice head start in the economic race, and will probably do quite well. Nevertheless, it is unlikely that their earnings histories will match those of their prominent mothers and fathers. The economic performance of the children of highly successful parents will probably revert somewhat toward the lower average in the population. Similarly, even though the children of less-skilled parents are themselves likely to be less skilled, it is unlikely that the children will be as unskilled as the parents, and again there is a reversion toward the population average. Regression toward the mean resembles a double-sided magnet: it pulls the economic status of the children toward the mean of the population, regardless of where the parents start out.

This phenomenon occurs because parental skills and family background are not the only factors that influence the intergenerational transmission of skills. Many other unknown and random variables also enter the process, including luck and imperfect genetic transmission of ability, motivation, and drive. These extraneous factors imply that the children of parents who reside at either tail of the skill distribution will probably lie closer to the middle of that distribution. Andrew Carnegie tried to summarize this process in a famous quip: "Three generations from shirtsleeves to shirtsleeves."[9]

It is important to disentangle these two effects—the relative improvement that probably occurs between the first and second generations, and the phenomenon of regression toward the mean—to understand the long-run economic progress of immigrant households. To see why, recall that the comparison of immigrants in 1940 with second-generation workers in 1970 suggested that this particular second generation experienced slightly less economic progress than the rest of the economy. In 1940, however, immigrants were very skilled and had high earnings, and the phenomenon of regression toward the mean suggests that their children should be more "average-looking." And this regression toward the mean could outweigh whatever benefits might have accrued from the head start that was presumably enjoyed by the second generation.

There is another—and much more important—reason for determining the rate of regression toward the mean. Some ethnic groups enter the United States doing very well in the labor market, while other groups perform very poorly. Part of these ethnic differences will likely be transmitted to their offspring. The melting pot metaphor argues that ethnicity is not "sticky": ethnic differences disappear in a relatively short time, and all the groups eventually become indistinguishable from the mean of the American population. There is, therefore, another way of thinking about the notion of the melting pot. If regression toward the mean is an important phenomenon, the differences observed among ethnic groups in the first generation will not last long, and an immigrant's ethnic background will have little influence on economic outcomes in future generations. To some extent, the melting pot metaphor is just a repackaging of the concept of regression toward the mean.

SOCIAL MOBILITY BETWEEN THE FIRST AND SECOND GENERATIONS

There is substantial dispersion in the relative wage of ethnic groups in both the first and second generations (see Table 7-1). In 1970, for instance, immigrants from Canada earned 21 percent more than the typical worker in the third generation, while immigrants from Mexico earned 28 percent less. In 1998, second-generation workers from Canada earned 16 percent more than the typical worker in the third generation, while second-generation Mexicans earned 20 percent less. Recall that the "baseline" group of third-generation workers includes *all* persons who were born in the United States and had native-born parents, regardless of their ethnic background. In short, the third-generation group makes up the bulk of the "native" population.

How much of the ethnic differences that exist among immigrants persist into the second generation? Figure 7-2 shows the link for a large number of national origin groups, over both the 1940–70 period and the 1970–98 period.[10] There is an obvious and strong positive correlation between the

TABLE 7–1
Relative Wages of Selected Ethnic Groups in the First
and Second Generations, 1970–98

Country of birth	Percent wage gap between immigrant group and typical third-generation worker in 1970	Percent wage gap between second-generation group and typical third-generation worker in 1998
Canada	21.0	16.0
Cuba	−18.9	−18.0
Dominican Republic	−30.6	−13.0
El Salvador	1.6	2.1
France	28.0	−6.2
Germany	21.9	17.6
Greece	−3.9	31.8
Haiti	−21.6	−27.8
India	27.6	23.1
Ireland	5.3	28.2
Italy	4.2	13.3
Jamaica	−17.8	−6.3
Mexico	−27.6	−19.7
Nicaragua	−5.9	−7.4
Norway	35.1	−4.7
Philippines	−12.9	−17.0
Poland	8.6	33.6
Portugal	−17.6	−4.9
Spain	−10.7	−36.5
Switzerland	41.2	66.7

Sources: Calculations from the 1970 Public Use Microdata Sample of the U.S. Census and the pooled 1996–98 Current Population Surveys (Annual Demographic Files).

Notes: The data refer to salaried men who are twenty-five to sixty-four years old and are employed in the civilian sector. The "third generation" contains all workers who are U.S.-born and have U.S.-born parents, regardless of their ethnic background.

average skills of the ethnic groups in the two generations: the groups that did well in the first generation also did well in the second.

The upward-sloping trend line illustrated in Figure 7-2 summarizes the statistical relationship that links the relative wages of the two generations.[11] The slope (or steepness) of this trend line provides valuable information about the intergenerational link. This slope is sometimes called the *intergenerational correlation* in skills.[12] If the trend line were flat, it would indicate that there is no connection between the average skills of the ethnic groups in the second generation and the average skills of the immigrant groups. In this case, the intergenerational correlation would be zero, and there would be complete regression toward the mean. No matter how well or how poorly the immigrant groups did in the labor market, second-generation ethnic groups would end up with similar wages. If the trend line were relatively steep, there would then be a substantial link between average wages in the

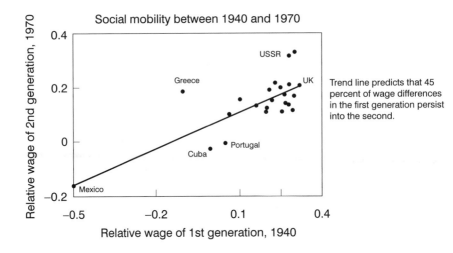

Trend line predicts that 45 percent of wage differences in the first generation persist into the second.

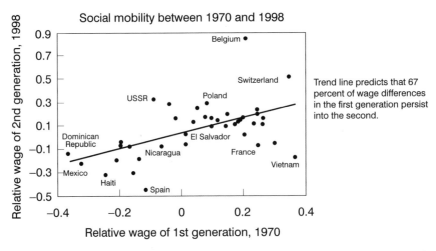

Trend line predicts that 67 percent of wage differences in the first generation persist into the second.

FIGURE 7-2. Social mobility between immigrants and their children, 1940–70 and 1970–98.

Sources: George J. Borjas, "The Intergenerational Mobility of Immigrants," Part 1, *Journal of Labor Economics* 11 (January 1994), p. 125; and additional calculations from the 1970 Public Use Microdata Sample of the U.S. Census and the pooled 1996–98 Current Population Surveys (Annual Demographic Files).

Notes: The data refer to salaried men who are twenty-five to sixty-four years old and are employed in the civilian sector. The relative wage gives the log point differential between the average worker in a particular group and the typical "third-generation" worker, where the third generation contains all workers who are U.S.-born and have U.S.-born parents, regardless of their ethnic background. The trend lines come from regressions that are (approximately) weighted by the sample size of the national origin group.

first and second generations. If the intergenerational correlation were equal to one, for instance, there would be a perfect correlation between the skills of the two generations: if one immigrant group earned 30 percent more than another immigrant group, the two groups would also be 30 percentage points apart in the second generation.[13] In sum, the intergenerational correlation measures the intergenerational stickiness in ethnic differences in the labor market. The higher the intergenerational correlation, the greater the stickiness.

Discussions of intergenerational progress are often couched in terms of "social mobility," a term that is typically taken to mean the extent to which a new generation can escape its past. There is little social mobility, for example, when the children of doctors become doctors, the children of plumbers become plumbers, and the children of farm laborers labor on the farm. In contrast, there is a great deal of social mobility when the parent's occupation or wage has little impact on the types of jobs performed by their children or on their children's wages.

The intergenerational correlation and the rate of social mobility are reverse sides of the same coin. For example, suppose that the trend line were perfectly flat and the intergenerational correlation were zero. There would then be perfect social mobility, in the sense that the skills of immigrant groups would play no role in determining the economic outcomes of the second generation. On average, second-generation workers would experience the same economic outcomes regardless of whether their parents originated in Mexico or in the United Kingdom. The second generation, in effect, would be able to escape its ethnic past. In contrast, suppose the trend line were very steep and the intergenerational correlation equaled one. There would not be any social mobility because ethnicity is destiny: the economic outcomes in the immigrant generation would completely determine how the groups do in the second. The children of Mexican immigrants, like their parents, would have relatively few skills, while the children of British immigrants, like their parents, would be highly skilled.

It turns out that the intergenerational correlation between the first and second generations was .45 over the 1940–70 period, and .69 over the 1970–98 period.[14] In rough terms, therefore, the intergenerational correlation between the skills of the first and second generations is about halfway between zero and one. What does this mean? An intergenerational correlation of .5 essentially implies that half of the skill differential between any two groups in the first generation persists into the second generation. If the average wage of two ethnic groups is 30 percentage points apart in the first generation, the average wage of the two groups will be about 15 percentage points apart in the second. There is some social mobility, but it is far from perfect because ethnicity is still an important determinant of labor market outcomes in the second generation.

As I noted earlier, the connection between the average skills of the first and second generations depends not only on the rate of regression toward the mean, but also on whether the second generation has a relative head start—an excess gain relative to the progress experienced by other generations. One can get a simple estimate of this head start by looking at the trend lines that link the relative wages of immigrants and of their children (again, see Figure 7-2). Consider the relation between the relative wages of immigrants in 1970 and the relative wages of their children in 1998. The trend line predicts that if a particular immigrant group—such as immigrants from El Salvador in the figure—had started out with the same wage as the third generation in 1970 (and had a relative wage of zero), the children of this group would earn about 4 percent more than the third generation by 1998. In other words, the children of immigrants who looked just like "native" workers when they first entered the country would outperform the rest of the economy by about 4 percentage points.

In sum, there is some advantage to being the first members of the immigrant household to be born in the United States, but not much. And ethnic background is an important determinant of socioeconomic outcomes in the second generation. About 50 percent of the skill differences found among ethnic groups in the first generation persist into the second.

THE FIRST GREAT MIGRATION

Ethnicity matters in the first generation. And it also matters in the second. To establish how long a person's ethnic background keeps on mattering, one can track the economic performance of the children and grandchildren of the immigrants who entered during the First Great Migration at the beginning of the twentieth century. Prior to the First Great Migration, immigration to the United States was relatively small. On average, about 1.7 million persons entered the country in each decade between 1820 and 1880.[15] The First Great Migration—which began around 1880—led to an explosion in the number of immigrants: five million persons arrived in the 1880s, four million in the 1890s, nine million between 1901 and 1910, and an additional six million in the 1910s.

The 1910 Census provides some information on the skill composition of many of the immigrants who were part of the First Great Migration (see Table 7-2).[16] Not surprisingly, immigrants and natives had very different economic experiences in 1910. The two groups had different skills, lived in different areas, and held different types of jobs. For example, although 37 percent of white native men worked in agricultural jobs, only 17 percent of immigrants worked in agriculture. Nearly half of the immigrants worked in manufacturing, as opposed to only a quarter of natives. And at a time when 28 percent of natives lived in the 230 largest cities, over half of the immigrants resided in those cities. The First Great Migration, therefore, was essen-

TABLE 7–2
Characteristics of the First Great Migration, 1910

	White natives	Immigrants
Literacy rate (percent)	95.8	86.9
Percent wage gap between		
immigrants and white natives	—	8.4
Percent residing in:		
Northeastern region	25.7	47.2
Southern region	29.6	4.4
Large cities	28.1	53.7
Percent employed:		
In agriculture	36.9	16.7
In manufacturing	26.4	44.3
As laborers	14.1	24.0

Source: George J. Borjas, "Long-Run Convergence of Ethnic Skills Differentials: The Children and Grandchildren of the Great Migration," Industrial and Labor Relations Review 47 (July 1994), p. 556.

Note: The data refer to working men who are twenty-five to sixty-four years old.

tially an urban phenomenon clustered in the manufacturing sector at a time when the native work force was overwhelmingly agricultural and resided outside urban areas.

Immigrants were also less skilled than natives. One-quarter of the immigrants living in the United States in 1910 were laborers, as compared to only 14 percent of white natives. And 87 percent of immigrants were literate (that is, they knew how to read and write some language), as compared to 96 percent of natives. Although the 1910 Census data does not report a worker's earnings, one can obtain a summary measure of economic performance by assigning each worker the average wage in the worker's occupation.[17] Using this wage measure, it turns out that immigrants, on average, earned about 8 percent less than natives.[18]

The Children of the First Great Migration

Not surprisingly, there were sizable ethnic differences in schooling and wages among the ethnic groups that made up the First Great Migration (see Figure 7-3). For instance, 45 percent of Mexican immigrants, 74 percent of Polish immigrants, and 99 percent of English immigrants knew how to read and write some language. The wage differentials in the first generation were equally large: English immigrants earned 13 percent more than the typical worker in the labor market at that time, Portuguese immigrants earned 13 percent less, and Mexican immigrants earned 23 percent less.[19]

As I argued earlier, the tracking of households across Censuses can provide valuable information about the intergenerational progress experienced by immigrants. One can then use the 1940 Census to measure the skills and eco-

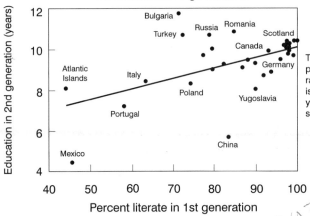

Education across generations

Trend line predicts that a 20-point difference in literacy rates in the first generation is associated with a one-year education gap in the second.

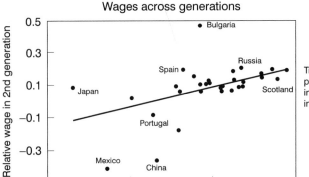

Wages across generations

Trend line predicts that 60 percent of wage differences in the first generation persist into the second.

FIGURE 7-3. The children of the First Great Migration.

Source: George J. Borjas, "Long-Run Convergence of Ethnic Skills Differentials: The Children and Grandchildren of the Great Migration," *Industrial and Labor Relations Review* 47 (July 1994), pp. 561–562.

Notes: The data refer to working men who are twenty-five to sixty-four years old. The relative wage gives the log wage differential between a particular group and the typical worker in the labor market at that point in time. The trend lines come from regressions that are (approximately) weighted by the sample size of the national origin group.

nomic performance of the children of the First Great Migration. It turns out that much of the dispersion across ethnic groups persisted into the second generation. Second-generation workers whose parents originated in Scotland had three more years of schooling than those whose parents originated in Portugal, and five more years than those whose parents originated in Mexico. Similarly, second-generation English workers earned about 19 percent more than the average worker in 1940, while second-generation Portuguese immigrants earned about 8 percent less.

Figure 7-3 clearly shows that the children of immigrant groups that had high literacy rates would eventually attain more education, and that the children of high-wage immigrant groups would eventually have higher wages. In fact, the trend line linking literacy rates and educational attainment across generations indicates that a 20 percentage point difference in literacy rates between two immigrant groups in 1910 is associated with a difference of about one year of schooling for their children.[20] Because differences in literacy rates of 20 percentage points among the first-generation ethnic groups were common, the intergenerational link in skills generated substantial differences in educational attainment among the groups in the second generation. Similarly, the trend line linking wages across generations indicates that about 60 percent of the earnings gap between any two immigrant groups persisted into the second generation.

The historical record shows that the skill differentials across ethnic groups introduced by the First Great Migration did not disappear within one generation. It is also remarkable that the intergenerational correlation between the average skills of immigrants and their children was roughly constant through the entire twentieth century.[21] At least half of the wage gap between any two ethnic groups in the first generation persisted into the second, regardless of whether the immigrants arrived in the early 1900s, prior to 1940, or in the 1960s. This historical experience suggests that half of the sizable skill differentials that exist among the immigrant groups in the Second Great Migration will likely persist into the second generation.

The Grandchildren of the First Great Migration

To determine if the ethnic skill differentials introduced by the First Great Migration continued beyond the second generation, one can move forward in time to about 1985 and assess how third-generation workers performed in the U.S. labor market at that time. The sample of grandchildren from the First Great Migration is drawn from the General Social Surveys.[22] The sample includes persons who are U.S.-born and have U.S.-born parents, but have at least one foreign-born grandparent. All respondents in this survey were asked to report their ancestry. One can then use the self-reported ethnic background to classify the worker into one of the ethnic groups that made up the First Great Migration.[23]

There clearly exist some skill differences among third-generation ethnic groups—although these differences are far smaller than the ones observed in the first and second generations (see Figure 7-4). Even after three-quarters of a century, however, one can still see a positive correlation between the average skills of the original immigrant groups and the average skills of the corresponding third-generation ethnic groups. The trend line linking educational attainment across generations indicates that a 20 percentage point differential in literacy rates among immigrant groups in 1910 is associated with about a half-year difference in educational attainment among the third-generation ethnic groups in 1985.[24] Recall that a 20 percentage point difference in literacy rates in 1910 implied a one-year difference in the educational attainment among second-generation groups. In effect, the regression toward the mean that occurs between the second and third generations cuts the remaining skill differential between any two ethnic groups by half.

Similarly, the trend line linking wages across the generations suggests that 22 percent of the wage gap observed between any two groups in the immigrant generation persisted into the third. Recall that roughly half of the wage gap between any two immigrant groups disappears between the first and second generations. It seems that about half of what remains in the second generation disappears between the second and the third.

The historical record suggests one broad generalization. The "half-life" of ethnic skill differentials is roughly one generation—roughly half of the ethnic differences in skills disappears in each generation. Put differently, a 20 percentage point wage gap among ethnic groups in the immigrant generation implies a 10-point gap among second-generation groups, and a 5-point gap among third-generation groups. In other words, the intergenerational correlation linking the average skills of ethnic groups between any two generations is about .5, and this correlation is roughly constant over time.

The conclusion that ethnic skill differentials have a half-life of one generation has important implications for any assessment of the long-run impact of the Second Great Migration. In 1990, some immigrant groups earned substantially more than other groups. For instance, Canadian immigrants earned twice as much as Mexican immigrants and 75 percent more than Haitian immigrants, while Italian immigrants earned 70 more than Laotian immigrants and 50 percent more than Chinese immigrants.

What does the historical experience suggest about the relative economic status of the descendants of today's disadvantaged immigrant groups? If the historical pattern holds, the third-generation descendants of today's Canadian immigrants will earn about 25 percent more than the descendants of today's Mexican or Haitian immigrants around the year 2070.

Is this rate of social mobility high or low? The answer depends on one's perspective. It seems that it might take over a century for the huge ethnic skill differentials introduced by the Second Great Migration to disappear. In the overall scheme of things, this is not a very long time. In the social and political context of the United States, however, one hundred years is a long

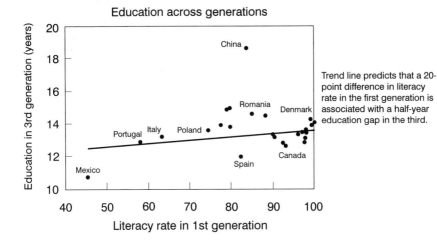

Education across generations

Trend line predicts that a 20-point difference in literacy rate in the first generation is associated with a half-year education gap in the third.

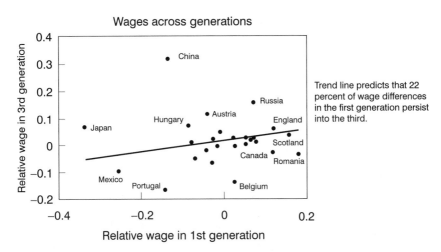

Wages across generations

Trend line predicts that 22 percent of wage differences in the first generation persist into the third.

FIGURE 7-4. The grandchildren of the First Great Migration.

Source: George J. Borjas, "Long-Run Convergence of Ethnic Skills Differentials: The Children and Grandchildren of the Great Migration," *Industrial and Labor Relations Review* 47 (July 1994), p. 569.

Notes. The relative wage gives the log wage differential between a particular group and the typical worker in the labor market at that point in time. The trend lines come from regressions that are (approximately) weighted by the sample size of the national origin group.

time indeed. In the past, ethnic and racial differences in socioeconomic outcomes have profoundly changed social and political dynamics, and have had far-reaching repercussions. If nothing else, the Second Great Migration has set the stage for yet another spin in this unpredictable game of ethnic roulette.

The Social Mobility of African Americans

Many observers often contrast the historical experience of immigrant progress in the twentieth century to that of the African American population—with the immigrant path typically seen as the "model" of social mobility. It is typically claimed that while immigrants were able to improve their economic situation, black economic status remained relatively stagnant.[25] This differential pattern of social mobility is sometimes attributed to racial discrimination and other constraints that prevented blacks from having full access to the opportunities afforded immigrants.

Blacks started out the twentieth century with a much greater economic disadvantage than the immigrants who made up the First Great Migration. In 1910, only 68 percent of blacks were literate, as compared to 87 percent of immigrants and 96 percent of white natives. Similarly, blacks earned about 27 percent less than immigrants and 34 percent less than white natives. In fact, of the thirty-two national origin groups that made up the bulk of the First Great Migration, only one (Japanese immigrants) earned less than blacks. The African American population clearly had a lot more catching up to do.

The trend lines linking the skills of immigrants to those of their descendants can be used to predict how blacks would have performed if they had experienced the same intergenerational progress as the immigrant groups. By comparing this prediction to what blacks actually experienced, one can then determine if black progress differed significantly from that of immigrants.

If an immigrant group had started out in 1910 with a 68 percent literacy rate—similar to that of blacks—the trend line in Figure 7-3 predicts that the children of this immigrant group would have had three more years of schooling than blacks by 1940.[26] In other words, blacks experienced much less social mobility—in terms of educational attainment—than immigrants who shared the same initial conditions. Similarly, an immigrant group that had the same initial wage disadvantage as blacks in 1910 would have earned about 25 percent more than blacks by 1940. Again, blacks experienced substantially less economic progress than the white ethnic groups.

It turns out, however, that these differences in social mobility narrow substantially when the prediction is conducted over the entire 1910–85 period. If an immigrant group had started out in 1910 with the black economic disadvantage, the children in the third generation would have had one more year of schooling and earned only about 3 percent more than blacks actually did.

Clearly, there was a fundamental shift in the process driving the social mobility of black households in the period after World War II. This shift is probably related to the desegregation of schools, the rising quality of educational opportunities for black children, the enactment and enforcement of civil rights legislation, and the migration of blacks from the rural South to manufacturing jobs in northern cities.[27] All of these changes improved the economic situation for black workers, and evened out the playing field. Because of these historical events, there is little evidence to support the hypothesis that the social mobility of the children and grandchildren of immigrant households greatly surpassed that of the African American population over the course of the twentieth century.

WELFARE USE ACROSS GENERATIONS

By now, there is little doubt that skill differences across ethnic groups persist for at least three generations. It is reasonable to suspect that ethnic differences in many other socioeconomic traits may also persist over time. One particular outcome that plays a crucial role in the immigration debate is immigrant participation in welfare programs. As I showed in the last chapter, there are huge differences in welfare use among national origin groups, raising the possibility that many of these differences will be transmitted to the second generation, and perhaps making some immigrant groups long-run captives of the welfare state.

Although it is too early to establish how the children of the Second Great Migration will adapt to the presence of generous welfare benefits, the available evidence does not paint an optimistic picture: ethnic differences in welfare use tend to persist across generations.

In 1970, there were sizable differences in welfare use among the ethnic groups in the immigrant population. By 1998, there was similar dispersion in the second generation (see Figure 7-5). For example, only 2 percent of second-generation households originating in India received cash benefits, as compared to 9 percent for households originating in Honduras, and 14 percent for households originating in Mexico.[28] In fact, the figure shows that the same ethnic groups have a high chance of receiving cash benefits in both the first and second generations. The trend line linking welfare use in the two generations implies that a 10 percentage point difference in welfare use between any two groups in the first generation is associated with an 8.2-point difference in the second.[29] The intergenerational correlation in welfare use, therefore, is far stronger than the intergenerational correlation in educational attainment or wages, essentially helping to transmit all of the ethnic differences in welfare use from one generation to the next.

Immigration imposes a substantial short-run fiscal burden on natives living in the main immigrant-receiving states, particularly in California. By the late 1990s, about 28 percent of immigrant households in California, as compared to 20 percent of immigrant households outside California, received some type of welfare benefit. It is difficult to predict what will happen to the children of these households because of the major changes enacted in the welfare

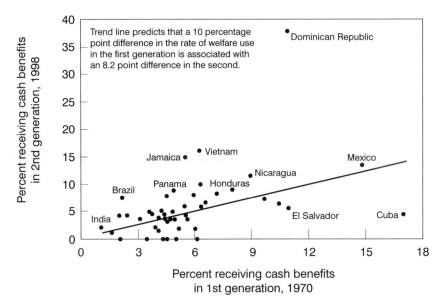

FIGURE 7-5. Welfare participation in first- and second-generation households.

Sources. Calculations from the 1970 Public Use Microdata Sample and the pooled 1996–98 Current Population Surveys (Annual Demographic Files).

Notes. The data refer to households where the head of the household is at least eighteen years old. The trend line comes from a regression that is weighted by the sample size of the national origin group.

reform legislation of 1996. This legislation made fundamental changes in the types of welfare programs that will be made available, in the way that the programs will be funded, and in the eligibility requirements for both immigrants and natives. These changes suggest that the historical record on the intergenerational stickiness of welfare use may provide little information about future trends. Nevertheless, the strong intergenerational link in welfare use indicates that the Second Great Migration will probably impose a long-run fiscal burden on the taxpayers who reside in the main immigrant-receiving states.

THE SIMMERING POT

The key message is simple. Ethnicity matters, and it matters for a very long time. The vivid metaphor of the melting pot—where all the differences across ethnic groups melt away in a relatively short time—is not entirely right. A better metaphor is one of a "simmering pot," where the ethnic differences dissolve slowly.

The Second Great Migration introduced many new ethnic groups into the American mosaic, and also introduced substantial ethnic differences in skills and economic outcomes. How will the simmering pot transform these differences over the course of the twenty-first century? One could easily argue that the historical record does not provide a good guide for predicting the future for many reasons, including the following:

- The structure of the American economy changed dramatically in the last decades of the twentieth century.
- The expansion of the welfare state has radically altered the set of economic incentives facing disadvantaged groups, and the long-run consequences of welfare dependency are still not well understood.
- The Second Great Migration is much more dominated by a few ethnic groups than the First Great Migration ever was. In 1990, for example, Mexicans made up almost 30 percent of the immigrant population. In contrast, Germans and Russians—the two largest groups of the First Great Migration—accounted for only 15 and 12 percent of the immigrant population, respectively. The lack of diversity in the post-1965 immigrant flow may greatly reduce the incentives for assimilation by allowing some ethnic groups to essentially develop separate-enclave economies and societies.
- The First Great Migration was followed by an enforced moratorium on immigration, and this breathing period may have fueled the assimilation process by cutting off the supply of new workers to ethnic enclaves, and by reducing the economic and social contacts between the immigrants and the "old country."
- And the social pressures for assimilation and acculturation have all but disappeared. If anything, the programs that can be classified under the broad umbrella of affirmative action actively encourage persons to retain some types of racial and ethnic identities.

Yet, even if all of these concerns are put aside, the implications of the historical record are still disturbing. The Second Great Migration has set the stage for ethnic differences in economic outcomes that are likely to be a distinctive feature of the American economy throughout the twenty-first century. These ethnic differences will almost surely be dominant features of the social and political landscape in the United States. In other words, the long and bumpy ride has just begun.

Ethnic Capital

THE NOTION THAT social, cultural, and economic differences between natives and immigrants fade over the course of a few generations is the essence of the melting pot metaphor. Over time, the children and grandchildren of immigrants move out of ethnic enclaves, discard their social and cultural ties to the source countries, and experience social and economic mobility. After a few decades, the melting pot "forges" the American-born descendants of the immigrants into new men and women, and they become indistinguishable from the native population.

The evidence presented in the last chapter suggests that a new metaphor is needed to describe the immigrant experience in the long run—a "simmering pot" where ethnic differences dissolve slowly over time. The historical record of earlier immigrant waves shows that over half of the skill differentials between any two ethnic groups in the first generation persists into the second, and over half of what remains in the second persists into the third.

The conclusion that ethnicity "sticks" seems to contradict a large academic literature that examines the socioeconomic links between parents and children.[1] These studies typically find that the correlation between various measures of parental socioeconomic achievement—such as education and earnings—and the children's achievement may not be very strong. Typically, only about 20 to 40 percent of the differences in achievement between any two parents persist into the next generation.

The evidence presents a puzzle. How can one reconcile the relatively weak transmission that takes place between parents and children with the relatively strong transmission in ethnic socioeconomic characteristics? In other words, how can it be that only about 20 to 40 percent of parental differences in skills are transmitted to the children, but at least half of the ethnic differences in the immigrant generation survive into the second generation?[2]

To solve this puzzle, I will argue that a person's ethnic background—*in and of itself*—influences the process of social mobility. In particular, the skills of the next generation depend not only on what parents do but also on the characteristics of the ethnic environment where the children are raised. A highly advantaged ethnic environment—where most parents are college graduates, for example—imbues the children who grow up in that environment with valuable characteristics that enhance the children's socioeconomic achievement later in life. In contrast, disadvantaged ethnic environments—where most parents may be high school dropouts or welfare recipients—imbue the children raised in those environments with characteristics that impede future socioeconomic achievement. In effect, the ethnic environment is like glue in the process of social mobility, ensuring that the average characteristics of the ethnic group do not change much from generation to generation.

WHAT IS ETHNIC CAPITAL?

As I have just noted, there is an empirical puzzle to reconcile: about 20 to 40 percent of the skill differences between parents are typically transmitted to their children, but at least half of the average skill differential between any two ethnic groups persists into the next generation.

One way of making sense of this conflicting evidence is to recognize that ethnicity matters—above and beyond what parents do for their children. A child's education, occupation, and earnings, for instance, are partly determined by the investments that parents make. Many parents devote a large amount of time and effort to investing in their children's human capital. The parents read stories at bedtime, they help with homework, and they provide valuable information about (and connections to) particular types of jobs. Such parental activities typically improve the children's socioeconomic outcomes.[3]

Parents also allocate substantial financial resources to their children. Many parents choose to live in neighborhoods that offer better public schools— and pay dearly for their choice, because housing in those neighborhoods is typically more expensive. Some parents send their children to exclusive private schools or hire tutors to help in the children's intellectual development. All of these activities can be viewed as investments in the children's human capital, investments that presumably increase the child's economic potential later on.

These parental activities create the links in the chain connecting the socioeconomic achievements of parents and children. Skilled parents typically earn more and can better afford to invest in their children's human capital. Skilled parents typically live in better neighborhoods; they send their kids to private schools; they hire tutors; and they engage in many other costly activities that augment the children's human capital. In the end, it is reasonable to suspect that the children of highly skilled parents will also tend to be highly skilled, generating the positive intergenerational correlation that is so often observed within the family.[4]

The influences that affect a child's socioeconomic development, however, are not confined to those that are transmitted within the household. In other words, parental inputs are not the only factors that determine how children perform in school and in the labor market. Ethnic influences also matter.

To illustrate, consider two hypothetical families. Suppose that each of these two families has a husband, a wife, and a child and that the husband and wife are both high school graduates. In fact, suppose that the families are alike in *almost* every respect—the parents do the same kinds of jobs, they have the same earnings, and so on. The two families, however, differ in one key characteristic: their ethnicity. The families belong to different ethnic groups and expose their children to different ethnic influences. The parents in the first family were born in Mexico and live in one of the many barrios sprinkled across the eastern Los Angeles basin. The parents in the second family were born in Korea, and they live in one of the Korean enclaves located in Orange County, just south of Los Angeles. Because both families "look alike" in terms of parental socioeconomic status, one might expect that their children would also tend to look alike. In other words, the children should complete about the same number of years of schooling and face roughly similar labor market opportunities.

This expectation, however, hinges crucially on the idea that parental influences are the only factors that determine the child's socioeconomic development. It seems reasonable to suspect that the children in these two families might turn out quite differently because they belong to different ethnic groups and are being exposed to different ethnic experiences. The two ethnic groups, for instance, may differ in their attitudes towards education and work. Workers in the two ethnic groups certainly differ in their occupational distributions, so that each child is getting different messages about the types of work that people "usually" do, as well as making different types of job connections. And the two groups provide different types of role models as the children go about their everyday activities within the ethnic enclave.

Define *ethnic capital* as the whole set of ethnic characteristics—including culture, attitudes, and economic opportunities—that the children in particular ethnic groups are exposed to. I want to argue the obvious: ethnic capital influences the socioeconomic development of children.[5]

To illustrate the link between ethnic capital and social mobility, return to the hypothetical Mexican and Korean families. Even though the parents in these two families are high school graduates, the child in the Mexican household will likely grow up in an ethnic enclave where many of the neighbors are high school dropouts and where few of the child's friends go on to college. In contrast, the child in the Korean household will likely grow up in an area where many neighbors have some college education and where many of the child's friends will go on to college.

If ethnic capital matters—in other words, if exposure to different types of ethnic influences has an effect on social and economic development—the two children in this hypothetical example are on different socioeconomic paths, and these paths will lead to very different life experiences. The Mexican child will be continually exposed to the cultural and economic contacts that are common among less educated workers, while the Korean child will be exposed to the contacts that are common among college graduates. The continual exposure to a particular type of ethnic capital tends to "pull" the child toward the average or norm in that ethnic group. In other words, ethnic capital is like a magnet—attracting the child toward the socioeconomic outcomes experienced by the typical person in the particular ethnic group. In the end, even though both children come from households that have a similar socioeconomic background, the Mexican child will have a larger chance of dropping out from high school and the Korean child will have a larger chance of going on to college.

Ethnic capital, in effect, puts the brakes on social mobility. The more important ethnic capital is, the more likely that a gap in educational attainment will show up among children who belong to different ethnic groups—even if the parents have comparable skills. In addition, the more important ethnic capital is, the more likely that the gap in the average skills of ethnic groups will persist across generations. Because the children of particular ethnic groups tend to follow the *group's* footsteps, ethnic capital provides the mechanism that lowers the flame under the melting pot from a full boil to a slow simmer.

The idea that ethnic capital matters sheds some light on the intergenerational link in educational attainment between parents and children, as well as on the link in many other socioeconomic characteristics. For instance, ethnic groups tend to cluster in particular occupations. In 1990, 9 percent of Mexican immigrant men were farm workers, 5 percent were construction laborers, and 4 percent were janitors and cleaners. In contrast, 7 percent of Korean immigrant men were supervisors and proprietors, 6 percent were managers and administrators, and 4 percent were postsecondary teachers.[6] These ethnic differences in occupational choice imbue the ethnic environment with particular types of information and job contacts about employment opportunities. As a result, ethnic capital could easily explain why the different career choices made by ethnic groups persist over time.

It is also well known that many of the friends in a child's social circle have the same ethnic background as the child. A sociological study of social contacts among U.S.-born white children in upstate New York indicated that half of all nonrelated childhood friends belonged to the same ethnic group.[7] These friendships form the peer group or reference group that defines behavioral norms for the child, and obviously influence the child's socioeconomic development.

Friends also matter in more direct ways. They probably provide the best information about all kinds of income opportunities, ranging from job openings to welfare programs to illegal activities. In fact, friends are a key source of job referrals, and these job referrals have a particularly good chance of ending up as successful job contacts.[8] Because our friends know our likes and dislikes, a friend's job referral has much greater value than an ad in the classified pages. Similarly, employers are more willing to take a closer look at a job applicant when the applicant comes with a recommendation from someone the employer already knows or employs. The link among ethnicity, friendships, and job contacts probably explains why members of particular ethnic groups often "take over" employment in particular factories or occupations. In Houston, for example, a relatively small migrant flow of Guatemalan

Mayas that began with the migration of a single person in 1978 held most of the maintenance jobs in a large supermarket chain by the late 1980s.[9]

The impact of ethnic capital on social mobility is an example of what economists call "spillover effects," or externalities. An externality occurs when a decision that someone else makes—such as how much schooling to attain, which occupations to enter—spills over and affects us. Because of the close cultural and social links that often exist within ethnic groups, ethnicity has a spillover effect on the socioeconomic achievement of persons in that group.

Ethnic capital is just a special type of what has come to be known as "social capital" in modern sociology. The late sociologist James Coleman argued that the culture in which the individual is raised, or social capital, can be thought of as a form of human capital common to all members of that peer group.[10] Social capital has spillover effects because it alters the social and economic opportunities available to members of the group.

William Julius Wilson's classic study of the black underclass in *The Truly Disadvantaged* also uses the notion of spillover effects to explain the poor social and economic outcomes experienced by many blacks in the United States.[11] Wilson argues that the economic situation of young blacks in poor neighborhoods is worsened because they are not exposed to "mainstream role models that help keep alive the perception that education is meaningful, that steady employment is a viable alternative to welfare, and that family stability is the norm."[12] He concludes: "In a neighborhood with a paucity of regularly employed families and with the overwhelming majority of families having spells of long-term joblessness, people experience a social isolation that excludes them from the job network system that permeates other neighborhoods and that is so important in learning about or being recommended for jobs that become available in various parts of the city."[13]

Finally, many recent studies of economic development—collectively known as "the new growth theory"—use the notion of spillover effects to explain why some countries grow richer, while other countries remain poor.[14] These studies argue that high levels of human capital within a country spill over onto the decisions of other persons in that economy, making them more productive and encouraging even more human capital accumulation and investment in research and development. As a result, countries with high levels of human capital can keep their economic advantage over long periods of time, while poorer countries fall further behind.

I began the discussion of the concept of ethnic capital by noting an empirical puzzle: the intergenerational correlation between the skills of parents and children is relatively small, but the average skill differences among ethnic groups tend to persist across generations. Ethnic capital provides a simple explanation of this puzzle. Ethnic influences have spillover effects on members of the ethnic group, and these influences can have a substantial impact on the group's social mobility—above and beyond the impact of parental influence. As I noted earlier, ethnic capital acts like a magnet. It makes it harder for persons belonging to a particular ethnic group to deviate from that group's norm.

Finally, it is worth emphasizing that the intergenerational transmission of ethnic capital is a double-edged sword. The spillovers that occur within ethnic groups help transmit *both* good and bad socioeconomic characteristics. The spillover effects might increase the educational attainment of the children and improve their employment prospects when they grow up. Spillover effects, however, can also help transmit welfare dependence or a higher incidence of teenage pregnancy. Regardless of whether the traits that are being transmitted through these ethnic spillovers are beneficial or harmful, the end result is the same: ethnic capital helps ensure that ethnic differences persist across generations.

EVIDENCE ON ETHNIC CAPITAL

Is there any evidence that the socioeconomic performance of children depends not only on parental inputs but also on the characteristics of the ethnic environment where the child was raised? More precisely, do children belonging to more advantaged ethnic groups do better than children belonging to less advantaged groups—even after adjusting for differences in the skills of the parents?

Two widely used surveys, the General Social Surveys (GSS) and the National Longitudinal Surveys of Youth (NLSY), provide detailed information on the skills of the child, the skills of the parents, and the ethnic background of the household.[15] These surveys report the respondent's educational attainment and occupation as well as the educational attainment and occupation of the respondent's father.[16] The occupational data can be used to calculate a measure of "occupational earnings" by assigning each worker the average earnings of persons employed in the particular occupation.[17] Ethnic capital is then defined as either the average education or the average wage of the ethnic group in the parental generation.

Not surprisingly, there is a great deal of dispersion in educational attainment and wages across ethnic groups in these data. The important question, however, is whether these differences persist across generations because of the influence of ethnic capital.

It is easy to illustrate the influence of both parental characteristics and ethnic capital on social mobility (see Figure 8-1).[18] The top panel of the figure—where each point in the diagram represents a father-child pair in the General Social Surveys—relates the children's wage with the father's wage, after adjusting for differences in ethnic background. This figure, in effect, illustrates the link between the wages of fathers and children *within* a particular ethnic group. There is an obvious positive correlation: the children of high-wage fathers tend to earn more. In fact, the trend line suggests that a 10 percent increase in the father's wage raises the child's wage by 1.7 percent.

Put differently, if one compares two parents who belong to the same ethnic group but whose wages differ by 10 percent, the wage of the children in these two families will tend to differ by about 2 percent.

The parent's socioeconomic achievement is not the only factor that determines the child's wage; ethnic capital, or the mean wage of the ethnic group in the parental generation, also matters. The bottom panel of the figure—where each point in the diagram represents an ethnic group—shows ethnic capital at work. This figure shows the connection between the ethnic group's mean wage in the children's generation and its mean wage in the parent's generation—after adjusting the data so that all fathers in all ethnic groups have the same wage. Even after adjusting for differences in the father's wage, children belonging to high-wage ethnic groups earn more. The trend line indicates that a 10 percent increase in the mean wage of an ethnic group in the parental generation increases the wage of the children in that group by about 2.9 percent. It seems that the spillovers that occur within the ethnic group are at least as important as the transmission of skills from father to child.

Finally, the *sum* of these two effects—the correlation between the children's skills and parental skills, and the correlation between the children's skills and ethnic capital—has an important interpretation. It turns out that this sum measures the intergenerational correlation in the *mean* skills of the ethnic group—precisely the type of intergenerational correlation that I discussed at length in the previous chapter.[19] If, on average, there is a 10 percent wage gap between two ethnic groups in the parental generation, the data indicate that there will be a 4.6 percent wage gap between these two groups in the children's generation (the sum of 1.7 percent and 2.9 percent). In short, about half of the difference in the mean wage between any two ethnic groups in one generation persists into the next generation. And about half of this persistence can be attributed to the spillover effects of ethnicity on social mobility.

Figure 8-2 summarizes some of the additional evidence available on the role played by ethnic capital in the process of social mobility.[20] For instance, 70 percent of the differences in the average wage among ethnic groups in the National Longitudinal Surveys are transmitted from generation to generation, with about half of this "stickiness" attributable to the spillover effects of ethnic capital. Similarly, 50 percent of the differences in educational attainment across ethnic groups in the General Social Surveys survive across generations, and half of this persistence occurs because of ethnic capital.

So what is the bottom line? Skill differentials across ethnic groups tend to persist across generations, and much of this persistence arises because ethnicity matters, and it matters above and beyond parental inputs. In an important sense, ethnicity is like glue: it has spillover effects that stick for a long time. These ethnic spillover effects help "prop up" the skills of persons who belong to advantaged groups, slowing down the natural process of regression toward the mean. The same spillover effects help "keep down" the skills of

Relation between the wages of fathers and children,
adjusted for differences in ethnic background

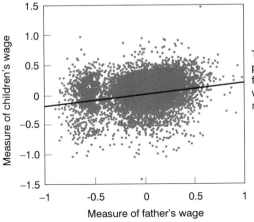

Trend line predicts that a 10
percent wage gap between two
fathers leads to a 1.7 percent
wage gap between their
respective children.

Relation between the average wage of the
children in an ethnic group and ethnic capital,
adjusted for differences in parental skills

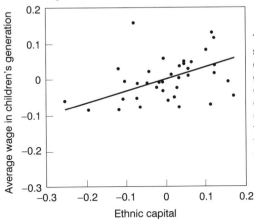

Two children have equally
skilled parents but belong to
different ethnic groups. The
groups differ in their ethnic
capital; on average, one group
earns 10 percent more than the
other. The trend line predicts
that there will be a 2.9 percent
wage gap between the two
children.

FIGURE 8-1. The link among children's wages, father's wages, and ethnic capital.
   Sources: George J. Borjas, "Immigrant Skills and Ethnic Spillovers," *Journal of Population Economics* 7 (June 1994), p. 107. The data are drawn from the General Social Surveys.
   Notes: The regression model relates the children's log wage to the log wage of the father
and to ethnic capital, defined as the mean log wage of the ethnic group in the parental
generation. The regression also controls for age and gender. The top panel illustrates the
relation between the children's wage and the father's wage, adjusted for differences in
ethnic background and all other variables in the regression model. The bottom panel illustrates the relations between the children's wage and ethnic capital, adjusted for differences
in parental skills and all other variables in the model.

Measure of skills

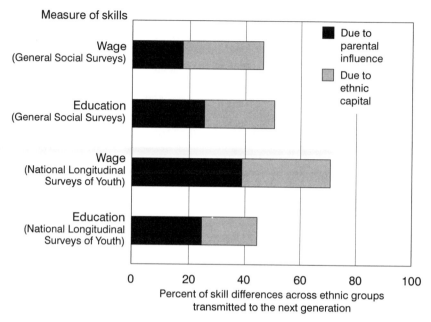

FIGURE 8-2. The impact of parental skills and ethnic capital on the children's skills.
  Sources: The evidence from the General Social Surveys is drawn from George J. Borjas, "Immigrant Skills and Ethnic Spillovers," *Journal of Population Economics 7* (June 1994), p. 107. The evidence from the National Longitudinal Surveys of Youth is drawn from George J. Borjas, "Ethnicity, Neighborhoods, and Human-Capital Externalities," *American Economic Review* 85 (June 1995), p. 383.
  Note: Depending on whether the socioeconomic outcome is educational attainment or the wage, ethnic capital is defined as the mean education or as the mean log wage of the ethnic group in the parent's generation.

persons belonging to disadvantaged groups, again arresting the natural process of regression toward the mean. In effect, ethnic capital simultaneously creates both a glass ceiling and a glass floor, preventing workers from deviating too much from the norms of their ethnic group. In an important sense, ethnic capital makes it harder to escape the economic destiny implied by one's ethnic background.

Ethnic Capital across Generations

As social, cultural, and economic assimilation occurs, the importance of the ethnic enclave diminishes, exposure to ethnic role models becomes less frequent, and there is more intermarriage across ethnic groups.[21] One might then expect that the children of later generations would be getting a more mixed ethnic "signal" and the link between ethnic capital and social mobility would weaken and eventually disappear.

  The data collected by the General Social Surveys can differentiate workers who belong to two distinct generations of U.S.-born workers: those in the second generation (who had at least one parent born abroad) and those in the third generation (whose parents were born in the United States but who had at least one grandparent born abroad). One can then estimate the intergenerational correlations between children's socioeconomic outcomes and parental skills and ethnic capital for each of these two generations separately.

Not surprisingly, ethnic spillovers play an important role in the socioeconomic development of the children of immigrants, and a weaker role in the development of the grandchildren of immigrants (see Figure 8-3).[22] Almost 60 percent of the differences in educational attainment among ethnic groups in the first generation, for instance, are transmitted to their children, with almost three-quarters of this transmission attributable to ethnic capital. In contrast, half of the differences in educational attainment in the second generation are transmitted to the third, but only about half of this correlation can be attributed to ethnic capital. Although the evidence is consistent with the notion that ethnic spillovers become less important over time, it is worth noting that these spillovers seem to matter even in the third generation. Put differently, even after the immigrant family has been in the United States for several decades, the "norms" of the ethnic group still influence the process of social mobility.

ETHNIC CAPITAL AND WELFARE DEPENDENCY

We have seen that ethnic capital influences the social mobility of ethnic groups in important ways. Even after adjusting for differences in parental skills, children who belong to disadvantaged ethnic groups will probably have less education and earn less than children who belong to more advantaged ethnic groups.

This is not the end of the story, however. The same types of ethnic spillovers that alter the incentives to go to school or enter particular occupations will influence many other aspects of socioeconomic achievement.[23] I have already established that there is a great deal of variation in welfare use among ethnic groups in the immigrant generation, and that these ethnic differences in welfare use seem to persist between the first and second generations.

Can the intergenerational persistence of ethnic differences in welfare use be attributed to ethnic spillovers? Put differently, do ethnic spillovers play an important role in creating and sustaining a "culture of dependence" in a particular ethnic group?[24] The development of such a culture would have disturbing implications for the social and economic impact of the Second Great Migration in the long run—and would surely play a major role in the direction of immigration policy.

The data collected by the National Longitudinal Surveys of Youth allow a partial investigation of the link between ethnicity and welfare dependence. Respondents in this survey were fourteen to twenty-two years old at the time the survey began in 1979, and 80 percent of these "children" lived with at

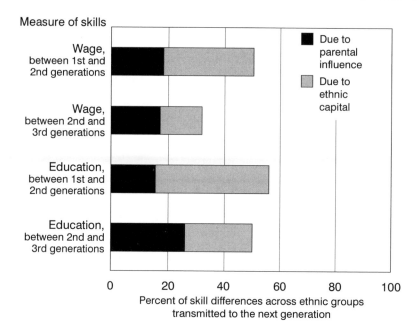

Measure of skills

FIGURE 8-3. The changing impact of ethnic capital across generations.

Sources: George J. Borjas, "Immigrant Skills and Ethnic Spillovers," *Journal of Population Economics* 7 (June 1994), p. 109. The data are drawn from the General Social Surveys.

Note: Depending on whether the socioeconomic outcome is educational attainment or the wage, ethnic capital is defined as the mean education or as the mean log wage of the ethnic group in the parent's generation.

least one of their parents at the time of the initial survey. In this subsample of children who initially lived with their parents, the survey also collected information on whether the *parents* received welfare benefits in 1979.[25] The respondents in the survey were interviewed annually throughout much of the 1980s and 1990s, which yielded information on their life experiences long after they had left their parents' residence and established their own households.

It turns out that there is a strong positive correlation between the children's receipt of AFDC benefits in 1989 and that of the parents in 1979—even after adjusting for measures of parental skill and ethnic background. A 10 percentage point increase in the probability that the parents received welfare in 1979 translates to a 1.5 percentage point increase in the probability that the child received benefits in 1989.[26]

It also turns out that ethnic capital—defined as the fraction of the ethnic group that received welfare in the parental generation—has a far stronger effect on the children's propensity to receive AFDC benefits.[27] A 10 percentage point difference in the rate of welfare use between any two ethnic groups generates a 5.9 percentage point difference in the probability that the chil-

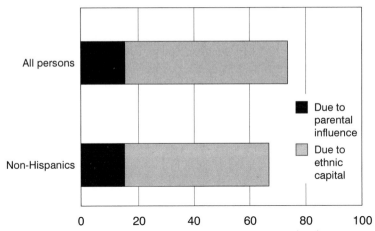

FIGURE 8-4. The intergenerational transmission of welfare recipiency.

Sources: George J. Borjas and Glenn T. Sueyoshi, "Ethnicity and the Intergenerational Transmission of Welfare Dependency," *Research in Labor Economics* 16 (1997), pp. 280, 283. The data are drawn from the National Longitudinal Surveys of Youth.

Notes: The correlations are obtained from regression models that relate the person's welfare participation in 1989 to whether the parents received welfare in 1979, and to ethnic capital, defined as the welfare participation rate of the ethnic group in the parental generation. The regression models also adjust for age, gender, the educational attainment of the father, an indicator of whether the parents worked in 1979, the mean educational attainment of the ethnic group in the parental generation, and the mean labor force participation rate of the ethnic group in the parental generation.

dren of these two groups receive benefits—even after adjusting for whether or not the parents were enrolled in the program in 1979.[28] In short, children who grow up in an ethnic environment where welfare use is widespread are themselves very likely to eventually enter the welfare system.

The sum of these two correlations has an important interpretation: it gives the "total" intergenerational correlation in the proportion of the ethnic group that receives welfare (see Figure 8-4). Suppose that the rate of welfare use in one ethnic group in the parental generation exceeds the rate of use in another group by 10 percentage points. The available evidence then suggests that the welfare recipiency rates of these two groups will be 7.4 percentage points apart in the next generation. In other words, about three-quarters of the ethnic differences in the receipt of AFDC benefits survived between one generation and the next, and much of this persistence occurred because ethnic spillovers help transmit some type of "attachment" to the welfare system across generations.[29]

It is important to stress that even though the evidence clearly indicates that ethnic differences in welfare recipiency are "sticky," it does not state *why* this stickiness arises. It may be that enrollment in some welfare programs—like entering particular types of occupations—provides information that the people who live outside of the ethnic environment are simply unaware of. It may also be that long-term exposure to welfare programs reduces the stigma that inhibits many potential participants from entering the system in the first place.

Regardless of why the stickiness arises, the evidence is clear. First, the children of welfare households are more likely to become welfare recipients. Second, and equally important, growing up in an ethnic environment characterized by welfare dependence probably has a large effect on welfare participation in the next generation. It seems that a disadvantaged ethnic environment has harmful consequences on members of that group for a very long time.

An Alternative Interpretation: Measurement Error

Because the finding that ethnic spillovers influence social mobility has potentially important implications, it is worth considering if the evidence can be attributed to a spurious correlation between ethnic capital and the skills of children. Such a spurious correlation could easily arise if parental skills are measured with error.

The measurement error interpretation of the evidence presented in this chapter goes as follows. It is well known that children err frequently when they attempt to report retroactively their parent's socioeconomic achievement, such as the parent's education, occupation, or earnings. This type of measurement error would typically generate a statistical bias, and the badly measured variable would seem to have little impact on socioeconomic outcomes. In other words, because there is so much "noise" in the measure of parental skills, the observed correlation between parental skills and children's socioeconomic achievement will probably understate the true correlation.

I defined ethnic capital as the average socioeconomic achievement of members of the ethnic group in the parental generation. This measure of ethnic capital effectively "averages out" skills over a group of people who are roughly similar because they all share the same ethnic background. Even though any particular child in that group would report the parent's skills with error, the average across all members of the group washes out some of the noise. As a result, ethnic capital could have an impact on social mobility not because ethnic spillovers matter but because ethnic capital may be a good proxy for parental outcomes.

This interpretation of the results is particularly relevant in light of recent evidence that measurement error in parental skills does, in fact, lead to a substantial understatement of the correlation between the earnings of fathers and sons. Prior to these "revisionist" studies, it was generally believed that the intergenerational correlation between fathers and sons was on the order of .2.[30] The recent studies, which typically average parental earnings over a number of years, report much higher intergenerational correlations, on the order of .3 to .4.[31]

Although it is very difficult to isolate the role played by measurement error in generating the correlation between social mobility and ethnic capital, it is unlikely that the impact of ethnic capital can be attributed solely to measurement error. For example, much of the evidence reported in this chapter suggests that ethnic capital matters at least as much as parental skills in the social mobility process.

As a purely mathematical fact, it turns out that ethnic capital could not be that important unless there is a *lot* of noise in measures of parental skills. In fact, to explain the results solely through measurement error, one would have to argue that over half of the variation in observed measures of parental skills—such as the father's education or wage—must be due to measurement error, rather than to true differences in skills across parents.[32] Put differently, a measurement error interpretation of the evidence would probably require much more error in the data on parental skills that what is typically found there.[33]

The construction of the NLSY data also allows the use of an alternative method for netting out the spurious correlation induced by measurement error. Because of the way that the survey was collected, the data contain a large number of siblings: 27 percent of the respondents have one sibling in the sample, and an additional 19 percent have at least two. And each sibling was asked *independently* to report the father's education and earnings, as well as ethnic background.[34]

The correlation among the siblings' responses is high, but it is not perfect. For example, the correlation between one sibling's report of the father's education and the other sibling's report is .9. The availability of several sources of information for parental skills can be used to determine if measurement error biases the findings. The statistical technique essentially uses the several pieces of information available for the same variable (such as the father's education) to correct the estimated correlations for potential sources of misreporting.[35]

Not surprisingly, the correlation between the children's and the father's skills rises after one adjusts for measurement error. In the absence of any adjustment, 3.8 percent of a 10 percent wage gap between any two parents is transmitted to the children. The adjustment for measurement error implies that 4.8 percent of the gap is transmitted to the children.[36] However, the correlation between the children's socioeconomic achievement and ethnic capital barely changes. A 10 percent difference in the average wage of two ethnic groups in the parental generation implies a 3.2 percent wage differential among the children when there is no adjustment for measurement error, and a 3.0 percent differential when the data are adjusted. In short, it is unlikely that measurement error can be used as a scapegoat to explain the existence of a strong correlation between children's socioeconomic outcomes and the "norms" of the ethnic group in the parental generation. A more credible interpretation is simply that ethnic spillovers exist and play an important role.

Summing Up

The evidence linking social mobility and ethnic spillovers raises a number of difficult issues for social policy. Since the 1960s, many localities in the United States have dealt with a related problem—the clustering of minority children in segregated schools—by busing children across neighborhoods. By integrating the school system, busing presumably exposes the minority children to different (and better?) social and economic opportunities than they would face in their isolated ghettos.

Although such a "mixing" could, in principle, benefit society in the long run, it clearly has distributional consequences, and these are precisely the consequences that drive the political debate over the role of immigration and ethnicity in American society. If nothing else, the social, demographic, and political consequences of busing have shown that policies designed to address the impact of ethnic spillovers on social mobility will surely have many unintended consequences.

In the end, the link between ethnic capital and social mobility raises a number of questions that have yet to be addressed in the immigration debate. How should the government respond—*if at all*—to the ethnic spillovers that lower the flame under the melting pot? And, if the government's objective is to speed up the assimilation process, how can it ensure that persons in less advantaged ethnic groups get exposed to more advantaged environments?

CHAPTER 9

Ethnic Ghettos

ETHNIC SPILLOVERS matter—and they seem to matter a lot, accounting for about half of the correlation between the mean skills of ethnic groups across generations. But *why* do ethnic spillovers matter? How exactly are the social, cultural, and economic ties that bind together an ethnic group transmitted across generations?

In this chapter, I argue that ethnic neighborhoods—those geographic concentrations of barrios, ghettos, and enclaves scattered across American cities—are incubators for the intergenerational transmission of ethnic capital.[1] These neighborhoods provide a close-knit and geographically compact community where members of the same ethnic group interact closely and frequently, influencing one another's behavior, marrying one another, and transmitting valuable information about economic opportunities through the social web that makes up the ethnic network. And these spillover effects have crucial implications for a wide array of issues in social policy, ranging from the creation and growth of a social underclass to the study of how distinct cultures and languages can exist and persist in the United States.[2]

Parents know that ethnic spillovers influence social mobility. Because parents care about the well-being of their children, they will choose to live in those neighborhoods that they can afford *and* that offer a particular "menu" of ethnic opportunities—namely, the ethnic traits and socioeconomic contacts they wish to transmit to their children. These parental decisions, in turn, determine how ethnic groups are clustered in the United States, and often ensure that ethnic differences are not quickly eliminated by the melting pot.

This chapter documents a number of related facts. First, there is a lot of ethnic residential segregation in the United States. Not surprisingly, persons of Mexican ancestry live near other persons of Mexican ancestry, persons of Italian ancestry live near other persons of Italian ancestry, and so on. More interesting, however, is the fact that ethnic segregation remains strong across generations. To a remarkable extent, the ethnic characteristics of the neighborhoods where people choose to live resemble those of the neighborhoods where their parents lived. Finally, because few persons in the less advantaged ethnic groups can afford to escape the neighborhoods where they live, ethnic ghettos make it easy for ethnic capital to perpetuate the socioeconomic differences observed across ethnic groups from generation to generation.

In the end, the chapter asks a simple question, Are ethnic ghettos good or bad?[3] This question, however, does not have a simple answer. Ethnic ghettos can be good or bad, *depending on who you are and which group you belong to.*

If one happens to be a highly skilled worker in a highly advantaged ethnic group, ethnic ghettos provide a terrific head start in the economic race: the ethnic spillovers from other members of the ethnic group will greatly benefit the children of that group. However, if one happens to be a less-skilled worker in a disadvantaged ethnic group, ethnic ghettos may be socioeconomic traps: they are hard to escape, and the ethnic spillovers will inevitably hamper the social mobility of the next generation.

ETHNIC SEGREGATION

It is well known that blacks and Hispanics experience a great deal of residential segregation in the United States—and that this "ghettoization" has characterized American neighborhoods for many decades. In 1990, for example, the typical African American lived in a neighborhood where 56 percent of the population was black, and the typical Hispanic lived in a neighborhood that was 42 percent Hispanic.[4] What is less well known is that there is also a great deal of residential segregation among immigrants, among the children of immigrants, and among ethnic groups in general.

The general perception of ethnic residential segregation in policy discussions is imprecise because this type of segregation—unlike that of blacks or Hispanics—is very hard to measure and has not been studied as frequently. To illustrate the pattern of ethnic residential segregation in the United States, for example, one needs information on whether persons are foreign-born, on the ethnic ancestry of persons in the population, and on the characteristics of the neighborhoods where people live.

Because of confidentiality concerns, however, most data surveys in the United States do not report *any* information on the socioeconomic characteristics of the neighborhoods where the survey respondents live. In fact, the last U.S. Census that contained publicly available information on both personal and neighborhood characteristics was a data file constructed from the 1970 enumeration.[5] These data not only contained the personal demographic variables typically available in Census data, such as schooling and earnings, but also grouped individuals into one of 42,950 "neighborhoods." The neighborhoods were contiguous, relatively compact, roughly the size of a Census tract, and had an average population of four thousand persons. This Census file also contained detailed information about the socioeconomic attributes that characterized the neighborhood of residence, such as the fraction of persons who were either first- or second-generation Americans, the fraction of persons who were college graduates, the fraction of persons unemployed, and so on.

One can use these data to document the residential segregation of the first and second generations in 1970.[6] Not surprisingly, there is a great deal of residential segregation in *both* the first and second generations (see Figure 9-1). The average immigrant present in the United States in 1970 resided in a

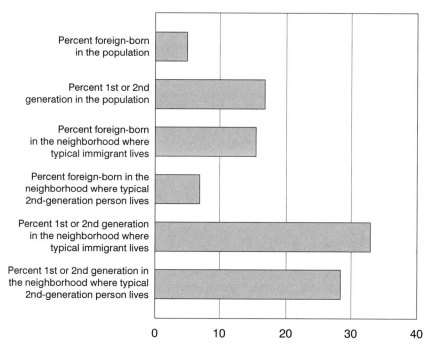

FIGURE 9-1. Residential segregation in the first and second generations, 1970.
Sources: George J. Borjas, "Ethnicity, Neighborhoods, and Human-Capital Externalities," *American Economic Review* 85 (June 1995), p. 368. The data are drawn from the 1970 Public Use Microdata Sample of the U.S. Census (Neighborhood File).
Note: The data refer to persons who are eighteen to sixty-four years old.

neighborhood where 15 percent of the population was foreign-born, even though only 5 percent of the population was foreign-born at that time. Similarly, the typical immigrant lived in a neighborhood where 33 percent of the population was either first- or second-generation, at a time when only 17 percent of the population was first- or second-generation.[7]

The clustering of immigrant families into what can be broadly described as "immigrant neighborhoods" is also apparent in the second generation. The average second-generation American resided in a neighborhood that was 28 percent first- or second-generation. There seems to be little mobility out of these ethnic neighborhoods between the first and second generations.

Because the data do not provide any information on ancestry past the second generation, it is impossible to determine how the pattern of residential segregation changes beyond the second generation for most groups. Such long-term changes, however, can be documented for the Hispanic population, the vast majority of whom are foreign-born or have parents or grandparents who are foreign-born.[8] It turns out that there is a lot of residential segregation in the Hispanic population, even in the third generation (see Figure 9-2). The average Hispanic immigrant lives in a neighborhood that is 35

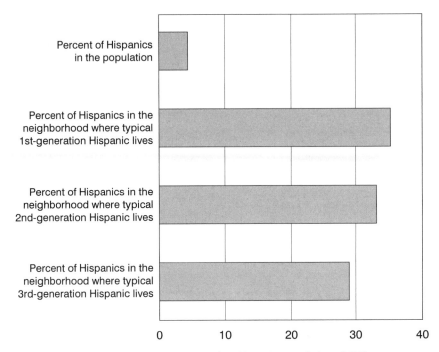

FIGURE 9-2. Residential segregation in the Hispanic population, 1970.
Sources. George J. Borjas, "Ethnicity, Neighborhoods, and Human-Capital Externalities,"
American Economic Review 85 (June 1995), p. 368. The data are drawn from the 1970 Public
Use Microdata Sample of the U.S. Census (Neighborhood File).
Note: The data refer to persons who are between eighteen to sixty-four years old.

percent Hispanic; the second-generation Hispanic lives in one that is 33 percent Hispanic; and the third-generation Hispanic lives in one that is 29 percent Hispanic. In 1970, Hispanics made up only 4 percent of the population.
The clustering of Hispanics into the barrios, therefore, seems to be prevalent
and long lasting.

A major drawback of the Census data is that they portray ethnic residential
segregation as of 1970, just before immigration began its resurgence in the
United States.[9] More recent surveys can be used to update the picture—
although the available surveys tend to have much smaller samples than the
Census data (and hence are less reliable). For example, a specially designed
version of the data contained in the National Longitudinal Surveys of Youth
(NLSY) identifies the subset of persons who resided in the same zip code in
1979. Because the young men and women in this survey were fourteen to
twenty-two years old in 1979, many of the children in the panel were still
living with their parents. These data can be used to determine if these young
persons grew up near other persons who shared the same ethnicity.[10] And,
because the children have been interviewed many times since then, it is also

TABLE 9–1
Residential Segregation for Selected Ethnic Groups, 1979

Ethnic ancestry	Ethnic group's share of the population	Ethnic group's share of the population in the neighborhood where the average person in the group lives	Percent living in "ethnic" neighborhood
Black	14.9	63.6	79.4
Cuban	0.4	33.3	66.7
English	18.9	23.9	22.1
Filipino	0.4	5.0	20.5
German	17.4	25.7	28.4
Irish	11.0	14.3	18.7
Italian	6.2	16.3	49.6
Mexican	4.2	50.3	83.8
Other Hispanic	0.9	9.3	52.3
Polish	3.1	12.8	43.0
Portuguese	0.6	19.7	66.0
Puerto Rican	1.2	29.8	80.2
Russian	0.6	0.3	10.6
Scottish	1.5	4.6	35.2
All groups	—	—	48.0

Sources. George J. Borjas, "To Ghetto or Not to Ghetto: Ethnicity and Residential Segregation," *Journal of Urban Economics* 44 (September 1998), p. 240. The data are drawn from the National Longitudinal Surveys of Youth (NLSY).

Notes. The "ethnic group's share of the population in the neighborhood where the average person lives" should be interpreted as follows: the average black person lives in a neighborhood where 63.6 percent of the people are black, the average Cuban lives in a neighborhood where 33.3 percent of the people are Cuban, and so on. The "percent living in 'ethnic' neighborhood" gives the percent of the group that lives in a neighborhood where the share of the ethnic group in the population is at least twice as large as one would expect from a random sorting.

possible to measure the ethnic composition of the neighborhoods chosen by the children once they grew up and set up their own households.

There is clear evidence of ethnic residential segregation in this survey (see Table 9-1). The average black grew up in a neighborhood that was 64 percent black, the average Mexican in one that was 50 percent Mexican, the average Italian in one that was 16 percent Italian, and the average Portuguese in one that was 20 percent Portuguese. For most of the groups, this clustering is far greater than what one would expect to find if the ethnic and racial groups were randomly distributed across zip codes in the United States.

The survey data can be used to calculate a simple measure of residential segregation for the ethnic group. Define a particular person as living in an ethnically segregated neighborhood if a disproportionately large fraction of the neighborhood's population shares the person's ethnic background. For example, the fraction of persons of Italian ancestry in the national population is about 6 percent. A person of Italian ancestry would be living in an ethnically segregated neighborhood if Italians made up, say, at least *twice* that fraction of the population in the neighborhood—or 12 percent. By this definition, it turns out that 50 percent of the persons of Italian ancestry are living in "Italian neighborhoods." Similarly, persons of Mexican ancestry make up only 4 percent of the national population. Classify a particular Mexican as living in a segregated neighborhood if Mexicans make up at least 8 percent of the neighborhood's population (twice what one would expect if Mexicans were randomly sorted across neighborhoods). By this definition, 84 percent of the Mexicans in the survey grew up in Mexican neighborhoods. In fact, almost half of the persons grew up in segregated neighborhoods—in the sense that the share of the ethnic group in the neighborhood's population was at least twice as large as one would expect from a random sorting.

The available evidence, therefore, indicates that residential segregation is prevalent in the United States. Immigrants and their children tend to cluster in immigrant neighborhoods, and these neighborhoods tend to contain clusters of particular ethnic groups. In an important sense, segregation by race and ethnicity defines the invisible line that creates a neighborhood. These neighborhoods effectively insulate people of similar ethnic backgrounds, and foster a set of cultural attitudes, social contacts, and economic opportunities that affect workers throughout their lives. Ethnic residential segregation provides the building blocks for the social networks that allow ethnic capital to permeate cultural and economic interactions within the ethnic group, and to influence the process of social mobility.

Ethnic Segregation across Generations

The evidence from the 1970 Census suggests that there may be a great deal of "stickiness" in ethnic residential segregation across generations. One can obtain a much better picture of this intergenerational persistence from the data provided by the National Longitudinal Surveys of Youth. Because this survey follows the same persons over time, one can determine how the characteristics of the neighborhood where the child grew up compare to those of the neighborhood where the child eventually ends up.

As noted above, the data began to be collected in 1979, when the young men and women were, on average, eighteen years old. Consider the subsample of young persons who were living with their parents at that time, so that the decision of where to live was clearly made by the parents. By 1992, these persons were, on average, thirty-one years old, and they were making their own decisions about the type of neighborhood where they wished to live and raise *their* children.

It turns out that there is a very strong link between ethnic segregation in the neighborhoods that the parents chose and in the neighborhoods that the children chose once they grew up.[11] For instance, 66 percent of the children who grew up in an ethnically segregated neighborhood lived in an ethnically segregated neighborhood when they grew up. In contrast, only 20 percent of the children who grew up in an integrated neighborhood chose to live in a segregated neighborhood by 1992.[12]

Part of the intergenerational persistence in ethnic segregation arises because the parents (in 1979) and the children (in 1992) may have been living in exactly the same neighborhood. In fact, about 39 percent of the persons in the survey lived in the same zip code in those two years. The ethnic composition of most neighborhoods probably changes very slowly over time, and it is costly for persons to leave the neighborhood where they grew up—both financially and in terms of the dislocation suffered when persons leave an area where they have well-established social and economic networks. As a result, the intergenerational correlation in ethnic segregation arises partly because of the inertia in the residential location decision.

It turns out, however, that there is a strong link in ethnic segregation even among households that lived in different zip codes in the two years (so that the parents made a particular residential choice in 1979 and the children made a different choice in 1992). About 57 percent of the children who moved out of a segregated neighborhood ended up in a segregated neighborhood, as compared to only about 21 percent of the children who grew up in an integrated neighborhood. In short, parents and children make residential location choices that are not all that different in at least one key characteristic, the ethnic composition of the neighborhood.

ETHNIC CAPITAL AND NEIGHBORHOOD EFFECTS

"Neighborhood effects"—as the term is generally used in academic studies—are the impact of certain socioeconomic characteristics of the neighborhood where persons grow up or currently live on social and economic outcomes. Suppose, for example, that a particular racial or ethnic group now lives in a neighborhood where most families receive public assistance, so that welfare dependence is an accepted part of the social and cultural milieu. Because of that group's continued exposure to welfare use, its members might feel little social stigma when applying for and receiving public assistance. Moreover, their neighbors would be very helpful in the process: they could provide a lot of information about the eligibility rules, about the types of programs available, and about the way the game is played at the welfare office—which social workers to approach, say, and which to avoid. In the end, persons in that group will probably have a disproportionately high chance of receiving public assistance simply because they live in a neighborhood where a disproportionate number of families already receive welfare.

The role played by these types of neighborhood effects in determining many socioeconomic outcomes is currently the subject of intensive research—and contentious debate—in social science.[13] The typical study correlates how a particular person behaves—in terms, for example, of educational attainment or criminal activity—with measures of educational attainment or criminal activity in the neighborhood where he or she grew up or currently resides. In effect, the local environment is viewed as a form of social capital that affects the behavior of all persons residing in that neighborhood. And, in fact, there is substantial evidence linking neighborhood characteristics to teenage pregnancy, criminal behavior, educational attainment, and welfare recipiency, although there is a great deal of disagreement over how to interpret this evidence.

The data clearly indicate that ethnic groups cluster in particular neighborhoods: Italians live near other Italians, Portuguese near other Portuguese, Cubans near other Cubans, and so on. Moreover, there is a lot of similarity in the socioeconomic outcomes of persons within ethnic groups. Most Indian immigrants, for example, have college diplomas, while most Salvadoran immigrants are high school dropouts. A neighborhood's population, therefore, not only tends to be characterized by a particular type of ethnic "look," but also by a particular type of socioeconomic class. When choosing where to live, persons cluster not only by ethnicity but also by skill level or class, so that unskilled ethnic groups tend to mix together in low-income neighborhoods and skilled ethnic groups tend to live in high-income neighborhoods.

This characteristic of neighborhoods raises an important question: is it the neighborhood's ethnicity that influences social mobility, or is it the neighborhood's socioeconomic class? Because ethnic groups are so geographically concentrated and because neighborhoods are also segregated by class, it might seem as if ethnic capital matters when, in fact, it is just socioeconomic class that matters. In other words, the correlation between ethnic capital and the children's socioeconomic outcomes may simply be "covering up" a neighborhood effect: growing up in poor neighborhoods is not good for one's socioeconomic health.

Ethnic capital might still matter, *above and beyond neighborhood effects,* if contacts within an ethnic group in a particular neighborhood are more frequent or more influential than contacts across ethnic groups in that neighborhood. Children who belong to a particular ethnic group are then exposed to a different set of values, social contacts, and economic opportunities than children who belong to other ethnic groups and who grow up in the same neighborhood. In other words, just knowing which neighborhood a child grew up in would not provide sufficient information to summarize the impact of the social and economic environment on social mobility.

If ethnicity did not have a direct impact on intergenerational mobility, adjusting for differences in the relevant neighborhood characteristics, such as mean income and education in the neighborhood, should account for much of the correlation between ethnic capital and the children's socioeconomic achievement. In fact, the available evidence confirms that there is a

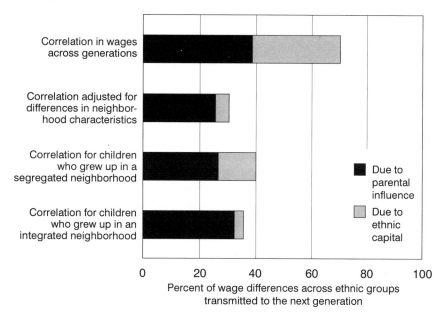

FIGURE 9-3. Ethnic capital and neighborhood effects.

Sources: George J. Borjas, "Ethnicity, Neighborhoods, and Human-Capital Externalities," *American Economic Review* 85 (June 1995), pp. 383, 385. The data are drawn from the National Longitudinal Surveys of Youth (NLSY).

Notes: Ethnic capital is defined as the mean log wage of the ethnic group in the parent's generation. The correlations that adjust for differences in neighborhood characteristics come from a regression model that includes indicators for the neighborhood where a particular person grew up.

very strong link between neighborhood effects and the correlation between ethnic capital and social mobility (see Figure 9-3).[14] About 70 percent of the wage differentials across ethnic groups in the parental generation are transmitted to the children's generation, with roughly half of this persistence attributable to the influence of ethnic capital on social mobility. If one adjusts for differences in the socioeconomic characteristics of the neighborhood—so that the correlations are effectively being calculated within the subsample of persons who live in the *same* neighborhood—the influence of ethnic capital diminishes considerably.[15]

The evidence, therefore, strongly suggests that almost all of the impact of ethnic capital on social mobility can be attributed to the fact that ethnic groups with similar socioeconomic characteristics tend to cluster in the same types of neighborhoods, ensuring that the children are exposed to roughly similar sets of economic opportunities, regardless of their ethnic background. In other words, it seems as if it is socioeconomic class that truly matters, rather than ethnicity.

In view of this fact, it is worth asking if ethnicity—in and of itself—plays any role whatsoever in social mobility, above and beyond the influence of parents and neighborhoods. If ethnicity is to play an independent role, it would most likely be found among children who grow up in a segregated ethnic environment. These children will probably have (and be influenced by) more frequent social and economic contacts with members of their own ethnic group.

It turns out that the effect of ethnic capital on social mobility is strongest and the effect of parental skills is weakest for children who grow up in highly segregated neighborhoods (again, see Figure 9-3). For example, about 35 percent of the wage differences across ethnic groups survive across generations when children are raised in integrated neighborhoods—where contacts within a particular ethnic group would presumably be relatively rare—and less than 10 percent of the persistence can be attributed to ethnic capital. In contrast, about 40 percent of the ethnic wage differentials survive for children who are raised in segregated neighborhoods—where they will encounter many other persons who belong to their ethnic group—and over a third of this stickiness can be attributed to ethnic capital.[16]

As the neighborhood becomes more segregated and the influence of ethnic spillovers rises, the influence of the parents on social mobility declines correspondingly. It seems, therefore, that peer influences "take over" as the neighborhood becomes more segregated. Put differently, parents matter most when there are few members of the ethnic group around to provide ethnic role models.

The evidence, therefore, suggests that ethnic residential segregation has a substantial impact on the social mobility of immigrant families in the United States. The influence of the melting pot is weakest for immigrants who tend to live in highly segregated neighborhoods. The more intense the ethnic clustering in the immigrant generation, the longer it takes for the melting pot to do its job of dissolving the ethnic differences and forging the "new Americans."

SPILLOVERS WITHIN AND ACROSS ETHNIC GROUPS

Up to this point, I have emphasized that ethnic capital has spillover effects *within* an ethnic group. It is also possible, however, that there are spillovers across ethnic groups. After all, a person of Italian ancestry living in a neighborhood with a strong Irish presence may be influenced not only by the cultural, economic, and social networks that bind together the Italians in the neighborhood, but also by the networks that bind the Irish.

One can use the data from the National Longitudinal Surveys of Youth to determine if such cross-group spillover effects exist, and if they are as influential as the ones that occur within an ethnic group. For any particular child in these data, one can determine which ethnic groups were present in the neighborhood where the child grew up. The typical neighborhood, however, cannot be neatly defined in terms of ethnic categories. A neighborhood, for example, may be predominantly Italian and Irish, but also contain some persons of Mexican ancestry, a few Filipinos, and a number of Koreans. It seems sensible to suppose that the young Italian will probably be most influenced by the largest non-Italian influence in the neighborhood.

The socioeconomic achievement of children would then depend on the socioeconomic achievement of the parents, on the socioeconomic achievement of the child's own ethnic group, and on the socioeconomic achievement of the other ethnic group that the child was most exposed to. It turns out that there are in fact spillover effects both within an ethnic group and across ethnic groups. The correlation between the children's education and the father's education is about .23. The correlation between the children's education and the ethnic capital of the "own" ethnic group is about .22. And the correlation between the children's education and the ethnic capital of the "other" ethnic group is about .12. In short, both the ethnicity of the child and the ethnicity of the neighbors influence social mobility. And, although the cross-group effect is weaker than the own-group effect, it is still surprisingly strong.[17]

There is little doubt, therefore, that the ethnic composition of a neighborhood influences social mobility in subtle and significant ways. Ethnic spillovers matter a great deal when the ethnic group is disproportionately represented in the neighborhood where the children grew up. And these spillovers occur both within an ethnic group (such as the influence of Italian ethnic capital on a child of Italian ancestry), as well as across ethnic groups (such as the influence of Irish ethnic capital on an Italian child who lives in an Irish neighborhood).

To GHETTO OR NOT TO GHETTO?

Because exposure to various ethnic cultures and attitudes influences social mobility, parents have strong incentives to pick and choose from the menu of ethnic influences offered by different neighborhoods. Parents of Italian ancestry who want their children influenced by their Italian ethnic capital will want to take into account the fact that the child will be influenced by the ethnic capital of the non-Italian persons in the neighborhood. Suppose, for instance, that the parents are considering moving to one of two neighborhoods. The population in each of the neighborhoods is 50 percent Italian. In the first neighborhood, the remaining population is predominantly Korean; in the other neighborhood, the remaining population is predominantly Portuguese. Parents know that the choice between these two neighborhoods may well influence the social mobility of their children. Because parents care about their children's socioeconomic achievement, it is clear that parents will want to choose particular types of ethnic neighborhoods and avoid others. Such incentives probably play an important role in determining how families choose to segregate themselves across neighborhoods in the United States.

   After all, everyone wants to live in a good neighborhood. Families who belong to disadvantaged ethnic groups will want to escape the poor communities and move into those neighborhoods where highly skilled groups reside. Such a move would expose their children to beneficial ethnic spillovers, and improve their children's socioeconomic achievement. At the same time, however, families who belong to highly skilled ethnic groups will want to segregate themselves by excluding persons who belong to disadvantaged ethnic groups and might have a harmful influence on their children's social mobility. To the extent possible, these well-off ethnic groups build ethnic enclaves that have sturdy cultural and physical barriers to prevent the entry of other groups. The explosive growth of zoning restrictions and gated communities in many parts of the United States reflects this desire on the part of well-situated families to "close out" the outside world and screen the types of influences that their children are exposed to.

   A particular family's choice of neighborhood, however, is constrained by economic realities. Many Americans may want to live in Beverly Hills or Scarsdale, or perhaps in one of those fancy gated communities that are guarded around the clock, but only those families who can afford it can actually move there. The resulting competition for "quality" neighborhoods raises the cost of housing in those neighborhoods. As a result, few persons in the disadvantaged ethnic groups will be able to escape the ghettos and barrios where their ethnic groups are clustered. Only the most skilled persons in the disadvantaged ethnic groups can afford to move into the better neighborhoods, and expose their children to other ethnic influences that might improve the children's socioeconomic achievement. In contrast, the most skilled persons belonging to the most advantaged ethnic groups will want to *and can afford to* remain segregated, and will choose to live in neighborhoods where their ethnic groups are overrepresented.

   Because of these financial constraints, one should observe systematic differences both within and across ethnic groups in the extent to which particular families "choose" to reside in ethnically segregated neighborhoods. Not surprisingly, residential segregation—in the sense that the family lives in a neighborhood where the ethnic group is disproportionately represented—is most common among persons who belong to disadvantaged ethnic groups.[18] At the same time, however, the most skilled persons in the disadvantaged ethnic groups often take the opportunity to move to less segregated neighborhoods. For example, a 10 percentage point increase in the wage of a worker belonging to a disadvantaged ethnic group *reduces* the probability of ethnic segregation by about 3 percentage points. In contrast, high-wage persons who belong to advantaged ethnic groups often take the opportunity to stay put, and live in a segregated neighborhood. A 10 percentage point increase in the wage of someone who belongs to an advantaged ethnic group *raises* the chances that the family will live in a segregated neighborhood by about 1 percentage point.[19]

In effect, each family in each ethnic group faces a simple question: to ghetto or not to ghetto? Because of ethnic spillovers, the collective answers to this question have effects that extend far beyond what happens within that family. The impact extends to other families in the ethnic group, as well as to families in other ethnic groups.

These residential segregation decisions help build the links in the chain that connects the socioeconomic achievements of ethnic groups across generations. And these links explain why the melting pot does not quickly eliminate the differences across ethnic groups, but rather puts those differences into what a movie buff would call a slow fade. Few persons in disadvantaged ethnic groups can afford to live in better neighborhoods and expose their children to the beneficial ethnic influences that might improve their socioeconomic achievement. Instead, the children in disadvantaged ethnic groups, by and large, tend to be exposed to the same spillovers that their parents were exposed to, ensuring that the socioeconomic traits of the ethnic group persist for yet another generation. In contrast, many persons in advantaged ethnic groups can afford to move to better neighborhoods. In these neighborhoods, the children are exposed to beneficial spillovers not only from their own ethnic group, but from other advantaged groups as well. This ensures that the children in advantaged ethnic groups are exposed to the same types of beneficial ethnic influences that their parents were exposed to, enhancing the children's human capital.

For better or worse, the interactions between residential segregation and ethnic capital generate a recurring cycle. In this long-running play, ethnic influences—both good and bad—play the same role generation after generation. If, through the accident of birth, one happens to be born into a disadvantaged ethnic group, the cycle is vicious; it is hard to escape the economic fate implied by one's ethnic background, and the children in these groups will often experience poor socioeconomic achievements. If, however, one happens to be born into an advantaged ethnic group, the cycle is virtuous: it is also hard to escape one's ethnic fate, but the children of this group are instead "sentenced" to a life of economic privilege.

Even the most casual observer of American life at the end of the twentieth century must be struck by the rapid growth of ethnic enclaves in many cities. For the most part, the new immigrants live, work, and raise their children in these enclaves. If the historical record is any guide, these children will probably move to neighborhoods that have roughly the same ethnic characteristics as the ones where they grew up. As a result, these ethnic enclaves provide the scaffolding for the social and economic networks that will likely influence the lives of the children and grandchildren of the Second Great Migration far into the twenty-first century.

The Goals of Immigration Policy

UP TO THIS POINT, I have attempted to document the economic impact of immigration on the United States. It is now time to change gears and simply ask, What should the United States do about it?

As I have emphasized many times, facts alone do not have any implications for immigration policy. The country must first decide what it is that the policy should accomplish. Depending on the objectives, the same set of facts can have very different policy implications. For example, if the goal were to relieve the tax burden on native-born taxpayers, it would be fiscally irresponsible to admit millions of less-skilled immigrants who have a high propensity for participating in public assistance programs. In contrast, if the goal were to help the poor of the world by giving many of them an opportunity to live and work in the United States, the increased cost of maintaining the welfare state would be the price that Americans would have to pay for their generosity.

Unfortunately, much of the debate over immigration policy is conducted in a vacuum—there is seldom any mention of the policy goals. In this chapter, I provide a framework for thinking about what the goals should be. I will argue that rather than worrying about the symptoms of current immigration—that the United States admits too many unskilled workers or that too many immigrants receive welfare—the immigration debate should have a very different question at its core: *whom should the United States care about?* Immigration policies designed to improve the well-being of the native-born population will often favor the entry of different numbers and different types of persons than policies that emphasize the well-being of the immigrants.

So why do participants in the immigration debate keep dodging the question, Who matters? Because any particular objective that the country chooses—or, more precisely, any particular group of persons that the country chooses to favor when setting immigration policy—raises difficult ethical questions about the type of country that the United States is and the type of country that the United States wishes to be.

THE COMPONENTS OF AN IMMIGRATION POLICY

The initial symbolism behind the Statue of Liberty had nothing to do with immigration—the French gave it to the American people as a representation of "Liberty Enlightening the World." The symbolism of the monument, however, changed permanently once a plaque engraved with Emma Lazarus's poem, "The New Colossus," was attached to the wall inside the pedestal of the statue.[1] Her call to other countries for "the huddled masses" and "the wretched refuse" made the Statue of Liberty a shining beacon to potential migrants from across the world.

The United States does indeed offer unequaled social, political, and economic opportunities to anyone lucky enough to enter its borders—regardless of that person's social and economic standing in the source countries. In an important sense, the American dream promises a "memory-less" opportunity. The limits imposed by the social and economic status of immigrants in their home countries matter little in the United States. After migration, life starts anew, and anything seems possible.

Because of these opportunities, many more people want to come to the United States than the country has been willing to admit. In November 1998, for example, the State Department was processing the visa applications filed twenty years earlier, on July 15, 1978, by Filipino-born U.S. citizens who wanted to sponsor the entry of their siblings. These long queues, moreover, probably underrepresent the demand for entry visas. There are probably millions more who do not bother to apply because they know that they cannot qualify under current regulations—or might have to wait decades for a chance to enter the country. Consider, for example, the "diversity" lottery that the United States held annually in the 1990s. Each year, some visas were made available to persons originating in "countries with low rates of immigration to the United States." Persons living in the eligible countries could apply for a random chance at winning one of the coveted green cards. Potential migrants applied for the 1997 drawing by submitting an application between October 24, 1997, and November 24, 1997. This lottery drew 3.4 million qualified applications for the fifty thousand available visas.[2]

Few serious participants in the immigration debate advocate completely open borders to solve this imbalance between the supply of entry visas and the demand for those visas. An important—and influential—exception is the editorial page of the *Wall Street Journal*, which has run a Fourth of July editorial proposing a new constitutional amendment: "There shall be open borders."[3]

Of course, the editorial stand of the *Wall Street Journal* partly reflects the economic interests of that paper's constituency, the business community that would obviously gain from paying lower wages to workers. Almost everyone else in the immigration debate, however, recognizes that immigration policy must *discriminate*—where I use this charged word in the old-fashioned sense of "using good judgment" to allocate the limited number of entry visas among the many applicants.

Because many more people want to live in the United States than the country is willing to admit, immigration policy has to specify a set of rules that can help selectively pick and choose from the many applicants. These rules may stress family ties (as is currently done), or national origin (as used to be done), or socioeconomic characteristics (as is done in other countries). In the end, these rules will inevitably stress a combination of characteristics that Americans deem culturally, economically, and politically desirable, and that are consistent with the country's values and beliefs. Because there are only a limited number of visas, the policy has to restrict or prohibit the entry of many classes of persons. Inevitably, difficult choices have to be made.

Ultimately, every immigration policy must answer two distinct questions:

• How many immigrants should the United States admit?
• Which types of persons should be awarded the scarce entry visas?

It is useful to think of immigration policy as setting out a formula that gives "points" to visa applicants on the basis of various characteristics, and then sets a passing "grade." The variables in the formula determine *which* types of persons will be let into the country, while the passing grade determines *how many* persons will be let in. The policy advocated by the *Wall Street Journal*, for example, sets a passing grade of zero and essentially grants points to any live body that can somehow reach the U.S. borders.

For the most part, the policy that has regulated entry into the United States since 1965 uses a formula that has only one variable, indicating whether the visa applicant has a family member already residing in the United States. In rough terms, an applicant who has a relative in the country gets one hundred points, passes the test, and is admitted. An applicant who does not gets zero points, fails the test, and cannot migrate legally. In addition, the post-1965 policy does not set strict restrictions on the number of immigrants. In the typical language of late twentieth-century bureaucratese, there are "pierceable caps"—or, put differently, numerical caps that are not really caps because they do not set out any numerical limits. These caps allow the number of visas allocated to particular groups (such as the ones granted to close relatives of U.S. citizens) to expand with demand.

Admittedly, this description is a very simplistic summary of current policy. There are a lot of bells and whistles that feed an entire industry of immigration lawyers, and that make the immigration statutes almost as complicated and as long as the federal tax code. Current policy, for instance, awards different numbers of points to applicants depending on whether the sponsor is a U.S. citizen or a permanent resident and on whether the family connection is a close one (such as a parent, spouse, or child) or a more distant one (a sibling). Generally, these nuances help determine the speed with which the visa is granted, with closer family connections leading to speedier entry. In addition, a limited number of visas are distributed on the basis of skill characteristics, but these select workers made up only 7 percent of the immigrant flow in the early 1990s.[4]

Although the United States does not admit officially to using a point system in awarding entry visas, other countries proudly advertise their formulas through the web sites of their respective immigration agencies. The comparison of point systems across countries reveals that the United States—relative to other countries—emphasizes family ties between persons currently in the country and potential migrants in awarding entry visas.

Canada, Australia, and New Zealand use more complex formulas, which include the applicant's educational background, occupation, English language proficiency, and age as well as family connections. In the late 1990s, New Zealand's immigration policy seemed to be the most creative, setting up financial incentives designed to speed along the process of assimilation. New Zealand required that the "principal" immigrant in the household be proficient in the English language, but allowed this principal immigrant to bring in family members who were not proficient in English. However, a family member who could not pass the "English standard" at the time of entry had to post a bond of $20,000 in the local currency (U.S. $11,000). If this family member passed an English test within three months after arrival, the entire bond was refunded. If the family member failed this test at the three-month point but passed it within a year after arrival, the government refunded 80 percent of the bond. If the family member failed to meet the English standard within a year after arrival, the family forfeited the entire bond. New Zealand's immigration policy gives a whole new meaning to the old cliché that "it pays to learn."

Sometimes a host country chooses to "sell" visas. For instance, a private consulting firm recently placed an ad in the *Times* of Oman offering "U.S. Green Cards for Anyone Who Can Show U.S. $500,000."[5] The United States allocates ten thousand entry visas annually for wealthy foreign investors (and their families) who create at least ten full-time jobs in the United States by investing $1 million. The "purchase price" is reduced to $500,000 if the investment is made in a high unemployment area. The investor visa scheme can be interpreted as a particular type of point system: a person can buy the requisite number of points needed for entry for $500,000. It seems, however, that the United States has set its admission price far too high. In 1996, only 936 such visas were sold. Canada sells the entry visa at a much lower price: the investor must be willing to invest only $250,000 in Canadian currency (U.S. $160,000).

Many people, particularly economists, would probably support the idea of an open market for most visas—not just those that are traded under the investor program.[6] After all, if bread, butter, and the proverbial widget can be bought and sold in the open market—and this solution seems to work pretty well in allocating these goods among the many consumers who want them— why not also sell the limited number of entry visas that the United States makes available every year? The United States, for example, could announce at the beginning of each year that it is willing to sell visas at, say, $50,000 per visa. Those who want to migrate to the United States at that price would then enter the marketplace.

The market for widgets "works" because it allocates the available supply of widgets to those consumers who most value them and are willing and able to pay the going price. Even though all consumers would presumably love to own more widgets, some consumers simply cannot afford to buy a lot of them. The going price for widgets rations the scarce supply among the many potential buyers. It turns out that this market solution is "efficient," in the sense that no other allocation of widgets to consumers would generate a larger economic pie. In other words, the *total* gains accruing to the consumers and produces of widgets are largest when widgets are exchanged in the open market. This fact, however, does not imply that the allocation of widgets to consumers is "fair." Buyers with a lot of money end up with a lot of widgets; buyers with little money end up with few, if any, widgets.

In a similar vein, an open market for visas would ensure that only those persons who most value the visas would be willing to pay the entry price. In other words, only those immigrants who feel that their entering the United States is worth more than $50,000 will buy the visas. And just as the widget market leads to an efficient allocation of the widgets available in the economy, the market for visas would also lead to an efficient allocation of the available visas. In fact, the visa market would maximize the *total* gains accruing to those who immigrate to the United States and to the U.S. Treasury.[7]

From a purely economic perspective, this market approach would solve a lot of the problems created by immigration. It would provide an "impartial" judge to distribute the scarce entry visas among the many potential buyers; it would generate additional revenues for the federal government; and it would filter the applicant pool to ensure that only those who most valued entry into the United States would actually get into the country.

Selling visas in the open market, however, also raises a number of problems. For instance, there are obviously many persons in the source countries who probably would never have the chance to accumulate enough money to bid successfully in this marketplace. In fact, it is likely that most of the ancestors of the current American population would have been unable to buy such visas. Per capita income in many of the developing countries is so low that most visa applicants in those countries would have to work several lifetimes to be able to afford a visa selling for what most Americans would consider a modest price.

Although this concern is serious, it is not insurmountable. The price for a visa could be set as a percentage of the source country's per capita income. Suppose, for instance, that the United States set the price at twice the level of per capita GDP. In the mid-1990s, this pricing scheme would have had the typical French immigrant paying $53,000 for a visa, and the typical Filipino immigrant paying only $2,000.

A potentially more serious problem with an open market for visas is that such a policy would not necessarily increase the skill level of the immigrant population. The immigrants who would buy the visas are the ones who would gain the most by migrating. Suppose that economic conditions in the United States—relative to the rest of the world—are such that the country attracts less-skilled workers from the source countries. Those American employers who have much to gain from an increase in the number of less-skilled workers would quickly learn that they could influence outcomes in the visa market. Although these types of workers would typically lack the funds to buy a visa, their future American employers could help finance the purchase. These loans, of course, would eventually have to be repaid by the immigrants.

An open market for visas, therefore, may have an unfortunate by-product: it could potentially reintroduce a form of "indentured servitude" into the history of immigration in the United States.[8] But such types of contracts *already* exist between many immigrants and the persons who paved the way for their entry into the country. By bringing these contracts to the open, and subjecting them to strict government regulation, an open market for visas could actually improve the living conditions of the immigrants as they attempt to pay off the loans.[9]

Because an open market for visas may not increase the skill level of the immigrant flow, there would still be reasons to be concerned about the adverse impact of immigration on less-skilled native workers and on expenditures in social services. These concerns, however, could again be easily handled by the market approach. Before announcing the going price for a visa, the government agency in charge could calculate the "net" cost of admitting immigrants into the United States. This calculation would contrast all of the costs and benefits that can be attributed to immigration, including expenditures on public assistance programs and education, the tax revenues collected from immigrants, the wage reduction suffered by native workers, and so on. The government agency would then set a price that reflected the net cost of admitting an immigrant. And the revenues from selling visas could be redistributed to the workers who would be adversely affected by immigration and to the taxpayers who would bear the burden of funding a more expensive welfare state.[10]

In short, many of the potential objections that one could raise to an open market for visas can be easily disposed of. And yet, despite the logical appeal and apparent benefits of the market approach, this type of proposal does not seem to go far in the political debate.

The problem is that an open market for visas brings into the open a number of moral questions that cannot be easily dismissed in the policy discussion. Difficult moral issues sometimes surface when one attempts to extend the paradigm of market economics from the traditional issues of selling bread, butter, and widgets, to the sale of such things as human organs and visas. Although the sale of kidneys, livers, and visas may be the economist's favorite solution to the very difficult problem of how to allocate these scarce resources in a democratic society, the proposals tend to share a moral blind spot. Many persons—myself included—feel that there are some things that *should not be* for sale. Put simply, life and liberty should not be for sale in nations that value the sanctity of individuals. Similarly, the hard-fought rights granted by American citizenship should not be sold in the open market. As a result, policy proposals that push the idea of an open market for visas are often not taken very seriously in the immigration debate, precisely because many people have a strong moral repugnance to what may be perceived as an implicit market for human beings and for what it means to be an American.

So What Do Americans Want?

Immigration policy can be viewed as a formula that awards points to various characteristics of visa applicants and sets a passing grade to help a country select from the many applicants. The formula implied by what is known about the economic impact of immigration will depend entirely on what determines the "social welfare," the well-being of the United States. In other words, what kind of country does the United States want to be? And what kind of country do Americans wish to live in?[11]

The social welfare of the United States obviously depends on much more than dollars and cents. It turns out, however, that it is quite difficult to figure out what type of immigration policy is in the national interest—*even when one focuses only on economic issues.*[12] To see why, divide the world into three distinct constituencies: persons now living in the United States (who, in the context of the current discussion, I will call the natives), the immigrants to be admitted, and those who remain in the source countries. One could easily imagine that the social welfare of the United States depends, to some extent, on the economic well-being of each of these groups.[13] The country would presumably be happier if all three groups were living in relative comfort.

Any attempt to design an immigration policy quickly encounters a difficult obstacle: what is the nature of the tradeoff among the well-being of natives, the well-being of immigrants, and the well-being of the population in the rest of the world? Consider, for instance, a policy that admits highly skilled engineers. Such a policy would probably be in the interest of the bulk of the native population—although American engineers would surely disagree. At the same time, many of the foreign engineers who are lucky enough to get one of the entry visas would probably jump at the opportunity to move to the United States. But many of the persons who remain in the source countries would probably be worse off; they would have to do without some of the infrastructure (and economic benefits) that the engineers could have created. To determine if this policy is worth pursuing, one needs to know exactly *whose* economic welfare the United States should take most into account when setting policy. In other words, the construction of an immigration policy requires assigning weights to the well-being of the three constituencies, with these weights deciding the relative importance of each group in determining the social welfare of the United States.

Different political, economic, and moral arguments can obviously be used to derive definitions of the national interest that would attach different weights to the groups. In some scenarios, the well-being of natives would dominate the calculation; in other scenarios, the well-being of the immigrants or of the persons left behind in very poor countries might dominate.

I think that most participants in the immigration debate have historically attached the largest—and perhaps the only—weight to the economic well being of natives. This is not surprising. After all, the goals and aspirations of the native population drive American politics. It is probably the case that many native voters have parochial interests, in the sense that they care most about their own economic status. The competition for the political support of natives ensures that U.S. immigration policy will inevitably reflect the self-interest and concerns of these voters.

As long as immigration is motivated by the search for better economic opportunities, it is reasonable to suspect that immigration also improves the economic well-being of the immigrants. The United States, perhaps alone among the world's developed countries, is perceived as the "last frontier" by the many foreigners who, through an unlucky circumstance at birth, were born in countries with oppressive political systems or in countries that fail to provide the social and economic opportunities that those persons seek. If the immigrants are not better off after they enter the United States, they are always free to go back or try their luck elsewhere—and indeed, many do.

It is easy to see how the well-being of immigrants might enhance the social welfare of the United States, a country that has had a two-century–old love-hate affair with immigration. Immigrants could increase the *country's* well-being because their presence helps nourish some great American traditions and values: the tradition of providing shelter to those most in need and the values underlying the American dream—that "only in America" can someone arrive penniless from a poor country and rise to become the CEO of a multinational corporation in a few years.

Finally, there are the billions of persons who remain in the source countries. They have little hope (or desire) of migrating either to the United States or to any place else. Nevertheless, U.S. immigration policy affects them in many ways. The United States might choose to drain their labor markets of particular types of skills and abilities. Such a drain would probably have a detrimental effect on economic growth in those countries. Similarly, the principles of free trade first enunciated by David Ricardo almost two centuries ago suggest that the world would be much richer if there were no national borders to interfere with the free movement of goods and people. By prohibiting the immigration of many persons, the United States inevitably shrinks the size of the world economic pie, reducing the economic opportunities that could be available to many persons in the source countries.

In short, even if the United States were a "caring" nation—in the sense that all of the groups counted in the calculation of the country's social welfare or well-being—there would still be difficult choices to make. Pursuing a particular immigration policy might help one or two of the three groups but hurt the other(s). As a result, the adoption and implementation of any specific immigration policy will likely leave winners and losers in its wake. This simple fact forces the American people to make an uncomfortable calculation. The gains that accrue to the winners have to be compared with the losses suffered by the losers, and the country then has to decide whose well-being counts more.

A Particular Weighting Scheme

Most discussions of immigration policy "run" with one of the facts about the economic impact of immigration—that immigrants reduce the wage of native workers, or that more recent immigrants tend to be relatively less skilled—to propose some type of reform in immigration policy. Such a hasty approach, however, is fundamentally dishonest because it leaves out of the discussion some of the key assumptions made by those who propose particular policy reforms. To design an immigration policy based on what is known about the economic impact of immigration, one must first explicitly decide how to weigh the well-being of the three groups that potentially determine the social welfare of the United States. Different weighting schemes will spin the same facts in different ways and result in different immigration policies.

Consider, for instance, the fact that immigrant participation in welfare programs has risen greatly over time. As I argued earlier, this fact has different policy implications depending on whether the weighting scheme emphasizes the economic well-being of the native population or the economic well-being of the immigrants. Those who put a greater weight on the economic well-being of natives would find the welfare use of immigrants distressing, and would recommend that fewer poor immigrants be admitted. Those who put a greater weight on the economic well-being of immigrants would welcome the use of the welfare state to help poor people from across the world, and might encourage the entry of even more poor immigrants.

Inevitably, different participants in the immigration debate will assign different weights to the three groups. So it is fruitless to devote much time and effort to intellectual exercises that want to uncover the "true" weighting scheme—the scheme that actually determines social welfare in the United States. Perhaps the only thing that all of the participants might agree on is that the well-being of the native population should matter in any calculation of the nation's social welfare. But the participants would then quickly begin to quarrel over how much it should matter.

In my view, many participants in the immigration debate—although seldom saying so explicitly—have a particular weighting scheme in mind: the United States should be concerned only with the economic well-being of the native population.

My perception that the economic interests of the native population are all that matter in setting immigration policy is certainly debatable. Moreover, this particular vision of the country's national interest (like any other vision of the national interest) inevitably raises a difficult moral question: is it "just" for the United States to act selfishly and ignore the well-being of everyone else in the world when setting immigration policy? Nevertheless, this approach provides a good starting point for organizing one's thoughts about the type of immigration policy that the United States should pursue.

Before moving on, let me clarify some issues. As I noted earlier, the "natives" that influence the social welfare of the country include all persons present in the United States at a particular point in time, regardless of where they were born. This native population must decide what type of immigration policy to pursue in the future.

Second, saying that the United States should design an immigration policy that benefits natives does *not* necessarily imply that natives are oblivious to what happens to the economic status of persons in other countries. For instance, the well-being of natives in the United States depends critically on having friendly neighbors—neighbors living in countries that are politically stable and economically vibrant. If Mexico were to suddenly become an unfriendly neighbor, the cost of controlling the southern border would probably be far greater than the cost of admitting millions of less-skilled Mexican immigrants. By admitting these immigrants, the United States effectively gives Mexico a "safety valve" that relieves many of the social and economic pressures on that country. The United States might bear some short-term losses from this type of migration, but it also has much to gain by having a more stable neighbor. In the end, the United States would be willing to admit millions of Mexican immigrants, not because the Mexican immigrants benefit greatly or because Mexico itself benefits (both of which are probably true), but because it is in the selfish interests of American natives to do so.

Finally, by proposing that the country's social welfare depends only on the well-being of the native population, it might seem that I am ignoring a basic lesson of American history. As is often said, the United States is a nation of immigrants. And one interpretation of American history might be that the United States admitted millions of immigrants because it is a generous country that wanted to share its wealth and good fortune with the huddled masses from around the world. In other words, the social welfare of the United States depends on more than making the native population rich and happy; it also depends on sharing the wealth with some of the less fortunate persons from around the world.

That might be a correct interpretation of American history. But it is also possible that throughout much of the past two centuries, the persons who inhabited the United States at the time found it beneficial to open up the borders. The land had to be tamed, the frontier had to be conquered, and the railroads had to be built. All of these activities required a lot of labor and brute force—far more than the small population of the young country could conceivably provide. Admitting millions of the tired and the poor, though a noble and generous gesture, also coincided quite well with the selfish interests of natives *at that time*. As a result, one can interpret the symbolism of the Statue of Liberty in a different and more cynical way: Give me your tired and your poor. The country *needs* them.

It is an intriguing historical coincidence that once the need for millions of less-skilled workers began to subside, around the beginning of the twentieth century, the United States also became much less tolerant of immigration. And soon thereafter, the country imposed severe limits on the numbers and types of persons who would be admitted.

Both versions of American history probably contain a kernel of truth. The United States is a very tolerant nation when it comes to immigration—far more than tolerant than most other countries. And as the country perceives itself, more than its social welfare—its very sense of being—depends on providing shelter and opportunity to many persons from abroad, and on granting admission tickets to the American dream. *But* the country also becomes much more tolerant about immigration when the immigrants serve a particular economic purpose.

There is little need to take sides in this historical debate. I would argue that it is still worthwhile to investigate the type of immigration policy that the country *would* pursue if all it cared about were the economic well-being of the native population. If the American people eventually wanted to include other factors in the definition of the country's social welfare, the United States could then adjust the proposed immigration policy accordingly. One can, in effect, use the immigration policy that maximizes the economic well-being of natives as a yardstick—a standard that can be used to measure the economic consequences of pursuing other goals.

Efficiency versus Distribution

Even if the country's social welfare depends only on the economic well-being of the native population, there is still one additional question to address. *Which* dimension of economic well-being matters most in determining social welfare: the per capita income of natives or the distribution of income in the native population? As I have shown, immigration may raise the per capita income of natives, but this does not mean that all natives gain equally. Admitting less-skilled immigrants, for example, reduces the income accruing to less-skilled natives, but increases the income accruing to capitalists or skilled natives by even more. Any evaluation of the impact of immigration policy, therefore, has to be conducted on two very different economic dimensions: the size of the economic pie and the splitting of the pie.

The evidence on the economic impact of immigration suggests that the net gains from immigration tend to be small, so it is doubtful that these gains could determine the direction of immigration policy. The truly important economic impact of immigration is that it changes the way the pie is split. The immigration of less-skilled workers redistributes wealth from unskilled to skilled natives, from workers to the owners of firms, and from taxpayers who bear the burden of paying for the social services used by immigrants to consumers who use the goods and services produced by immigrants.

These distributional effects often drive the political debate over many social policies, and immigration policy is no exception. Let me make the point even clearer: the debate over immigration policy is *not* a debate over whether the entire country is made better off by immigration. The gains from immigration seem much too small, and could even be outweighed by the cost of providing increased social services. The debate over how many and which types of immigrants to admit is best viewed as a tug-of-war between those who gain from immigration and those who lose from it. And this fact goes a long way toward explaining why some Americans favor the continued entry of large numbers of immigrants, while others favor cutting off the flow.

Despite the importance of these distributional issues, it is fair to say that most economists typically ignore these concerns when evaluating alternative social policies. Alternative policies are typically ranked solely in terms of their effect on per capita income, with policies that lead to larger increases in incomes being considered better policies (that is, "more efficient"), regardless of their impact on the distribution of wealth. In other words, the typical approach favored by economists would suggest an even narrower definition of the social welfare of the United States: social welfare depends only on the level of per capita income in the native population. Under this definition, the "best" immigration policy is the one that generates the highest per capita income for natives. One could easily justify this approach because a larger economic pie makes it possible to redistribute income from the winners to the losers so as to make every native in the United States better off. It is worth noting, however, that such redistribution seldom takes place; those who gain from immigration typically keep the bulk of the gains, while those who lose from immigration simply have to make do in the new, and less beneficial, economic environment.

The long-running debate over international trade is instructive and illustrates how, in the words of John Maynard Keynes, "practical men, who believe themselves to be quite exempt from any intellectual influences, are usually the slave of some defunct economist."[14] The economic case for free trade is clear and has been part of the political culture for almost two centuries.[15] When the United States began to import large numbers of Japanese cars, many workers in the American auto industry probably lost their jobs, and eventually ended up in lower-paying positions. The losses suffered by these unlucky workers, however, were more than offset by the benefits accruing to consumers, who could now buy better and cheaper cars.[16]

Because most economists tend to view the world through a somewhat peculiar prism—a definition of the nation's social welfare that emphasizes the size of the economic pie—the economic argument in favor of free trade is crystal clear. Free trade is "efficient"—it is a good policy because it increases per capita income.

At the same time, however, this narrow focus on economic efficiency misses the point of the political debate over free trade. A long line of political figures—from Alexander Hamilton in the eighteenth century to Andrew Jackson in the nineteenth to Theodore Roosevelt at the beginning and Dick Gephardt and Pat Buchanan at the end of the twentieth century—have raised serious questions about the wisdom of free trade. In recent years, these doubts have often stressed the distributional impact of trade—the potential for some workers to be left behind by the rush to a global economy.[17]

Both sides of the modern debate over free trade are right. There *are* efficiency gains from trade. *And* some workers do lose substantially. The two sides, however, differ in their perception of what determines the country's social welfare. The proponents of free trade attach greater weight to efficiency; the opponents attach greater weight to distributional issues.

Obviously, there is no simple way of determining what is most important in determining the nation's social welfare: efficiency or distribution. Each American would probably assign different weights to these two dimensions of economic well-being. Some will value the rapid growth in per capita incomes that free trade promises—perhaps in the hope that the rising tide will lift all boats. Others will be more concerned about the workers who lose their job and are left behind. One thing is clear, however. Distributional issues play a crucial role in the political arena. And one misses the entire point of the political debate, in either trade or immigration, by ignoring the fact that these policies often make some persons better off at the same time that they make other persons worse off.

The Moral Consequences of Immigration Policy

In this discussion, I have tried hard to straddle the very thin line between the setting of immigration policy based solely on the economic impact of immigration and the fact that the adoption of such a policy raises a number of ethical issues. But it would be foolish to ignore that any assignment of weights among the three groups that could potentially affect the social welfare of the United States—the natives, the immigrants, and the rest of the world—evokes difficult questions of morality and justice. Who should have first claim over the product of the American economy? Is it "just" to favor some persons over others? Is it "fair" to deny some persons the opportunity to partake in the American dream? Is it "right" to build barriers between countries? Although economics often frames the discussion of immigration issues, these moral questions also play an important role in the debate.

Most people take it for granted that there is no such thing as a universal right to migrate to other places. My ability to move across places *within* the United States is restricted. I have no right to pack my belongings and set up shop in my neighbor's backyard. Political philosophers have long speculated about these thorny issues.[18] Inevitably, there is quite a bit of disagreement over what makes a "just" and "right" immigration policy, and about the limits that distributive justice places on a sovereign state's authority to determine who can and cannot become a member of the "club," the group of natives who inhabit that country.[19]

The source of the disagreement can be described in terms of a simple parable.[20] Suppose there is a world with two distinct geographic areas. At the beginning of time, these areas are identical in every way—size, physical endowments, weather, population, human capital, and so on. At the starting line, therefore, there are two parallel and identical economies about to embark into history.

The race is on. Through random luck and the infinite possibilities introduced by different types of social interactions, the two countries inevitably develop slightly different social, economic, and political systems. Over time, these differences are amplified as each country's population invests in the types of skills and activities that are rewarded in their particular environments. After many years, the two hypothetical countries look quite different. One country has high per capita income and a rapidly growing economy; the other has low per capita income and a stagnant economy.

Do the persons residing in the rich country then have an obligation to admit immigrants from the poor country?

The "correct" answer depends greatly on how one feels about the right of persons to have *equal opportunities* versus the right to have *equal outcomes*. Those Americans who believe in equal opportunity might argue that the persons in the rich country are not obligated to accept any of the immigrants who want to come from the poor country. Everyone had the same chances at the outset, and some groups just happened to make more efficient use of the resources at their disposal. In contrast, those Americans who believe in equal outcomes would assert that all individuals currently living in this hypothetical universe have identical claims on the economic resources available. An open-border immigration policy (or free trade) would tend to equalize the resources available to the populations of the two countries.

Many participants in the immigration debate would probably argue that the relation between these two hypothetical economies should be guided by the principle of "mutual aid," best illustrated by the parable of the Good Samaritan. A Samaritan walking along a road meets a man who has been robbed, beaten, and left half-dead by a band of thieves. The principle of mutual aid states that the Samaritan has a moral responsibility to help. But how far does this responsibility extend? Must the Samaritan welcome the man into his home, feed and clothe the man, and then set the man on his way? Or must the Samaritan welcome the man into his home and then proceed to split his entire wealth with the man?

It is well beyond the scope of this book to address the deep philosophical and moral concerns raised by these questions. So I will leave it to others to determine if the immigration policies implied by the country's desire to make its native population better off are morally defensible.

But I would argue that although these moral issues may influence the direction and tone of the immigration debate, as well as determine the likelihood that some policies are adopted or rejected, it is still valuable to describe the type of immigration policy that the United States would pursue if it wanted to maximize the economic well-being of its native population. As I noted earlier, that policy sets the standard by which one can measure the cost borne by the American people if the country deviates from that goal. Such deviations might well be the just and right thing to do—and their cost may be easy to justify by appealing to a higher cause than dollars and cents. But the American people should be fully informed about the price that they will have to pay.

CHAPTER 11

A Proposal for an Immigration Policy

I HAVE SUMMARIZED the evidence. And I have argued that it is worthwhile to assume that immigration policy should strive to maximize the well-being of the native population.

In this chapter, I sketch the parameters of an immigration policy that achieves this goal. The chapter does not provide a nuts-and-bolts description of the optimal immigration policy in the sense of describing, in excruciating detail, how a new-and-improved immigration statute should be written. Rather, the discussion focuses on the general principles that are at stake. Although I touch on some of the issues that arise with refugee policy and with illegal immigration, the discussion is mostly confined to the link between the evidence and the type of immigration policy that the United States should adopt to regulate the entry of legal permanent immigrants.

Throughout the 1980s and 1990s, the United States admitted about 730,000 legal immigrants, over 100,000 refugees, and at least 200,000 illegal aliens per year, and many of these immigrants were relatively unskilled. In this chapter, I will argue that an immigration policy better attuned to the country's national interest—which, *by assumption*, is to maximize the economic well-being of natives—would probably grant fewer entry visas, and that most of the successful visa applicants would be more skilled.

THE ECONOMIC IMPACT OF IMMIGRATION

The academic literature investigating the economic impact of immigration on the United States grew rapidly in the past decade. This new research established a number of stylized facts that will influence the immigration debate in years to come:

- The relative skills of successive immigrant waves declined over much of the post-war period.
- Because the newest immigrant waves start out with such an economic disadvantage and because economic assimilation does not occur rapidly, the earnings of the newest arrivals will remain far below those of natives throughout much of their lives.
- The decline in the relative economic performance of immigrants can be attributed to a single factor, the changing national origin mix of the immigrant population.
- The large-scale migration of less-skilled workers probably had an adverse impact on the economic opportunities of less-skilled natives.

- The new immigrants have relatively high rates of welfare use. As a result, immigration places a substantial fiscal burden on the most affected localities and states.
- There are economic benefits to be gained from immigration, but the net (measurable) benefits are small, on the order of .1 percent of GDP annually. The main economic impact of immigration is distributional: immigration redistributes wealth away from workers who compete with immigrants to those who use immigrant services.
- There exists a strong positive correlation between the average skills of ethnic groups in the first and second generations, so the huge skill differentials observed among today's foreign-born groups will almost certainly become tomorrow's differences among American-born ethnic groups.
- Ethnic capital, the set of socioeconomic characteristics that characterizes the ethnic group, affects the social mobility of members of that group. These spillovers help explain why ethnic skill differentials tend to persist from generation to generation.
- Ethnic neighborhoods isolate the cultures and attitudes of particular ethnic groups. The ethnic spillovers associated with ethnic capital are mainly transmitted through these ethnic enclaves.

These are the facts that rekindled the debate over immigration policy in the United States, and that will determine the direction and resolution of this debate.

Which Immigrants Should the United States Admit?

Suppose that the goal of immigration policy were to maximize the economic well-being of the native population, where the native population includes all persons currently residing in the United States. And suppose that native economic well-being depends both on per capita income and on the distribution of income in the native population. In other words, the optimal immigration policy should make natives wealthier, but should not increase the income disparity among workers already in the country. What type of immigration policy should the United States then pursue? More specifically, which types of immigrants should the country admit, skilled or unskilled workers?

A strong case can be made that the social welfare of the United States—*as I have defined it*—would increase if the country adopted an immigration policy that favored the entry of skilled workers. The argument in favor of this policy contains two distinct parts. Consider first how the fiscal impact of immigration affects the economic well-being of natives. Skilled immigrants earn more, pay higher taxes, and require fewer social services than less-skilled immigrants. Put differently, skilled immigration increases the after-tax income of natives, while the tax burden imposed by the immigration of less-skilled workers probably reduces the net wealth of native taxpayers. From a fiscal perspective, therefore, there is little doubt that skilled immigration is a good investment, particularly when compared to the immigration of less-skilled workers.

The fiscal impact of skilled immigration also has desirable distributional consequences. Because the income tax is progressive, high-income workers pay a larger fraction of their income in taxes. For any given amount of government expenditures, an increase in the size of the skilled (and well-paid) work force would increase the share of taxes paid by the group of skilled workers. As a result, skilled immigration would lower the tax burden of less-skilled natives.

The second part of the case for skilled immigration rests on how immigrants alter the productivity of the native work force and of native-owned firms. These productivity effects depend entirely on how the skills of immigrants compare to those of natives. Skilled native workers, for example, have much to gain when less-skilled immigrants enter the United States. Skilled natives can specialize in their professions, while the immigrant work force complements the native work force by taking on a variety of service jobs. It does not seem farfetched to assume that the American work force, particularly when compared to the work force of many source countries, is composed primarily of "skilled" workers. On aggregate, therefore, it would seem as if the typical American worker would gain from and would prefer to have *unskilled* immigration.

But that is not the end of the story. Immigration also affects the profits of native-owned firms. Firms that use less-skilled workers in the production line, such as sweatshops, gain from the immigration of the less-skilled. Other firms, however, might be better off with skilled immigrants. In fact, many studies of the American economy suggest that there is more complementarity between skilled labor and capital than between unskilled labor and capital. In other words, the machines and capital that are now used in the production process become more productive when combined with a skilled worker than with an unskilled worker. Most firms, therefore, would gain more if the immigrant flow were composed of skilled workers.[1]

In short, there is a conflict between the type of immigrant that the "typical" native worker favors and the type of immigrant that the "typical" firm favors. The typical native worker would be better off with unskilled immigrants, while the typical native-owned firm would be better off with skilled immigrants. Because the productivity of capital is very sensitive to the presence of skilled workers, the evidence tends to suggest that per capita income in the United States would rise most if immigration policy favored skilled persons.

The gains from skilled immigration could be even larger if immigrants had "external effects" on native productivity. One could argue, for example, that immigrants bring in knowledge, skills, and abilities that natives lack, and that natives can somehow pick up this know-how by interacting with immigrants. In fact, many of the arguments that stress the beneficial impact of immigrants on particular industries—such as the role played by immigrants in the creation and growth of Silicon Valley—stress these types of externalities. Although there is no evidence that such externalities exist, it seems reasonable to suspect that these gains would be larger if natives were to interact with highly skilled immigrants.

The production complementarities between immigrants and natives, therefore, increase the per capita income of native workers most when the immigrant flow is composed of skilled workers. Moreover, if the social welfare of the country improves with less, rather than more, income inequality, the entry of skilled workers clearly has preferable distributional consequences. An influx of skilled workers would narrow the income gap between skilled and unskilled workers in the United States. On both efficiency and distributional grounds, therefore, it would seem that social welfare increases most when the immigrant flow is skilled.

THE POINT SYSTEM

How can the United States select skilled workers from the pool of visa applicants? In the past few decades, Australia, Canada, and New Zealand have all instituted point systems that reward certain socioeconomic traits in the admissions formula.

In Canada, for example, a hypothetical person who is forty-eight years old (which just happens to be my age as I write this) gets two points—out of a possible ten. This hypothetical person gets another sixteen points if he or she happens to have a doctorate. Further, he or she gets one point for being an economist (out of a possible ten for occupational background), eight points for having more than four years of work experience, nine points for being fluent in the English language (but not in French), zero points for not having any relatives in Canada (out of a possible five), and so on. After all is said and done, this hypothetical person (who just happens to share all of my relevant socioeconomic characteristics) would get sixty-seven points. Unfortunately, the Canadian point system demands that a visa applicant get 70 out of a possible 112 points, so this hypothetical person is denied entry into Canada.

Any point system will obviously seem quite arbitrary and lead to somewhat inscrutable conclusions: why can't *I* migrate to Canada? Moreover, it turns out that if I had been a social worker instead of a social scientist, I would have obtained a total of seventy-one points, and passed the test.

Despite its arbitrariness, the Canadian point system performs a useful function: it selects those immigrants who the Canadian authorities decided were most beneficial for the country. By restricting the entry of persons who are "too old" or "too unskilled" or "doing the wrong kind of job," the point system attempts to match immigrant skills with labor market needs and reduces the fiscal burden that immigration would place on Canada's generous system of public assistance.

A point system has many imperfections. A few hapless government bureaucrats have to sit down and decide which characteristics will enter the admissions formula, which occupations are the ones that are most beneficial, which age groups are to be favored, how many points to grant each desired characteristic, and so on. In Canada, for example, the list of occupations and the points granted to each occupation stretches through ten pages. By their very nature, most of these decisions are bound to be arbitrary and clearly stretch the ability of bureaucrats to determine labor market needs well beyond their limit.

The point system also emphasizes easily observable characteristics in the admissions formula—such as age, education, experience, and occupation. These characteristics help determine our economic opportunities, but they are not the only things—in fact, they are not even the main things—that matter. Differences in education, age, and occupation explain only about a third of the variation in earnings across workers in the United States.[2] Put differently, a full two-thirds of the differences in worker productivity are explained by other factors—factors that neither economists nor immigration officials can easily observe. Because the point system must inevitably rely on characteristics that are easy to measure, it misses those intangibles that are the main determinants of what makes some workers successful and others unsuccessful.

Despite these serious imperfections, the point system has two things going for it: it is simple, and it works. As Canada's experience shows, the point system does a good job at screening the applicant pool, and generates a more skilled immigrant flow than a system that does not use any skill filters.

The Canadian experience suggests that the United States could probably increase the skill level of its immigrant population by adopting a point system that relies on a few socioeconomic characteristics—such as education, age, and a measure of English proficiency. The formula could also award points to workers in "urgently needed" occupations, to applicants who have a job offer prior to entry, and to persons who already have relatives living in the United States. In short, the adoption of a point system need not mean that family connections with U.S. residents will cease to matter in awarding entry visas. Rather, it would mean that family connections will no longer be the *only* thing that matters.

In 1997, the United States began to take some tentative (though very indirect) steps toward using information about the economic potential of migrants in its immigration policy. Sponsors of new immigrants, the family members who already live in the United States and want to bring in their relatives, must meet certain financial requirements. The sponsor's household income must typically exceed 125 percent of the poverty line, so that if a married couple with two children wants to sponsor the entry of two additional relatives, the household's annual income would have to exceed $26,000.

This type of filter, however, bases the decision of whether to award an entry visa on the *sponsor's* socioeconomic characteristics, rather than the applicant's. There is probably a positive correlation between the two sets of characteristics—the relatives of highly educated sponsors, for instance, tend to be highly educated. It would be preferable, however, to stress the economic potential of the *actual* immigrants. After all, these are the persons who will have the largest impact on the economic well-being of natives.

Finally, it is worth stressing that adopting a point system addresses only the "demand side" of the immigration problem. In the end, the United States can attract only those immigrants who wish to enter the country—regardless of what the admissions formula says. For many reasons, including the narrowing of the income gap between the United States and most other industralized countries, the United States seems to attract less-skilled workers originating in developing countries. If a skills-based point system were adopted, the demand side of the "immigration market" would grant most visas to skilled workers, but it might be the case that relatively few skilled workers want to migrate to the United States.

There is a possibility, therefore, that adopting such a point system might greatly reduce the number of immigrants admitted, simply because many of the persons who might meet the requirements would not bother to apply for entry. I do not view this potential outcome as a flaw of the point system. It simply means that the types of workers the United States wants to "buy" are not available at the price the country is willing to offer. When such things happen in other markets, consumers typically do one of two things. First, they might raise the price they are willing to pay. The United States could offer financial incentives to the immigrants it truly wants—as Australia did for many years when it chose to pay some immigrants for the expense of getting there. Alternatively, consumers might withdraw from the market. The United States could simply wait for economic conditions to change until it can again recruit the types of workers who would be most beneficial for the country.

NATIONAL ORIGIN AND THE POINT SYSTEM

Even though the point system would clearly introduce a much-needed skill filter into immigration policy, it is important to be candid about the way such a system would actually work. In particular, one should not overlook the fact that any point system that places a heavy emphasis on such characteristics as education and English language proficiency will have a huge impact on the national origin mix of the immigrant flow. Most likely, the predominance of Mexican immigrants and of immigrants from some other developing countries will decline substantially.

To get a rough idea of this impact, consider the following exercise. Suppose the United States adopted a point system that emphasized only three variables: educational attainment, English language proficiency, and age at time of entry. Persons who had at least a high school diploma would get fifty points; persons who were proficient in the English language would get twenty-five points; and persons who were under forty years of age would get twenty-five points. Finally, the passing grade would be set at seventy-five points (out of a possible total of one hundred points). Suppose now that this point system had been in place in 1990. What fraction of the immigrants who actually entered the country between 1985 and 1990 would have qualified for entry, and how would this fraction have varied among national origin groups?

As Table 11-1 shows, about 41 percent of the immigrants who actually entered the country in the late 1980s would have failed this test—which essentially restricts entry to persons who are high school graduates and either speak English or are relatively young. Even more striking are the differences in the "failure rate" across national origin groups. Almost three-quarters of the Mexicans who entered the country at that time would have failed to get an entry visa, as compared to 30 percent of Italians and 12 percent of Canadians. As a result, even though Mexican immigrants accounted for 18 percent of the actual immigrant flow in the late 1980s, they would have accounted for less than 8 percent if this point system had been in effect.

Of course, this mechanical exercise does not present a complete picture of what would actually happen. After all, the adoption of such a point system would tend to change the applicant pool, and perhaps encourage more skilled persons to apply for entry, since they no longer would have to pass the current test of having relatives already residing in the United States. Nevertheless, the point system would have a disproportionate impact on applicants from developing countries simply because a relatively small percentage of the population in those countries has completed a high school education.

Inevitably, many opponents of a skills-based point system will bitterly proclaim such systems to be inherently racist. The *Oxford English Dictionary* defines racism as "the theory that distinctive human characteristics and abilities are determined by race." A skills-based point system gives equal opportunity to all persons who have equal skills—regardless of race or national origin. Such an immigration policy affects the race and ethnicity of the immigrant population because skills tend to vary systematically across source countries. As long as the United States pursues an immigration policy that favors the admission of skilled workers, it is inevitable that persons who originate in countries with abundant human capital will be overrepresented in the immigrant flow.

Moreover, a bias toward particular national origin groups arises even in point systems that stress factors other than the skills of visa applicants. For instance, an admissions formula that favors applicants with relatives already residing in the United States gives an advantage to those ethnic groups that have recently migrated to the United States. In 1990, only 15,000 adult immigrants had been born in Bangladesh (a country with nearly 130 million

TABLE 11–1
Effect of a Hypothetical Point System on the National Origin Mix of the
1985–90 Immigrant Flow

Country of origin	Percent of group that fails the test	Percent of immigrants originating in country	Percent of qualified immigrants originating in country
All countries	40.7	—	—
Europe			
France	7.4	0.6	0.9
Germany	14.4	0.6	0.9
Greece	30.6	0.3	0.3
Ireland	9.6	0.7	1.0
Italy	29.5	0.5	0.6
Portugal	70.1	0.5	0.2
United Kingdom	6.2	0.6	0.9
Americas			
Canada	12.2	1.8	2.7
Cuba	66.6	1.1	0.6
Dominican Republic	58.4	2.0	1.4
El Salvador	77.0	2.9	1.1
Haiti	54.1	1.2	1.0
Mexico	74.6	18.4	7.9
Nicaragua	56.6	1.7	1.2
Asia			
China	42.9	4.7	4.6
India	18.8	3.9	5.3
Korea	29.3	3.9	4.6
Vietnam	62.5	2.7	1.7
Philippines	15.0	5.8	8.3

Source: Calculations from the 1990 Public Use Microdata Sample of the U.S. Census.

Notes: The data refer to immigrants who are twenty-five to sixty-four years old at the time of entry. The point system is defined as follows: 50 points if high school graduate, 25 points if under age forty, 25 points if fluent in English; the passing grade is 75 points.

inhabitants), and fewer than 200 adult immigrants had been born in the Democratic Republic of the Congo (a country with about 50 million inhabitants). A point system that stresses family connections makes it almost impossible for persons born in those countries to enter the United States.

Diversity and the Point System

An important lesson of the evidence summarized in this book is that socioeconomic differences among ethnic groups will tend to persist across generations when the groups are isolated in ethnic enclaves. It is not clear that natives benefit from such ethnic isolation. On the one hand, the production complementarities between immigrants and natives persist as long as immigrants do not "become like" natives. On the other hand, greater inequality—

particularly in socioeconomic status among ethnic groups—can lead to many social problems, including an increased likelihood of ethnic conflict.[3]

Choosing sides on this issue, therefore, partly signals how one balances the beneficial gains from having immigrants who differ from natives with the adverse distributional impact of ethnic isolation. There is little direct quantitative evidence on the cost of ethnic isolation—though I suspect the cost may be quite large. But the available evidence on the gains from production complementarities between immigrants and natives suggests that these gains are small. Therefore, it seems prudent to conclude that the country should pursue policies that discourage the balkanization of the American population into ethnic groups with competing interests and different cultures.

How can immigration policy influence the long-run dynamics of social mobility? The simplest way is to encourage diversity in the national origin mix of the immigrant flow. Ethnic differences are most likely to persist among groups that are clustered in the ethnic enclaves that isolate particular ethnic characteristics, including language, culture, and attitudes. These ethnic enclaves, in effect, incubate ethnic differences, and impede the operation of the melting pot.

As the size of a particular ethnic group increases, immigrants and their descendants find it more profitable to isolate themselves into an enclave and create parallel markets that coexist with the mainstream economy. For the most part, members of the ethnic group remain within the enclave, where they work, buy goods, and make most of their social and economic exchanges. In other words, in a large enclave, the immigrants can become one another's accountants, doctors, and plumbers. The fact that the enclave provides many social and economic opportunities means that the immigrants have few incentives to learn the tools, including the language and cultural norms, of the mainstream economy—tools that would allow them to trade with the outside world. As a result, the native population gains little from the presence of these immigrants, and may lose much as the country becomes a collection of separate and distinct ethnic groups.

The cultural and economic hold of the ethnic enclave on its members could be greatly reduced by limiting the number of visas that are granted to any particular national origin group. There would be greater incentives for the residents of the enclave to trade with the mainstream economy—as well as with other immigrant groups—when the enclave is too small to sustain all the trades and activities that the residents may wish to carry out. In other words, immigrants living in relatively small enclaves quickly learn that it pays to become integrated with the mainstream economy.

These considerations suggest that no ethnic group should be allowed to become large enough to sustain a permanent and economically viable ethnic enclave within the United States. In other words, no nationality, culture, or language should dominate the immigrant flow. The point system could encourage ethnic diversity by limiting the number of visas granted to applicants from any given country to 5 percent of the total number available.[4]

Ironically, "diversity pays" in a sense that is at complete odds with what is typically implied by those who favor multiculturalism. Diversity pays because it ensures commonality.

The Point System and Immigrant-Dependent Industries

It is often claimed that certain industries in the United States would cease to exist—or at least would have to change radically—if immigration did not provide a continuing supply of cheap workers to those industries. The stereotypical industry is agriculture. Nearly two-thirds of farm workers in the United States, and 90 percent of those in California, are foreign-born. The United States, in fact, is a net exporter of *hand*-harvested fruits and vegetables.[5]

It is worth noting that immigrant-dependent industries employ both less-skilled and highly skilled workers. The debate over the expansion of the H-1B ("high-tech") temporary visa program in 1998 illustrates the economic issues at stake. Employers of software programmers and engineers insisted that their industries were plagued by chronic and severe labor shortages, shortages that could be resolved only by an increased supply of foreign-born "high-tech braceros."[6] Workers already employed in those industries responded that the labor shortage was a figment of the employers' imagination, designed simply to increase the supply of workers so that the firms could hire cheaper programmers and engineers. Prior to 1998, the United States granted sixty-five thousand annual temporary visas to high-tech workers. The debate ended with Congress voting to increase the number of temporary visas granted to high-tech workers to about 115,000 annually for three years.

A skills-based point system that ignores the existing clustering of immigrants in certain industries when awarding entry visas will obviously have a disproportionate effect on those industries. The point system, and a substantial cut in illegal immigration, would effectively stop the supply of foreign-born workers into U.S. agriculture. In principle, one could soften the impact of the point system on the immigrant-dependent industries by making specific provisions that would grant additional points to "urgently needed" workers who bring in specific types of skills.

Before such exemptions are routinely granted, however, one should consider whether the exemptions improve social welfare. Adam Smith's warning is as valid today as it was back in 1776: "People of the same trade seldom meet together, even for merriment and diversion, but the conversation ends in a conspiracy against the public, or in some contrivance to raise prices."[7] Organizations of employers in each industry would like to claim that their particular industry faces a particularly serious labor shortage, that the shortage has important social and economic consequences for the nation, and that the shortage can be solved only by bringing in more of the types of workers that they tend to hire. A detached observer should point out, however, that the additional supply of workers in the industry would likely reduce the wages of workers in that industry, and increase the profits of the firms that claim to represent the national interest.

It is certainly the case that the agricultural industry could not survive as it is currently structured if a skills-based point system were adopted and if the illegal alien flow were curtailed. For example, the domestic production of hand-harvested fruits and vegetables would probably disappear were it not for the presence of tens of thousands of immigrants in the fields of California and other agricultural states. But it is also worth asking a different question: does it make sense for the United States, a country with a relative abundance of skilled labor, to be in the business of exporting hand-harvested fruits and vegetables?

It is hard to believe that the United States has a comparative advantage at growing these products. And it makes little sense for the country to attempt to produce domestically every good and service that consumers demand. Some goods are best produced abroad, and it may be in the national interest to import those goods. In other words, if the United States wishes to maximize the size of the economic pie available to its population, it should use its available resources efficiently. It is wasteful to devote many resources— resources that could be put to better uses—to the production of goods that can be much more cheaply manufactured in a different physical and economic environment.

Even putting aside the fact that it might be best to import some of the goods produced by the immigrant-dependent industries, one could still argue that what is good for the employers in those industries need not be good for the country. For instance, the agricultural firms that hire seasonal workers in California ignore the fact that the immigrants probably impose a costly externality on the native population during the off-season. Although many of the immigrants whom these firms employ during the season return to their home countries after the harvest, some of the immigrants probably end up in the cities and towns of California and other states, increasing the demand for social services in many localities.[8]

In addition, the immigrant-dependent industries and the consumers of the products they produce would surely adapt to a different economic environment if the skills-based point system were adopted. The industries would investigate the adoption of alternative methods of production, methods that they had previously ignored because of the almost limitless supply of cheap labor. In fact, some firms in these industries could adopt capital-intensive technologies that might allow them to become competitive in the world market for the goods they produce. Consumers would also adapt. If a particular product became too expensive because the good could no longer be produced domestically with cheap labor, consumers would shift their demand to substitutable products that served the same needs.

How Many Immigrants Should the United States Admit?

In theory, the United States should admit an immigrant whenever the immigrant makes a positive contribution to the economic well-being of natives. As long as the contribution of an additional immigrant exceeds the costs imposed by that immigrant, the United States should let the person in.[9]

Even though the evidence on the economic impact of immigration provides a clear road map for thinking about the type of immigrant who should be admitted into the country, it provides few guidelines for coming up with the "magic number" of immigrants. The academic literature is not at the point where one can estimate the relevant costs and benefits with any reasonable degree of confidence, and then use these estimates to grind out a magic number. Moreover, even if all Americans agreed that immigration should increase the well-being of the native population, there would be a lot of haggling over the weight that should be attached to efficiency versus distributional issues.

I have argued that the nation's social welfare would be increased most by admitting skilled immigrants, as long as social welfare depends on larger per capita incomes and less, rather than more, income inequality in the society. Admitting skilled immigrants would likely reduce the earnings of skilled native workers, but would increase the earnings of other workers and of native-owned firms by more—raising per capita income in the native population. The twin goals of efficiency and a more equitable income distribution could then be attained by the same policy tool: admitting skilled immigrants.

In a typical year during the 1980s and 1990s, the United States admitted 730,000 legal immigrants, over 100,000 refugees, and at least 200,000 illegal aliens. Not counting the refugees, therefore, the policies that regulated legal and illegal immigration let in almost one million immigrants annually. Are one million immigrants "too many" or "too few" relative to the magic number that would maximize social welfare?

It is tempting to interpret the emotional debate over the social, political, and economic consequences of immigration as a sign that the United States is admitting too many immigrants. The symptoms include the strong political support given by California voters to Proposition 187, which denied certain benefits to illegal aliens; Congressional action that bans many types of public assistance and social benefits to illegal aliens; the welfare reform legislation of 1996, which made it more difficult for legal immigrants to qualify for public assistance; and the recommendation by the Commission on Immigration Reform to cut the number of legal immigrants to about 550,000 per year.[10] However, one can also interpret most of these policy actions as responses to the perception that the United States is admitting the "wrong type" rather than the "wrong number" of immigrants.

An alternative way of posing the question is to imagine a counterfactual: what would be the nature of the immigration debate if the immigrant flow were composed of one million highly skilled workers? I think the United States would still be in the midst of a debate, and perhaps an even more heated debate. After all, this type of immigration would have substantial distributional consequences on some well-organized and highly vocal constituencies. The political reactions of some professional groups—such as engineers, computer programmers, and mathematicians—to the economic impact of increased immigration in their fields stress precisely these distributional impacts (immigration lowers wages), and suggest that, if anything, the debate would probably be conducted at an even higher decibel level.

A flow of one million skilled workers per year would probably have a very large effect on the earnings of skilled workers already in the country. To get a rough sense of the magnitude, suppose the United States were to enact an immigration policy that admitted only college graduates, and that this policy were to stay in effect for two decades. By the year 2020 or so, roughly fifteen million skilled workers would have been added to the work force (assuming that 75 percent of the immigrants were working at that time). There were roughly thirty million college graduates working in the country in 1998. Immigration would effectively increase the supply of college graduates by 50 percent. The available evidence suggests that a 10 percent increase in labor supply may reduce the wage of competing native workers by 3 percent. A 50 percent increase in the skilled labor supply would then reduce the wage of college graduates by 15 percent.

This reduction in the returns to a college education would probably influence the college enrollment decisions of many native students. After all, going to college is expensive, both in terms of tuition and in terms of the potential earnings that students forgo while in school. If a particular social policy were to reduce the returns to such an investment by 15 percent, many students would probably respond by deciding not to get a college education at all. In fact, the available evidence suggests that a 15 percent decline in the wage of college graduates would reduce the number of young persons enrolled in college by between 15 to 30 percent.[11] Moreover, disadvantaged native students would probably be most sensitive to the decline in the returns to college, and their enrollment rates would probably drop the most. These are the students, after all, who can least afford to attend college and who would quickly discover that the shrinking returns to a college education do not justify the cost.

In view of the ongoing debate over the impact of affirmative action on the college enrollment rates of minorities, many Americans would not view such an outcome as beneficial.[12] As a result, even though some narrowing of the wage gap may be desirable, too large a narrowing is not. And, in my view, a 15 percent cut in the salary of college workers is sufficiently large to be worrisome. It is also worth adding that such a wage cut would make it difficult, if not impossible, to muster much political support for an immigration policy that admitted one million skilled workers annually.

There is, therefore, some limit to how much immigration should narrow income inequality. It is not beneficial for the United States to enact social policies that reduce the wage gap between skilled and unskilled workers "too much."[13] But it is difficult to determine precisely what that wage gap should be unless one is willing to inject a great deal more information into how the country's social welfare is determined. Those who feel very strongly that the wage distribution should be roughly egalitarian would recommend that many skilled immigrants be admitted, while those who feel just as strongly that there should be substantial rewards for differences in human capital would recommend that relatively few skilled immigrants be admitted. Because of this inherent uncertainty, no academic study has attempted to predict, purely on the basis of the evidence, what the number of skilled immigrants should be.

I tentatively conclude, however, that it is reasonable to interpret part of the passion in the immigration debate as indicating that an immigrant flow of one million persons per year is "too large"—regardless of its skill composition—and that it creates substantial economic, political, and social dislocations.

But let me be completely candid about my recommendation. There is no objective yardstick that I can use to determine what the right number of immigrants should be. My recommendation is based less on the available evidence, and more on how *I* balance the value of the efficiency gains from immigration with what is "fair" to the population of native skilled workers. Other participants in the immigration debate could reasonably disagree with my pick of the magic number. Those who believe that there should be a much greater narrowing of the wage gap between skilled and unskilled workers—and who are willing to accept a correspondingly large reduction in the number of natives who choose to attend college—would advocate a large immigrant flow. In contrast, those who believe that immigration should not narrow the wage gap substantially and that it should have less influence on the college enrollment decisions of native students would advocate a smaller immigrant flow.

Choosing the magic number of skilled workers—that number where the nation gains from immigration and where the distributional impact can be handled within the existing political framework—is bound to be a painful process of trial and error. A good place to start might be to let in around 500,000 legal immigrants per year—roughly the number recommended by the Commission on Immigration Reform, and about a 33 percent cut from the average number of legal immigrants admitted annually during the 1980s and 1990s (net of refugees). This number also happens to be the average number of immigrants who entered the United States during the 1970s, a period of high immigration (relative to earlier decades), when the debate focused solely on the perceived problem of illegal immigration.

Finally, it makes little sense to legislate a magic number that would be set in stone, unresponsive to changes in economic conditions in the United

Table 11–2
Illegal Immigration in the United States, October 1996

	Number of illegal aliens
Total	5,000,000
"Top five" countries of origin	
Mexico	2,700,000
El Salvador	335,000
Guatemala	165,000
Canada	120,000
Haiti	105,000
"Top five" states of residence	
California	2,000,000
Texas	700,000
New York	540,000
Florida	350,000
Illinois	290,000

Source: U.S. Immigration and Naturalization Service, *Statistical Yearbook of the Immigration and Naturalization Service, 1996* (Washington, D.C., 1997), p. 198.

States. The number of immigrants that maximizes the social welfare of the country is probably smaller when the economy is weak and larger when the economy is strong. The point system, therefore, should take account of macroeconomic conditions in the United States, such as the aggregate unemployment rate, before setting the passing grade. If the unemployment rate is high, the passing grade should be higher and fewer immigrants should be admitted. For example, when the economy is near full employment and the unemployment rate is less than 6 percent or so, 500,000 entry visas could be awarded; the number of visas might decline to 450,000 if the unemployment rate rose to 7 percent, and so on. At some point, the unemployment rate might be sufficiently high that it might not be in the national interest to admit any immigrants that year. Of course, it is also probably the case that few immigrants might want to come to the United States during such a severe recession.

Illegal Aliens

Five million illegal aliens lived in the United States in 1996 (see Table 11-2).[14] Their number grows by about 300,000 per year. And these numbers are on top of the three million illegal aliens who were granted amnesty in the late 1980s.

The common perception of an illegal alien is of someone who avoided inspection at the time of entry because he or she lacked the necessary documents for legal entry (such as a passport and a visa). The Immigration and

Naturalization Service refers to these persons as EWIs, for "entry without inspection." The stereotypical EWI is a Mexican immigrant running across the border. Many illegal aliens, however, had a legal visa when they first entered, such as a student's visa or a tourist's visa, but simply remained in the country long after their visas expired. The illegal alien flow, therefore, can originate anywhere. And, in fact, almost half of the illegal alien population is *not* of Mexican origin.

The United States attracts illegal aliens for many reasons. First, persons originating in many source countries have strong economic incentives to enter the United States—regardless of whether they can get a visa or not. Per capita income in the United States is at least three times larger than in Mexico. Even after netting out the cost of illegal immigration, such as getting to the U.S. border and payments to *coyotes* (the experienced guides who help the illegal aliens across the border), the income differential between the two countries remains exceptionally high.

Second, black markets arise whenever government regulations prevent people from voluntarily exchanging goods and services. Although it is illegal to buy drugs and sex, many people still desire those goods, and black markets arise to satisfy the illicit demand. Illegal immigration is no different. Immigration policy prohibits the entry of many persons, but these persons still wish to live in the United States. As long as the potential immigrants believe that the cost of participating in this black market is relatively low, they will come. In fact, there are few penalties imposed directly on the illegal aliens who are caught by the Border Patrol. When they are apprehended, they are simply put on the first plane or bus that goes back to their source country. Once there, the aliens are free to try to reenter the United States whenever the opportunity arises.

Third, it is no secret that many American employers benefit greatly from the entry of illegal aliens. This vast pool of workers lowers wages and increases profits in the affected industries. Even though it is illegal for employers to "knowingly hire" illegal aliens, the chances of getting caught are negligible and the penalties are trivial.[15] Newly hired workers must offer proof that they are U.S. citizens, are permanent legal residents, or have visas permitting them to work in the United States. Employers must then complete forms for each new employee certifying that the relevant documents were reviewed. The statutes, however, have a huge loophole, one that essentially permits anyone to hire an illegal alien. Employers need only to certify that they reviewed the documents that described the legal status of job applicants. The employer is not required to keep copies of these documents for inspection. Hence there is practically no chance of detecting employers who decide to hire illegal aliens after "reviewing" the documents provided by willing co-conspirators.[16]

Finally, the United States does a notoriously poor job at controlling its borders. In fact, few other countries have been so lackadaisical about border control. Although the number of agents in the Border Patrol rose rapidly in the 1990s (from about three thousand in 1990 to near ten thousand by 1998), the Mexican–U.S. border is 1,950 miles long.[17]

A number of highly publicized Border Patrol operations in the mid-1990s, such as Operation Hold the Line in El Paso and Operation Gatekeeper in San Diego, attempted to curtail illegal immigration by providing an around-the-clock Border Patrol presence in some of the stretches that illegal aliens typically used to cross the border.[18] These operations seem to have been effective in the targeted areas, but many observers suspect that some of the illegal aliens eventually entered the United States by crossing the border in those areas that were less heavily patrolled. A Binational Study of Migration, commissioned by the governments of Mexico and the United States, concluded that "the United States border enforcement strategies begun in 1994 are affecting migration patterns, but not preventing unauthorized entry."[19] Moreover, tighter controls on the U.S.–Mexico border do not address the problem of how to curtail the number of visa overstayers, who account for about half of the illegal aliens in the United States.

Any serious reform of immigration policy—and any attempt to adopt a skills-based point system—is doomed to failure unless the problem of illegal immigration is also resolved. A well-designed immigration policy may not have the desired effect on the social welfare of the United States if the border is porous. Illegal immigration can effectively unravel the social and economic effects of that policy. Illegal immigration is also unfair and unjust. Both the moral and the political legitimacy of immigration restrictions come into question if one can get to the front of the immigration queue by simply breaking the law. Finally, illegal immigration may be the root cause of substantial social and ethnic conflict, particularly in California, where the voters, fed up with government inaction on this issue, enacted Proposition 187 in 1994. This proposition denied many locally provided benefits to illegal aliens—including a public education.[20]

Proposition 187, in fact, raises fundamental questions about how far the United States can go—or *should* go—in controlling the illegal alien flow. Much has been made, for instance, about the rights and wrongs of denying a public education to the children of illegal aliens. The supporters of Proposition 187 argued that illegal aliens should not be entitled to attend public schools, that illegal immigration has unalterably lowered the quality of education in California schools, and that such a ban might reduce the incentives for illegal aliens to migrate to the United States. After all, illegal immigration from Mexico responds to the price of *tomatoes* in the United States—apprehensions rise when the price is high and American farms pay more to harvest the crops.[21] If aliens respond to the price of tomatoes, they would surely respond to the cut in education benefits.

The opponents of the proposition argued that it is morally wrong to kick children out of school and that, in any case, it makes economic sense to provide illegal aliens with free schooling. Preventing illegal aliens from getting a high school diploma today will only buy the United States more poverty, welfare, and crime in the future.

Putting the moral issues aside, barring illegal aliens from public schools may not be the most effective way of stopping the illegal flow. Many of the children who live in households headed by illegal aliens were born in the United States and are American citizens—courtesy of the Fourteenth Amendment to the Constitution.[22] The denial of public education affects a relatively small part of the illegal population, and would likely not deter the migration of single persons and childless couples.

The United States could probably deter many more illegal aliens by imposing substantial penalties on the employers who hire them. These firms—large agricultural enterprises, sweatshops, and native households that hire illegal aliens as maids or nannies—get the bulk of the gains from illegal immigration, but bear few of the costs. The demand for illegal aliens would probably drop dramatically if the government began to bill the owners of the fields where the aliens toil and the families who hire illegal servants for the expenses incurred by public schools and Medicaid.

There should also be some penalties assessed on the illegal aliens themselves. It is sometimes recommended that illegal aliens, when caught, should be sent for a few days to some type of detention center, so that they can pay for their crime through a short incarceration. The problem with this proposal is that it is very expensive to send a person to jail. In 1997, it cost $59.83 to send a person for one day to a federal prison.[23] If every apprehended illegal alien (and there were 1.6 million of them in 1996) were forced to spend two weeks in a federal prison, the total bill would be around $1.3 billion—assuming that no new prisons have to be built. It is unclear, therefore, whom this incarceration actually punishes, the illegal alien or the taxpayer.

One alternative might be to punish the illegal aliens by hitting them where it hurts the most, in the pocketbook. Federal law, for example, routinely allows the confiscation of much of the property used by drug dealers in their illegal business activities. The application of this principle to illegal immigration would imply that the aliens could be fined for their illegal activities (such as working in the United States) through the confiscation of their assets prior to deportation. The assets that would revert to the U.S. treasury could include bank accounts, cash, automobiles, and the right to collect social security benefits upon retirement (if the illegal alien had somehow been issued a valid social security number). These penalties would probably move the economic activities of the illegal alien population further into the underground economy. But the financial penalties—if accompanied by a strong effort at detecting and apprehending the aliens—could trim the economic benefits associated with migrating to the United States, and reduce the size of the illegal alien flow.

Ultimately, any serious attempt to resolve the illegal alien problem faces a crucial obstacle. There must be a simple way of determining who is an illegal alien, and who is not. After all, it is unreasonable to increase the penalties on employers who hire illegal aliens if it is difficult for employers to determine the legal status of a particular job applicant. The United States has yet to grapple with this troublesome detail, which raises the specter of a national identification system.

The United States has a somewhat paradoxical attitude on this issue. Most Americans probably have a libertarian streak that immediately rejects the notion of living in a country where one has to carry a card that provides information to potential employers about whether one is legally entitled to work. Yet most Americans carry credit cards that are scanned regularly whenever goods and services are purchased. The information provided by that scanning—including the type of purchase, the amount, and the location—triggers a computer "prediction" of whether the credit card actually belongs to the person who is carrying it. If, given the past consumption history of the authorized credit card holder, the computer concludes that the person at the store is buying the wrong things, or buying them in the wrong place, or going on an unexplained shopping spree, it will signal the shopkeeper to check for identification.

Regardless of one's position on the critical issue of a national identification system, the basic dilemma is clear. The illegal alien problem will remain a problem as long as the United States skirts the central question of how to identify who is a legal resident and who is not.

Finally, it may be possible to encourage the parties involved in the immigration debate to take illegal immigration more seriously by linking the point system for legal immigration with the size of the illegal alien flow. Suppose, for example, that the United States were to adopt a system that granted 500,000 legal visas each year. Each of these slots would become much more valuable if the government "taxed" the number of legal visas available every time an illegal alien entered the country. The Immigration and Naturalization Service might report that 200,000 illegal aliens had entered the country in any given year. The point system could then be adjusted so that only 300,000 legal visas would be granted.

This "tax" would introduce a number of important incentives into the enforcement of immigration policy. First, it would make the country aware of the opportunity cost of illegal immigration. In other words, by looking the other way and letting in 200,000 illegal aliens, Americans would be forgoing the economic benefits that could be provided by 200,000 well-chosen immigrants. Second, firms that employ immigrants would have to "compete" over their share of entrants. Even though some firms might benefit from the less-skilled illegal aliens, many other firms would want to see the entry of the skilled legal immigrants that they prefer to hire. Finally, the immigrant community already in the United States would have a strong incentive to stop the illegal alien flow, since each illegal alien who entered the country would make it that much harder for the relatives of current U.S. residents to enter, even if the relatives were highly skilled.

REFUGEES

From a moral perspective, persons seeking refuge from political oppression and persecution in foreign countries have a very strong claim to visas that allow them to enter the United States.[24] Often, the lives of these persons are endangered; they have lost the means to support themselves and their families; and they lack even the most basic political freedoms. Although there are some glaring exceptions, the United States has, in fact, taken this responsibility seriously throughout much of its history, providing a safety haven to wave after wave of refugees. Nearly 1.8 million refugees and asylees were admitted between 1980 and 1996.[25] In a typical year, the president (in consultation with Congress) sets an annual limit on the number of refugees to be granted admission, and determines how these visas will be distributed across parts of the world. In 1996, the admission ceiling was 90,000 with 25,000 visas granted to East Asia and 45,000 to Eastern Europe and the former Soviet Union.

Participants in the immigration debate—despite their disagreements over the objectives and parameters of immigration policy—have seldom argued over the country's moral responsibility to accept refugees. Nevertheless, there is an unresolved operational question in refugee policy, a question that is likely to play an ever-larger role in the debate: *who* is a refugee? Were the immigrants from Cuba during the Mariel flow in 1980, to take one particular example, fleeing political oppression, or were they fleeing poor economic conditions? Why were they considered refugees and welcomed with open arms, while Haitians fleeing equally oppressive economic conditions were denied refugee status?

Despite the lofty moral aspirations—and despite the veneer of humanitarianism that envelops most discussions of refugee policy—it is probably safe to conclude that the determination of refugee status mostly reflects the objectives of American foreign policy and domestic political forces.[26] Prior to 1980, the United States defined a refugee as a person fleeing a communist country, a communist-dominated area, or the Middle East. The Refugee Act of 1980 redefined a refugee as someone who is residing outside his or her country of nationality, and who is unable or unwilling to return because of a "well-founded fear of persecution on account of race, religion, nationality, membership in a particular social group, or political opinion."[27]

A good example of how the post-1980 definition adjusts to the changing political winds occurred in 1995. Prior to that time, persons fleeing the communist regime in Cuba were automatically granted asylum once they reached the United States. To reduce the chances of a new boatlift originating in Cuba—and its potentially devastating effect on Florida's political landscape—President Clinton unilaterally reversed this decades-long policy in 1995 by proclaiming that Cuban citizens would no longer receive preferential treatment in their applications for asylum.[28]

Admission under refugee status has certain advantages for the entrant. To a large extent, persons who do not have relatives in the United States, and who do not qualify for any of the few employment-based visas, find that obtaining a refugee or asylee visa provides the only way to enter the country legally. Second, refugees are immediately entitled to a vast array of social services unavailable to other immigrants—and sometimes even to natives. These services are costly. In 1995, the Office of Refugee Resettlement spent almost $400 million providing cash and medical assistance to refugees, as well as English language training and employment-related services.[29]

Needless to say, the United States should continue its tradition of offering refuge to those in need. Nevertheless, there are two issues in refugee policy that are worth keeping in mind. The evidence indicates that refugees are very likely to be enrolled in welfare programs. Even after ten years in the United States, 16 percent of Vietnamese refugees, 24 percent of Cambodian refugees, and 34 percent of Laotian refugees were still receiving public assistance.[30] Moreover, the refugees' exceptional use of welfare programs (relative to that of other immigrants and natives) cannot be attributed solely to differences in socioeconomic characteristics, such as education and household composition. Refugee households continue to be relatively heavy users even after one adjusts for those differences. It seems to be counterproductive to expose refugees to the welfare state so soon after entry into the country. It would be preferable to eliminate this particular "favor" to refugees, and simply provide the same types of assistance required by other immigrants in similar economic circumstances.

Second, and far more important, is the direction of the political debate over the definition of a refugee. There was little discussion of this issue during the cold war: the United States automatically offered refuge to all those fleeing communist regimes. This consensus, however, collapsed with the end of the cold war, and the operational meaning of the definition is now up for grabs. In the 1990s, the debate took a somewhat ominous turn by introducing differences in cultural norms as a way of defining refugee status. Consider, for example, the debate over whether women who live in cultures that perform genital mutilation qualify for refugee status. An immigration tribunal in the United States eventually granted asylum to one such woman who had fled her homeland to escape the ritual.[31] Abstracting from the specifics of this case, the ruling raises a fundamental question: Are people who live in societies that have norms of conduct, rules of behavior, and religious or cultural rites that are foreign, if not abhorrent, to most Americans entitled to seek refuge in the United States? And if so, how offensive must the norms of conduct be to qualify? For instance, do families residing in countries where the children are regularly sent off to work at the age of ten (or even earlier) qualify for refugee status in the United States?

There may be a danger in extending the umbrella of refugee status to those persons who live under cultural or social norms that Americans consider offensive. The broader definition of what constitutes a refugee is obviously ripe for abuse, and could be used to justify awarding refugee status to millions of persons who are now subjected to many types of offensive behavior. The danger, of course, is that the looser the definition of refugee status, the harder it becomes to maintain the political legitimacy of programs that pay special attention to a particular class of immigrants. And the harder it might be to give refuge to those who really need it when events warrant it.

Conclusion

THE UNITED STATES has been populated by many recurring waves of immigrants, each contributing a particular set of abilities and traits that helped shape the nation. By 1776, on the eve of the signing of the Declaration of Independence, about one million persons had already migrated to what would eventually become the United States.[1] Immigration continued sporadically for the next century; sometimes the faucet was on, and sometimes it was just a trickle. Throughout much of the century, however, the immigrant flow was relatively small, averaging about 170,000 immigrants annually between 1820 and 1880.

The First Great Migration, which began around 1880 and ended abruptly in 1924, fundamentally changed how the United States viewed immigration and its contribution to American society. This historic movement of peoples from many countries brought almost twenty-six million persons to the United States, and altered the course of American social and economic history throughout the twentieth century.

The First Great Migration was—and remains—an exceptional event in human history. Never before had such large population movements occurred over such long distances and in such a short period. Remarkably, it took only a century for history to repeat itself. The Second Great Migration began at the end of the 1960s, and has yet to subside. By the time the twenty-first century begins, almost thirty million persons will have migrated to the United States as part of this flow.

The United States is only now beginning to observe the economic, cultural, and social consequences of the Second Great Migration. Regardless of how immigration policy changes in the future, the Second Great Migration has already set in motion a series of events that will alter the social and economic structure of the United States not only in our generation, but for our children and grandchildren as well.

For better or worse, economic issues often frame the immigration debate. And the weapons of choice in this debate are statistics produced by economic research, with all sides marshaling facts and evidence that support particular policy goals. Will the available evidence influence the direction of the immigration debate? And, perhaps more important, *should it*?

I believe that it will and that it should. Overall, the evidence suggests that Americans would be better off if the immigrant flow were more skilled. And it can be plausibly argued that a slightly smaller immigrant flow might be beneficial for the country.

But history suggests that major changes in immigration policy occur only sporadically in the United States. Therefore, the road ahead, as the political consensus crystallizes around a new and improved policy, is long and fraught with dangers.

The economic impact of immigration is essentially a distributional one. Immigration shifts wealth away from those who compete with the skills and abilities that immigrants bring into the country, and toward those who employ or use those immigrant resources. As with many redistribution schemes, the people who lose from immigration tend be quite diffused—there are many of them, they are dispersed geographically, and they are not well organized. In contrast, the winners are much more concentrated and better organized—many immigrants tend to be employed in a few industries, and employers in those industries probably gain substantially.

The political lines, therefore, are clearly drawn. But the dangers that lie ahead do not come only from those who call loudly and often for extreme immigration restrictions, such as a closing of the border. The dangers also arise because there are powerful interest groups that gain substantially from current immigration policy. And these groups seem unable—or are unwilling—to see the cost that immigration imposes on other segments of society, and have considerable financial incentives and resources to influence the course of the debate and to ensure that the current policy remains in place.

The adverse effects of the Second Great Migration will not go away simply because some people do not wish to see them. They will continue to accumulate. In the short run, these interest groups will likely succeed in delaying the day of reckoning. In the long run, their impact is much more perilous. For the longer the delay, the greater the chances that when immigration policy finally changes—as it surely must—it will undergo a seismic shift. That shift may, as in 1924, give those who advocate a closing of the border the victory that has long eluded them, and prevent many Americans from enjoying the many benefits that a well-designed immigration policy could bestow on the United States.

Such an outcome would be extremely unfortunate. Immigration has blessed the United States throughout much of its history. Every country is, if one goes back far enough into history, a nation of immigrants. But the United States is unique in this regard. No other nation has offered such a beacon of hope and aspirations to tens of millions of persons from around the world. And nowhere has this beacon shone on for so long. Without the dreams and toil of the millions of immigrants who tamed and harvested the land and helped build great cities "from sea to shining sea," the United States could not offer today such a wonderful and unrivaled mix of cultural and economic opportunities.

Unless the United States chooses a wise immigration policy in the future, there is a real chance that there simply will be no immigration at all. That would leave many people—the immigrants who could benefit greatly from the opportunity of sharing in the American dream and who could, in turn, benefit the American people—forever knocking on heaven's door.

CHAPTER 1
REFRAMING THE IMMIGRATION DEBATE

1. This anecdote has long made the rounds among participants in the immigration debate. Former Secretary of State Cyrus Vance has confirmed the details (letter to author, June 3, 1998). The incident has also been publicly mentioned by Zbigniew Brzezinski, President Carter's advisor on national affairs; see "Fifty Years after Yalta: Europe's and the Balkan's New Chance" (speech by Zbigniew Brzezinski before the Free and Democratic Bulgaria Foundation, Sofia, April 1, 1995). The Jackson-Vanik amendment linked the granting of equal tariff privileges to communist countries to their emigration policies. The amendment was enacted in 1974, and was co-sponsored by Representatives Henry Jackson and Charles Vanik.

2. Letter of Benjamin Franklin to Peter Collinson, May 1753. This letter is excerpted in Edith Abbott, ed., *Historical Aspects of the Immigration Problem* (New York: Arno Press and the New York Times, 1969), pp. 415–416.

3. U.S. Bureau of the Census, *Statistical Abstract of the United States, 1997* (Washington, D.C., 1997), p. 9.

4. By definition, 10 percent of the natives are in each decile of the native wage distribution.

5. The trend would be even more striking if the calculation included the illegal alien population because illegal immigration is disproportionately of Mexican origin. At the same time, however, the large number of illegal aliens who were granted amnesty in the early 1990s distorts the trend. The Immigration and Naturalization Service defines their year of entry as the year when the application for permanent residence was approved, rather than as the year when they first actually entered the United States.

6. Peter Brimelow, *Alien Nation: Common Sense about America's Immigration Disaster* (New York: Random House, 1995).

7. James P. Smith and Barry Edmonston, eds., *The New Americans: Economic, Demographic, and Fiscal Effects of Immigration* (Washington, D.C.: National Academy Press, 1997), p. 121. This prediction depends crucially on the assumption that the descendants of Asians or Hispanics will themselves be Asians or Hispanics. The validity of this assumption is questionable, particularly since there is already some intermarriage across the groups, and it is unclear how the children of these mixed marriages should be classified or will classify themselves.

8. The National Academy study also estimated the long-run fiscal impact by "tracking" a hypothetical immigrant household over a three-hundred-year period following the immigrant's entry. This dynamic exercise revealed that admitting one immigrant today yields an $80,000 fiscal surplus at the national level. The long-run net benefit from immigration, however, arises mainly because the numerical exercise assumed that the federal government will put its fiscal house in order in the year 2016, and pass a huge tax increase to ensure that the debt-GDP ratio remains constant after that point.

9. William Julius Wilson, *The Truly Disadvantaged: The Inner City, the Underclass, and Public Policy* (Chicago: University of Chicago Press, 1987); and Douglas S. Massey and Nancy A. Denton, *American Apartheid: Segregation and the Making of the Underclass* (Cambridge: Harvard University Press, 1993).

10. Note that, in this context, the group of "natives" is defined to include all persons living in the country regardless of where they were born. This is the group that will enter whatever cost-benefit calculation the country chooses to make when it determines immigration policy in the future.

11. The "probably" arises because economic theory suggests that an open-border policy would maximize the world gross domestic product. In principle, one could then take this bigger economic pie and redistribute it so that every person in the world would be slightly better off. In practice, however, political considerations probably make it impossible to design and implement this type of redistribution scheme.

CHAPTER 2
THE SKILLS OF IMMIGRANTS

1. James P. Smith and Barry Edmonston, eds., *The New Americans: Economic, Demographic, and Fiscal Effects of Immigration* (Washington, D.C.: National Academy Press, 1997), p. 392. The opposition of skilled natives to immigration rises substantially when the immigrant flow is highly skilled and competes directly with clearly identifiable and highly vocal groups of American workers, such as computer programmers, academic mathematicians, or engineers. The heated debate over the expansion of the H-1B visa program in 1998 illustrates this point. This program allows the temporary entry of highly skilled workers in particular high-tech occupations. Not surprisingly, industry organizations, such as the Information Technology Association of America, argued that there were severe labor shortages, but these claims were typically not supported either by the data or by the workers in those industries, who would face stiffer labor market competition. The April 24, 1998, issue of the *Congressional Quarterly Researcher* contains a number of articles related to this debate.

2. The data are drawn from the 1960–90 Public Use Microdata Samples (PUMS) of the U.S. Census and the 1996–98 Annual Demographic Files of the Current Population Surveys (or the March CPS). These data contain information on the skills and labor market characteristics of millions of workers in the United States. Persons who are not citizens or who are naturalized citizens are classified as immigrants; all other persons are classified as natives. The calculations use a 1 percent random sample of native and immigrant workers in each Census (except in 1980 and 1990, when the immigrant extracts form a 5 percent random sample), and the entire samples of the CPS. Unless otherwise noted, the wage data in all of the surveys refer to the hourly wage rate, adjusted for inflation using the CPI-U cost-of-living index. The three CPS data sets are pooled, and are referred to as the 1998 data. Although some of the variables reported in the Census (such as the wage) refer to the year prior to the survey, I avoid confusion by always referring to the data in terms of the survey year.

3. The statistics reported in Table 2-1 refer to persons aged twenty-five to sixty-four who work in the civilian sector, are not self-employed, and do not reside in group quarters. Self-employed workers are omitted because their income reflects both the worker's human capital and any return to physical capital invested in the business.

The available data do not distinguish between these two sources of income. Including the self-employed in the calculations would not appreciably improve the relative income of immigrants. Immigrants are more likely to be self-employed throughout much of the period, but self-employed workers sometimes report lower incomes than do salaried workers. Although the table presents the trends for both men and women, the discussion in the text emphasizes the male differential for two reasons. First, the trends in the sample of working women are generally similar—though not as striking—as those found among men. More important, a relatively large number of women do not work and these nonworking women are not selected randomly from the population of all women. As a result, the wage differential between native- and foreign-born women may partly reflect differences in the variables that motivate some women to work, such as household composition, the number and age of the children, and the earnings of the husband, rather than any underlying skill differences. Detailed studies of skill differences between immigrant and native women are given by Edward Funkhouser and Stephen J. Trejo, "Labor Market Outcomes of Female Immigrants in the United States," in *The Immigration Debate: Studies on the Economic, Demographic and Fiscal Effects of Immigration*, ed. James P. Smith and Barry Edmonston (Washington: National Academy Press, 1998), pp. 239–288; and Robert Schoeni, "Labor Market Assimilation of Immigrant Women," *Industrial and Labor Relations Review* 51 (April 1998): 483–504.

4. Some observers deemphasize the observed decline in *relative* skills and stress instead that the educational attainment of immigrants was rising throughout the post-1965 period; see, e.g., Julian Simon, *Immigration: The Demographic and Economic Facts* (Washington, D.C.: Cato Institute, 1995); and John J. Miller, *The Unmaking of Americans: How Multiculturalism Has Undermined America's Assimilation Ethic* (New York: Free Press, 1998), p. 214. The improvement in the absolute level of immigrant skills—by itself—is not an important determinant of the economic impact of immigration. As I noted earlier, what matters is how the skill distribution of immigrants compares to that of natives. To see why, suppose that all of the immigrants who entered the United States between 1940 and 1990 had twelve years of schooling. The economic impact of immigration, however, would differ greatly over time because most natives in 1940 were high school dropouts, while most natives in 1990 had some college education.

5. Barry R. Chiswick, "The Effect of Americanization on the Earnings of Foreign-Born Men," *Journal of Political Economy* 86 (October 1978): 897–921, introduced this hypothesis to explain why, in the 1970 Census cross-section, the earnings of immigrant workers eventually caught up with and overtook the earnings of native workers; see also Geoffrey Carliner, "Wages, Earnings, and Hours of First, Second and Third Generation American Males," *Economic Inquiry* 18 (January 1980): 87–102. These studies greatly influenced the vast academic literature that estimates the correlation between earnings in the United States and the number of years that have elapsed since migration.

6. George J. Borjas, "Assimilation, Changes in Cohort Quality, and the Earnings of Immigrants," *Journal of Labor Economics* 3 (October 1985): 463–489, initially proposed this alternative interpretation of the data. A large academic literature debates the validity of the two alternative interpretations. Representative studies include Barry R. Chiswick, "Is the New Immigration Less Skilled than the Old?" *Journal of*

Labor Economics 4 (April 1986): 168–192; Robert J. LaLonde and Robert H. Topel, "The Assimilation of Immigrants in the U.S. Labor Market," in *Immigration and the Work Force: Economic Consequences for the United States and Source Areas,* ed. George J. Borjas and Richard B. Freeman (Chicago: University of Chicago Press, 1992), pp. 67–92; Andrew Yuengert, "Immigrant Earnings, Relative to What? The Importance of Earnings Function Specification and Comparison Points," *Journal of Applied Econometrics* 9 (January-March 1994): 71–90; George J. Borjas, "Assimilation and Changes in Cohort Quality Revisited: What Happened to Immigrant Earnings in the 1980s?" *Journal of Labor Economics* 13 (April 1995): 201–245; Edward Funkhouser and Stephen J. Trejo, "The Labor Market Skills of Recent Male Immigrants: Evidence from the Current Population Survey," *Industrial and Labor Relations Review* 48 (July 1995): 792–811; and Harriet Orcutt Duleep and Mark C. Regets, "The Decline in Immigrant Entry Earnings: Less Transferable Skills or Lower Ability?" *Quarterly Review of Economics and Finance* 37 (Special Issue Supplement, 1997): 189–208.

7. Carl C. Brigham, *A Study of American Intelligence* (Princeton, N.J.: Princeton University Press, 1923).

8. John Higham, *Strangers in the Land: Patterns of American Nativism, 1860–1925* (New York: Atheneum, 1963), presents a detailed discussion of how these studies influenced the immigration debate. Richard J. Herrnstein and Charles Murray, *The Bell Curve* (New York: Free Press, 1994), p. 5, argue that the publication of Brigham's book came far too late to play a significant role in the debate. Finally, Stephen J. Gould, *The Mismeasure of Man* (New York: Norton, 1981), pp. 222–233, presents a highly critical appraisal of this line of research.

9. Brigham, *Study of American Intelligence*, pp. 155, 209–210.

10. See, e.g., Nancy Clelland, "Immigrants Are $30 Billion Plus for the Nation, Study Contends," *San Diego Union Tribune*, May 25, 1994, p. A-1; and Marc Sandalow, "Immigrants Don't Hurt Economy," *San Francisco Chronicle*, May 25, 1994, p. A3.

11. Michael J. Fix and Jeffrey Passel, *Immigration and Immigrants: Setting the Record Straight* (Washington, D.C.: Urban Institute, 1997), p. 36.

12. Ibid., p. 39 (emphasis in original).

13. The sample of most recent immigrants in the Census data consists of persons who arrived in the country in the five years prior to the Census. The sample of most recent immigrants in the Current Population Surveys consists of persons who entered the country either after 1990 (in the 1996 CPS) or after 1992 (in the 1997 and 1998 CPS).

14. Some studies report that there might have been a slight turn of the long-run downward trend in the early 1990s. But this result hinges crucially on the data set being analyzed. The most recent data available from the Current Population Surveys (through 1998) suggests that if such a turnaround occurred, it did not continue into the late 1990s. See Funkhouser and Trejo, "Labor Market Skills of Recent Male Immigrants"; Alan Barrett, "Did the Decline Continue? Comparing the Labor Market Quality of United States Immigrants from the Late 1970s and Late 1980s," *Journal of Population Economics* 9 (April 1996): 55–63; and Guillermina Jasso, Mark R. Rosenzweig, and James P. Smith, "The Changing Skills of New Immigrants in the United States: Recent Trends and Their Determinants," in *Issues in the Economics of*

Immigration, ed. George J. Borjas (Chicago: University of Chicago Press, forthcoming 2000).

15. U.S. Immigration and Naturalization Service, *Statistical Yearbook of the Immigration and Naturalization Service, 1996* (Washington, D.C., 1997), p. 198.

16. The thirteen countries are Afghanistan, Bulgaria, Cambodia, Cuba, Czechoslovakia, Ethiopia, Hungary, Laos, Poland, Romania, Thailand, the former Soviet Union, and Vietnam.

17. Smith and Edmonston, *New Americans,* p. 193. This particular exercise in the National Academy's report formed the basis of the earlier and more extensive work of Barrett, "Did the Decline Continue?"

18. It is unclear if the occupation reported by the immigrant is the occupation where the person worked prior to migration or the intended occupation in the United States.

19. It would be interesting to track this cohort of immigrants into the 1980s and 1990s. Because of changes in coding procedures, however, the available surveys do not identify this particular immigrant cohort in data collected after 1970.

20. Quoted in Miller, *Unmaking of Americans,* pp. 7, 12. For additional examples of the emotional reactions typically encountered in the debate over assimilation, see Georgie Ann Geyer, *Americans No More: The Death of Citizenship* (New York: Atlantic Monthly Press, 1996); Joel Millman, *The Other Americans: How Immigrants Renew Our Country, Our Economy, and Our Values* (New York: Viking, 1997); and Peter D. Salins, *Assimilation, American Style* (New York: Basic Books, 1996).

21. Quoted in Peter Brimelow, *Alien Nation* (New York: Random House, 1995), p. 115. The multicultural perspective on assimilation issues seems to have some adherents in the Immigration and Naturalization Service, which has seriously considered eliminating the "citizenship test" that immigrants take as part of the naturalization process. This test encourages immigrants to acquire some basic knowledge about the political institutions of the country. Sample questions include: What are the three branches of the U.S. government? Who was the first president? What is the capital of the state where you live?

22. Donald L. Horowitz, *Ethnic Groups in Conflict* (Berkeley: University of California Press, 1985), presents an encyclopedic study of the determinants and consequences of ethnic conflict. The essay begins by stating that "the importance of ethnic conflict as a force shaping human affairs, as a phenomenon to be understood, as a threat to be controlled, can no longer be denied" (p. xi). In another provocative analysis, historian Arthur Schlesinger concludes: "The historic idea of a unifying American identity is now in peril in many arenas. If separatist tendencies go unchecked, the result can only be the fragmentation, resegregation, and tribalization of American life." See Arthur M. Schlesinger, Jr., *The Disuniting of America: Reflections on a Multicultural Society* (New York: Norton, 1992), pp. 17–18.

23. Gilles Grenier, "The Effects of Language Characteristics on the Wages of Hispanic American Males," *Journal of Human Resources* 19 (Winter 1984): 35–52. See also Walter McManus, William Gould, and Finis Welch, "Earnings of Hispanic Men: The Role of English Language Proficiency," *Journal of Labor Economics* 1 (April 1983): 101–130; Walter S. McManus, "Labor Market Costs of Language Disparity: An Interpretation of Hispanic Earnings Differences," *American Economic Review* 75 (September 1985): 818–827; Barry R. Chiswick and Paul W. Miller, "Language in

the Immigrant Labor Market," in *Immigration, Language and Ethnicity, Canada and the United States*, ed. Barry R. Chiswick (Washington, D.C.: American Enterprise Institute, 1992), pp. 229–296; and Barry R. Chiswick and Paul W. Miller, "The Endogeneity between Language and Earnings: International Analyses," *Journal of Labor Economics* 13 (April 1995): 246–288.

24. Evelina Tainer, "English Language Proficiency and Earnings among Foreign-Born Men," *Journal of Human Resources* 23 (Winter 1988): 108–122.

25. U.S. Department of Commerce, *The Foreign-Born Population in the United States*, U.S. Bureau of the Census Report 1990 CP-3-1 (Washington, D.C., 1993), p. 129. Persons who filled out the 1990 Census questionnaire were asked to report "how well" each person in the household spoke English. The possible answers were Very well, Well, Not well, and Not at all.

26. Alejandro Portes, "The Social Origins of the Cuban Enclave in Miami," *Sociological Perspectives* 30 (Fall 1987): 340–372.

27. Walter S. McManus, "Labor Market Effects of Language Enclaves: Hispanic Men in the United States," *Journal of Human Resources* 25 (Spring 1990): 228–252.

28. Edward P. Lazear, "Culture and Language," *Journal of Political Economy*, forthcoming 1999.

29. A few studies have investigated other channels of economic assimilation. Immigrants, for example, might acquire human capital by searching for job opportunities in various regions of the country, and resettling in those areas that offer the best opportunities. But Ann P. Bartel, "Where Do the New U.S. Immigrants Live?" *Journal of Labor Economics* 7 (October 1989): 371–391, finds that during the 1970s immigrants arrived in a small number of gateway cities, and tended to stay there. A relatively large number of immigrants also return to school after arrival in the United States; 17 percent of the immigrant men (aged sixteen to sixty-four) who migrated between 1985 and 1990 were enrolled in school in 1990. See Julian R. Betts and Magnus Lofstrom, "The Educational Attainment of Immigrants: Trends and Implications," in Borjas, *Issues in the Economics of Immigration*.

30. The assumption has its roots in economic theory. In the standard model of a free-market economy, the market wage equals the additional revenue generated by the last worker hired. Presumably, more productive workers can generate more revenue and hence would earn a higher wage.

31. Detailed descriptions of these trends are given by Kevin M. Murphy and Finis Welch, "The Structure of Wages," *Quarterly Journal of Economics* 107 (February 1992): 215–326; and Lawrence F. Katz and Kevin M. Murphy, "Changes in the Wage Structure, 1963–87: Supply and Demand Factors," *Quarterly Journal of Economics* 107 (February 1992): 35–78. Surveys of this vast literature are given by Frank Levy and Richard J. Murnane, "U.S. Earnings Levels and Earnings Inequality: A Review of Recent Trends and Proposed Explanations," *Journal of Economic Literature* 30 (September 1992): 1333–1381; and Lawrence F. Katz and David H. Autor, "Changes in the Wage Structure and Earnings Inequality," in *Handbook of Labor Economics*, ed. Orley Ashenfelter and David Card (Amsterdam: North-Holland, forthcoming 1999).

32. Barry T. Hirsch and David A. Macpherson, *Union Membership and Earnings Data Book: Compilations from the Current Population Survey* (Washington, D.C.: Bureau of National Affairs, Inc., 1998), p. 11.

33. Moreover, some of these factors might explain particular aspects of the increase in wage inequality, but not others. For example, international trade might explain the increasing wage gap between college graduates and high school graduates, but would probably not account for increased inequality within a skill group. A widely cited allotment among the various causes appeared in the 1997 *Economic Report of the President* (p. 175), where a very informal poll of a small number of economists attending a conference at the Federal Reserve Bank of New York concluded that about half of the increase in inequality can be attributed to skill-biased technological change, about 10 percent to immigration, about 10 percent to trade, and about 10 percent to deunionization.

34. The wage structure changed in different ways for various age-education groups, with more-skilled groups experiencing larger wage growth between 1970 and 1990. One can then use the wage growth observed in particular age-education cells among native workers to deflate the wage growth of immigrants in the same age-education cells. See Borjas, "Assimilation and Changes in Cohort Quality Revisited," for details.

35. Moreover, the data do not indicate a substantially faster process of economic assimilation when they are adjusted to account for changes in the wage structure; see ibid.

36. George J. Borjas and Bernt Bratsberg, "Who Leaves? The Outmigration of the Foreign-Born," *Review of Economics and Statistics* 78 (January 1996): 165–176. The out-migration rate is calculated by first estimating the number of legal immigrants who should be present in the United States after adjusting for mortality. This information is then compared with the Census enumeration after accounting for the presence of "nonimmigrants," such as illegal aliens, foreign students, and foreign executives. Semiofficial estimates of the out-migration rate are presented in U.S. Immigration and Naturalization Service, *Statistical Yearbook of the Immigration and Naturalization Service, 1996*, p. 196. See also Guillermina Jasso and Mark R. Rosenzweig, "Estimating the Emigration Rates of Legal Immigrants Using Administrative and Survey Data: The 1971 Cohort of Immigrants to the United States," *Demography* 19 (August 1982): 279–290; Robert Warren and Jennifer Marks Peck, "Foreign-Born Emigration from the United States," *Demography* 17 (February 1980): 71–84; and Robert Warren and Ellen Percy Kraly, *The Elusive Exodus: Emigration from the United States*, Population Trends and Public Policy Occasional Paper no. 8 (Washington, D.C.: Population Reference Bureau, March 1985). The data do not provide any information on whether the immigrants who leave the United States are returning to their home countries or migrating elsewhere.

37. U.S. Department of Commerce, *U.S. Population Estimates by Age, Sex, Race, and Hispanic Origin: 1990 to 1996*, U.S. Bureau of the Census Report PPL-57 (Washington, D.C., March 24, 1997). An equivalent restatement of the assumption is that roughly 25 percent of the immigrants who entered the country in the 1980s and 1990s eventually leave the United States.

38. In the words of the Immigration and Naturalization Service: "Partly because of inherent methodological difficulties, data on emigration from the United States are not being collected." See U.S. Immigration and Naturalization Service, *Statistical Yearbook of the Immigration and Naturalization Service, 1996*, p. 197.

39. The most careful study of the skill composition of the out-migrants is given by Fernando Ramos, "Out-Migration and Return Migration of Puerto Ricans," in Borjas and Freeman, *Immigration and the Work Force*, pp. 49–66. Because Puerto Rico is a U.S. possession, the Puerto Rican and U.S. censuses provide valuable information on the characteristics of Puerto Ricans in the United States versus those of Puerto Ricans who remained in their homeland, as well as on the characteristics of Puerto Ricans who returned to Puerto Rico after living in the United States for a brief period. Ramos finds that Puerto Rican "immigrants" in the United States are relatively unskilled, but that the return migrants are relatively more skilled than the typical immigrant. See also George J. Borjas, "Immigrant and Emigrant Earnings: A Longitudinal Study," *Economic Inquiry* 27 (January 1989): 21–37; and Jasso and Rosenzweig, "Estimating the Emigration Rates of Legal Immigrants Using Administrative and Survey Data."

40. Smith and Edmonston, *New Americans*, p. 205.

CHAPTER 3
NATIONAL ORIGIN

1. John Higham, *Strangers in the Land: Patterns of American Nativism, 1860–1925* (New York: Atheneum, 1963), gives an interesting analysis of the immigration debate that led to the enactment of the 1924 legislation. E. P. Hutchinson, *Legislative History of American Immigration Policy, 1798–1965* (Philadelphia: University of Pennsylvania Press, 1981), provides an encyclopedic account of the evolution of immigration policy up to the enactment of the 1965 Amendments.

2. U.S. Immigration and Naturalization Service, *Statistical Yearbook of the Immigration and Naturalization Service, 1996* (Washington, D.C., 1997), p. 34. The period referred to is 1994–96, so the statistics are unaffected by the large number of illegal aliens who received amnesty and were awarded permanent residence in the early 1990s.

3. U.S. Immigration and Naturalization Service, *Statistical Yearbook of the Immigration and Naturalization Service, 1996*, p. 198.

4. The national origin distribution for the 1991–96 period is distorted by the large number of illegal aliens who received amnesty through the Immigration Reform and Control Act, and who were granted permanent residence status in the early 1990s. The INS defines the time of entry of a legal immigrant as the time that he or she receives permanent residence status, and this is not necessarily the same as the year the person actually entered the country.

5. The historic shifts initiated by the First Great Migration—in terms of the number and national origin mix of immigrants—were accompanied by substantial changes in the skill endowments of the immigrant flow; see Paul H. Douglas, "Is the New Immigration More Unskilled than the Old?" *Journal of the American Statistical Association* 16 (June 1919): 393–403. The perceived or actual impact of these changes became a central issue in the debate over immigration policy, culminating in the enactment of the national origins quota system during the 1920s. An interesting summary of the findings in the forty-one–volume report of the Dillingham Commission (set up by Congress in 1907 to investigate the impact of immigration) is given by

Jeremiah W. Jenks and W. Jett Lauck, *The Immigration Problem* (New York: Funk and Wagnalls, 1917).

6. George J. Borjas, "The Economics of Immigration," *Journal of Economic Literature* 32 (December 1994): 1677–1717, p. 1686.

7. The National Academy discussion is based on a more detailed exercise conducted by George J. Borjas, "The Economic Impact of Immigration" (Class Notes, Harvard University, 1996). The close link between the changing national origin mix of immigrants and the decline in relative economic performance was first documented by George J. Borjas, "National Origin and the Skills of Immigrants in the Postwar Period," in *Immigration and the Work Force: Economic Consequences for the United States and Source Areas*, ed. George J. Borjas and Richard B. Freeman (Chicago: University of Chicago Press, 1992), pp. 17–47; and Robert J. LaLonde and Robert H. Topel, "The Assimilation of Immigrants in the U.S. Labor Market," in Borjas and Freeman, *Immigration and the Work Force*, pp. 67–92.

8. The average relative wage is a weighted average of the relative wage of each of the groups, where the weight is the share of the immigrant population that belongs to each group. The 1990 wage differential between immigrants and natives calculated in the National Academy report differs slightly from the one reported in the last chapter because the two studies use different random samples of native workers.

9. The counterfactual wage is a weighted average of the relative wage of each group, where the weights are the shares of each group in the 1970 immigrant population. An alternative counterfactual would take the relative wages of the various groups in 1970 as given (rather than 1990), and calculate the predicted wage for a particular national origin mix. The numerical answers from the two exercises are not identical, but they lead to the same general result, that the change in the national origin of immigrants is the main determinant of the decline in immigrant skills. Borjas, "National Origin and the Skills of Immigrants in the Postwar Period," also shows that the conclusions are unchanged when the exercise uses countries of origin, rather than continents, for classifying national origin.

10. These data are drawn from Robert J. Barro and Jong-Wha Lee, "International Comparisons of Educational Attainment," *Journal of Monetary Economics* 32 (December 1993): 363–394.

11. The trend line comes from a regression that relates the mean educational attainment of the immigrant group in the United States to the years of schooling completed by the average adult man in the source country. The regression coefficient is .88, with a standard error of .15. The regression is weighted by the sample size of the national origin group and has 67 observations.

12. These statistics are obtained by taking a weighted average of the Barro-Lee measure of educational attainment in the adult male population of the source countries as of 1985, where the weights are the shares of the immigrant population originating in the source country at a particular point in time.

13. David Card, "The Causal Effect of Education on Earnings," in *Handbook of Labor Economics*, vol. 3, ed. Orley Ashenfelter and David Card (Amsterdam: North Holland, forthcoming 1999), surveys this extensive literature. Julian R. Betts and Magnus Lofstrom, "The Educational Attainment of Immigrants: Trends and Implications," in *Issues in the Economics of Immigration*, ed. George J. Borjas (Chicago: Uni-

versity of Chicago Press, forthcoming 2000), report that the rate of return to education is lower for immigrants than for natives, regardless of where the immigrants obtained their education.

14. George J. Borjas, "Self-Selection and the Earnings of Immigrants," *American Economic Review* 77 (September 1987): 531–553; and Guillermina Jasso and Mark R. Rosenzweig, "What's in a Name? Country-of-Origin Influences on the Earnings of Immigrants in the United States," *Research in Human Capital and Development* 4 (1986): 75–106.

15. The trend line comes from a regression that relates the age-adjusted 1990 relative wage of immigrants who entered between 1985 and 1989 to the source country's (log) per capita GDP, Gini coefficient, and distance from the United States and the average educational attainment of the group. The age-adjusted wage is obtained from a regression that controls for variables indicating if the worker is twenty-five to thirty-four, thirty-five to forty-four, forty-five to fifty-four, or fifty-five to sixty-four years old. The per capita GDP is measured as of 1985; the Gini coefficient is measured as of 1980. The regression has 75 observations and is weighted by the sample size of the national origin group. The regression coefficients (and standard errors) are as follows: log per capita GDP, .149 (.023); Gini coefficient, −.003 (.002); distance in thousands of miles, −.023 (.010); and educational attainment, .094 (.010). Figure 3-2 illustrates the relation between relative wages and per capita GDP after controlling for all the other variables in the regression model. The coefficient of per capita GDP would rise to .202 (.033) if the educational attainment variable were not included in the regression model. See George J. Borjas, "The Economic Progress of Immigrants," in Borjas, *Issues in the Economics of Immigration*, for a more detailed analysis of these data.

16. These statistics are obtained by taking a weighted average of the 1985 per capita GDP across countries, where the weights are the country's share of the immigrant flow in the United States in a particular year.

17. U.S. Bureau of the Census, *Statistical Abstract of the United States, 1997* (Washington, D.C., 1997), p. 839. The (purchasing-power–parity basis) per capita GDP of the United States in 1995 was $26,438, while that of Mexico was $7,387.

18. Letter of Benjamin Franklin to Peter Collinson, May 1753. This letter is excerpted in Edith Abbott, *Historical Aspects of the Immigration Problem* (New York: Arno Press and the New York Times, 1969), pp. 415–416.

19. Quoted in David M. Kennedy, "Can We Still Afford to Be a Nation of Immigrants?" *Atlantic Monthly*, November 1996, p. 54.

20. Borjas, "Self-Selection and the Earnings of Immigrants," provides a technical discussion of the types of selection generated by income-maximizing behavior on the part of potential migrants.

21. George Psacharopoulos, *Returns to Education: An International Comparison* (San Francisco: Jossey-Bass, 1973), estimates the rate of return to education in many countries.

22. Ronald G. Ehrenberg and Robert S. Smith, *Modern Labor Economics*, 6th ed. (Reading, Mass: Addison-Wesley, 1997), pp. 558–561, present a clear discussion of how a Gini coefficient is defined and calculated. The regression coefficient is −.014, with a standard error of .003. The regression also holds constant the log per capita

GDP in the source country and the distance between the source country and the United States. The regression has 75 observations and is weighted by the sample size of the national origin group.

23. The Gini coefficients for Mexico and the United Kingdom are 57.9 and 23.3, respectively.

24. Additional evidence that measures of income inequality in the source country are negatively correlated with the earnings of immigrants in the United States is reported by George J. Borjas, "Immigration and Self-Selection," in *Immigration, Trade, and the Labor Market*, ed. John M. Abowd and Richard B. Freeman (Chicago: University of Chicago Press, 1991), pp. 29–76; and Deborah A. Cobb-Clark, "Immigrant Selectivity and Wages: The Evidence for Women," *American Economic Review* 83 (September 1983): 986–993. J. Edward Taylor, "Undocumented Mexico-U.S. Migration and the Returns to Households in Rural Mexico," *American Journal of Agricultural Economics* 69 (August 1987): 626–638, gives a case study of migration in a rural Mexican village, and concludes that Mexicans who migrated illegally to the United States are less skilled, on average, than the typical person residing in the village. This type of selection is consistent with the fact that Mexico offers a relatively high rate of return to skills. Alan M. Barrett, "Three Essays on the Labor Market Characteristics of Immigrants" (Ph.D. diss., Michigan State University, 1993), shows that immigrants who enter the United States using a family reunification visa have relatively lower earnings if they originate in countries where there is a great deal of income inequality.

25. Betts and Lofstrom, "Educational Attainment of Immigrants," tab. 9.

26. Stephen J. Trejo, "Why Do Mexican Americans Earn Low Wages?" *Journal of Political Economy* 105 (December 1997): 1235–1268, p. 1256. As a comparison, Trejo shows that whites earn about 31 percent more than blacks, but less than a third of this gap can be attributed to differences in observable human capital. See also Cordelia W. Reimers, "Labor Market Discrimination against Hispanic and Black Men," *Review of Economics and Statistics* 65 (November 1983): 570–579. Peter Skerry, *Mexican Americans: The Ambivalent Minority* (New York: Free Press, 1993) gives a broad account of the economic experiences and the cultural and political attitudes of the Mexican-American population.

27. Barry R. Chiswick, "An Analysis of the Earnings and Employment of Asian-American Men," *Journal of Labor Economics* 1 (April 1983): 197–214.

28. Studies that investigate ethnic differences in wage growth include Borjas, "Economic Progress of Immigrants"; Harriet Orcutt Duleep and Mark C. Regets, "Immigrant Entry Earnings and Human Capital Growth: Evidence from the 1960–1980 Censuses," *Research in Labor Economics* 16 (1997): 297–317; and Robert F. Schoeni, Kevin F. McCarthy, and Georges Vernez, *The Mixed Economic Progress of Immigrants* (Santa Monica, Calif.: RAND Corporation, 1996).

29. For example, one point in the figure would be the group of Mexican immigrants who were twenty-five through thirty-four years old when they entered the United States between 1975 and 1979.

30. The trend line comes from a regression of the rate of wage growth on the log of the entry wage. The regression also includes variables indicating the age at the time of entry. The regression has 246 observations and is weighted by the sample size

of the immigrant cohort. The coefficient of the log entry wage is .13, with a standard error of .11. Note that this coefficient is not statistically different from zero. See Borjas, "Economic Progress of Immigrants," for methodological details.

31. See LaLonde and Topel, "Assimilation of Immigrants in the U.S. Labor Market"; and Duleep and Regets, "Immigrant Entry Earnings and Human Capital Growth." Both of these studies report a negative correlation between the entry wage and the wage growth of immigrant cohorts within particular education groups.

32. The trend line comes from a regression of the rate of wage growth on the log of the entry wage and on the average educational attainment of the immigrant cohort at the time of entry. The regression also includes variables indicating the age at the time of entry. The regression has 246 observations and is weighted by the sample size of the immigrant cohort. The coefficient of the log entry wage is −.43, with a standard error of .06. See Borjas, "Economic Progress of Immigrants," for methodological details. Note that the analysis of wage convergence in the immigrant population has much in common with the literature that estimates cross-country regressions to determine the rate of convergence in per capita income across countries; see, e.g., Robert J. Barro, *Determinants of Economic Growth: A Cross-Country Empirical Study* (Cambridge: MIT Press, 1997); and Gregory N. Mankiw, David Romer, and David N. Weil, "A Contribution to the Empirics of Economic Growth," *Quarterly Journal of Economics* 107 (May 1992): 407–438. These studies typically correlate the growth rate in per capita GDP with initial levels of per capita GDP and find a weak positive correlation that turns negative when the regression controls for the initial human capital stock of the country.

33. In contrast, if one wants to design social policies that would improve the economic status of immigrants in the United States, the adjusted correlation illustrated in Figure 3-5 provides very valuable information. Investments in human capital that equalize the skills of the various immigrant groups soon after they enter the United States would go a long way toward reducing long-run wage inequality in the immigrant population.

34. See, e.g., Alejandro Portes, ed., *The Economic Sociology of Immigration: Essays on Networks, Ethnicity, and Entrepreneurship* (New York: Russell Sage Foundation, 1995); and Alejandro Portes and Rubén G. Rumbaut, *Immigrant America: A Portrait*, 2d ed. (Berkeley: University of California Press, 1996).

35. George J. Borjas, *Friends or Strangers: The Impact of Immigrants on the U.S. Economy* (New York: Basic Books, 1990), p. 90, surveys the related evidence indicating that immigrants who live in areas with high immigrant populations have lower wages than other immigrants.

36. The trend line comes from a regression that relates the rate of wage growth of an immigrant cohort in the first ten years in the United States to the source country's (log) per capita GDP, Gini coefficient, distance from the United States, and a Herfindahl index measure of the degree of geographic clustering of the ethnic group at the state level. The regression also includes variables indicating the age at the time of entry and the year of entry. The regression has 749 observations and is weighted by the sample size of the immigrant cohort. The coefficient of the Herfindahl index is −.16, with a standard error of .06. The Herfindahl index is defined as follows. Let p_j be the fraction of an immigrant group (defined by national origin and year of arrival)

that lives in state *j*. The index is obtained by summing the square of p_j across states. The Herfindahl index takes on a value of one if a particular immigrant group resides only in one state. The Herfindahl index for natives is .04. See Borjas, "Economic Progress of Immigrants," for methodological details.

37. Maria La Ganga, "Bilingual Ed Initiative Wins Easily," *Los Angeles Times*, June 3, 1998, p. A1.

38. This test is available online at the web site of Citizenship and Immigration Canada, the government agency responsible for immigration issues.

39. The scores refer to the point system in effect in mid-1998. The points allocated to particular factors, as well as the passing grade, are under continuous evaluation by the Canadian authorities and change frequently.

40. Michael Baker and Dwayne Benjamin, "The Performance of Immigrants in the Canadian Labor Market," *Journal of Labor Economics* 12 (July 1994): 369–405, present a detailed analysis of the changes in immigrant skills experienced by Canada during the 1971–86 period. It turns out that the adoption of the point system in the early 1960s did not halt the deterioration in the relative skills of immigrants admitted to Canada. Part of the problem is that the fraction of "independent immigrants" admitted to Canada (and hence the fraction that is filtered by the point system) has declined steadily over time. Although both Canada and the United States experienced a deterioration of immigrant skills during the same period, the downward trend was much steeper in the United States.

41. Borjas, "Economics of Immigration," p. 1694.

42. Barro and Lee, "International Comparisons of Educational Attainment."

43. Harriet Orcutt Duleep and Mark C. Regets, "Some Evidence on the Effect of Admission Criteria on Immigrant Assimilation," in *Immigration, Language and Ethnicity, Canada and the United States*, ed. Barry R. Chiswick (Washington, D.C.: American Enterprise Institute, 1992), pp. 410–439; and George J. Borjas, "Immigration Policy, National Origin, and Immigrant Skills: A Comparison of Canada and the United States," in *Small Differences That Matter: Labor Markets and Income Maintenance in Canada and the United States*, ed. David Card and Richard B. Freeman (Chicago: University of Chicago Press, 1993), pp. 21–43. The trend line in the figure comes from a regression of the educational attainment of immigrant groups in the United States on the educational attainment of the immigrant group in Canada. The regression has 15 observations and is weighted by the sample size of the national origin group. The slope coefficient is 1.20, with a standard error of .37. See Borjas, "Immigration Policy, National Origin, and Immigrant Skills," p. 32, for methodological details.

44. Statistics Canada, *1996 Census Nation* tables; available at Canada Statistics web site.

45. This argument assumes that the United States and Canada offer relatively similar economic opportunities to potential migrants.

46. Borjas, "Immigration Policy, National Origin, and Immigrant Skills," shows that if the immigrant flow in Canada had the same national origin mix as that of the United States, the relative wage of immigrants in Canada would be as low as that of immigrants in the United States.

47. Peter Brimelow, "Afterword to the Paperback Edition," in *Alien Nation: Common Sense about America's Immigration Disaster* (New York: HarperCollins, 1996), pp. 277–300, discusses this point in the context of the reaction to the initial publication of his book.

CHAPTER 4
THE LABOR MARKET IMPACT OF IMMIGRATION

1. F. Bowen, "Immigration and Wages," originally published in *North American Review* (1852), excerpted in *Historical Aspects of the Immigration Problem*, ed. Edith Abbott (New York: Arno Press and the New York Times, 1969), pp. 291–292.

2. Thomas J. Espenshade, ed., *Keys to Successful Immigration: Implications of the New Jersey Experience* (Washington, D.C.: Urban Institute Press, 1997), pp. 94–95.

3. To my knowledge, no academic studies attempted to estimate this statistical relationship prior to 1982; see Jean Baldwin Grossman, "The Substitutability of Natives and Immigrants in Production," *Review of Economics and Statistics* 54 (November 1982): 596–603, for the first published study. The academic literature, however, has grown rapidly since then.

4. George J. Borjas, *Friends or Strangers: The Impact of Immigrants on the U.S. Economy* (New York: Basic Books, 1990), p. 81.

5. Rachel Friedberg and Jennifer Hunt, "The Impact of Immigration on Host County Wages, Employment and Growth," *Journal of Economic Perspectives* 9 (Spring 1995): 23–44, p. 42.

6. James P. Smith and Barry Edmonston, eds., *The New Americans: Economic, Demographic, and Fiscal Effects of Immigration* (Washington, D.C.: National Academy Press, 1997), p. 220.

7. William Frey, "The New White Flight," *American Demographics* 16 (April 1994): 40–48.

8. Ann P. Bartel, "Where Do the New U.S. Immigrants Live?" *Journal of Labor Economics* 7 (October 1989): 371–391.

9. In 1950, the states with the highest foreign-born shares in the population were New York (21 percent), Connecticut (17 percent), Massachusetts (17 percent), Rhode Island (16 percent), and New Jersey (15 percent).

10. In contrast, New York's share of foreign-born persons rose from 24 to 32 percent, Chicago's rose from 12 to 17 percent, and Houston's rose from 9 to 17 percent. The only large metropolitan area outside California that experienced a Southern California–like influx was Miami, where the immigrant share rose from 41 to 53 percent.

11. The early estimates of spatial correlations used cross-sectional data, estimating the correlation between the wage level in a particular locality and a measure of immigrant penetration at a point in time. Later studies estimated the correlation between the *change* in the wage level in a particular locality and the *change* in the number of immigrants over some period of time.

12. See, for example, some of the results reported in Joseph G. Altonji and David Card, "The Effects of Immigration on the Labor Market Outcomes of Less-Skilled Natives," in *Immigration, Trade, and the Labor Market*, ed. John M. Abowd and Richard B. Freeman (Chicago: University of Chicago Press, 1991), pp. 201–234.

Donald Huddle, "The Costs of Immigration" (photocopy, Carrying Capacity Network, Washington, D.C., July 1993), makes selective use of the Altonji-Card evidence in his calculation that immigrants impose a $40 billion burden on natives.

13. Borjas, *Friends or Strangers*, chap. 4, surveys this literature.

14. I converted the regression coefficients reported by Robert F. Schoeni, "The Effect of Immigrants on the Employment and Wages of Native Workers: Evidence from the 1970s and 1980s" (photocopy, RAND Corporation, March 1997), into units that are more easily interpretable. Schoeni relates the wage of white native workers to the immigrant share (the fraction of the population in the labor market that is foreign-born). To translate the Schoeni results into the units used in Table 4-1, I multiplied his regression coefficients by $1/(1 + x)^2$, where x gives the number of immigrants per native in the labor market. I assumed that $x = .1$.

15. The correction uses a statistical procedure called instrumental variables. This two-stage procedure involves predicting the immigrant penetration in particular labor markets, and then correlating these predictions with the labor market outcomes experienced by native workers. A widely cited application is presented in Altonji and Card, "Effects of Immigration on the Labor Market Outcomes of Less-Skilled Natives," pp. 219–221. Altonji and Card predicted the 1970–80 change in the share of immigrants in a metropolitan area by using information on the immigrant share in 1970 and its square.

16. This change in the regional wage structure was first documented by George J. Borjas, Richard B. Freeman, and Lawrence F. Katz, "How Much Do Immigration and Trade Affect Labor Market Outcomes?" *Brookings Papers on Economic Activity* 1 (1997): 1–67.

17. The data underlying the figure are adjusted for interstate differences in the educational attainment of native men by aggregating across different education cells, using a fixed weight of the native education distribution. See ibid., pp. 17–20, for details.

18. The trend line illustrated in the top panel of Figure 4-3 is estimated from a regression that relates the rate of wage growth in the 1980s to the rate of wage growth in the 1970s. The regression coefficient is −1.33, with a standard error of .14. The trend line is obtained by weighting each state's observation by the population of the state. It turns out that this negative correlation did not exist between the 1960s and the 1970s; the correlation in wage growth between those two decades was nearly zero.

19. The trend line illustrated in the bottom panel of Figure 4-3 is estimated from a regression that relates the change in the number of immigrants per native worker during the 1980s with the change in the number of immigrants per native worker during the 1970s. The regression coefficient is 1.07, with a standard error of .06. The trend line is obtained by weighting each state's observation by the population of the state.

20. David Card, "The Impact of the Mariel Boatlift on the Miami Labor Market," *Industrial and Labor Relations Review* 43 (January 1990): 245–257.

21. Related studies of natural experiments in immigration include Jennifer Hunt, "The Impact of the 1962 Repatriates from Algeria on the French Labor Market," *Industrial and Labor Relations Review* 45 (April 1992): 556–572; and William J. Carrington and Pedro de Lima, "The Impact of 1970s Repatriates from Africa on

the Portuguese Labor Market," *Industrial and Labor Relations Review* 49 (January 1996): 330–347. Neither study finds a substantial impact of immigration on the affected local labor markets.

22. Joshua D. Angrist and Alan B. Krueger, "Empirical Strategies in Labor Economics," in *Handbook of Labor Economics*, vol. 3, ed. Orley Ashenfelter and David Card (Amsterdam: North-Holland, forthcoming 1999).

23. There is little documentation of where the potential refugees eventually ended up. Many of them were probably deterred from starting the hazardous journey; some returned to Cuba after being intercepted; and others were eventually admitted to the United States. In May 1995, the Clinton administration agreed to admit the 21,000 Cubans who were still being held at Guantanamo Bay. Because it took so many months for all these events to unfold, no local labor market in the United States faced a sudden and large increase in labor supply—as had been the case with the Mariel flow. Beginning in May 1995, the United States also changed its decades-long policy of automatically granting asylum to Cubans fleeing the Castro regime, and began to intercept and repatriate those Cubans who attempted to leave the island. See Steve Fainaru, "U.S. Policy on Cubans Reversed," *Boston Globe*, May 3, 1995, p. 1.

24. The data reported in Table 3-2 are drawn from the Current Population Surveys, which implies that the calculations of the Miami unemployment rates are based on relatively small samples. As a result, the standard errors are relatively large and the hypothesis that the 1993–95 change in Miami's black unemployment rate was similar to that experienced by the comparison cities cannot be rejected in a strict statistical sense. The t-statistic testing whether the black unemployment rate grew faster in Miami is 1.70. See Angrist and Krueger, "Empirical Strategies in Labor Economics," for details.

25. The few studies that attempt to determine if native migration decisions are correlated with immigration have yielded a confusing set of results. See, e.g., Randall K. Filer, "The Impact of Immigrant Arrivals on Migratory Patterns of Native Workers," in *Immigration and the Work Force: Economic Consequences for the United States and Source Areas*, ed. George J. Borjas and Richard B. Freeman (Chicago: University of Chicago Press, 1992), pp. 245–269; William H. Frey, "Immigration and Internal Migration 'Flight' from US Metropolitan Areas: Toward a New Demographic Balkanization," *Urban Studies* 32 (May 1995): 733–757; and Richard Wright, Mark Ellis, and Michael Reibel, "The Linkage between Immigration and Internal Migration in Large Metropolitan Areas in the United States," *Economic Geography* 73 (April 1997): 234–254. Filer finds that metropolitan areas where immigrants cluster had lower rates of native in-migration and higher rates of native out-migration in the 1970s; Frey finds a strong negative correlation between immigration and the net migration rates of natives in the 1990 Census; and Wright, Ellis, and Reibel report a positive correlation between the in-migration rates of natives to particular cities and immigration flows in the 1980s.

26. This section is based on the discussion by Borjas, Freeman, and Katz, "How Much Do Immigration and Trade Affect Labor Market Outcomes?" pp. 25–38.

27. The decline in the 1990s is partly attributable to the deep recession that hit California around 1990.

28. Card, "Impact of the Mariel Boatlift on the Miami Labor Market," p. 255.

29. The trend line is estimated from a regression where the dependent variable is the annualized 1970–90 change in the native population as a fraction of the state's population in 1970, and the independent variable is the annualized 1970–90 change in the immigrant population as a fraction of the state's population in 1970. The regression coefficient is .78, with a standard error of .53. The trend line is obtained from a regression that is weighted by the population of the state, and that has 51 observations.

30. David Card, "Immigrant Inflows, Native Outflows, and the Local Labor Market Impacts of Higher Immigration" (National Bureau of Economic Research Working Paper no. 5927, February 1997).

31. The trend line is estimated from a regression where the dependent variable gives the annualized 1970–90 change in the native population as a fraction of the state's population in 1970 minus the 1960–70 change in the native population as a fraction of the state's population in 1960, and the independent variable gives the annualized 1970–90 change in the immigrant population as a fraction of the state's population in 1970 minus the 1960–70 change in the immigrant population as a fraction of the state's population in 1960. The regression coefficient is − .76, with a standard error of .29. The trend line is obtained from a regression that is weighted by the population of the state, and that has 51 observations.

32. Daniel S. Hamermesh, "Immigration and the Quality of Jobs," in *Help or Hindrance: The Economic Implications of Immigration for African-Americans*, ed. Daniel S. Hamermesh and Frank Bean (New York: Russell Sage, 1998), pp. 75–106.

33. The complete list of immigrant-intensive industries includes personal services, agriculture, business and repair services, retail trade, and manufacturing. See Borjas, Freeman, and Katz, "How Much Do Immigration and Trade Affect Labor Market Outcomes?" p. 9, for additional details.

34. George J. Borjas, Richard B. Freeman, and Lawrence F. Katz, "On the Labor Market Impacts of Immigration and Trade," in Borjas and Freeman, *Immigration and the Work Force*, pp. 213–244. Related applications of the factor proportions approach include Richard B. Freeman, "Manpower Requirements and Substitution Analysis of Labor Skills: A Synthesis," *Research in Labor Economics* 1 (1977): 151–183; and George E. Johnson, "The Demand for Labor by Educational Category," *Southern Economic Journal* 37 (October 1970): 190–204.

35. The validity of the approach also depends on a number of technical assumptions. These assumptions include a detailed description of how labor inputs (and capital) are transformed into a single aggregate output, the aggregation of workers of heterogeneous skills into two groups (skilled and unskilled), and the requirement that natives and immigrants within each skill group be equally productive. The calculations then require information on the actual change in the relative number of immigrants for each skill group, and an estimate of how relative wages respond to the change in relative supplies. Borjas, Freeman, and Katz, "How Much Do Immigration and Trade Affect Labor Market Outcomes?" pp. 39–46, provide a technical discussion of the issues involved.

36. Lawrence F. Katz and Kevin M. Murphy, "Changes in the Wage Structure, 1963–87: Supply and Demand Factors," *Quarterly Journal of Economics* 107 (Febru-

ary 1992): 35–78; and Kevin M. Murphy and Finis Welch, "The Structure of Wages," *Quarterly Journal of Economics* 107 (February 1992): 215–326.

37. Per-Anders Edin and Bertil Holmlund, "The Swedish Wage Structure: The Rise and Fall of Solidarity Wage Policy?" in *Differences and Changes in Wage Structures*, ed. Richard B. Freeman and Lawrence F. Katz (Chicago: University of Chicago Press, 1995), pp. 307–343; Richard B. Freeman and Karen Needels, "Skill Differentials in Canada in an Era of Rising Labor Market Inequality," in *Small Differences That Matter*, ed. David Card and Richard B. Freeman (Chicago: University of Chicago Press, 1993), pp. 45–67; Dae-Il Kim and Robert Topel, "Labor Markets and Economic Growth: Lessons from Korea's Industrialization, 1970–1990," in Freeman and Katz, *Differences and Changes in Wage Structures*, pp. 227–264; and John Schmitt, "The Changing Structure of Male Earnings in Britain, 1974–88," ibid. pp. 177–204.

38. David A. Jaeger, "Skill Differences and the Effect of Immigrants on the Wages of Natives" (photocopy, U.S. Bureau of Labor Statistics, 1996), presents some evidence indicating that immigrant and native workers who have the same level of education have roughly similar productivities.

39. These are "approximate" percentage changes; the wage data actually refer to differences in log points.

40. To isolate the labor market effects of post-1979 immigration, the simulation defines all persons present in the United States as of 1979 as natives.

41. Studies of labor demand suggest that the wage ratio of unskilled to skilled workers falls by 32.2 percent when the ratio of unskilled to skilled workers increases by one unit (from, say, one unskilled worker per skilled worker to two unskilled workers per skilled worker). To obtain the impact of immigration on the relative wage, one multiplies this "relative wage elasticity" of −.322 by the change in factor proportions, which is approximately 17 percentage points. See Borjas, Freeman, and Katz, "How Much Do Immigration and Trade Affect Labor Market Outcomes?" pp. 48–50, for details.

42. The classification actually breaks the data into high school "equivalents" (all workers with twelve or fewer years of schooling and one-half of those with some college) and college "equivalents" (all workers with at least a college degree and one-half of those with some college). Katz and Murphy, "Changes in the Wage Structure," argue that this classification of skills may be useful in some contexts. The estimate of the relative wage elasticity for these two groups is −.709.

43. Card, "Immigrant Inflows, Native Outflows, and the Local Labor Market Impacts of Higher Immigration," p. 2; and John DiNardo, "Comments and Discussion," *Brookings Papers on Economic Activity* 1 (1997), p. 75.

44. Borjas, Freeman, and Katz, "How Much Do Immigration and Trade Affect Labor Market Outcomes?" pp. 10–12.

45. Ibid., pp. 10–14.

46. Ibid., pp. 56–61. Richard B. Freeman, "Are Your Wages Set in Beijing?" *Journal of Economic Perspectives* 9 (Summer 1995): 15–32, summarizes the evidence on the labor market impacts of trade.

47. The economic effects of immigration and trade will differ, however, because some goods are not "tradable." These goods, such as plumbing, gardening, and child

care, have to be produced within the United States. Immigrants can compete in these markets, but trade cannot provide those services.

CHAPTER 5
THE ECONOMIC BENEFITS FROM IMMIGRATION

1. James P. Smith and Barry Edmonston, eds., *The New Americans: Economic, Demographic, and Fiscal Effects of Immigration* (Washington, D.C.: National Academy Press, 1997), p. 384.

2. George Gilder, "Geniuses from Abroad," *Wall Street Journal*, December 18, 1995, p. A14.

3. Detailed expositions of the model are given by Ronald G. Ehrenberg and Robert S. Smith, *Modern Labor Economics*, 6th ed. (Reading, Mass.: Addison Wesley, 1997), chap. 2; and George J. Borjas, *Labor Economics* (New York: McGraw-Hill, 1996), chap. 5. The simulations presented in this chapter calculate the economic benefits of immigration within a competitive, market-clearing framework. By focusing on a competitive economy with market clearing and full employment, the analysis ignores the potentially harmful effects of immigration when there is structural unemployment in the economy and jobs might be "prizes" that are captured partly by immigrants.

4. There also exist models of international trade where the country gains but no workers lose. These models typically require that the traded goods not be produced in the United States. This assumption, however, is false for many of the goods that the United States imports. A good introduction to international trade theory is given by Wilfred J. Ethier, *Modern International Economics*, 3d ed. (New York: W. W. Norton, 1995).

5. The immigration surplus isolates the economic gains accruing to natives in the United States. The calculation, therefore, ignores the impact of immigration both on the immigrants themselves and on the persons who remain in the source countries.

6. George J. Borjas, "The Economic Benefits from Immigration," *Journal of Economic Perspectives* 9 (Spring 1995): 3–22, presents a technical discussion of how the immigration surplus arises in a market economy. A number of technical assumptions are required to derive the formula: (1) the production process uses two inputs, capital and labor; (2) the capital stock is fixed, and natives own all of the capital; (3) the production technology has constant returns to scale, so that if the capital stock and the number of workers were to double, the quantity of output produced would also double; (4) all workers, whether immigrants or natives, have the same skill level; and (5) all workers are willing to work at the going wage. Because of the assumption that the capital stock is fixed, this formula provides an estimate of the immigration surplus in the short run, before the rest of the economy can adjust to the immigrant influx.

7. See David H. Autor, Lawrence F. Katz, and Alan B. Krueger, "Computing Inequality: Have Computers Changed the Labor Market?" *Quarterly Journal of Economics* 113 (November 1998): 1169–1213.

8. Recall that immigration increased the supply of high school dropouts by about 21 percent and that of college graduates by about 4 percent. The 17 percent relative increase in the supply of high school dropouts lowered their relative wage by about

5 percentage points. So a 10 percent increase in the number of immigrants would be roughly expected to reduce the wage by about 3 percent. Daniel S. Hamermesh, *Labor Demand* (Princeton, N.J.: Princeton University Press, 1993), chap. 3, provides an extensive survey of estimates of the responsiveness of wages to changes in supply. Hamermesh concludes that a 10 percent increase in the supply of workers most likely leads to a 3 percentage drop in the wage.

9. The exact formulas giving the net change in the incomes of native workers and capitalists are as follows: Change in the income accruing to native workers as a fraction of GDP = $-se(1-m)$, and Change in the income accruing to capitalists as a fraction of GDP = $se(1-.5m)$, where s is labor's share of income, e gives the percent drop in the wage attributable to immigration, and m is the fraction of the labor force that is foreign-born; see Borjas, "Economic Benefits from Immigration," for details.

10. Smith and Edmonston, *New Americans*, p. 6, conclude that "the domestic gain may run on the order of $1 billion to $10 billion a year."

11. Spencer Abraham, "Immigrants Bring Prosperity," *Wall Street Journal*, November 11, 1997, p. A18 (emphasis added).

12. U.S. Department of Commerce, *The Black Population of the United States: March 1997 (Update)*, P20–508 (Washington, D.C., June 1998), tab. 12. The data refer to salaried persons aged twenty-five through sixty-four. For a more detailed discussion of the gains and losses accruing to blacks, see George J. Borjas, "Do Blacks Gain or Lose from Immigration?" in *Help or Hindrance? The Economic Implications of Immigration for African-Americans*, ed. Daniel S. Hamermesh and Frank D. Bean (New York: Russell Sage Foundation, 1998), pp. 51–74.

13. The available estimates of the black-white wealth, or net worth, ratio range from .18 to .27; see Francine D. Blau and John W. Graham, "Black-White Differences in Wealth and Asset Composition," *Quarterly Journal of Economics* 105 (May 1990): 321–339; and James P. Smith, "Racial and Ethnic Differences in Wealth in the Health and Retirement Survey," *Journal of Human Resources* 30 (Supplement 1995): S158–S183.

14. It is worth emphasizing that the native-born black population is just one of many native groups that are "labor-intensive." If one conducted this type of cost-benefit analysis for other native groups that are labor-intensive (which would presumably include most subgroups of native workers), the same general finding would emerge: Immigration is not beneficial for groups that are long on labor and short on capital. It is also important to note that the back-of-the-envelope calculation uses a number of assumptions that might not accurately reflect the operation of the U.S. economy. For example, many of the gains from immigration that initially go to capitalists are eventually redistributed to consumers (in the form of lower prices for the goods that immigrants produce). As a result, African American natives get additional gains because they profit from these lower prices. There is no direct evidence on the magnitude of these price effects. Moreover, if many of the goods and services produced by immigrants cater to the demands of high-income native workers, the price effects will tend to disproportionately favor the white native population.

15. U.S. Department of Commerce, *The Foreign-Born Population in the United States*, Bureau of the Census Report 1990 CP-3-1 (Washington, D.C., 1993); and U.S. Bureau of the Census, *Statistical Abstract of the United States, 1992* (Washington, D.C., 1992), pp. xii–xiii.

16. Although the argument abstracts from foreign investments, these flows could be included in a more general model without changing the basic conclusion.

17. In technical terms, the aggregate production function has constant returns to scale, so that a doubling of all inputs doubles output.

18. Nothing would change if the two economies were integrated. Suppose, for example, that native firms hire all the immigrant workers and that immigrant firms hire all the native workers. Each economy will still generate only $7 trillion in national income, and the distribution of income between immigrants and natives will remain unaffected.

19. See George J. Borjas, "The Economic Analysis of Immigration," *Handbook of Labor Economics*, ed. Orley Ashenfelter and David Card (Amsterdam: North-Holland, 1999), for a technical discussion of this issue. The key theoretical result is that the immigration surplus equals zero if the rate of return to capital in the United States is reequilibrated back at the "world price" after the immigrant supply shock. This result arises because the immigration-induced capital flows reestablish the capital-labor ratio that existed in the United States prior to immigration, and the native wage remains unchanged. In the end, natives neither gain nor lose from immigration. The empirical evidence, however, suggests that capital is somewhat immobile across countries; see Martin S. Feldstein and Charles Horioka, "Domestic Savings and International Capital Flows," *Economic Journal* 90 (June 1980): 314–329.

20. This argument also implies that the impact of immigration on the income distribution becomes much less important over time.

21. Michael Fix and Jeffrey S. Passel, *Immigration and Immigrants: Setting the Record Straight* (Washington, D.C.: Urban Institute, May 1994), p. 49.

22. Julian Simon, *Immigration: The Demographic and Economic Facts* (Washington, D.C.: Cato Institute, 1995), p. 4. See also Stephen Moore, "Return of the Nativists," *American Spectator*, June 1996, p. 22.

23. Elhanan Helpman and Paul R. Krugman, *Market Structure and Foreign Trade* (Cambridge: MIT Press, 1985).

24. Edward P. Lazear, "Diversity and Immigration," in *Issues in the Economics of Immigration*, ed. George J. Borjas (Chicago: University of Chicago Press, forthcoming 2000), presents a theoretical (and technical) discussion of the economic gains that might arise from the interaction of persons from different cultures. Lazear's study, however, does not attempt to estimate what those potential gains might be in the case of the United States.

25. It can be also argued that immigration injects the economy with a group of persons who are very responsive to differences in economic opportunities across states. Since the immigrants are incurring a substantial cost in their migration, they might as well move to the state that provides the best economic opportunities. Immigrants would then make up a disproportionate bulk of the "marginal" persons who chase better economic opportunities and help equalize wages across areas. As a result, immigration into the United States speeds up the rate of wage convergence across regions and improves labor market efficiency. It is difficult to estimate precisely the magnitude of this gain because the calculation requires information on how long it would take for wage differentials across regions to disappear if there were no immigration. A rough calculation, however, suggests that this gain in economic efficiency may be of the same order of magnitude as the immigration surplus. See George J. Borjas,

"Does Immigration Grease the Wheels of the Labor Market?" (photocopy, Harvard University, April 1998).

26. The assumption that there are only two skill groups is obviously a drastic simplification of the real economy. But more complex models, which would allow for more skill groups, are difficult to manipulate, and often do not provide a fruitful way of measuring the economic impact of particular social policies. This family of economic models is now frequently used for simulating the impact of immigration on the U.S. labor market. See, e.g., Borjas, "Economic Benefits from Immigration"; George E. Johnson, "Estimation of the Impact of Immigration on the Distribution of Income among Minorities and Others," in Hamermesh and Bean, *Help or Hindrance? The Economic Implications of Immigration for African-Americans*, pp. 17–50; and George J. Borjas, Richard B. Freeman, and Lawrence F. Katz, "How Much Do Immigration and Trade Affect Labor Market Outcomes?" *Brookings Papers on Economic Activity* 1 (1997): 1–67. The simulation reported here uses data drawn from Borjas, "Do Blacks Gain or Lose from Immigration?"

27. Hamermesh, *Labor Demand*, chap. 3.

28. I showed earlier that African American natives lose from immigration because they are less likely to own capital, and it is the capitalists who typically have the most to gain from an increase in the number of workers. African American natives will also lose from immigration because their skills are more likely to resemble those of immigrants. In terms of the definition of skill groups used in the simulation, 50 percent of natives are unskilled, 70 percent of immigrants are unskilled, and almost 65 percent of African American natives are unskilled. In the short run, the immigration deficit in the black population—after accounting both for blacks' lack of capital ownership and for the relative similarity in the skills of blacks and immigrants—is between $4 billion and $13 billion annually. Put differently, immigration reduces black annual income by between $100 to $400 per person. For more details, see Borjas, "Do Blacks Gain or Lose from Immigration?"

29. The discussion initially ignores the role of capital in the production process.

30. A review of the empirical evidence on the capital-skill complementarity hypothesis is given by Hamermesh, *Labor Demand*, chap. 3. A historical perspective on the emergence of capital-skill complementarity in the U.S. economy is given by Claudia Goldin and Lawrence F. Katz, "The Origins of Technology-Skill Complementarity," *Quarterly Journal of Economics* 113 (August 1998): 693–732.

31. David M. Kennedy, "Can We Still Afford to Be a Nation of Immigrants?" *Atlantic Monthly*, November 1996, pp. 52–68.

32. Goldin and Katz, "Origins of Technology-Skill Complementarity," p. 694. See also John A. James and Jonathan S. Skinner, "The Resolution of the Labor-Scarcity Paradox," *Journal of Economic History* 45 (September 1985): 513–540.

CHAPTER 6
IMMIGRATION AND THE WELFARE STATE

1. See, e.g., Francine D. Blau, "The Use of Transfer Payments by Immigrants," *Industrial and Labor Relations Review* 37 (January 1984): 222–239; Leif Jensen, "Patterns of Immigration and Public Assistance Utilization, 1970–1980," *International Migration Review* 22 (Spring 1988): 51–83; and Marta Tienda and Leif Jensen,

"Immigration and Public Assistance Participation: Dispelling the Myth of Dependency," *Social Science Research* 15 (December 1986): 372–400. George J. Borjas and Stephen J. Trejo, "Immigrant Participation in the Welfare System," *Industrial and Labor Relations Review* 44 (January 1991): 195–211, reported some of the initial evidence that raised concerns about rising welfare use in the immigrant population.

2. The AFDC program, which has been replaced by the Temporary Assistance for Needy Families (TANF) program by the 1996 welfare reform, was targeted to single women with small children. The SSI program is targeted mainly to disabled and elderly persons. The general assistance program is typically administered at the county level, and is targeted to families with short-run needs. See U.S. House of Representatives, *Background Material and Data on Programs within the Jurisdiction of the Committee on Ways and Means* (Washington, D.C., 1996), for an encyclopedic description of all means-tested programs.

3. Ibid., pp. 1319–1320.

4. The data are drawn from the 1970–90 Public Use Microdata Samples of the U.S. Census and the 1996–98 Annual Demographic Files of the Current Population Surveys. The 1970 Census data consist of a .1 percent random sample of native households and a 2 percent random sample of immigrant households. The 1980 Census data consist of a .1 percent random sample of native households and a 5 percent random sample of immigrant households. And the 1990 Census data consist of a .5 percent random sample of native households and a 5 percent random sample of immigrant households. The three CPS data sets are pooled, and are referred to as the 1998 data. A household is classified as an immigrant household if the household head was born outside the United States and is either an alien or a naturalized citizen. All other households are classified as native households. The year of immigration of the household is determined by the household head's year of arrival in the United States. The empirical analysis is restricted to households that do not reside in group quarters and are headed by persons who are at least eighteen years old. George J. Borjas, "Immigration and Welfare, 1970–1990," *Research in Labor Economics* 14 (1995): 251–280, presents a more detailed discussion of the Census data.

5. The sample of newly arrived immigrants in the 1970, 1980, and 1990 Census data consists of persons who arrived in the country in the five-year period prior to the Census. The sample of newly arrived immigrants in the Current Population Surveys consists of persons who entered the country either after 1990 (in the 1996 survey) or after 1992 (in the 1997 and 1998 surveys).

6. The tracking procedure raises the likelihood that the same groups are being compared over time. In 1990, for example, the immigrant sample would contain households that entered between 1965 and 1969 and where the head is thirty-eight to fifty-four years old, and the native sample would contain households where the head is in this age range. Borjas, "Immigration and Welfare," shows that other immigrant cohorts (who arrived in different years or at different ages) exhibit the same pattern of assimilating into welfare. There are differences in the assimilation pattern between immigrants who originate in refugee-sending countries and immigrants who do not. The nonrefugees tend to exhibit the pattern illustrated in Figure 6-2. The refugees enter the country with very high rates of welfare use, and those rates remain high throughout their lives.

7. This provision of immigration law went into effect in 1882. Between 1971 and 1980, the last year for which data are reported, only thirty-one persons were deported for being a public charge; see U.S. Immigration and Naturalization Service, *Statistical Yearbook of the Immigration and Naturalization Service, 1996* (Washington, D.C., 1997), p. 183.

8. Although the analysis of welfare participation is typically conducted at the household level, this approach is somewhat problematic. A household is typically defined as an immigrant household when the head of the household is foreign-born. But this household may contain a few native-born persons, and it is unclear if one should count the welfare use of these natives as immigrant or native use. See Frank D. Bean, Jennifer V. W. Van Hook, and Jennifer E. Glick, "Country of Origin, Type of Public Assistance, and Patterns of Welfare Recipiency among U.S. Immigrants and Natives," *Social Science Quarterly* 78 (June 1997): 432–451, for a more detailed analysis of this issue, and of how different definitions can change the size of the immigrant-native welfare gap. Immigrant households are also somewhat larger than native households, increasing the likelihood that someone in an immigrant household receives some type of assistance. Nevertheless, many welfare programs—such as housing assistance and food stamps—are targeted to the household, not to individual persons. Although the data based on whether a particular person receives assistance leads to a more optimistic portrayal of welfare use in the immigrant population in the 1970s and 1980s, this is no longer true by the 1990s. The 1996–98 Current Population Surveys indicate that 5.4 percent of foreign-born *persons* received cash benefits, as compared to 4.2 percent of native-born persons; that 10.5 percent of immigrants received Medicaid, as compared to 7.8 percent of natives; and that 10.7 percent of immigrants participated in some public assistance program, as compared to 8.1 percent of natives.

9. The immigrant-native welfare gap, however, was still far smaller than the respective welfare gap between black and white households in the native population. In 1998, 34 percent of black native households received some type of assistance, as compared to 12 percent of white native households.

10. George J. Borjas and Lynette Hilton, "Immigration and the Welfare State: Immigrant Participation in Means-Tested Entitlement Programs," *Quarterly Journal of Economics* 111 (May 1996): 575–604, p. 584. After accounting for all of the means-tested programs, the welfare gap grew significantly between the mid-1980s—when data on immigrant use of "in-kind" transfers began to be collected—and the late 1990s. In the mid-1980s, "only" about 18 percent of immigrants and 15 percent of natives participated in some welfare program.

11. U.S. Department of Health and Human Services, Office of Refugee Resettlement, *Refugee Resettlement Program, 1995* (Washington, D.C., 1995), p. 8.

12. The Current Population Surveys do not contain any information on the type of visa used by a particular household to enter the country. To approximate the refugee population, I classified all households who originated in the main refugee-sending countries as refugee households, while households originating in all other countries were classified as nonrefugee households. The main refugee-sending countries over the 1970–90 period were Afghanistan, Bulgaria, Cambodia, Cuba, Czechoslovakia, Ethiopia, Hungary, Laos, Poland, Romania, Thailand, the former Soviet Union, and Vietnam.

13. A classic critique of the welfare state is given by Charles A. Murray, *Losing Ground: American Social Policy, 1950–1980* (New York: Basic Books, 1984). Robert Moffitt, "Incentive Effects of the U.S. Welfare System: A Review," *Journal of Economic Literature* 30 (March 1992): 1–61, reviews the scholarly literature on this controversial subject.

14. These data are formally known as the Surveys of Income and Program Participation (SIPP), and are analyzed in Borjas and Hilton, "Immigration and the Welfare State."

15. Adjusting for state of residence is important because immigrants cluster in very few states—and two of those states, California and New York, have relatively generous welfare programs.

16. Michael Baker and Dwayne Benjamin, "The Receipt of Transfer Payments by Immigrants in Canada," *Journal of Human Resources* 30 (Fall 1995): 650–676, investigate the relationship between immigration and welfare in Canada. They find that immigrants in Canada (which uses a point system based on observable socioeconomic characteristics to award some of the entry visas) are less likely to receive welfare benefits than natives.

17. U.S. House of Representatives, *Background Material and Data on Programs within the Jurisdiction of the Committee on Ways and Means*, pp. 437, 913.

18. U.S. Central Intelligence Agency, *Handbook of International Economic Statistics* (Washington, D.C., 1997). The per capita income data adjust for international differences in purchasing power.

19. Quoted in Peter Brimelow, "Milton Friedman at 85," *Forbes*, December 29, 1997, p. 52.

20. U.S. Immigration and Naturalization Service, *Statistical Yearbook of the Immigration and Naturalization Service, 1996*, p. 196.

21. Patricia B. Reagan and Randall J. Olsen, "You Can Go Home Again: Evidence from Longitudinal Data" (photocopy, Ohio State University, September 1996).

22. This evidence should be interpreted cautiously. It is only a correlation, and there are difficult causality issues that are not addressed. It may be that immigrants who expect to leave the United States in the near future are more likely to enter the welfare rolls because they do not want to make the requisite investments in human capital that may be required by American employers. Under this interpretation, it is not welfare that deters out-migration, but rather the prospect of out-migration that improves the opportunities provided by the welfare state relative to those found in the labor market.

23. In principle, what matters is the interstate variation in AFDC benefit levels after adjusting for cost-of-living differences across states. Although there are no widely accepted state-specific price deflators, the Bureau of Labor Statistics does provide deflators for specific cities and broadly defined regions. Using these deflators to adjust the data does not alter the basic fact that California's benefit structure changed drastically over the period, and that the state had become nearly the most generous in the nation by 1990.

24. Alaska was the only state that surpassed California's generous AFDC benefits in 1990.

25. Rebecca Blank, "The Effect of Welfare and Wage Levels on the Location Decisions of Female Households," *Journal of Urban Economics* 24 (September 1988):

186–211; James Walker, "Migration among Low-Income Households: Helping the Witch Doctors Reach Consensus" (photocopy, University of Wisconsin, Madison, 1993). Some evidence in favor of a magnetic effect in the native population is reported in Bruce D. Meyer, "Do the Poor Move to Receive Higher Welfare Benefits" (photocopy, Northwestern University, July 1998).

26. There is also a marked difference between the geographic sorting of new immigrants who are welfare recipients and that of immigrants who have been in the country for at least ten years. The earlier immigrants behave more like the natives who are "stuck" in their state of residence and do not find it worthwhile to move across state lines searching for higher welfare benefits. In particular, 34 percent of the "older" immigrants who received welfare lived in California, as compared to 26 percent of those who did not. The geographic clustering is also evident in the demographic group that should be most sensitive to interstate AFDC benefit differentials: female-headed households with children under eighteen years of age. In 1990, 10 percent of the native households in this group that received welfare lived in California, as compared to 11 percent of the native households that did not. Among new immigrants, 31 percent of the households that did not receive welfare lived in California, as compared to 41 percent of the ones that did. See George J. Borjas, "Immigration and Welfare Magnets," *Journal of Labor Economics* (forthcoming 1999), tab. 2, for details.

27. See, e.g., Douglas S. Massey, "The Settlement Process among Mexican Migrants to the United States," *American Sociological Review* 51 (October 1986): 670–684; and Douglas S. Massey and Felipe Garcia España, "The Social Process of International Migration," *Science*, August 14, 1987, 733–738.

28. Don Barnett, "Their Teeming Shores," *National Review*, November 1, 1993, pp. 51–55; and Norman Matloff, "From 'Jiu Ji Jin' to 'Fu Li Jin': Some Chinese Immigrants Mistakenly See Welfare as a 'Fringe Benefit,'" *New Democrat*, November 1994, pp. 23–25.

29. Borjas and Hilton, "Immigration and the Welfare State," pp. 596–599.

30. Although this strong correlation is consistent with the existence of information networks within the immigrant community, organized along national origin lines, this is not the only interpretation of the evidence. The correlation between how a national origin group has behaved in the past and how new additions to that group behave in the present can also arise because of some unobserved factors that simply lead to a higher propensity for receiving particular types of aid among all members of that group.

31. Wendell Primus, "Immigration Provisions in the New Welfare Law," *Focus* 18 (Fall/Winter 1996–97): 14–18, p. 14.

32. The legislation also tightened the rules for sponsorship. The income of persons who wish to sponsor the entry of family members must exceed 125 percent of the poverty line. The sponsors must also file affidavits of support that are legally binding, making the sponsor financially liable for many of the expenses incurred by the immigrant.

33. U.S. Immigration and Naturalization Service, *Statistical Yearbook of the Immigration and Naturalization Service, 1996*, p. 146. The rapid increase in the number of petitions has also been attributed to politically motivated programs that sought to increase the number of registered voters prior to the 1996 presidential election; see

Mirta Ojito, "A Record Backlog to Get Citizenship Stymies 2 Million," *New York Times*, April 20, 1998, p. A1.

34. Jeffrey S. Passel and Rebecca L. Clark, "How Much Do Immigrants Really Cost? A Reappraisal of Huddle's 'The Costs of Immigrants' " (photocopy, Urban Institute, Washington, D.C., February 1994); Donald Huddle, "The Costs of Immigration" (photocopy, carrying Capacity Network, Washington, D.C., July 1993). A good review of the methods and assumptions used in these accounting exercises is given by Thomas MaCurdy, Thomas Nechyba, and Jay Bhattacharya, "An Economic Framework for Assessing the Fiscal Impacts of Immigration," in *The Immigration Debate: Studies on the Economic, Demographic and Fiscal Effects of Immigration*, ed. James P. Smith and Barry Edmonston (Washington: National Academy Press, 1998), pp. 13–65.

35. James P. Smith and Barry Edmonston, eds., *The New Americans: Economic, Demographic, and Fiscal Effects of Immigration* (Washington, D.C.: National Academy Press, 1997), chaps. 6, 7. Although I was a member of the National Academy panel that wrote the report, the two chapters on the fiscal impact of immigration were prepared by other panel members, mainly Robert Inman (an economist at the University of Pennsylvania), Thomas Espenshade (an economist at Princeton University), and Ronald Lee (an economic demographer at the University of California, Berkeley). The key papers used by the National Academy panel in preparing the final chapters on the fiscal impact of immigration were Deborah L. Garvey and Thomas J. Espenshade, "Fiscal Impacts of Immigrant and Native Households: A New Jersey Case Study," in Smith and Edmonston, *Immigration Debate*, pp. 66–119; Michael S. Clune, "The Fiscal Impacts of Immigrants," in ibid., pp. 121–182; and Ronald D. Lee and Timothy W. Miller, "The Current Fiscal Impact of Immigrants and Their Descendants: Beyond the Immigrant Household," ibid., pp. 183–205.

36. For some of the state and local government expenditure and tax programs, the National Academy had reasonably good information on immigrant participation. For example, there are data available that indicate how many immigrant children are enrolled in school, how many of these children are in bilingual programs, how many immigrants are covered by Medicaid, how much immigrants earn, and so on. For other programs, however, the data are sketchy. There is no evidence, for example, on how immigrants affect the cost of providing garbage collection. The typical assumption for these programs was that if immigration increased the population of a state by 10 percent, the cost of providing these services also rose by 10 percent. In effect, the analysis assumed that the cost of providing the services to additional persons (immigrants) equals the average cost of providing these services to the native population. Although it is difficult to verify this assumption for every single government program, it is probably not a bad approximation for the aggregate sum of all the programs provided by state and local governments.

37. Smith and Edmonston, *New Americans*, p. 284.

38. California Department of Finance. "Educating Illegal Immigrants" (Technical Notes to the Governor's Budget 1994–95, Sacramento, California, January 19, 1994).

39. Smith and Edmonston, *New Americans*, pp. 276, 281.

40. Alan L. Gustman and Thomas L. Steinmeier, "Social Security Benefits of Immigrants and U.S. Born," in *Issues in the Economics of Immigration*, ed. George J.

Borjas (Chicago: University of Chicago Press, forthcoming 2000), present a careful analysis of the fiscal impact in the "middle run," by calculating how the current immigrant population will affect expenditures in the social security system as they reach retirement age.

41. The present value calculation discounts the receipts and expenditures in future years at a 3 percent annual rate.

42. Not surprisingly, the long-run benefit differs significantly among different types of persons. Immigrants who are high school dropouts generate a long-run fiscal burden of $13,000, while immigrants who have some college education generate a long-run fiscal surplus of nearly $200,000.

43. The specific assumption is: "Starting in 2016, and thereafter, fiscal policy will hold the debt/GDP ratio constant at the level of 2016." See Smith and Edmonston, *New Americans*, p. 325.

44. Ibid., p. 337.

45. Ibid., p. 343. If the simulation focuses only on the first twenty-five years after the immigrant enters the country, the $80,000 net gain becomes an $18,400 net loss.

CHAPTER 7
SOCIAL MOBILITY ACROSS GENERATIONS

1. Barry Edmonston and Jeffrey S. Passel, "Immigration and Immigrant Generations in Population Projections," *International Journal of Forecasting* 8 (November 1992): 459–476, p. 471.

2. Classic expositions of the assimilation hypothesis are given by Robert Park, *Race and Culture* (Glencoe, Ill: Free Press, 1975); and Milton Gordon, *Assimilation and American Life* (New York: Oxford University Press, 1964).

3. Nathan Glazer and Daniel P. Moynihan, *Beyond the Melting Pot: The Negroes, Puerto Ricans, Jews, Italians, and Irish of New York City* (Cambridge: MIT Press, 1963), p. xcvii.

4. The debate over the validity of the melting pot hypothesis continues in the sociological literature. For instance, Richard D. Alba, *Ethnic Identity: The Transformation of White America* (New Haven, Conn.: Yale University Press, 1990), stresses the convergence that occurred among groups of European origin. Studies that stress the persistent differences include Reynolds Farley, "Blacks, Hispanics, and White Ethnic Groups: Are Blacks Uniquely Disadvantaged?" *American Economic Review* 80 (May 1990): 237–241; and Stanley Lieberson and Mary C. Waters, *From Many Strands: Ethnic and Racial Groups in Contemporary America* (New York: Russell Sage Foundation, 1988). See also Joel Perlmann, *Ethnic Differences: Schooling and Social Structure among the Irish, Italians, Jews, and Blacks in an American City, 1880–1935* (New York: Cambridge University Press, 1988); and Stephen Steinberg, *The Ethnic Myth: Race, Ethnicity, and Class in America* (Boston: Beacon Press, 1989).

5. Barry R. Chiswick, "Sons of Immigrants: Are They at an Earnings Disadvantage?" *American Economic Review* 67 (February 1977): 376–380; and Geoffrey Carliner, "Wages, Earnings, and Hours of First, Second and Third Generation American Males," *Economic Inquiry* 18 (January 1980): 87–102.

6. Beginning in 1980, the Census stopped collecting information on the birthplace of a person's parents. Instead, the Census began to report the ethnic ancestry.

This key change in the survey instrument implies that there is now some information on national origin for all persons, but that the information provided is likely to be imprecise (relative to the information gathered when persons are specifically asked to name the country where their parents were born). In 1994, the Current Population Surveys began to collect information on a person's birthplace, as well as on the birthplace of the person's parents.

7. The linkage between parents and children across censuses can be improved in a number of ways. For example, the children of immigrants aged twenty-five to forty-four in 1940 are likely to be relatively young in 1970, while the children of immigrants aged forty-five to sixty-four in 1940 are likely to be relatively older in 1970. The results, however, are not very sensitive to the adoption of alternative tracking procedures; see George J. Borjas, "The Intergenerational Mobility of Immigrants," Part 1, *Journal of Labor Economics* 11 (January 1993): 113–135.

8. The study of how various personal traits and socioeconomic characteristics are transmitted across generations has a long history, beginning with the famous study by Sir Francis Galton, "Regression towards Mediocrity in Hereditary Stature," *Journal of the Anthropological Institute of Great Britain and Ireland* 15 (1886): 246–263, where he measured the correlation between the heights of children and parents. Recent studies of the intergenerational transmission of skills include Gary S. Becker and Nigel Tomes, "Human Capital and the Rise and Fall of Families," Part 2, *Journal of Labor Economics* 4 (July 1986): S1–S39; Gary Solon, "Intergenerational Income Mobility in the United States," *American Economic Review* 82 (June 1992): 393–408; and David J. Zimmerman, "Regression toward Mediocrity in Economic Stature," *American Economic Review* 82 (June 1992): 409–429. Gary Solon, "Intergenerational Mobility in the Labor Market," in *Handbook of Labor Economics*, vol. 3, ed. Orley Ashenfelter and David Card (Amsterdam: North-Holland, forthcoming 1999), surveys this literature.

9. This quip has its origins in a Lancashire proverb that Carnegie liked to quote: "There's nobbut three generations atween clog and clog."

10. The ethnic background of second-generation Americans is determined by the father's country of birth (unless only the mother is foreign-born, in which case it is determined from the mother's country of birth). See Borjas, "Intergenerational Mobility of Immigrants," for more details on the analysis of the 1940–70 data; see also David Card, John DiNardo, and Eugena Estes, "The More Things Change: Immigrants and the Children of Immigrants in the 1940s, the 1970s, and the 1990s," in *Issues in the Economics of Immigration*, ed. George J. Borjas (Chicago: University of Chicago Press, forthcoming 2000), for an analysis of the trends between 1970 and the 1990s.

11. The trend line comes from a regression where the dependent variable gives the average log wage of second-generation workers from a particular source country in 1970 or in 1998 (relative to the wage of the third generation); and the independent variable gives the average log wage of first-generation workers from that source country in 1940 or in 1970 (relative to the wage of the third generation). See Borjas, "Intergenerational Mobility of Immigrants," for additional details about the specification and estimation of the regression model.

12. The slope coefficient of the regression equals $\rho\sigma_2/\sigma_1$, where ρ is the correlation between the average skills of the groups in the first and second generations, σ_1 is the

standard deviation of the mean skills of ethnic groups in the first generation, and σ_2 is the standard deviation of the mean skills of ethnic groups in the second generation. The regression coefficient is exactly equal to the "intergenerational correlation" only if the standard deviation of mean skills is constant across generations.

13. The trend line would have a 45-degree angle when the intergenerational correlation equals one.

14. The estimated trend lines are as follows. In the 1940–70 period, the intercept is .07 (with a standard error of .02), and the slope coefficient is .45 (.07). In the 1970–98 period, the intercept is .04 (.02), and the slope coefficient is .69 (.10). The 1940–70 regression is estimated using twenty-three national origin groups, while the 1970–98 regression uses forty-one national origin groups. The regressions are estimated using generalized least squares to account for the sampling error in the dependent variable. The regressions include only the national origin groups that have sufficient observations to allow a statistically reliable analysis. Several studies also report that the intergenerational correlation in educational attainment is somewhat smaller, on the order of .3 to .4. See, e.g., Card, DiNardo, and Estes, "The More Things Change." One possible interpretation of this finding is that the measure of educational attainment is "top-coded"—educational attainment cannot go over twenty years of schooling. The compression of the huge differences in skills that exist among ethnic groups into a relatively narrow range can reduce the estimate of the intergenerational correlation. Finally, as pointed out in note 12, the regression coefficient linking the average earnings of the group across generations can vary over time—even if the underlying intergenerational correlation (ρ) is relatively constant. In particular, the regression coefficient will tend to be larger when the earnings inequality among ethnic groups increases across generations. The standard deviation of log earnings for the first generation in 1940 is .17, and the standard deviation for the second generation in 1970 is .15; the standard deviation for the first generation in 1970 is .19, and the standard deviation for the second generation in 1998 is .23. Because of these trends, much of the increase in the regression coefficient from .45 to .69 over the two sample periods can be attributed to the rising wage inequality across ethnic groups. Using the definition presented in note 12, one can show that ρ equals .51 in the 1940–70 period, and .57 int eh 1970–98 period. Card, DiNardo, and Estes, ibid., present a detailed discussion of this statistical issue.

15. U.S. Immigration and Naturalization Service, *Statistical Yearbook of the Immigration and Naturalization Service, 1996* (Washington, D.C.: GPO, 1997), p. 25.

16. See George J. Borjas, "Long-Run Convergence of Ethnic Skill Differentials: The Children and Grandchildren of the Great Migration," *Industrial and Labor Relations Review* 47 (July 1994): 553–573, for a more detailed discussion. It is important to note that the First Great Migration did not stop in 1910. An additional eight million persons migrated between 1911 and 1924, when restrictive new immigration policies went into effect.

17. Borjas, "Long-Run Convergence of Ethnic Skill Differentials," pp. 556–557, discusses the imputation procedure in detail. The 1910 Census also does not provide any measure of educational attainment, for either native or immigrant workers.

18. Detailed studies of the skill differences that existed between immigrants and natives at the beginning of the twentieth century include Francine D. Blau, "Immigration and Labor Earnings in Early Twentieth Century America," *Research in Popu-*

lation Economics 2 (1979): 21–41; Barry Eichengreen and Henry A. Gemery, "The Earnings of Skilled and Unskilled Immigrants at the End of the Nineteenth Century," *Journal of Economic History* 46 (June 1986): 441–454; and Joseph Ferrie, "Immigrants and Natives: Comparative Economic Performance in the United States, 1850–1860 and 1965–1980," *Research in Labor Economics* 16 (1997): 319–341.

19. Borjas, "Long-Run Convergence of Ethnic Skill Differentials," pp. 558, 560. To maintain comparability with the wage data available in the 1910 Census, I created an occupational wage for each worker in the 1940 Census by assigning each worker the average wage rate in his occupation.

20. The regression relating the average educational attainment of the ethnic group in the second generation to the literacy rate of the group in the first generation has a slope coefficient of 5.12, with a standard error of .96. The regression relating the average log occupational wage of the group in the second generation to the average log occupational wage of the group in the first generation has a slope coefficient of .60, with a standard error of .14. The regressions are estimated using generalized least squares to account for the sampling error in the dependent variable; see Borjas, "Long-Run Convergence of Ethnic Skill Differentials," p. 563. The regressions are estimated using thirty-two national origin groups; these groups accounted for over 99.5 percent of the immigrants who entered the country between 1880 and 1910.

21. See Card, DiNardo, and Estes, "The More Things Change," for a detailed discussion of this point.

22. The General Social Surveys (GSS), conducted by the National Opinion Research Center at the University of Chicago, contain a series of cross-sections that have been collected annually since the early 1970s. Each cross-section consists of a survey of over one thousand persons. See James Allan Davis and Tom W. Smith, *General Social Surveys, 1972–1989, Cumulative Codebook* (Chicago: National Opinion Research Center, 1989), for a more detailed description of the data. The empirical evidence reported in this chapter is based on data drawn from the pooled 1977–89 waves of the GSS. The calculations use the sample of all working persons aged eighteen to sixty-four.

23. The GSS does not contain specific information on the place of birth of the individual's parents or grandparents (other than whether they were born in the United States), so it is not possible to ascertain the exact national origin of the person. The person's ethnicity, therefore, is obtained from the individual's response to the question, "From what countries or part of the world did your ancestors come?" Although most persons in the sample gave only one response to the question, some gave multiple responses. These multiple answers may arise because of intermarriage across national origin groups. I used the main ethnic background (as identified by the respondent) to classify the GSS respondents into one of the ethnic groups in the First Great Migration. Because of the classification system used by the GSS, and because of the relatively small sample sizes available in these data, it was possible to identify only twenty-two ethnic groups of third-generation workers. Lieberson and Waters, *From Many Strands*, discuss some of the problems caused by the errors that inevitably occur when persons are asked to self-report their ancestry.

24. The regression linking the average educational attainment of the group in the third generation and the literacy rate of the group in the first generation has a slope coefficient of 2.53, with a standard error of 1.78. The regression linking the average

log occupational wage of the group in the third generation and the average log occupational wage of the group in the first generation has a slope coefficient of .22, with a standard error of .11. The regression is estimated using generalized least squares to account for the sampling error in the dependent variable. For details, see Borjas, "Long-Run Convergence of Ethnic Skill Differentials," p. 569.

25. Thomas Sowell, *Ethnic America* (New York: Basic Books, 1981).

26. Borjas, "Long-Run Convergence of Ethnic Skill Differentials," pp. 570–571.

27. See Stanley Lieberson, "Generational Differences among Blacks in the North." *American Journal of Sociology* 79 (November 1973): 550–565; David Card and Alan B. Krueger, "School Quality and Black-White Relative Earnings: A Direct Assessment," *Quarterly Journal of Economics* 107 (February 1992): 151–200; James P. Smith and Finis R. Welch, "Black Economic Progress after Myrdal," *Journal of Economic Literature* 27 (June 1989): 519–564; and James J. Heckman and Brook S. Payner, "Determining the Impact of Federal Anti-discrimination Policy on the Economic Status of Blacks: A Study of South Carolina," *American Economic Review* 79 (March 1989): 138–177.

28. A household is classified as first-generation if the head of the household is foreign-born. The household is classified as second-generation if the head was born in the United States but either parent of the head was foreign-born. A detailed analysis of the intergenerational link in welfare use is given by George J. Borjas and Glenn T. Sueyoshi, "Ethnicity and the Intergenerational Transmission of Welfare Dependency," *Research in Labor Economics* 16 (1997): 271–295.

29. The trend line comes from a regression that relates the welfare participation rate of the second generation to that of the group in the first generation. The coefficient is .82, with a standard error of .10. The regression is weighted by the sample size of the immigrant group, and has forty-nine observations.

CHAPTER 8
ETHNIC CAPITAL

1. Theoretical discussions of intergenerational income mobility include Gary S. Becker, *A Treatise on the Family* (Cambridge: Harvard University Press, 1981), chap. 7; Gary S. Becker and Nigel Tomes, "Human Capital and the Rise and Fall of Families," *Journal of Labor Economics* 4 (July 1986): S1–S39; and Arthur Goldberger, "Economic and Mechanical Models of Intergenerational Transmission," *American Economic Review* 79 (June 1989): 504–513. Recent empirical studies include Kenneth A. Couch and Thomas A. Dunn, "Intergenerational Correlations in Labor Market Status: A Comparison of the United States and Germany," *Journal of Human Resources* 32 (Winter 1997): 210–232; John Fitzgerald, Peter Gottschalk, and Robert Moffitt, "An Analysis of the Impact of Sample Attrition on the Second Generation of Respondents in the Michigan Panel Study of Income Dynamics," *Journal of Human Resources* 33 (Spring 1998): 300–344; Gary Solon, "Intergenerational Income Mobility in the United States," *American Economic Review* 82 (June 1992): 393–408; and David J. Zimmerman, "Regression toward Mediocrity in Economic Status," *American Economic Review* 82 (June 1992): 409–429. Gary Solon, "Intergenerational Mobility in the Labor Market," in *Handbook of Labor Economics*, vol. 3, ed. Orley

Ashenfelter and David Card (Amsterdam: North-Holland, forthcoming 1999), surveys the literature.

2. This difference is related to the discussion of ecological correlations in the sociology literature. See W. S. Robinson, "Ecological Correlations and the Behavior of Individuals," *American Sociological Review* 15 (June 1950): 351–357; and Leo A. Goodman, "Some Alternatives to Ecological Correlation," *American Sociological Review* 18 (December 1953): 663–664.

3. See the Fall 1994 issue of the *Journal of Human Resources* for a recent collection of articles showing the link between parental investments and such traits as child height, ability, educational attainment, and labor supply,

4. Some observers would argue that part of the correlation arises because of the genetic transmission of ability. All that is required in the present context is that there be *some* link between parental skills and the children's skills. Therefore, there is no need to enter the contentious debate over the respective roles of nature versus nurture. For a good introduction to recent developments in this debate, see Richard J. Herrnstein and Charles A. Murray, *The Bell Curve: Intelligence and Class Structure in American Life* (New York: Free Press, 1994); Russell Jacoby and Naomi Glauberman, *The Bell Curve Debate: History, Documents, Opinions* (New York: Times Books, 1995); and Bernie Devlin et al., eds., *Intelligence, Genes, and Success: Scientists Respond to The Bell Curve* (New York: Springer, 1997). James J. Heckman, "Lessons from the Bell Curve," *Journal of Political Economy* 103 (October 1995): 1091–1120, gives a technical discussion of the issues.

5. George J. Borjas, "Ethnic Capital and Intergenerational Mobility," *Quarterly Journal of Economics* 107 (February 1992): 123–150, presents a more detailed (and technical) development of this hypothesis.

6. These statistics are calculated from the 1990 Public Use Microdata Sample of the U.S. Census, and give the employment shares in the top three occupations for each ethnic group.

7. Richard D. Alba, *Ethnic Identity: The Transformation of White America* (New Haven, Conn.: Yale University Press), 1990.

8. Harry J. Holzer, "Search Method Use by Unemployed Youth," *Journal of Labor Economics* 6 (January 1988): 1–20.

9. Roberto Suro, *Strangers among Us: How Latino Immigration Is Transforming America* (New York: Knopf, 1998), chap. 3.

10. James S. Coleman, "Social Capital in the Creation of Human Capital," *American Journal of Sociology* 94 (Supplement): S95–S120. The term "social capital" was introduced by Glenn C. Loury, "A Dynamic Theory of Racial Income Differences," in *Women, Minorities, and Employment Discrimination*, ed. Phyllis A. Wallace and Annette A. LaMond (Lexington, Mass.: Lexington Books, 1977), pp. 153–186. Loury used the concept to illustrate how racial income differences can persist over time because of spillover effects within racial groups—essentially the same idea that is captured by the ethnic capital hypothesis. Shelly Lundberg and Richard Startz, "On the Persistence of Racial Inequality," *Journal of Labor Economics* 16 (April 1998): 292–323, present a recent application of this framework. The concept is also at the core of Robert Putnam's famous "bowling alone" metaphor describing the link between social capital and declining civic participation; see Robert D. Putnam, "Bowling Alone: America's Declining Social Capital," *Current* 373 (June 1995): 3–10.

11. William Julius Wilson, *The Truly Disadvantaged: The Inner City, the Underclass, and Public Policy* (Chicago: University of Chicago Press, 1987).

12. Ibid., p. 56.

13. Ibid., p. 57.

14. Robert E. Lucas, "On the Mechanics of Economic Development," *Journal of Monetary Economics* 22 (July 1988): 3–42; and Paul M. Romer, "Increasing Returns and Long-Run Growth," *Journal of Political Economy* 94 (October 1986): 1002–1037.

15. The GSS is a series of cross-sections, each containing about one thousand persons, collected annually by the National Opinion Research Center at the University of Chicago. The NLSY is a panel of over twelve thousand persons aged fourteen to twenty-two at the time of the initial survey in 1979, and these same persons have been surveyed many times since then. The analysis reported in this section pools persons aged eighteen to sixty-four from the 1977–89 waves in the GSS, and uses the 1990 wave of the NLSY (by which time only 5 percent of the sample were still enrolled in school). The person's ethnicity in these surveys is defined from the response to the question, "From what countries or part of the world did your ancestors come?" or "What is your origin or descent?" Although most persons in these samples gave only one response to the question, some gave multiple responses. In those cases, I used the main ethnic background (as identified by the respondent) to classify persons into ethnic groups. A potentially important problem is that there could be a lot of self-selection in how persons choose to identify themselves. In particular, only those persons with the strongest ethnic roots will respond that they are Russians, or Germans, or Mexicans. This self-identification could potentially bias the results.

16. Similar types of results are obtained when one correlates the children's outcomes with the characteristics of the mother (or with an average of the father and mother's characteristics). See David Card, John DiNardo, and Eugena Estes, "The More Things Change: Immigrants and the Children of Immigrants in the 1940s, the 1970s, and the 1990s," in *Issues in the Economics of Immigration*, ed. George J. Borjas (Chicago: University of Chicago Press, forthcoming 2000).

17. The 1970 U.S. Census was used to calculate the mean log earnings in each three-digit occupation.

18. The regression model used to estimate the trend lines illustrated in Figure 8-1 is

$$y_{ij} = \alpha + \beta_1 x_{ij} + \beta_2 \bar{x}_j + \text{other variables} + \text{random term},$$

where y_{ij} gives the socioeconomic outcome of child i in ethnic group j, x_{ij} gives the socioeconomic outcome of the father of this child, and $\bar{x}_j$ gives the mean of the socioeconomic outcome in group j in the parental generation (or ethnic capital). The other variables included in the regression are age, age squared, gender of respondent, and dummy variables indicating the GSS cross-section from which the observation was drawn. The trend line illustrated in the top panel of the figure isolates the relationship between the child's outcome and the father's outcome, holding constant all the other variables in the regression, and its slope estimates the parameter β_1. The trend line in the bottom panel isolates the relationship between the child's outcome and the measure of ethnic capital, holding constant all the other variables in the regression, and its slope estimates the parameter β_2.

19. Abstracting from the other variables in the model, the previous note specifies the regression equation as

$$y_{ij} = \alpha + \beta_1 x_{ij} + \beta_2 \bar{x}_j + \text{random term.}$$

One can aggregate this regression model within an ethnic group to obtain

$$\bar{y}_j = \alpha + (\beta_1 + \beta_2)\bar{x}_j + \text{random term,}$$

where $\bar{y}_j$ gives the mean socioeconomic outcome in ethnic group j in the children's generation. The regression of mean outcomes across the two generations, therefore, has a slope equal to the sum of the two coefficients.

20. The standard errors for the correlations between children's skills and father's skills are around .01 in the GSS and around .05 in the NLSY. The standard errors for the correlations between children's skills and ethnic capital lie around .06 in the GSS, .05 in the NLSY for the education measure of skills, and .16 in the NLSY for the wage measure of skills.

21. Paul R. Spickard, *Mixed Blood: Intermarriage and Ethnic Identity in Twentieth-Century America* (Madison: University of Wisconsin Press, 1989).

22. The standard errors for the correlations between children's skills and father's skills are between .02 and .03. The standard errors for the correlations between children's skills and ethnic capital are around .07 for the education measure of skills, and around .10 for the wage measure. Because the standard errors of the ethnic capital correlations are relatively large, one cannot reject the hypothesis that the impact of ethnic capital on children's skills is the same across generations. The trend in the correlation, however, does suggest that ethnic spillovers tend to matter less the longer the household has lived in the United States.

23. For instance, there is a strong positive intergenerational correlation in the "civic culture" of ethnic groups, at least in terms of their voter turnout and such activities as reading the newspaper every day; see Thomas W. Rice and Jan L. Feldman, "Civic Culture and Democracy from Europe to America," *Journal of Politics* 59 (November 1997): 1143–1172.

24. An extensive literature in sociology analyzes the related issue of a "culture of poverty." See Oscar Lewis, *Five Families: Mexican Case Studies in the Culture of Poverty* (New York: Basic Books, 1959); and Oscar Lewis, *La Vida: A Puerto Rican Family in the Culture of Poverty—San Juan and New York* (New York: Random House, 1966). A collection of essays that criticize this approach is given by Eleanor Burke Leacock, ed., *The Culture of Poverty: A Critique* (New York: Simon & Schuster, 1971).

25. The parental household is classified as being on welfare if the parents received any type of public assistance income in the previous calendar year.

26. The standard error is .1 percent.

27. The average characteristics for the ethnic group were calculated from a sample of households drawn from the 1980 Public Use Microdata Sample of the U.S. Census, where the household head is between thirty-five and sixty-four years old. This age restriction makes it more likely that the persons in the Census sample can be the parents of the NLSY children. See George J. Borjas and Glenn T. Sueyoshi, "Ethnicity

and the Intergenerational Transmission of Welfare Dependency," p. 275, for additional details.

28. The standard error is 2.5 percent.

29. There is also evidence that the intergenerational persistence in welfare use affects not only whether a particular household enters the welfare system but also the duration of the welfare spell. See Borjas and Sueyoshi, "Ethnicity and the Intergenerational Transmission of Welfare Dependency," pp. 284–289.

30. Becker and Tomes, "Human Capital and the Rise and Fall of Families."

31. Joseph G. Altonji and Thomas A. Dunn, "Relationship among the Family Incomes and Labor Market Outcomes of Relatives," *Research in Labor Economics* 12 (1991): 269–310; Solon, "Intergenerational Income Mobility in the United States"; and Zimmerman, "Regression toward Mediocrity in Economic Status." Note that the measurement error problem addressed by averaging out the parent's earnings over a period of time is the one caused by transitory changes in earnings. Fitzgerald, Gottschalk, and Moffitt, "Analysis of the Impact of Sample Attrition on the Second Generation of Respondents in the Michigan Panel Study of Income Dynamics," have argued that the intergenerational correlation between the earnings of the parents and those of the children is probably around .3, once the data properly account for the attrition that inevitably occurs in longitudinal samples.

32. Borjas, "Ethnic Capital and Intergenerational Mobility," p. 142.

33. Measurement error in the schooling of survey respondents may account for only about 10 percent of the variance in schooling. There is less evidence, however, indicating how much of the variance in measures of parental skills can be attributed to measurement error. A detailed discussion of the available theory and evidence on measurement error is given by Joshua D. Angrist and Alan B. Krueger, "Empirical Strategies in Labor Economics," in *Handbook of Labor Economics*, ed. Orley Ashenfelter and David Card (Amsterdam: North-Holland, forthcoming 1999).

34. George J. Borjas, "Ethnicity, Neighborhoods, and Human-Capital Externalities," *American Economic Review* 85 (June 1995): 365–390.

35. This technique is known as "instrumental variables" in the econometrics literature. Orley Ashenfelter and Alan B. Krueger, "Estimates of the Economic Return to Schooling from a New Sample of Twins," *American Economic Review* 84 (December 1994): 1157–1173, use this methodology to analyze the impact of measurement error in educational attainment on estimates of the rate of return to schooling. Borjas, "Ethnicity, Neighborhoods, and Human-Capital Externalities," pp. 386–388, presents a detailed discussion of the statistical methodology and the results discussed in this section.

36. Borjas, "Ethnicity, Neighborhoods, and Human-Capital Externalities," p. 388.

CHAPTER 9
ETHNIC GHETTOS

1. There is a growing appreciation for the notion that the social, cultural, and economic environment—as determined by a person's neighborhood, associates, and friends—has a potentially large impact on socioeconomic outcomes. A good survey of the academic literature is given by Christopher Jencks and Susan E. Meyer, "The

Social Consequences of Growing Up in a Poor Neighborhood: A Review," in *Inner City Poverty in the United States*, ed. Laurance E. Lynn and Michael G. H. McGeary (Washington, D.C.: National Academy Press, 1990), pp. 111–186. There is, however, a heated debate over whether the measured impacts reflect a spurious correlation, induced by the possibility that the same unobserved factors that lead to particular location choices also lead to particular socioeconomic outcomes; see, e.g., William N. Evans, Wallace E. Oates, and Robert M. Schwab, "Measuring Peer Group Effects: A Study of Teenage Behavior," *Journal of Political Economy* 100 (October 1992): 966–991. A very critical, though technical, appraisal of the literature is given by Charles F. Manski, "Identification of Endogenous Social Effects: The Reflection Problem," *Review of Economic Studies* 60 (July 1993): 531–542.

2. See, e.g., Douglas S. Massey and Nancy A. Denton, *American Apartheid: Segregation and the Making of the Underclass* (Cambridge: Harvard University Press, 1993); William Julius Wilson, *The Truly Disadvantaged: The Inner City, the Underclass, and Public Policy* (Chicago: University of Chicago Press, 1987); and Edward P. Lazear, "Culture and Language," *Journal of Political Economy*, forthcoming, 1999.

3. David M. Cutler and Edward L. Glaeser, "Are Ghettoes Good or Bad?" *Quarterly Journal of Economics* 112 (August 1997): 827–872, present a valuable analysis of this question, in the context of black-white differences in economic opportunities.

4. David M. Cutler, Edward L. Glaeser, and Jacob L. Vigdor, "The Rise and Decline of the American Ghetto" (National Bureau of Economic Research Working Paper no. 5881, January 1997). A large literature documents the extent of residential segregation among blacks and Hispanics; see Nancy A. Denton and Douglas S. Massey, "Hypersegregation in United States Metropolitan Areas—Black and Hispanic Segregation along 5 Dimensions," *Demography* 26 (August 1989): 373–391; and Mark Alan Hughes and Janice Fanning Madden, "Residential Segregation and the Economic Status of Black Workers: New Evidence for an Old Debate," *Journal of Urban Economics* 29 (January 1991): 28–49.

5. Detailed information on the Neighborhood File of the 1970 Census is given in U.S. Bureau of the Census, *Supplement no. 1 to Public Use Samples of Basic Records from the 1970 Census: Description and Technical Documentation* (Washington, D.C., 1973).

6. As I emphasized in Chapter 7, a single Census snapshot cannot be used to determine the extent of intergenerational mobility in residential segregation. The second-generation adults enumerated in 1970 are unlikely to be the children of the adult immigrants enumerated at the same time. See George J. Borjas, "Ethnicity, Neighborhoods, and Human-Capital Externalities," *American Economic Review* 85 (June 1995): 365–390, for details.

7. It is also the case that even when immigrants or their children move to other neighborhoods in the United States, they tend to choose neighborhoods that look like the neighborhoods they just left, at least in terms of their "immigrant-ness." Immigrants who have lived in the same house for over ten years live in a neighborhood that is 33 percent first- or second-generation, while the corresponding statistic for immigrants who have lived in the house for less than three years is 32 percent. Finally, it is worth noting that although there is substantial residential segregation among first- and second-generation workers, it is not nearly as striking as that found among blacks. The average black in 1970 lived in a neighborhood where the population was

55 percent black. See Borjas, "Ethnicity, Neighborhoods, and Human-Capital Externalities," pp. 368, 370.

8. The General Social Surveys indicate that over 90 percent of persons who classified themselves as Hispanic in the early 1980s are foreign-born, have parents who are foreign-born, or have grandparents who are foreign-born.

9. The 1970 Census also does not provide any information on the ethnic ancestry of U.S.-born who have U.S.-born parents, making it impossible to measure the extent of segregation that occurs within particular ethnic groups.

10. To reduce costs, the NLSY surveyed other persons in the family unit who were in the "correct" age range (that is, ages fourteen to twenty-two in 1979). As a result, there are a large number of siblings in the data. To avoid the bias introduced by this sampling scheme, I calculated the residential segregation measures on the sample of nonrelated persons who resided outside the household unit.

11. George J. Borjas, "To Ghetto or Not to Ghetto? Ethnicity and Residential Segregation," *Journal of Urban Economics* 44 (September 1998): 228–253.

12. By definition, a person of, say, Italian ancestry lives in an "integrated" neighborhood if the fraction of persons in the neighborhood who have Italian ancestry is less than twice that found in the national population.

13. Representative studies include Anne C. Case and Lawrence F. Katz, "The Company You Keep: The Effects of Family and Neighborhood on Disadvantaged Youths" (National Bureau of Economic Research Working Paper no. 3705, May 1991); Mary Corcoran, Roger Gordon, Deborah Laren, and Gary Solon, "The Association between Men's Economic Status and Their Family and Community Origins," *Journal of Human Resources* 27 (Fall 1991): 575–601; Jonathan Crane, "The Epidemic Theory of Ghettos and Neighborhood Effects on Dropping Out and Teenage Childbearing," *American Journal of Sociology* 96 (March 1991): 1226–1259; and James E. Rauch, "Productivity Gains from Geographic Concentration of Human Capital: Evidence from the Cities," *Journal of Urban Economics* 34 (November 1993): 380–400.

14. The analysis uses the 1990 wave of the NLSY, by which time the respondents were twenty-five to thirty-three years old and only about 5 percent were still enrolled in school. The regressions also control for age, gender, whether the person is a first- or second-generation American, and whether the person was enrolled in school in 1990. See Borjas, "Ethnicity, Neighborhoods, and Human-Capital Externalities," for details.

15. The estimation strategy is to add a vector of 1,937 zip code fixed effects to the regression model, so that the estimated coefficients measure within-neighborhood intergenerational correlations. The correlation between the children's wage and the father's wage falls to .25 (with a standard error of .04), while the correlation between the children's wage and ethnic capital falls to .05 (with a standard error of .13).

16. These correlations are obtained from a regression model that analyzes the interaction of both the ethnic capital variable and the parental skills variable with dummy variables indicating the proportion of persons in the neighborhood who share the same ethnic background. The regression model also includes the dummy variables indicating the proportion of the neighborhood's population that belongs to the respondent's ethnic group. A neighborhood is defined as integrated if fewer than 5

percent of the neighborhood's population share the same ethnic background as the person; a neighborhood is defined as segregated if at least 33 percent of the neighborhood's population share the same ethnic background as the person. Although the results are suggestive, it is important to note that the standard errors of the coefficients are sufficiently large that one cannot reject the hypothesis that the correlations between the children's wage and ethnic capital are the same for persons who grew up in segregated neighborhoods and persons who grew up in integrated neighborhoods. One can, however, reject the hypothesis that the correlations between the children's education and ethnic capital are the same for persons who grew up in segregated neighborhoods, and persons who grew up in integrated neighborhoods. See Borjas, "Ethnicity, Neighborhoods, and Human-Capital Externalities," pp. 384–386, for additional details.

17. These cross-group effects persist even when the correlations are adjusted for differences in the socioeconomic characteristics of neighborhoods; see Borjas, "To Ghetto or Not to Ghetto?" pp. 242, 244.

18. An increase in ethnic capital—such as that associated with a 10 percentage point increase in the average wage of the ethnic group in the parental generation— reduces the probability that the child in the survey will eventually live in a segregated neighborhood by 18 percentage points (with a standard error of 3 percentage points). A family is defined as living in an ethnically segregated neighborhood if the fraction of the population in the neighborhood that belongs to the respondent's ethnic group is at least twice as large as would have been expected if the ethnic group were randomly allocated to the neighborhood. See ibid., p. 248, for more details on the regression model underlying the discussion.

19. The standard errors for these predicted changes in residential segregation are .7 percent for the disadvantaged ethnic group and 1.7 percent for the advantaged group. Note that the latter effect is not significantly different from zero.

CHAPTER 10
THE GOALS OF IMMIGRATION POLICY

1. Leslie Allen, *Liberty: The Statue and the American Dream* (New York: Simon and Schuster, 1985), pp. 37–38. The Statue of Liberty was unveiled on October 28, 1886. The plaque bearing Emma Lazarus's poem did not become a permanent fixture of the monument until 1903.

2. An additional 2.4 million visa applications were disqualified for various reasons. See "Results of the Diversity Immigrant Visa Program (DV-99)" (Statement of James B. Foley, Deputy Spokesman, U.S. Department of State, May 6, 1998, available at U.S. Department of State website).

3. "The Rekindled Flame," *Wall Street Journal*, July 3, 1990, p. A10.

4. Some of the visas handed out under the employment preference category are actually reserved for unskilled workers. In 1996, for example, 11,849 of the 117,499 visas awarded under the employment preferences were awarded to "needed unskilled workers" and their families.

5. William Branigin, "U.S. Issuing More Visas to Investors," *Washington Post*, December 29, 1997, p. A1.

6. The visa market has been a frequent recommendation of Gary Becker in his *Business Week* columns. These columns are collected in Gary S. Becker and Guity Nashat Becker, *The Economics of Life* (New York: McGraw-Hill, 1997).

7. An alternative interpretation of what "efficiency" implies in the visa market may be instructive. Suppose that one million persons are willing to buy visas at a price of $50,000. Consider now an alternative market structure. In particular, suppose the United States decides to sell one million visas and that instead of charging a flat price of $50,000, it can set a price that differs among buyers. The United States, in effect, would be a perfectly discriminating monopolist. Each of the million visa buyers would then be charged exactly the maximum amount that he or she was willing to pay to enter the country. All of the gains would then accrue to the U.S. Treasury, and it would be impossible to design an immigration policy that would let in one million persons and that would generate any additional gains for the United States.

8. Abbot Emerson Smith, *Colonists in Bondage: White Servitude and Convict Labor in America, 1607–1776* (Gloucester, Mass.: Peter Smith, 1965).

9. It is not uncommon to find immigrants working under brutal conditions to pay off the cost of moving to the United States. See, e.g., Deborah Sontag, "Captive in Queens: Dozens of Deaf Immigrants Discovered in Forced Labor," *New York Times*, July 20, 1997, p. A1; Frank Davies, "Feds Bust State Sex Slavery Ring," *Miami Herald*, April 24, 1998, p. A1; and William Branigin, "Sweatshop Instead of Paradise: Thais Lived in Fear as Slaves at L.A. Garment Factories," *Washington Post*, September 10, 1995, p. A1.

10. This type of calculation would probably indicate that the net cost of admitting one more immigrant depends on the immigrant's socioeconomic characteristics. Some immigrants might be quite beneficial for the United States, and the country might want to subsidize their entry. Other immigrants might be quite costly, and the country might like to discourage their entry. The United States could take advantage of these differences by price-discriminating: selling visas at different prices, depending on the characteristics of the visa buyer.

11. In the jargon of modern economics, what is the country's "social welfare function"?

12. The discussion in this section is based on George J. Borjas, "The New Economics of Immigration," *Atlantic Monthly*, November 1996, pp. 72–80.

13. I want to emphasize that the country's social welfare obviously depends on many noneconomic factors. These objectives are shaped by values, humanitarian concerns, and geopolitical considerations. A different mix of these objectives would obviously lead to a different immigration policy. As I show here, however, even a discussion that is very narrowly restricted to economic factors requires a number of important assumptions before one can make the "leap of faith" from research findings on the economic impact of immigration to the design of an immigration policy.

14. John Maynard Keynes, *The General Theory of Employment, Interest, and Money* (1936; reprint, New York: Harcourt, Brace and World, 1964), p. 383.

15. Douglas A. Irwin, *Against the Tide: An Intellectual History of Free Trade* (Princeton, N.J.: Princeton University Press, 1996).

16. Although the discussion captures the flavor of the simplest models of international trade, more complex models suggest that under some conditions, *all* workers

gain from trade. These models often stress externalities or the importation of goods that are not currently produced in the domestic economy.

17. Patrick J. Buchanan, *The Great Betrayal: How American Sovereignty and Social Justice Are Sacrificed to the Gods of the Global Economy* (Boston: Little, Brown, 1998). Dani Rodrik, *Has Globalization Gone Too Far?* (Washington, D.C.: Institute for International Economics, 1997), provides a rare discussion—within the mainstream of economic thought—that stresses these distributional impacts.

18. A good introduction is given by Joseph H. Carens, "Realistic and Idealistic Approaches to the Ethics of Migration," *International Migration Review* 30 (Spring 1996): 156–170. For a selection of different approaches to the moral issues involved, see Michael Walzer, *Spheres of Justice: A Defense of Pluralism and Equality* (New York: Basic Books, 1983); Will Kymlicka, *Multicultural Citizenship: A Liberal Theory of Minority Rights* (New York: Oxford University Press, 1993); and Jean Hampton, *Political Philosophy* (Boulder, Colo.: Westview Press, 1997).

19. A justification for various "rights" that might accrue to sovereign countries—particularly the right to select and reject certain types of potential migrants—is given by Joseph Raz and Avishai Margalit, "National Self-Determination," *Journal of Philosophy* 88 (September 1990): 439–461.

20. The parable is due to James M. Buchanan, "A Two-Country Parable," in *Justice in Immigration*, ed. Warren F. Schwartz (New York: Cambridge University Press, 1995), pp. 63–66. The issues involved become even harder to address when one allows for the fact that countries differ dramatically in their endowments of physical and human capital, and that these differences in "initial conditions" often generate great disparities in economic opportunities.

CHAPTER 11
A PROPOSAL FOR AN IMMIGRATION POLICY

1. The argument holds strictly when the capital stock in the United States is fixed. The gains to native-owned firms decline as the capital stock adjusts to the entry of immigrants.

2. A regression of the log wage rate on a worker's education, age, and an indicator of occupation (at the three-digit level) has an R^2 of .34. This regression uses a sample of native-born working men aged twenty-five to sixty-four drawn from the 1990 Census.

3. Denise DiPasquale and Edward L. Glaeser, "The Los Angeles Riot and the Economics of Urban Unrest," *Journal of Urban Economics* 43 (January 1998): 52–78

4. The United States already sets limits on the number of visas that can be granted to any country. The limit for each country is set at 7 percent of the immigrants admitted under the preference system. This cap is typically not binding, however, because close relatives can enter the United States regardless of how many other immigrants have already been admitted or where those immigrants originated. Since 1990, U.S. immigration policy has allocated a relatively small number of visas into a "diversity visas" category. In particular, fifty-five thousand visas are allocated to countries that were "adversely affected" by the 1965 Amendments. The stated objective of these visas is to increase the possibility that persons who originate in countries that are not

represented in the current immigrant flow—and hence have few relatives residing in the United States—will be able to enter the country. In 1998, no more than 3,850 (or 7 percent) of the diversity visas could be allocated to any country. During the initial years of the diversity program, however, over 40 percent of the visas were reserved for Irish citizens (courtesy of Senator Ted Kennedy's disproportionate influence over the drafting of immigration legislation).

5. J. Edward Taylor and Philip L. Martin, "The Immigrant Subsidy in U.S. Agriculture: Farm Employment, Poverty, and Welfare," *Population and Development Review* 23 (December 1997): 855–874.

6. The original bracero program was launched in 1942. This guest-worker program allowed the temporary migration of agricultural workers from Mexico. The program was abruptly terminated in 1962, presumably because the braceros depressed the earnings of workers in the U.S. agricultural industry.

7. Adam Smith, *The Wealth of Nations* (reprint, Chicago: University of Chicago Press, 1976), p. 144.

8. Taylor and Martin, "The Immigrant Subsidy in U.S. Agriculture."

9. This is just another application of a general principle of economic theory. The gains from a particular activity are maximized by conducting the activity up to the point where the marginal benefit (the gain from carrying out the activity one more time) equals the marginal cost (the additional cost incurred).

10. U.S. Commission on Immigration Reform, *Becoming an American: Immigration and Immigrant Policy* (Washington, D.C.: GPO, 1997), p. xix.

11. Richard B. Freeman, "Demand for Education," in *Handbook of Labor Economics*, vol. 1, ed. Orley C. Ashenfelter and Richard Layard (Amsterdam: North-Holland, 1986), p. 373. See also Robert J. Willis and Sherwin Rosen, "Education and Self-Selection," Part 2, *Journal of Political Economy* 87 (October 1979): S7-S36; and Thomas J. Kane, "College Entry by Blacks since 1970: The Role of College Costs, Family Background, and the Returns to Education," *Journal of Political Economy* 102 (October 1994): 878–911.

12. William G. Bowen and Derek Bok, *The Shape of the River: Long-Term Consequences of Considering Race in College and University Admissions* (Princeton, N.J.: Princeton University Press, 1998).

13. Even though the absence of a wage gap between skilled and unskilled workers would deter natives from acquiring skills, many foreign-born skilled persons would still be willing to immigrate as long as the income of skilled workers in the United States exceeded the income of skilled workers in the source countries (net of migration costs).

14. A good description of the methodologies used to calculate the number of illegal aliens is given in U.S. General Accounting Office, *Illegal Aliens: Despite Data Limitations, Current Methods Provide Better Population Estimates*, GAO/PEMD-93–25 (Washington, D.C., August 1993).

15. Remarkably, it was not illegal for firms to hire illegal aliens until 1988. Even though it was illegal for some persons to be in the United States, and it was illegal for those persons to work, firms were free to hire the illegal aliens. Since 1988, first-time offenders have been liable for fines ranging from $250 to $2,000 per illegal alien hired. Criminal penalties can be imposed on repeated violators when there is a "pat-

tern and practice" of hiring illegal aliens, including a fine of $3,000 per illegal alien and up to six months in prison.

16. Many studies have attempted to determine if the 1986 Immigration Reform and Control Act slowed down the illegal alien flow. These studies typically conclude that the legislation was a dismal failure; see Katharine M. Donato, Jorge Durand, and Douglas S. Massey, "Stemming the Tide? Assessing the Deterrent Effects of the Immigration Reform and Control Act," *Demography* 29 (May 1992): 139–157.

17. Most of the illegal crossings, however, take place over a relatively small area, stretching for about 165 miles. See Robert J. Caldwell, "Grading Gatekeeper: Tougher Border Enforcement Shows Promise but Remains Incomplete," *San Diego Union-Tribune*, August 10, 1997, p. G-1.

18. See Robert Suro, *Strangers among Us: How Latino Immigration Is Transforming America* (New York: Knopf, 1998), chap. 16, for a detailed discussion of the El Paso operation.

19. Quoted ibid., p. 273.

20. In the 1982 *Plyer v. Doe* decision, the U.S. Supreme Court ruled narrowly (on a 5-to-4 vote) that illegal aliens were entitled to a public education.

21. S. J. Torok and Wallace E. Huffman, "U.S.–Mexican Trade in Winter Vegetables and Illegal Immigration," *American Journal of Agricultural Economics* 68 (May 1986): 246–260. See also Gordon H. Hanson and Antonio Spilimbergo, "Illegal Immigration, Border Enforcement, and Relative Wages: Evidence," *American Economic Review*, forthcoming 1999.

22. This amendment states: "All persons born or naturalized in the United States, and subject to the jurisdiction thereof, are citizens of the United States and of the State wherein they reside." The amendment was enacted in 1868 to grant citizenship to the newly freed slave population.

23. Public Affairs Office, Federal Bureau of Prisons, telephone conversation with author.

24. Jules L. Coleman and Sarah K. Harding, "Citizenship, the Demands of Justice, and the Moral Relevance of Political Borders," in *Justice in Immigration*, ed. Warren F. Schwartz (New York: Cambridge University Press, 1995), pp. 18–62.

25. U.S. Immigration and Naturalization Service, *Statistical Yearbook of the Immigration and Naturalization Service, 1996* (Washington, D.C., 1997), pp. 95–96. The legal distinction between refugees and asylees depends on *where* the person applies for entry into the United States. The aliens who are outside the United States are typically called refugees, while the aliens who are already in the United States, and fear returning to their country of nationality, are called asylees.

26. A good description of the evolution of refugee policy is contained in Howard Adelman, ed., *Refugee Policy: Canada and the United States* (Staten Island, N.Y.: Center for Immigration Studies, 1991).

27. U.S. Department of Health and Human Services, Office of Refugee Resettlement, *Refugee Resettlement Program, Annual Report FY 1982* (Washington, D.C., 1983), pp. 1–2.

28. Christopher Marquis and Don Bohning, "Exiles, Key GOP Legislators Vow to Fight Clinton's Cuba Policy," *Miami Herald*, May 6, 1995, p. A22.

29. U.S. Department of Health and Human Services, Office of Refugee Resettlement, *Refugee Resettlement Program, FY 1995* (Washington, D.C., 1995), p. 8.

30. George J. Borjas, "Immigration and Welfare: 1970–1990," *Research in Labor Economics* 14 (1995): 253–282, p. 257.

31. Celia W. Dugger, "U.S. Grants Asylum to Woman Fleeing Genital Mutilation Rite," *New York Times*, June 14, 1996, p. A1.

CHAPTER 12
CONCLUSION

1. Bernard Bailyn, *Voyagers to the West: A Passage in the Peopling of America on the Eve of the Revolution* (New York: Vintage Books, 1986), pp. 25–26. The total number includes both voluntary and involuntary immigrants.